HISTORY OF THE AMERICAN CINEMA

Volume 8

1960–1969

Joe Buck (Jon Voight) and Ratso Rizzo (Dustin Hoffman) crossing the bridge toward 1970s cultural pessimisim in MIDNIGHT COWBOY, the Academy Award winner for best picture in 1969.

HISTORY OF THE AMERICAN CINEMA

CHARLES HARPOLE, GENERAL EDITOR

8
THE SIXTIES:
1960-1969

Paul Monaco

Charles Scribner's Sons

An Imprint of the Gale Group

NEW YORK • DETROIT

Credits and permissions can be found on p. 321 and should be
considered an extension of the copyright page.

Copyright © 2001 by Paul Monaco

Charles Scribner's Sons
1633 Broadway
New York, New York 10019

Gale Group
27500 Drake Road
Farmington Hills, Michigan 48331-3535

Printed in Canada

Printing Number
1   3   5   7   9   10   8   6   4   2

Library of Congress Cataloging-in-Publication Data

Monaco, Paul
    The sixties / Paul Monaco.
      p. cm. — (History of the American Cinema ; v. 8)
    Includes bibliographical references and index.
    ISBN 0-684-18416-8
      1. Motion pictures—United States—History. 2. Motion
    picture industry—United States—History. I. Title. II. Series.
PN1993.5.U6 H55   1990 vol. 8
791.43'0973—dc21

                       00-058372

Advisory Board

The Cinema History Project and the
History of the American Cinema
have been supported by grants from the
National Endowment for the Humanities and the
John and Mary R. Markle Foundation.

For Victoria

Contents

Acknowledgments

Shortly after my first major research trip in 1995 to the Center for the Study of the Motion Picture of the Academy of Motion Picture Arts and Sciences in Beverly Hills, I wrote a letter to the Center's director. In it, I complimented the entire staff for the kind, courteous, and conscientious service that had been extended to me consistently over a couple of weeks. The director wrote back to me, graciously thanking me for my letter, but also assuring me that she and the staff were just doing their jobs. Subsequently, I returned to the Center for several prolonged visits and follow-up trips. Perhaps they were only doing their jobs, but without all of the efforts of the founders and sustainers of that Center, along with the conscientiousness of each individual staff member there, this book would not exist.

Several other libraries and collections supplied access to their research collections, journals, papers, assorted materials, and books: The Library and Collection of the American Film Institute (Hollywood); the Cinema Studies Collection of the Doheny Library at the University of Southern California (Los Angeles); and the Libraries of the University of California, Los Angeles. I obtained photo illustrations for this volume from the collections of the Academy's Center for the Study of the Motion Picture (Beverly Hills) and the Photo Stills Collection of the Museum of Modern Art; especially as this project neared completion, Kristina Krueger was particularly helpful to me at the Center, as were Teri Geesken and Mary Corliss at MOMA. I obtained still other photographs from the Library of Congress, Mr. Roger Corman, and from a recent graduate of Montana State University, Matt Marshall. The dean of the Montana State University libraries, Bruce Morton, made available office space for me to dredge through the vast holdings of journals that came to Bozeman, Montana, on interlibrary loan.

Two separate Research/Creativity grants from the College of Arts and Architecture at Montana State University helped fund my research trips and my acquisition of photographs. Jean Koelzer, administrative assistant in the Department of Media and Theatre Arts at Montana State, was of great help in putting the final touches on the manuscript and bringing it all together. I appreciate the many hours, over the years, when I have had occasion to listen to both Andy Laszlo and Peter Fonda sharing their thoughts and insights on films from the 1960s with which they were involved. My thanks, also, to Michael Snow, who addressed to the general editor of this series and to myself a detailed letter about his experimental film work in the 1960s. Peter Lev, a great scholar and a longtime friend, has been a steady supporter of my research for this volume and also invited me to present a portion of my insights into "the Sixties" as a plenary speaker at the Film/Literature Conference at Towson University in late 1998. It was precisely the best time for me to do so: I used that occasion to solidify and finalize my thinking for this volume. My thanks also go to my wife, Victoria O'Donnell, for sharing her professional acumen with me and for lending to me her support in my research and writing.

As the lead author on this volume, I am grateful to the two other authors who contributed. Richard Barsam was involved with this project from its inception. Over an extended period of time, he has displayed enormous patience with a process to bringing this book to print. I cannot thank him enough for the good grace and professional collegiality that he put into writing and revising his section on the nonfiction film. By contrast, Walter Metz was enlisted late to the project and forced to complete his section on the avant-garde of the sixties in near-record time. I thank them both. My thanks, too, to Sonia Benson who completed the final copy editing and layout of the book.

Finally, I reserve my greatest thanks for John Fitzpatrick at Charles Scribner's Sons. As an editor he has been a prince. His comments on my sections of this book were always so thorough and lucid, so precise in their detail, and so insightful in their overview of where the manuscript was going and where it needed to go, that I cannot imagine anyone who could have done a better job. I know that John has labored long and hard to keep this series on course and that his task has not been easy. To him I extend my fondest appreciation for his brilliant criticisms and his indefatigable patience.

Contributors

PAUL MONACO is Professor of Cinema/Video and the head of Media and Theatre Arts at Montana State University, Bozeman. He is the author of *Understanding Culture, Society, and Television* and *Ribbons in Time: Movies and Society since 1945* and has twice received Fulbright fellowships to Germany.

RICHARD M. BARSAM, author of the chapter on nonfiction film, is Professor of Film Studies at Hunter College of the City University of New York.

WALTER METZ, author of the chapter on 1960s avant-garde film, is Assistant Professor of Motion Picture/Video/Theatre at Montana State University, Bozeman.

Introduction

"Not for the past five years has there been any doubt . . . that television has siphoned off the lowbrows and left theatre films on the high ground of art." So began an article by Gideon Bachman in the June 1, 1960 edition of *Variety*.[1] At almost the same time, in his doctoral dissertation written for the Faculty of Political Science at Columbia University, Frederic Stuart described three major impacts of television on Hollywood as the new decade began: 1) the breakup of the major studios had been accelerated; 2) the type of feature film being produced had changed; and 3) new technologies, such as widescreen, had been introduced.[2] From the newsprint of the premier trade tabloid of the entertainment industry to a scholarly treatise being defended at one of the nation's leading universities, the message was clear. As of 1960, the feature film industry in the United States was in the midst of a transition that was proving to be long and difficult. And Hollywood "restored" eventually would be a Hollywood substantially redefined and redirected. From a negative perspective, Hollywood would survive only as a shadow of its former self, absorbed into a corporate structure intent on packaging movies as part of a newly conceived commodity called "leisure," targeted extensively toward the growing adolescent and young adult populations of the industrial world. Viewed more favorably, the Hollywood feature film would reemerge at the end of the 1960s to fill a particular and distinguished niche among the growing range of aesthetic attractions available to increasingly affluent populations around the globe. The false hopes and genuine triumphs, as well as the fitful starts and firm directions of the feature film in the United States from 1960 through 1969, are the subject of the first section of this volume (chapters one through eleven).

There is a broad consensus among film historians that Hollywood experienced a transformation beginning in the late 1940s and the early 1950s that lasted well into the 1970s. There is less agreement, however, on which precise dates delineate the subcategories within this era. To cite several instances of the differences between historians, Gerald Mast offers one timeline (from 1953 to 1977) when Hollywood made a full transition to its redefined place in American culture and society during the "age of television."[3] In another of his books, however, Mast breaks down a similar period into "Hollywood in Transition: 1946–1965," and "Hollywood Renaissance: 1965–1976."[4] Another historian, Jack C. Ellis, dates the beginning of Hollywood's resurgence in 1963, two years earlier than Mast, arguing that this rebirth began with the critic Andrew Sarris's first articulation of the auteur notion of filmmaking that he had imported from France. Ellis maintained that auteurism, by emphasizing that moviemaking was dominated by the artistic vision of individual directors, provided the central mystique of the "New Hollywood."[5] The film historian Thomas Schatz, in contrast, identifies three distinct phases in the American cinema following World War II, each roughly a decade long—from 1946 to 1955, from 1956 to 1965, and from 1966 to 1975. Schatz typically divides American cinema history by the appearance of huge box office hits that strongly

influenced new directions for Hollywood production, such as THE TEN
COMMANDMENTS (1956), THE SOUND OF MUSIC (1965), and JAWS (1975).[6] Douglas
Gomery, in his survey of American cinema history, dates "the television era" as beginning in 1951 and concludes that "a new economics and sociology of Hollywood was in
play by 1975,"[7] while David A. Cook identifies a period lasting from 1952 to 1965 characterized primarily by Hollywood's attempts at technological innovations—especially
the exploitation of widescreen formats—to distinguish theatrical film releases from what
audiences could watch at home on television.[8] The more popular critic, Ethan Mordden,
however, locates the turning point for the American feature film precisely in the year
1960 with the release of Alfred Hitchcock's PSYCHO, which Mordden calls "a revolt
against the fascism of the studio heads and the Hollywood Production Code."[9] However,
in a 1959 essay, "The New Hollywood," Robert Brustein claimed that the feature film
industry in the United States had already destroyed its time-honored forms. According
to Brustein, then dean of the Yale Drama School, the demise of the major studios was
complete before 1960, and along with them went the production processes, artistic conventions, and themes that had defined Hollywood since its beginnings.[10]

The specifics of chronology are largely determined by where observers position
themselves and which indexes of change are noted to justify one interpretation or
another. Nonetheless, the history of the American cinema during the thirty-five years
after the end of World War II (1945–1980) has been divided into periods that are relatively well agreed upon. In this volume, the period from 1960 through 1969 is considered a coherent epoch, albeit a transitional one. Its coherence is defined by the
emergence of a cinema of sensation that begins with the famous shower scene in Alfred
Hitchcock's PSYCHO (1960), where Janet Leigh's character is stabbed to death. The new
cinema of sensation pioneered in this film grew up separate from the cinema of sentiment that had constituted the aesthetic core of classic Hollywood from the late 1920s
through the 1950s. The new aesthetic of sensation was defined by a speeded-up pacing,
the sweep of color production that all but eliminated black-and-white features from
Hollywood production, and an increased reliance on graphic visual and sound effects.
By 1969, when Sam Peckinpah's THE WILD BUNCH was released, that new aesthetic of
sensation was firmly established.

The aesthetics of this cinema of sensation moved away from the dialogue-based cinema that had dominated Hollywood production from the end of the 1920s into the
1960s. Perceptibly, visual and audio sensation began to coexist with—and even dis-
place—the narrative and dramatic demands of dialogue and scripting as the primary elements upon which the viewer's attention was focused in a feature film. The widescreen
aesthetic of the 1950s, and Hollywood experiments such as 3-D, either receded in significance or disappeared altogether during the 1960s. It was neither the spatial width
nor the depth perspective of the picture on the screen that gained aesthetic prominence
during the 1960s so much as a new editing style, which altered the temporal nature of
the American feature film. The distinct aesthetic that emerged was more strongly based
on how shots and scenes were constructed in terms of time, rather than on spatial relationships within visual shots, expanded aspect ratios for the screen size, or the appearance of increased depth perspective in the image.

In nonfiction film, the philosophic assertions and production techniques of direct cinema became prominent during the decade. The notion of the documentarian as an
observer of life and its processes largely displaced the traditional form of nonfiction film,
which emphasized a persuasive, voiced-over narrative that provided explanatory logic.

In the avant-garde cinema, experimental filmmaking entwined itself with contemporary movements in abstract art and performance, and developed conceptual and structural forms. Most importantly, however, the avant-garde cinema, centered almost entirely in New York City and San Francisco, provided a nexus for extending counterculture ideas well beyond the Beat movement of the 1950s and radically advanced alternative lifestyles and sexual identities. However, all these new directions of the 1960s, in each of the branches of the American cinema, were subsequently developed in ways that would be perceived as unfulfilled or distorted, or even as constituting outright betrayals of their original intention, by many of their innovators.

For Hollywood and the American feature film, the 1960s was a decade that ended in the midst of transitions that established no definitive direction for the future. Even the fiscal peril confronting the motion-picture production industry was not entirely overcome. Throughout the 1960s, the feature film industry in the United States continued to struggle with the competition of television and the decline of the domestic audience for theatrical movies. Early in the 1960s, moreover, Hollywood had been forced to take into account the growing and significant challenge of its European competition. The vitality of several film industries in Western Europe encouraged the perception that many foreign productions were setting new standards for sophistication and artistic achievement as well as increasing box-office competition for Hollywood. Faced with a malaise that had been growing in the feature film industry since television began siphoning off its mass audience, and further troubled by the European challenge, Hollywood made a number of major miscalculations in the early 1960s. The production of CLEOPATRA (1963)—a highly publicized, enormously expensive flop—only contributed to the growing perception among both Hollywood insiders and the nation's movie critics that European filmmakers were in some way ahead of their American counterparts. That CLEOPATRA cost more and lost more than any previous movie was only emblematic of Hollywood's troubles. That same year of 1963 showed an all-time low of 143 for the number of feature films produced in the United States.[11] Even though the number of productions started to increase the following year, it was far from certain whether Hollywood could regain its artistic reputation, or if it could continue to globally dominate cinema. For 1966, for example, Bosley Crowther, the highly influential movie critic for the *New York Times,* selected only three American-produced features on his list of the year's "Ten Best."[12]

In hindsight, the Hollywood feature film appears to have been struggling throughout the 1960s with the question of how to hold its audience by creating movies that might be positioned somewhere between being "arty" and "conventional." European directors dominated motion pictures aimed at the more mature and sophisticated "art" audiences. Such productions could hardly be imitated effectively by Hollywood. The European art film began in 1944 with neo-realism in Italy and remained linked to artistic concepts and intentions by dealing with the aftermath of World War II for nearly thirty years. Art films were produced by and for younger generations of Europeans who were still working through the moral legacy of that conflict on the continent. The aesthetics of the art film (e.g., neo-realism, auteurism, New Wave, engaged cinema) were rooted in Western European philosophy and collective experience in Western European nations after World War II in ways that Hollywood could neither duplicate nor imitate.

Television, on the other hand, provided conventional mass entertainment in infinitely greater abundance, as well as far more cheaply, than the movies. Hollywood's transition to new production formulas during the 1960s was not easy, and some of the spectacular

CLEOPATRA, *the greatest failure of the 1960s, was released in 1963—Hollywood's leanest year for film production.*

box-office successes of the decade did not necessarily provide formulas that assured the long-term recovery of feature film production in the United States. Looking back on the 1960s, the producer Ned Tanen argued that two of the decade's most profitable productions nearly destroyed the entire motion-picture industry in the United States: "THE SOUND OF MUSIC (1965) was a huge hit and all the studios tried to copy it . . . and all were commercial disasters. The second film was EASY RIDER (1969) which spawned the low-budget 'youth' movies . . . except most of the youth movies were so bad they were never even released."[13]

What films to make and the audience toward which to target them, of course, is the quintessential challenge faced by Hollywood in any era. The competition of television on the one hand, and the European art films on the other, along with America's shifting demographics throughout the 1960s and widespread cultural changes among young people, rendered the 1960s unusually trying and vexing for Hollywood. No decade in the twentieth century is so closely identified with social unrest in the United States, and few, if any periods in human history compare to the late 1960s for the speed and breadth of transformations in lifestyle and culture. One might be tempted to speculate on how Hollywood would have fared with its recovery and redirection in a less highly charged period of change, but such speculation is counter-historical. The 1960s provided abundant social and cultural grist for nonfiction films and experimental work, and both genres took up these challenges advantageously. For the American feature film, however, these years were difficult, indeed.

Historically, the decade was marked by an unprecedented string of assassinations, including the murders of President John F. Kennedy and his brother, U.S. Senator Robert F. Kennedy, civil rights leader Martin Luther King, Jr., and Nation of Islam leader Malcolm X. A landmark civil rights bill was passed by Congress in 1964 and signed into law, only to be followed by urban rioting that set cities ablaze from the nation's capital to the Watts section of Los Angeles. American military intervention in Southeast Asia beginning in 1965 became a divisive issue that polarized much of America, even if the images of an entire nation divided into two distinct and warring camps are largely exaggerated and inaccurate.[14] Nonetheless, the Vietnam War, and the protests that arose against it, inspired many to question the nation's sense of direction and basic institutions, and led to widespread challenges to fundamental values that were widely believed to constitute the "American way of life." A bipartisan foreign policy based on "containment of communism" that had prevailed since shortly after the end of World War II became widely opposed. The belief that the nation's affluence could be widely shared, hence providing a basis for social peace and domestic tranquillity, was seriously called into doubt. For most observers, the optimism that had dominated the public's perception of America and its role in the world during the 1950s was lost by the second half of the 1960s.

Along with the trials and tribulations of the American republic during the late 1960s, however, other factors fill in a more complete picture of the period's history and economics. As seen from many perspectives, the 1960s was a decade of positive social change, rapidly increasing affluence, and general well-being. The ten years from 1958 to 1968, for example, was a period of unprecedented economic prosperity. The spread of affluence and social mobility in the United States had never been greater. The brief presidency of John F. Kennedy (1961–1963) became linked in the collective memory with civil rights and ideas of social justice, although the most salient legislative accomplishment of his administration actually may have been a substantial federal tax reduction in 1963 that stimulated the nation's economy. Civil rights legislation and the "war on poverty" (and even final passage of the tax cut) were left to Kennedy's successor, Lyndon B. Johnson (1963–1968), who rallied Congress to act in memory of Kennedy. Johnson's pursuit of military intervention in Southeast Asia, however, so thoroughly compromised his presidency that he went from landslide electoral victory in 1964 to an early decision not to campaign for reelection in 1968.[15] The 1960s ended with conservative Republican Richard M. Nixon in the White House.

The 1960s, however, cannot be understood as a decade defined either by the broad sweep of American political and economic life, nor by the accomplishments and failures of the nation's presidents during the decade. The cultural historian Norman Cantor poignantly observed that in the late 1960s history reached a turning point, not only in the United States but in a substantial portion of the industrialized world, but did not turn.[16] Despite the cultural changes and political unrest of the 1960s neither the political nor the economic structure of the United States was transformed. The assaults upon capitalism and representative democracy failed. Indeed, social and cultural changes that spread farthest, fastest, and most tellingly across the United States were the shifts in mores, attitudes, and behaviors that constituted the "sexual revolution." The late 1960s in the United States proved far more revolutionary culturally than politically. Abbie Hoffman and his Chicago Seven cohorts (who upstaged the Democratic National Convention in 1968 with street demonstrations) were more effective at "street theater" than they were in assaulting the real bastions of establishment power. To say that the

Signs of social unrest. Cultural historian Norman Cantor observed that in the late 1960s, "history reached a turning point . . . but did not turn."

pursuit of pleasure transcended political ideology for most young Americans in the late 1960s is a truism, and not necessarily a negative one. It would be negative from a Marxist perspective, of course. But from a perspective anchored within the nexus of post-World War II American political, economic, social, and intellectual development, it was a logical consequence of the "American way of life." Far more young Americans found diversion during the late 1960s in "turning on and dropping out" than in becoming politically engaged and mounting the barricades.

While many of the public mythologies that had prevailed in the United States since the end of World War II were shaken to their roots during the 1960s, this fact did not derail the dominant culture in its continuing evolution toward non-ideological and apolitical responses to social and political causes. In many ways, American society and its core institutions were preserved intact in the late 1960s, while the nation's social and political conflicts were displaced to the combat field of America's "culture wars." Civil rights protests, political assassinations, antiwar protests, and the riot outside the 1968 Democratic Party convention in Chicago deservedly drew the headlines. Nonetheless, change in American society and culture was likely influenced as much or more by a decision made one day in 1960 by the Federal Drug Administration when it accepted the Searle Pharmaceutical Company's "synthetic anovulent" as an oral contraceptive pill, permitting its sale in the United States. The "birth control pill" offered highly reliable and relatively inexpensive birth control and appeared to involve none of the unromantic interference with sexual pleasure of previous contraceptive methods. The wellsprings of the sexual revolution were found in the small, round dispensers that made it easy for women to keep track of their intake; those pill dispensers likely were the truest symbols of deep cultural change and a shift in mores all across the United States.[17]

Low-budget feature films celebrating pleasure-seeking among young adults, such as MUSCLE BEACH PARTY, BIKINI BEACH, and BEACH BLANKET BINGO (all released between 1963 and 1965), pointed toward the abiding hedonistic social dynamic in American youth culture, in much the same way as the mayhem surrounding the American tour of the British rock group, the Beatles, in 1964.[18] At the same time, the world of experimental film portrayed the sexual revolution as radical, gay, and aggressively anti-conventional in films such as FLAMING CREATURES (1963), THE QUEEN OF SHEBA MEETS THE ATOM MAN (1963), BLOW JOB (1963), and SCORPIO RISING (1964). During the second half of the 1960s, cultural and political revolutionaries ostensibly coexisted, although sometimes uneasily, but in reality one form of rebellion far exceeded

The 1960s began with the government approving the birth control pill in 1960 and ended with a sexual revolution among young Americans: they "let it all hang out" at the Woodstock Music Festival in August 1969 and in Michael Wadleigh's documentary of the event.

the other. As Landon Y. Jones wrote in a seminal study of the post-World War II baby boomers and their impact on American society: "While the political revolution [of the 1960s] attracted the most fevered attention in the press and in the minds of the public, the cultural revolution was the most representative of the boom generation and the one that ultimately would come closest to prevailing."[19]

The American documentary film appeared ideally positioned to cut directly to the core of political and social issues. With television having largely taken over the dissemination of news and public information, however, and with documentary film's aesthetic impulses shifted toward observational filming techniques, nonfiction film in the United States during even the late 1960s remained relatively devoid of direct political engagement and the articulation of a clear ideology. Even the most radical agendas of the experimental filmmakers had more to do with building a sense of community based upon alternative sexuality and gender identity with small audiences on the edges of American culture than with advancing the dialectic of history and furthering the cause of the downtrodden. Hollywood feature films, moreover, avoided dealing directly with the great social and political issues of the 1960s almost entirely, although increasing numbers of them by the end of the decade began implicitly exploring the images and illusions of rapidly changing cultural attitudes and mores.

1

Hollywood Faces New Challenges

Hollywood's great and golden era was the two decades between the advent of synchronous sound motion-picture production in 1927 and the peak years for movie theater attendance in the United States, 1946–1948.[1] After 1948, the movie industry faced increasing challenges from many directions. Federal antitrust regulators successfully sued the major Hollywood companies on the grounds that their control of the production, distribution, and exhibition of American feature films constituted illicit collusion in restraint of trade and competition. Television, based on a technology invented in the late 1920s, began to be exploited commercially in the United States after World War II; as the medium grew pervasive, it drew much of the mass audience, especially the family audience, from the habit of moviegoing. Demographics and the social mobility of the growing American middle-class population further hampered the prospects for regaining the mass audiences that movies had attracted only a few years before.

As the vaunted major studios in Hollywood scrambled to respond to these massive challenges, their long-established system of production and employment unraveled during the 1950s. The vertical oligopoly of the major Hollywood companies—Paramount, Loew's (MGM), Warner Bros., 20th Century-Fox, RKO-Pathé, United Artists, Columbia Pictures, and Universal—over the production, distribution, and exhibition of motion pictures in the United States appeared to have ended by 1960. Forced by the federal courts, beginning with a 1948 decision, to divest themselves of their ownership of motion picture theaters around the country, the Hollywood majors were also ordered to end the practices of "blind" and "block" booking. These practices forced independent theater owners to either buy movies from majors as part of a package deal, or agree to rent films that they had no chance to preview.[2]

RKO-Pathé folded in 1958. Columbia and Universal, however, had never owned a substantial number of theaters. Moreover, for the remaining Hollywood majors there were different responses to court orders and consent decrees during the 1950s. While a couple of the companies moved quickly to sell off their movie theaters, others delayed in doing so. In essence, however, by 1960 the Hollywood majors were out of the business of owning movie theaters in the United States. That loss of direct control over the exhibition sector of the movie industry meant that the major producers of movies did not necessarily have guarantees for a film's exhibition. Nevertheless, it was clear that the

majors still controlled the distribution of feature films in the United States. Blind booking and block booking could be declared officially terminated, but the terms and conditions of movie rentals to theaters remained firmly in the hands of the major producers.[3]
By the late 1950s, that reality pointed toward the major studios increasingly placing their
emphasis on distribution and thinking more globally. Earnings abroad for the Hollywood
majors, in fact, surpassed their domestic revenues for the first time in 1958; that trend
continued every year throughout the 1960s.[4]

The Hollywood majors were not prevented from owning movie theaters in other
countries by court decisions in the United States. They all had well-established distribution and marketing branches in nearly all of the non-communist nations around the
globe. The growth of global demand for "entertainment product" also pointed toward
new areas of commerce related to the movies. The year 1960, for example, marked the
first time that American music producers reported that their overseas record sales surpassed those in the United States.[5] Television was spreading to other countries and con-
tinents as well, creating an ever-increasing demand for programming throughout the
1960s. Indeed, because the major Hollywood companies had long been well established
overseas, and because by 1960 over half of their total revenues came from abroad, they
became attractive targets for takeover by larger companies by the late 1960s.[6]

Despite having to divest themselves of movie theaters they owned in the United
States, and despite an enormous drop in the size of the domestic audience for the
movies throughout the 1950s, Hollywood major studios actually earned $1.5 billion in
1961—the highest amount earned since 1948. Half of those earnings were generated
outside the United States.[7] Furthermore, by 1965 the number of television sets in the
rest of the world exceeded those in the United States for the first time.[8]

The rapidly expanding global television market greatly increased the demand for
American movies. In 1966, shortly after becoming president of the Motion Picture
Association of America (MPAA), the trade organization representing the Hollywood
majors, Jack Valenti could boast, "The American movie is the world's most wanted
commodity."[9] Throughout the remainder of the decade, Valenti would focus his efforts
on developing Hollywood's global markets, concentrating on Japan, Formosa, the
Philippines, and Latin America, where there were growing populations and increasing
affluence.[10] Under Valenti's leadership the MPAA immediately began devoting
increased attention to its branch called the Motion Picture Export Association
(MPEA), which had been established right after World War II and held what constituted the equivalent of treaty-signing authority for film trade agreements with most of
the world's nations.[11]

Despite Hollywood's long-term global potential, however, the immediate prospects
for the American motion picture industry at the beginning of the 1960s were still considered bleak. The actual number of feature films being produced annually by the
Hollywood majors was falling. A studio such as Paramount, for example, which once had
produced more than a hundred films per year, averaged just fifteen features annually
during the 1960s.[12] The decline in the number of Americans going to the movies and the
erosion of the family habit of a weekly "night at the movies" in favor of staying home to
watch television for free meant that the double bill disappeared from most movie theaters. Rather than showing two features, exhibitors increasingly opted for the more efficient business practice of concentrating on exploiting the audience for a single major
feature. That shift had a double effect: fewer movies were being produced, and the business risk was increased on each of those being made.

For 1961, it was reliably estimated that three-quarters of the movies released by Hollywood lost money.[13] During the studio era, when most of the majors owned their own theater chains and when theaters still regularly showed double-bills, losses on individual productions were more easily covered by a studio's profitable films. While it was still intact and functioning, the Hollywood studio system had provided structural safeguards that amortized losses on some films against profits on others over the course of any given production year. By the early 1960s, in contrast, Hollywood was being transformed into a business where substantially fewer and fewer movies were being produced. As a result, the financial risk for each new production was greater (just as the potential for greater earnings increased). While a larger percentage of Hollywood features were losing money, the profit margins on the industry's successful features were increasing exponentially.[14]

At the beginning of the 1960s, the American feature film industry was considered to be beleaguered. However, it was not yet clear precisely what actions Hollywood needed to take to reverse its declining fortunes. Moreover, structural changes that were beginning to take hold in the movie business were not yet clearly recognized by most Hollywood insiders. Nonetheless, a fundamental shift was occurring in motion picture production that had to do with the potential profits to be earned in proportion to increased financial risk for any specific production. Put simply, as the stakes in each specific production rose, the rising production costs were accompanied by a more than commensurate increase in what a successful film could earn. From the beginning of the motion picture industry in the United States in 1895 up until the year 1960, only twenty movies grossed over $10 million. During the period 1960–1969, sixty more films recorded gross earnings in excess of that amount.[15]

Runaway Production

Increasing efforts to market Hollywood movies abroad was one major strategy for the American feature film industry in the late 1950s and the early 1960s. With these efforts came the accompanying decision to shift production itself overseas in order to reduce production costs. This practice, known as "runaway production," had become both widespread and highly controversial by the beginning of the 1960s.

Runaway production was predicated on several factors. Primarily, however, the costs for talent and technicians were considerably less anywhere abroad than they were in southern California. At the beginning of the 1960s, Hollywood producers and directors were engaged in constant struggles with the various Hollywood craft unions. Executives maintained that excessive labor costs were driving motion picture production out of the United States.[16] This line of argument continued throughout the 1960s and sometimes spilled over into internecine squabbles between different Hollywood guilds. Not long after he became the president of the Screen Actors Guild (SAG) in 1960, for example, Charlton Heston railed against the Screen Extras Guild for contributing to runaway production because "extras" had begun demanding too much for their services. That led to an ongoing feud between Heston and the Screen Extras Guild's president, Norman Stevans, that lasted nearly a decade.[17]

At the end of the 1950s and the beginning of the 1960s, in fact, Hollywood pioneered the practices of shifting production to places where labor was abundant and cheap and where local government offered substantial subsidies and tax breaks. By the 1980s, those business strategies would become common in other sectors of the American economy, as terms like "outsourcing" and "downsizing" came into vogue to describe manufacturers moving production abroad to hold down costs in an increasingly competitive global economy. Runaway production in the late 1950s and early 1960s intermeshed with the tendency of the Hollywood majors toward transforming themselves into businesses focused on the securing of production funds, the arranging of contracts, the supervising of productions, and on the marketing of the final product, rather than the actual producing of feature films. This transformation toward becoming managerial entities marked the primary shift of the major studios away from being labor intensive—i.e., characterized by large staffs on payrolls—toward becoming capital intensive with fewer and fewer employees overseeing larger and larger investments. Runaway production was a direct cause, as well as an effect, of this shift in the fundamental business of the Hollywood majors. As a result, the number of employees in southern California actually involved in the making of feature films was cut significantly. The impact on studio payrolls, especially with the loss of production technicians, was swift and dramatic. During the second week of March 1960 alone, 3,400 workers were laid off by the major Hollywood studios.[18]

The fundamental transformation occurring in the business profile of the Hollywood majors led to labor unrest in the early 1960s. The problems that exacerbated those labor tensions were largely blamed on runaway production. Trades people and union loyalists in the Los Angeles area began organizing to picket at theaters showing movies that had been produced abroad by the Hollywood majors.[19] Eventually, the national leadership of the AFL-CIO took up the cause by using its clout in the halls of Congress.[20]

Late in 1961, a House investigating committee chaired by Representative John Dent (Democrat, Pennsylvania) initiated formal congressional hearings on runaway production.[21] The well-publicized protests outside movie theaters and the congressional hearings accomplished little, however. There was a strong economic imperative for producers to seek lower labor costs in feature film production, and there were credible aesthetic arguments in favor of actually filming many movies in authentic locales as well. The critic and historian Charles Higham summarized the situation: "While the unions moaned, the moguls simply shifted one picture after another to European locations where labor was cheaper and crews could be kept to a minimum."[22]

THE ADVANTAGES OF RUNAWAY PRODUCTION

The shift of production overseas was facilitated by improved transportation and communication between the United States and Western Europe after World War II. Runaway production was fostered further by the various postwar protectionist schemes and governmental subsidies in Europe that applied to moviemaking, especially in Great Britain, Italy, and France. Hollywood companies were able to receive in 1962 alone over $5 million in direct governmental subsidies for the production of films in just those three nations. The nature of these subsidies, their amounts, and the methods by which they could actually be collected varied considerably from country to country. In some instances, a Hollywood major might have to work through a locally owned subsidiary that could "front" for the Hollywood production interests. In other places, Hollywood investments could be more direct, and studio executives back in southern California could exercise more control over the actual production process.

As a result of runaway production and the convoluted schemes by which movies were being produced abroad with American financing, the distinctions between what was

Representative John Dent (D-Penn.) chaired congressional
investigations into Hollywood's "runaway" production.

technically considered an American movie or a British, Italian, or French film started to erode. Because of the common language with the United States, this was most apparent in Great Britain. There, throughout the 1960s, a substantial portion of America's feature film production was carried out, in essence, as a subsidiary of Hollywood investment. A British subsidy law called the "Eady Plan" was intended to funnel governmental monies into movie production. Any producer could qualify to receive the monies even if the primary financing for a particular film came from non-British sources. Being able to take advantage of this scheme, Hollywood began to invest heavily and directly in production companies or individual productions in the United Kingdom.[23] In fact, when the American Film Institute announced its list of one hundred best American movies in 1998 there were three titles from the 1960s originally released with Great Britain credited as the producing nation. Those films were LAWRENCE OF ARABIA (1962), DR. STRANGELOVE, OR HOW I LEARNED TO STOP WORRYING AND LOVE THE BOMB (1964), and 2001: A SPACE ODYSSEY (1968).[24]

A variety of incentives, frequently related either with taxes or the foreign exchange rates on certain currencies, heavily favored local reinvestment by the major studios.

The "War Room" of the Pentagon as depicted in DR. STRANGELOVE, *made in England.*

Hollywood production found its closest partnership with the movie industry in the United Kingdom. As Chris Munsun noted in *The Marketing of Motion Pictures* (1969), "The financing of most British production by American companies is accomplished by a revolving system. Rental income earned by distribution subsidiaries of American companies are passed to the production companies and used to finance further production."[25] Although Great Britain remained Hollywood's most extensive partner in such productions, the filming of projects financed by Hollywood became common in France and Italy as well, and also in Spain and even North Africa. For the year 1960, forty percent of all movies financed by the Hollywood majors were shot overseas.[26] The following year, Hollywood companies produced 164 features in the United States and ninety abroad.[27] By 1960, annual film production in Italy had reached 114 features, with a majority of them having some Hollywood investment.[28] Even in France, despite the nationalist proclamations of President Charles de Gaulle and the country's legendary cultural chauvinism, Hollywood investment in movie production was significant. As late as 1967, an article published in *Variety* reported, "Three of ten French productions have some U.S. financing."[29] That percentage, however, was not even half the rate of Hollywood investment in feature films produced in Great Britain, where throughout the 1960s more than two-thirds of the films produced were financed entirely, or in part, by subsidiary companies owned and controlled by the Hollywood majors.[30]

Two decades later, the automobile industry in the United States would begin to define an "American-made" product by where it was assembled, regardless of where its major components were manufactured. The movie industry never reached that stage during the 1960s, although attributions of the country of origin for many movies became increasingly inconsistent, complex, and sometimes misleading. Exactly what was a Hollywood production and what was a "national" one (British, French, or Italian) became a real enough issue in the 1960s. In any number of instances it became a question that was difficult, if not impossible, to answer. As the national pedigree of many a particular movie was called into question, Hollywood's motion-picture production provided a precursor for the globalization of the world's economy that occurred in the last two decades of the twentieth century.

THE COMPLEXITIES OF RUNAWAY PRODUCTION

The overall artistic effect of runaway production on Hollywood features was even more difficult to assess than the convoluted economic relationships that developed between the film industries of numerous nations. As the film historian Richard Dyer MacCann argued persuasively, audiences after World War II came to appreciate, and to expect, real locations in the movies.[31] Films gained the look of authenticity by being shot in an actual locale, or in one closely resembling it, rather than on a studio set or a back lot. In this sense, runaway production contributed significantly to an emerging aesthetic that blended with the trend toward photographic naturalism in feature films. On the other hand, when sheer economic considerations displaced a production from utilizing a domestic location in the United States, the results could be negative. The critic Charles Higham, for example, maintains that the decision to film the movie version of LOLITA (1962, Stanley Kubrick) in England sacrificed "the grit of seedy American towns and the entire freeway culture which gave the book so much."[32]

There were no neat and easy answers to the aesthetic questions raised by runaway production. Some films depended on the convincing authenticity and realism of their locales. Others did not. No one, for example, appeared to mind that "Spaghetti Westerns" like A FISTFUL OF DOLLARS (1964), FOR A FEW DOLLARS MORE (1965), and THE GOOD, THE BAD, AND THE UGLY (1966) were filmed in Mediterranean locales, not the American West, nor that they featured international casts and utilized post-synchronized sound with few of the actors' original voices.[33]

The question of which films most effectively utilized foreign locations, however, gave way to the central financial question of whether over time runaway production really proved cost effective for Hollywood. The economics of runaway production were complex, for it soon became apparent to the industry that in the long run there was no guarantee that shooting a film where labor costs were lower necessarily reduced the production's total cost. Frequently, much longer shooting schedules were required to make a movie in a foreign country.[34] Foreign crews were often not as competent or effective as their American counterparts. Language barriers and governmental red tape interfered with a number of runaway productions. And even though transportation and communication were improving globally, serious problems and setbacks remained due to missed travel connections, mail that went astray, or interrupted telephone connections.

By the mid 1960s, evidence of a downturn in overseas production by the Hollywood majors was clear. Inconvenience and additional production costs were becoming a burden. Still, as late as 1970, at a meeting of film industry employees in Los Angeles, leaders of several Hollywood unions and guilds maintained that runaway production continued to account for nearly a third of Hollywood's annual feature production. Because of it, they maintained, unemployment among technicians and production personnel in Hollywood remained close to 40 percent.[35] Indeed, even at the very end of the 1960s, Hollywood producers were still investing upwards of $100 million annually in projects being filmed outside the United States.[36]

Television and a Changing Hollywood

Television's rapid growth in the United States during the 1950s, and not the film industry's transitory shift to runaway production, appeared to be the core of Hollywood's real dilemma at the beginning of the 1960s. In 1949, just 2 percent of households in the United States had a television set. Ten years later, 86 percent of households had at least one set.[37] Despite those statistics, some leaders in the motion picture industry argued publicly during the 1950s that television would never be able to successfully supplant moviegoing. They urged the industry to invest in such technologies as widescreen and 3-D to exploit the large size of the movie screen and distinguish the movie experience from anything that could be seen on television. As a result, many film historians maintained, Hollywood majors generally ignored television in favor of relying on schemes to save the American cinema.

More thorough research from the late 1980s and the early 1990s into the history of investment in production for television by the Hollywood majors, however, has documented that Hollywood was very much active in entering production for that medium. Additionally, executives wanted to exploit the medium to play movies that had been produced for theatrical release dating back well before the advent of commercial television. By the late 1950s, in fact, nearly every major motion picture studio was engaged in some sort of production for television.

Columbia and Universal, the so-called "second rank" Hollywood studios, had been limited historically in the venture capital available to them and had not owned their own theater chains. They were first to enter into producing programming for television in the early 1950s and were followed soon by richer, more firmly established and entrenched studios. Warner Bros., 20th Century-Fox, and Metro-Goldwyn-Mayer (MGM) all diversified into television production in 1955.[38] The relationship between the industries was convoluted from the beginning of broadcast television in the United States. The Hollywood establishment certainly saw in television an opponent that threatened the long-standing appeal of movies shown in theaters to a mass audience of all ages and soon recognized that the availability of television in nearly every American home would undermine, and perhaps eventually eliminate entirely, the social habit of regular family excursions to the movies.

The Hollywood majors never established a direct competition to the broadcast television networks (ABC, CBS, NBC, and, briefly, Dumont). Extensive talk about introducing some form of pay-per-view television originated in the mid 1950s. Pay-per-view television met strong resistance from the Federal Communications Commission (FCC) during the 1960s, even though the television networks were not restrained by federal regulators from becoming involved in film production. During the 1960s, pay-per-view television was promoted vigorously by the Screen Actors Guild; its president, Charlton Heston, constantly proselytized the idea. In essence, however, it became a cause promoted almost exclusively by actors and actresses. From the producers' perspective, the development of a pay-per-view television system as an alternative to free, advertising-supported broadcasts of the networks had no real allure.

While the major Hollywood companies continued to pay lip service to pay-per-television in concert with their perennial criticism of broadcast television, they evinced little real interest in tackling the challenge of launching and nurturing such an entirely new scheme.[39] Federal regulations that blocked such ideas as large screen television for movies theaters, and lack of venture capital and genuine interest by Hollywood majors in the development of pay-for-view television delayed it until the late 1970s, when it was spearheaded by Home Box Office (HBO), which was owned by media giant Time-Life, Inc.[40]

During the 1960s, the major Hollywood companies already invested in production for television seriously accelerated their strategy of greater integration with the newer medium. The entire matter of how much exposure films would get on television, and how such exposure might effect the motion picture business in general, was still vexing. Fear was common that the presence of movies on the little screen in everyone's home would further diminish the glamour and appeal of theatrical movies and their stars. The majors began creating ancillary branches of production that would make movies for television not necessarily intended for theatrical release. 20th Century-Fox, which experienced a sharp decline in its production of features for theatrical release during 1962 and 1963, began to reemerge in 1965 as a producer of films for television.[41] In 1966, Lew Wasserman of MCA/Universal Pictures reached an agreement with NBC to produce films exclusively for television broadcast.[42] By the end of the 1960s, the films produced by the Hollywood majors directly for television actually outnumbered Hollywood's theatrical releases being shown on the networks.[43]

From the opposite side of the new and emerging Hollywood, television networks explored inroads into motion picture production. In 1967, CBS bought the old Republic Pictures facilities, which had been closed since 1959, with the intention of self-producing feature-length movies for television. That same year, ABC established a similar subsidiary for feature-length movie production.[44] At this juncture in industry history, with no genuine hopeful signs for pay-per-view television on the horizon, the Screen Actors Guild finally reached a historic decision. Although expressing concern over "the danger in the networks entering filmmaking," the union chose in 1967 not to oppose either CBS or ABC in the courts.[45]

While misgivings and tensions abounded between various elements in the motion picture and television industries, by the end of the 1960s a symbiosis had developed between them. Television had taken away much of the mass audience from movies in the 1950s, only to become increasingly dependent on the motion picture industry's product and its production values for much of its prime-time programming by the end of the 1960s. Worldwide, the spread of television provided new markets for older American movies and stimulated audience interest in Hollywood's new releases. Over the course of the 1960s, the impact of television on the movies, and of the movies on TV, while always complicated (and sometimes contentious) had become, in essence, mutually beneficial.

Even as the major studios sought to develop strategies and technologies for producing theatrical movies different from what could be seen on television, they also began shifting resources toward television production. Still, their largest profits came from selling the rights to telecast films, including many older ones, originally produced for theatrical exhibition. The rapid rise of television during the 1950s and the increased demand from the television networks for films to broadcast posed a question to the entirety of the motion picture community: just who would reap what amounted to windfall profits on older films, many of which had little value for theatrical re-release, but could be marketed for television? In strong opposition to the collective interests of Hollywood's major companies, which stood to simply lap up these profits, the industry's actors and actresses stepped forward to claim a right to residual earnings from the television broadcast of older films.

THE SAG STRIKE OF 1960

At the end of 1959, the membership of the Screen Actors Guild (SAG) once more elected Ronald Reagan as their president. He had previously served in that role from 1947 to 1952. Reagan was called on to lead the organization in a showdown with producers over the issue of residual earnings for actors and actresses for their parts in films now being shown on television. This issue loomed especially large at the very end of the 1950s. The deterioration of the Hollywood studio system had substantially decreased the number of screen players under contract to the studios and was accompanied by a substantial downturn in the production of feature films in southern California. Focusing their demand on residuals for their performances in films produced since 1948 that were to be shown on television, SAG called for a strike at the beginning of 1960 against Hollywood's major production companies.[46]

Representatives of the major Hollywood studios maintained that this demand amounted to SAG members wanting to be paid twice for doing one job, since the actors had been compensated contractually at the time the films were originally produced. SAG, by contrast, maintained that actors and actresses were entitled to some of the profits that producers earned from the sale of television rights for films that were originally produced only for theatrical distribution. SAG argued that television exhibition created an entirely new category of earnings. Meanwhile, deeper battle-lines were being drawn between producers of films and actors over the extent to which motion-picture production was going to be influenced by thespians in the post-studio era.

The choice of Reagan to lead SAG through the first strike in its history was controversial. Reagan's critics assailed his presumed "sweetheart unionism" as toadying up to the producers. Charlton Heston, Reagan's immediate successor as SAG president, dismissed that view, claiming later that subsequent leftist leanings of the union membership effectively "rewrote the Guild's history" in order to discredit Reagan's leadership in successfully leading SAG to a negotiated resolution of the 1960 strike.[47] While the notion remains that Reagan was too inclined to compromise with the studio bosses, a balanced historical assessment of the eventual agreement that ended the strike suggests that its resolution was both reasonable and beneficial for both sides.

In March 1960, the Screen Actors Guild accepted a lump sum of $2.25 million from the studios to set up a health and welfare plan for its members, along with the guarantee that actors would share 6 percent of the producers' net revenues from the sale of a given film's rights for telecast. This 6 percent figure was arrived at by calculating a figure based on the gross earnings of any sale of a film's television rights less 40 percent.[48]

The agreement pleased producers by promptly clearing the way for the sale of television rights for all post-1948 Hollywood movies. Actors and actresses, meanwhile, were now guaranteed at least some earnings on their past work whenever their older films were shown on television. Residual agreements from future television earnings became commonplace in actors' and actresses' contracts. The guarantee of these new earnings from the sale of older films for telecast, in fact, contributed significantly to the rising financial fortunes of SAG members for the rest of the decade. Even though the number of moviegoers in the United States was plummeting, the gross earnings of SAG members were steadily increasing year by year, fueled primarily by earnings from residuals paid for telecasts of older films. Gross earnings rose 7 percent in 1966, 4 percent in both 1967 and 1968, and 7 percent in 1969.[49]

SAG President Ronald Reagan (center) *with union members Alexis Smith, Doris Day, and Jack Carson, winter 1960.*

Such broad statistics, however, provide only a general indication of the rising average earnings of actors in Hollywood features. More importantly, top actors and actresses gained greater influence and power over motion picture production as a whole. While the end of long-term player contracts with the studios threatened the security and livelihood of many, other Hollywood stars quickly became better paid and were increasingly able to be more selective in their choices of film roles. Hence, the most successful thespians rapidly gained influence, not only over their own financial fortunes, but increasingly over many creative aspects of the production process itself as well.

The Changing Hollywood Firmament

When Hollywood's longest-running player contract between Universal Pictures and actor Rock Hudson expired in 1965, the system that for five decades had bound and controlled major screen actors to specific studios was declared dead and buried.[50] The screen player contract system, however, had been undergoing substantial changes over the previous fifteen years. Well before the system was pronounced "ended," a combination of financial and contractual agreements had completely redefined the ways in which actors and actresses would be compensated and how they might influence production decisions. Emphasis on free-lance business arrangements in the industry and the rise of the production "deal" for securing the financing and distribution for a particular film translated into increased leverage, both financially and artistically, for the most sought-after stars. The competition for acquiring star talent increasingly became recognized as the most important single element in putting together a film package for production.[51] Hollywood's bankers increasingly put emphasis on a star's name in their consideration of whether or not to green-light a production for financing.[52]

During the 1960s the fundamental groundwork was laid out in Hollywood for the practices that increasingly permitted star players to dictate artistic choices in big budget productions and, in some instances, to refocus the creative elements in a film toward their role.[53] The end of long-term studio contracts was catalyst to shifting the fortunes of the most successful Hollywood actors and actresses toward becoming prominent players with substantial financial clout and increased artistic control over what the motion picture industry produced.[54]

The new, free-lance Hollywood of the 1960s also gave rise to new professions; the "line producer," for example, was essentially responsible for managing the bankers' and the producers' money throughout the actual process of a film production. The new free-lance system also spawned new kinds of tensions between writers, directors, and stars. No longer simply working on contract for studios, writers could negotiate greater leverage over decisions about how their work was brought to the screen and by whom. Directors frequently wanted a new and different kind of identification with a film, which was increasingly auteurist in nature.

As the 1960s ended, the importance of merchandising in the motion picture industry decidedly tilted the influence over production to the movie's star: Stars, alas, are marketable in ways that line producers, writers, and even directors are not. It was not long before the conglomerates (those large businesses that bought out the Hollywood majors in the late 1960s) figured out that the face of a film star (on book jackets, record albums, box tops, tee shirts, etc.) is the most product-like factor in a movie, and the performance of any major actor or actress in any given movie can be built upon in the future for other presentations (sequels, remakes, television presentations, etc.).[55]

ACTORS AS PRODUCERS

By 1960, it was already a well-established practice that studios worked with stars to finance movies, while stars increasingly called themselves producers and set up independent companies. United Artists, at its founding in 1919, had pioneered the idea of Hollywood screen players having the right to make the films they wanted within a limited framework. In the 1950s, United Artists came to the forefront in working out innovative financing deals as the studio era ended. The transformation of production to joint ventures that involved stars in increasingly important ways was piecemeal, but nonetheless steady. United Artists offered a percentage deal to enlist Gary Cooper to co-star with Burt Lancaster in VERA CRUZ (1953). In this kind of an arrangement the star typically received a 10 percent share as a "third party participant" with remaining earnings split between United Artists (which arranged the financing for the film) and the film's actual producer. The next year, Bryna Productions, founded by actor Kirk Douglas, entered negotiations with United Artists to the make THE VIKINGS, released in 1958. The range in which major stars might become producers or co-producers of major films proliferated quickly.[56]

Even while he was still "under contract" to Universal, Rock Hudson had established a degree of autonomy in 1960 by becoming the producer of record, through his

Seven Pictures Corporation (later renamed Gibraltar Films), of all the movies he would make during the next six years. Universal reliably supplied the financing and distribution arrangements for all of those productions.[57] In some instances, actors turned more truly independent by establishing their own production companies that more vigorously pursued alternatives to the studios for funding. John Wayne had founded his "Batjac" Production Company in 1951; by the mid 1960s it was so successful that Batjac had diversified into real estate, farming operations, apartment complex management, and publishing.[58] Wayne steadfastly maintained that the only true "independents" were those producers who, like himself, had taken the risk of establishing their own production organizations with full staffs. Nonetheless, although comparatively few actors or actresses matched the thoroughness with which Wayne pursued his business, the variety of motion-picture production entities either controlled or held in some way by Hollywood actors and actresses increased exponentially during the 1960s.[59] Veteran Hollywood producer Darryl F. Zanuck ridiculed Wayne for appropriating the powers of producer and director on THE ALAMO (1960), in which Wayne starred as well. Coming in 1960, however, Zanuck's criticism was belated. The floodgates in Hollywood were already open for nearly every sort of possible production arrangement whereby major actors and actresses might share in, or even control, the financial interest in a film.[60]

Veteran actor Gregory Peck (far right) in MAROONED *(1969). Although he still acted, Peck, like many male stars of his generation, had turned primarily to producing films during the 1960s.*

The Mirisch Brothers (left to right), *Marvin, Walter, and Harold.*

In one type of venture, for example, Marlon Brando signed a deal with Paramount to produce, direct, and star in ONE-EYED JACKS (1961), which was financed entirely by the studio. Brando received 100 percent of the movie's profits, while the studio earned revenues only from its distribution fees.[61] Brando next went on to produce and star in MUTINY ON THE BOUNTY (1962) and THE UGLY AMERICAN (1963). Both of those films, however, compromised him with the Hollywood establishment: MUTINY ON THE BOUNTY was a colossal financial failure, and THE UGLY AMERICAN was an anathema to many in the Hollywood establishment because they considered the movie anti-American. Those problems aside, the box-office and critical failure of Brando in BEDTIME STORY (1963) effectively placed his acting career in limbo for the second half of the 1960s.[62]

At least a half-dozen veteran actors—Cary Grant, Charlton Heston, William Holden, Burt Lancaster, Gregory Peck, and Frank Sinatra—found new opportunities to produce films in Hollywood they had never had before.[63] Indeed, for a while in the early to mid 1960s, the crossover of major actors and actresses of the waning studio era into producing became the Hollywood rule, not the exception. Many veteran actors chose new incarnations in Hollywood as producers as their screen careers faded. Nonetheless, their roles as producers and performers with creative control on productions were highly individual. Hollywood in the immediate post-studio era provided a free-lance environment that infrequently followed even its own fledgling models for doing business.

In the early 1960s, Hollywood suddenly found itself in a period where all sorts of production arrangements—and permutations of them—abounded. In his autobiography, for example, Charlton Heston recalls hesitatingly negotiating with the producer Samuel Bronston, who had devised an ingenious way for financing EL CID (1961), for any form of influence on the conditions of production. The very next year, Heston recalled, he came away from a luncheon with Bronston realizing he had granted to Bronston the authority for signing Ava Gardner to co-star with Heston in 55 DAYS AT PEKING (1963).[64] For other actors, however, such power was asserted more consciously and even before their careers had peaked. The Producers Guild of America honored Paul Newman as its producer of the year for 1968 (for RACHEL, RACHEL),[65] an undertaking that fell chronologically between his highly regarded acting roles in COOL HAND LUKE (1967) and BUTCH CASSIDY AND THE SUNDANCE KID (1969).

Along with the rise of "independent" production companies founded by prominent actors and actresses, an entire new branch of the movie production industry was created. Pioneered by Harold Mirisch in the early 1950s, and operated by him and his brothers, Walter and Marvin, the Mirisch Company was the prototype for providing business and legal services to the growing number of production ventures that were filmed independently but financed by a major studio.[66]

2

Changing Patterns of Production and the Arrival of the Conglomerates

Independent Filmmaking

During the 1930s and 1940s, seven major Hollywood studios had been responsible for producing two-thirds of the movies in the United States, including nearly all first-run films.[1] Still, there had always been room for independent producers who operated successfully along with several well-established but minor studios.[2] The decline of the Hollywood studio system during the 1950s, however, appeared to reverse this trend. By 1958, half of the features produced in the United States were "independent."[3] Two years later, two-thirds of the feature films being produced in the United States were attributed to 165 different production entities.[4] The major studios might have invested in nearly all of these productions and might have reached a distribution agreement with the producers of practically all of them before filming began. Still, the overwhelming majority of the productions were correctly called independent because they were produced outside the direct creative control of the studio. By 1960, the movie industry was well on its way toward a model of production in which practically each new movie was put together, packaged, and financed individually, with distribution arranged through one of Hollywood's major companies.[5]

By the mid 1960s, the major studios had already moved well beyond their traditional stock company model, in which producers, directors, writers, talent, and technical personnel were all studio employees on contract. Replacing that system was the practice of negotiating short-term contracts for each specific production. In this environment, a number of the successful studio producers went off on their own and became independents, even though they might continue to work in close concert with their former employer. Some of Hollywood's most successful actors were also setting up production companies of their own.[6] The most common new Hollywood model for production agreements was pioneered by United Artists, which began in the early 1950s to finance independent producers (sometimes backing them up to 100 percent) in return for a cut of the profits along with set distribution fees that were promised to the company.[7]

The emerging model for motion-picture production in the United States during the 1960s was based on "the deal" or "the package," a contractual agreement (often an oral contract) that brought together such diverse elements as a script, director, lead talent, and director of photography, among others, as a basis for securing financing and a distribution agreement from a major studio.[8] As this new system evolved, some projects might be pursued with little or no studio control over the actual production. "They'd never see a script," remarked George Axelrod, who in partnership with Frank Sinatra produced THE MANCHURIAN CANDIDATE (1962) for United Artists. "Once they ok'd [a project]," he continued, "they'd say, 'Goodbye, bring us a print.' It was a lovely way to work . . . . We were allowed to do wild things."[9]

Typically, however, such lassitude and freedom could hardly sustain the workings of a complex industry in which the unit costs of production were so high. The arrangements between individual producers and major Hollywood companies were nearly always unique, and frequently open to disagreement. As contracts and agreements became more detailed, lawyers and agents increasingly gained prominence in the motion picture industry. Typical of the changing Hollywood environment was the "change of elements" clause that came to be written into practically all movie production agreements. The clause ensured that while a project was in development and being offered around to different studios, it became impossible to change a major element—

Frank Sinatra (left, with Laurence Harvey) *acted in and co-produced THE MANCHURIAN CANDIDATE (1962).*

the script, the director, or the star—until after the first studio that was approached with the project was bought out. Such a clause assured that a significant position of strength was still held by the studio even in the planning stages of a project, no matter how and by whom it might eventually be financed. The Hollywood of the moguls was in decline, but studio control over the industry was shifting, not disappearing.[10]

Distribution was at the fulcrum of the changing Hollywood motion picture industry in the 1960s. All the majors were moving from company-owned pictures to those owned either partially or entirely by independent producers.[11] Some observers might argue in hindsight that the majors' concentration on motion picture distribution came about by default. They had been forced out of ownership of movie theaters by the federal courts, and although several companies had dragged their feet on selling off their theaters (20th Century-Fox, most notably) the divestiture was essentially complete by 1960. By contrast, distribution was an area of the business that had been left unchanged. Distribution was the most flexible and profitable branch of the motion picture business, especially in an era of rapidly changing audiences, tastes, and technologies.

The central importance of motion picture distribution, and control over it, was evidenced in many ways during the 1960s as the majors shifted from making movies to financing them. A suit by Samuel Goldwyn, Jr., against 20th Century-Fox was the first significant legal action filed in the motion picture industry in the 1960s. He claimed that through secret and monopolistic practices Fox had prevented him from distributing and exhibiting seven different features on which he had served as producer.[12] Although the case was settled out of court, as many similar cases would be, Goldwyn's complaint was emblematic of the central issue facing independent producers in a changing industry. As James B. Harris, the producer of LOLITA (1962) and THE BEDFORD INCIDENT (1965), summed up the situation, "It's great to be left alone when you're making a movie, but not when you're finished with it!"[13] A major studio might no longer supervise a production directly, but it still controlled the terms under which a finished movie reached the theaters. Control of distribution meant complete leverage over the promotion and exploitation of a film, which could greatly influence its draw of audiences.

The financial inducement and legal incentives were strong for establishing new motion-picture production companies. An expanding U.S. economy provided increasing venture capital, and after 1963 the federal tax codes provided considerable write-offs for motion-picture production and a shelter for such investments that ended only in 1976.[14] Just as the Hollywood majors began scrambling in the mid 1960s to find the right films for a drastically changed audience, the attraction grew as well of putting money into projects with independent production entities. However, the idea that independent production would necessarily translate into increased artistic freedom that would protect a significant number of projects from the worst vicissitudes of commercialism remained an illusion.[15]

The realities of feature film production transcended the avarice of moguls and the assembly-line practices of the studio era. Production values, not production procedures, fundamentally drove up the cost of making movies. Even for independents there was no avoiding the need to invest big money in a picture,[16] and, especially for independent producers, there loomed the inevitable problem of distributing, promoting, and exploiting a completed film effectively. Rather than leading American film toward more adventurous risk-taking, the demise of the studio system actually meant that in most cases hits could no longer be counted on to cover the losses of box-office failures. A picture-by-picture production system can be recognized, in hindsight, as pointing inevitably toward less room for experimentation and high-risk production and leading to greater emphasis on projects that stayed closer to tested formulas. Studios held control over creativity in the studio system, but nearly all movies were being made under an economic "big tent" that provided at least some protection for losses on individual films.

Even though the new Hollywood system was more tenuous and precarious, many observers who regard risk-taking as an element of creativity applauded the changes. Soon after he became president of the Motion Picture Association of America (MPAA) in 1966, Jack Valenti appraised the situation: "This business has changed. The old bankers in the East, big Moguls in the West, concept is dead. Now a fellow like Kirk Douglas can find a script he likes, find his own financing up to a point, hire a big studio that will do all the planning and set up exhibition. That opens up the way for creativity right down the line, and a chance to modernize some of the business techniques."[17]

The vocation of movie producer opened up in the 1960s to agents, actors, writers, directors, financiers, and former high-ranking production personnel at the studios. New producers needed industry connections, avenues for communication, and sufficient networking in Hollywood to put together a production package that could be sold to a major company. Personal links to executives at the major companies were always vital and provided the most important key to success. Other aspects and amenities of the business world were less important. Successful new producers emerged by being skilled at "packaging" creative talent and financing into a production deal. Those producers were not employees of the major studios, nor were they entrepreneurs in the traditional sense. They succeeded through personal contacts and their lifeline was the telephone. As Frank Yablans, one of the leading new producers of the 1960s, explained, "If someone could find a way of grafting a phone-jack to my ass, I wouldn't even need an office."[18]

AMERICAN INTERNATIONAL PICTURES

Not all feature production was financed by the major studios. By finding a specific niche and relentlessly exploiting it, the single most successful independent production company to thrive entirely outside the sphere of the Hollywood majors during the 1960s was American International Pictures (AIP). The company had been founded in the early 1950s by Samuel Z. Arkoff and Ben Nicholson, neither of whom was considered enough of an industry insider to have been invited to join the Academy of Motion Picture Arts and Sciences until well into the the next decade.[19] Nonetheless, by 1964 AIP was annually producing twenty-five feature films, a quantity that substantially outnumbered features being financed by any of the major Hollywood studios.[20]

AIP's foremost producer and director was Roger Corman, who became known to many in the industry during the mid 1960s as the "King of the Bs." As Corman himself pointed out, however, that nickname was a misnomer. By the time that he and AIP became prominent in Hollywood, the so-called "B" films, which were intended to run second on a double bill, had disappeared.[21] Corman's movies, like almost all of AIP's productions, were low budget and aimed primarily at the teenage audience that was growing exponentially in America's suburbs. Typical of these features was the company's most financially successful movie, THE WILD ANGELS (1966). Produced and directed by Corman and starring Peter Fonda and Nancy Sinatra, it was the largest grossing low-budget film yet. Even more surprisingly, it was a critical success. THE WILD ANGELS made it onto the program of the prestigious Venice International Film Festival in Italy, causing no small degree of consternation among representatives of the major Hollywood

Roger Corman, American International Pictures' prime producer/director, at work.

studios who were in attendance. Since THE WILD ANGELS portrayed what many critics considered an underside of American society better ignored, establishment Hollywood tended to condemn the movie as "unpatriotic."[22]

During the late 1950s and throughout the 1960s, American International Pictures made a specialty of this type of feature and called them "protest films," although great numbers of critics dismissed them as "motorcycle flicks."[23] Indeed, for such critics, AIP's approach to production was easily lampooned:

1. Spend no money.
2. Play up the basest, most sensationalist angle.
3. Exaggerate wildly in the advertising.
4. Book each film in as many theaters at once as possible, to forestall negative "word of mouth." This last idea, dubbed saturation booking, is the only film distribution scheme that implies a film is worthless.[24]

In spite of such negative characterizations, however, AIP's overall impact on the American feature film during the 1960s was highly salutary. The company's productions, especially those overseen by Corman, were frequently a springboard for talented young directors like Francis Ford Coppola, or promising acting talent like Jack Nicholson. Even when Roger Corman's last film at AIP, GAS-S-S-S (1970), failed at the box office, several young actors—Cindy Williams, Ben Vereen, Talia Shire, and Bud Cort, among the cast's twenty-five-year-old and under group that inherits the earth from tiresome older generations—were launched into successful screen-acting careers.[25] "You have to save your money so you can afford to work for (Roger Corman)," remarked Tina Hirsch, the highly regarded film editor, "but it's really worth it in many ways. The reason he turns out so many really good people is because he is willing to take a chance."[26]

In 1970 Corman formed his own company, New World Pictures, in partnership with his wife Julie and his brother Gene. New World carried on many of the practices that Corman had pioneered at American International Pictures, but without the same industry-wide impact that AIP exerted during the mid 1960s. As the movie business changed in the early 1970s, New World shifted away from production to increasingly become a distributor for foreign films released in the United States.[27]

CHILDREN OF HOLLYWOOD, OFFSPRING OF AIP

American International Pictures nurtured the careers of Peter Fonda and Dennis Hopper. Along with AIP veteran Jack Nicholson, they combined to play in EASY RIDER (1969), the most commercially successful, low-budget, "independent" production of the

Peter Fonda and Nancy Sinatra in THE WILD ANGELS, *the "biker flick" that made it onto the program of the Venice International Film Festival in Italy.*

1960s. Co-produced by Fonda and directed by Hopper, this movie appeared to many observers to successfully transcend the conventions and formulas of the "biker flick." Hollywood pundits and movie critics nationwide embraced EASY RIDER as a model for courageous low-budget production. At a time when pleas for authenticity and artistry reverberated among young moviegoing audiences, Fonda himself summed up his own interpretation of the film's potential for forging a new, independent spirit in the American cinema: "There's a better chance of honesty in a $400,000 picture than there is in a $2 million picture," he exclaimed.[28]

It is arguable, however, how truly "independent" this film was. EASY RIDER had wide box-office exposure domestically and globally only because of a distribution deal with Columbia Pictures that had been arranged between Fonda (the scion of acting legend Henry Fonda) and Bert Schneider, who happened to be the son of longtime Columbia Pictures Board President Abe Schneider. EASY RIDER was independent in its creative vision and had been produced on a low budget. That it succeeded so well, however, was still a function of this distribution deal with one of the majors.[29]

The new Hollywood production establishment took notice of the immediate box-office success of EASY RIDER. So, too, did Hollywood's critics, who believed that the film's appeal might be a beacon for a genuine breakthrough for independents and the advent of an alternative cinema based on low-budget production. Nonetheless, countervailing factors favored subtle adjustments in Hollywood, rather than radical transformations. Films meant to copy EASY RIDER fizzled at the box office. Independent producers had become commonplace in the American cinema throughout the 1960s, but feature film distribution remained unquestionably in the hands of the major studios. Moreover, none of the majors had disappeared. Instead, they were all being transformed during the late 1960s, becoming parts of far more wealthy and powerful commercial entities that could position these Hollywood companies to play a new and pivotal role in the emerging global entertainment industry.

Mergers and the Conglomerates

Variety's anniversary issue for the year 1966 listed ten items that constituted ferment in the motion picture and television industries during that year:

1. Election of Jack Valenti as President of MPAA.
2. Scrapping of the old Motion Picture Production Code.
3. MGM management in fight for its life.
4. Paramount absorbed by Gulf + Western.
5. THE SOUND OF MUSIC sets domestic box office record.
6. Columbia Pictures stock tenure offer by Swiss bank.
7. Formation of a fourth (television) network.
8. Bob Kinter (a vice president for programming) quits NBC.
9. Warner Bros. and CBS partner in film production experiment.
10. Exhibitors unite under NATO (National Association of Theater Owners).[30]

Each of these events was important in its own right, and several of them marked significant, or even definitive trends for the motion picture and television industries. None, however, was more significant for the future of the American feature film than the item buried in the middle of the list (at number 4). The takeover of one of the Hollywood majors by a corporation that had no prior experience or financial interest in the movie industry marked a dramatic shift in what Hollywood was and how Hollywood would carry out its business in the future.

Gulf + Western, which acquired Paramount in 1966, had its origins in the auto parts industry. It began as "Michigan Bumper" in the early 1950s. By the end of that decade it was established as a rapidly growing company that had acquired vast holdings in automobile accessories and supplies.[31] The company was headed by the Austrian-born Charles Bluhdorn. He had renamed his enterprise Gulf + Western in 1958 after acquiring Beard & Stone Electric of Houston, Texas, a manufacturing firm that made electronics for automobiles. The company's new name reflected the foreign-born owner's interpretation of his enterprise's geographic range: Houston, Texas = Gulf, and its Michigan home base = Western. Under his new corporate title Gulf + Western, Bluhdorn and his firm embarked on what was increasingly to become the company's speciality—the acquisition of controlling interest in profitable enterprises of all sorts. Gulf + Western was a forerunner in the practice of leveraged buyouts of various corporations. Operating in an increasingly diverse range of businesses, it provided a common model of entrepreneurial success for the last quarter of the twentieth century.[32]

Gulf + Western C.E.O. Charles Bluhdorn. Under Bluhdorn G+W became a forerunner in the practice of leveraged buyouts in an increasingly diverse range of businesses.

Gulf + Western's buyout of Paramount was the first in a rapid succession of acquisitions of controlling interests in the Hollywood majors by larger and wealthier corporations during the late 1960s. The prelude to this changing structure, however, dated back to 1959, when MCA (The Music Corporation of America) bought out Universal Pictures. The growth of MCA to a position where it could acquire Universal, moreover, was part of the larger story of the motion picture industry's transition during the 1950s. The breakup of the studio system immediately benefited the interests of talent agents, and the best and most powerful of agents were at the huge MCA agency.[33]

MCA was founded in the 1920s by a Chicago ophthalmologist named Jules Stein, who continued at the helm of the company through the 1950s. MCA's clout in the industry increased substantially in 1952 when the Screen Actors Guild agreed to a blanket waiver for MCA to represent talent and to produce television programming.[34] Largely as a result of that arrangement, MCA grew rich quickly. By 1959 it was in a position to purchase Universal Pictures.[35] This bold business move was engineered by Lew Wasserman, MCA's president since 1946. He pursued the acquisition as part of an overall scheme that included easing out the elderly Jules Stein from his position as chairman of the board at MCA.[36]

Universal had entered production for television in the early 1950s. Wasserman's vision for the 1960s entailed shifting Universal further toward television production with the intent of erasing almost entirely the sense of distinction between motion-picture production and production for television. Within three years of MCA's acquisition of Universal, Wasserman could boast, "In its heyday MGM . . . produced one hundred hours of film a year. Today, we make three hundred hours of film at Universal."[37] During that period between 1959 and 1962 MCA/Universal's earnings nearly doubled.[38]

By being the first of the Hollywood majors to achieve complete integration between motion picture and television production, the company carved out a profitable niche for itself. Wasserman's inspiration was one solution for Hollywood's business dilemma at the end of the 1950s and was widely admired within the industry. That admiration, however, did not extend beyond Hollywood to the halls of the U.S. Department of Justice. MCA/Universal's successes after the 1959 acquisition promptly drew the critical attention of the federal government's antitrust division. Faced with the threat of a government antitrust suit, the company divested itself entirely of its talent agency in 1962.[39]

Among the Hollywood majors, however, Universal took the road less traveled in the 1960s: first, by forging ahead with production for television, and then by reintegrating feature production for theatrical distribution back into its business mix toward the end of the decade. In doing so, Universal established a horizontal integration of the company's business that was exactly the opposite of the traditional, vertical monopoly that the Hollywood majors had held over the production, distribution, and exhibition of motion pictures, and which the federal courts had judged to be in constraint of trade. By mixing production for television with the production of feature films for theatrical release, Universal's losses on less successful productions could be covered by hits, costs could be spread out to cover high overhead, and Universal's facilities could be kept in constant use.[40]

PARAMOUNT AND GULF + WESTERN

The mergers and buyouts in Hollywood during the late 1960s were each different, and each had its own significance and importance for a changing industry. The takeover of Paramount by the auto parts supplier Gulf + Western was the first example of a buyout of a Hollywood major from outside the entertainment industry. An examination of the background of the buyout clarifies the motives behind all such Hollywood acquisitions in the late 1960s.

Gulf + Western's 1966 buyout of Paramount occurred immediately after the Hollywood major had first become the target of two Broadway producers, Cy Feuer and Ernest Martin. The pair, who jointly held a substantial block of Paramount stock, shaped an agreement with Herbert Siegel to acquire majority control of the company. Federal regulators, however, challenged Siegel's involvement in the deal because he held a majority interest in General Artists, a talent agency.[41] Eventually, conflict-of-interest claims against Siegel by the federal regulators did not hold up in court. While the court's decision on the regulators' challenge to Siegel was pending, Gulf + Western moved successfully on Paramount.[42] The targeting of Paramount for a buyout by several potential purchasers was common knowledge on Wall Street months before Gulf + Western made its move.[43]

Among Hollywood professionals, the acquisition was greeted with skepticism and suspicion often bordering on dismay.[44] A story circulated in Hollywood for years that Gulf +Western had acquired Paramount not for its value as a producer and distributor of movies, but rather as part of a larger financial intrigue aimed at accumulating enough capital assets to acquire New Jersey Zinc Company, which Gulf + Western coveted.[45] However, a review of the financial dealings of Gulf + Western clarifies that the acquisition of New Jersey Zinc was actually completed before the acquisition of Paramount.[46] Many movie industry pundits were still not certain that the company's interest was in film production and distribution. The acquisition of valuable real estate, along with the film library of Paramount that could be exploited in the rapidly expanding television market were believed to be the real prizes Gulf + Western was pursuing.[47]

It was widely known that the Hollywood majors had not been aggressive in exploiting their land holdings in southern California, or in closing down East Coast offices and consolidating management operations, or in marketing their array of older movies for television. Surely, each of those factors contributed to making them targets for buyout. The primary motive for the takeovers, however, was that any of these Hollywood companies could position their owners to thrive in an emerging new business sphere called "leisure"—favored by demographics and growing global affluence.

Gulf + Western's stewardship promptly placed Paramount at the center of what was labeled the company's "Leisure Time Group,"[48] in which the corporation invested heavily and developed quickly. Immediately, Gulf +Western added Desilu, a television production company and facility that had been founded by television stars Desi Arnaz and Lucille Ball. On the East Coast, Gulf + Western bought Madison Square Garden and acquired control of the arena's two main tenants, the New York Knicks professional basketball team and the New York Rangers professional hockey franchise. Ownership of Roosevelt Raceway, a harness racing track in suburban New York City, was added soon after. International Holiday on Ice, a traveling show of professional ice skaters, was the next purchase. The print media was not ignored: the specialty men's magazine *Esquire* was acquired, followed by Simon & Schuster Publishing and Monarch Books—all of which were added to the Leisure Group.[49] Under Gulf + Western, Paramount joined with an erstwhile competitor, Universal Pictures, in 1969 to open a new distribution company for the common market countries: Cinema International Corporation (CIC) was headquartered in the Netherlands.[50]

A 1971 Congressional report concluded that "Gulf +Western manages its acquisitions and assets on a decentralized basis."[51] In this regard, however, the corporation's buyout of Paramount was not typical. Gulf + Western CEO Charles Bluhdorn took a hands-on approach to Paramount's management, with one of his first moves at the studio being to replace the veteran production chief Howard Koch with Robert Evans, who was younger and had industry experience only as a minor actor and in 20th Century-Fox's international distribution division.[52] In the Hollywood community, however, Evans quickly became a figure who symbolized "the bridge between the business world at large and show business."[53] His powerful personality and his working methods reminded many observers of Hollywood's legendary first generation of moguls. Thus, the first major personnel appointment at Paramount by the "outsider" Bluhdorn was someone with a highly personal style and whose reach, both in the company and throughout Hollywood, was all-encompassing: "[Robert Evans] passes on the script, the producer, the director, and the cast," noted Gerald Clarke in a 1974 *Esquire* article. The gossip in industry circles about a "takeover" at Paramount by a production chief who wanted to

Paramount's new production chief Robert Evans mingling with the talent: (front left to right) *Lee Marvin, Evans, Barbra Streisand, Stanley Donnenfeld (studio vice president for administration), Clint Eastwood, and* (back, left to right) *Rock Hudson, John Wayne, and Yves Montand* (1969).

know only about the bottom line and profits at the expense of knowing nothing about the movies, could not have been less accurate.[54]

Claims that Gulf + Western acquired Paramount and quickly forgot about the studio, consigning its operations to accountants tallying the ledger sheets, were far from the truth. Bluhdorn followed Evans's every move carefully and was duly impressed when the young production chief brought in the very successful ROSEMARY'S BABY (1968, Roman Polanski). In some instances, Bluhdorn himself even made the final decision on whether or not to pursue a movie project. One of his biggest gaffes was turning down the production of FUNNY GIRL (1968) that was set to star Barbra Streisand. Bluhdorn decided that he could not satisfactorily answer his own question, "Who wants to hear this Jewish girl singing?" Columbia Pictures picked up the project and audiences all across America provided a resounding response.[55]

It was Bluhdorn who added the ambitious Frank Yablans to the Paramount production team,[56] and it was Bluhdorn who named the twenty-nine-year-old Stanley Jaffe as president of Paramount Pictures. Son of Leo Jaffe, the longtime board chairman of Columbia Pictures, Stanley Jaffe was a graduate of the Wharton School of Finance at the University of Pennsylvania.[57] Stanley Jaffe reflected the changing world of the Hollywood majors. In addition to genuine credentials in the increasingly sophisticated practices of contemporary business, he had connections in the industry. He had something else in his favor, too: his age. As Bluhdorn commented, "To me, Mr. Jaffe epitomizes what the motion picture business is all about today. He is a knowledgeable young man in an industry that is appealing, first of all, to the youth market."[58]

FOX ON THE RUN

The motives for the Gulf + Western acquisition of Paramount were emblematic of the string of acquisitions of the Hollywood majors by conglomerates in the late 1960s, but it was nonetheless a distinctive and *sui generis* purchase and takeover. The story of the fate of each of the major studios differed. Moreover, despite the widespread impression that Hollywood had been monolithic and single-minded historically, the majors did not necessarily mimic the business practices of one another even in the heyday of the studio era.

During the 1960s, such differences became even more apparent and telling. For example, 20th Century-Fox, which was controlled by the Zanuck family, took a wholly different approach than any of the other companies that were financially in the red at the beginning of the 1960s. After losing over $15 million on its motion-picture production and distribution activities in the fiscal year 1960, the company began to sell off stock and real estate to cover its shortfalls.[59] In April of 1961, 20th Century-Fox sold its 260-acre lot in west Los Angeles to ALCOA, an aluminum manufacturing company that developed the property into a commercial and residential community named "Century City."[60] The large profits from that land sale, however, did not suffice to reverse Fox's precarious financial situation. At the same time that the land deal was being completed, 20th Century-Fox was embarking on a film production that would prove disastrous. Indeed, the history of 20th Century-Fox in the 1960s was so bound up with the colossal failure of CLEOPATRA (1963) that the company's financial crisis through the rest of the decade can be understood in the ensuing bust-boom-bust cycle that began with that film.

Originally conceived as a relatively modest production that was to star Joan Collins, one of 20th Century-Fox's remaining contract players, CLEOPATRA escalated into a runaway fiasco starring Elizabeth Taylor, who was paid over a million dollars to play the lead role. Soon after Taylor came on board, she suffered a string of serious illnesses that delayed production. Once she was well enough for production to start, her romance with co-star Richard Burton and the resulting estrangement from her husband, Eddie Fisher, swept the media's fascination. The coverage of this romantic triangle reached a new high—or low—in celebrity journalism for the mainstream press. "Probably no news event in modern times has affected so many people personally," humorist Art Buchwald commented. "Nuclear testing, disarmament, Berlin, Vietnam, and the struggle between Russia and China are nothing comparable to the Elizabeth Taylor story."[61]

To what degree this publicity deluge, and its attendant turmoil, really affected the production is arguable. In the midst of the celebrity scandal, film critic William K. Zinsser wrote an article wondering why 20th Century-Fox hadn't already scrapped the project, which was clearly out of control.[62] Managing long production delays and 10,000 extras, the veteran producer Walter Wanger, who had "loaned" himself from his own production company to Fox for CLEOPATRA, lamented that the entire undertaking was "crazy."[63] With CLEOPATRA leading the way toward the abyss, the Hollywood industry appeared to be embarking on a reckless and irrational course that could cripple the entire American motion-picture industry. The production's "craziness" called into question the accountability and lines of responsibility in a production scheme improvised from a mixture of studio backing and independent production entities. For many, CLEOPATRA amounted to such an indictment of Hollywood in general that it raised fundamental questions about the industry and how long it could survive.

CLEOPATRA provided an interesting story and grist for the mill of Hollywood's critics. Its true significance for the institutional history of the industry, however, was its place in time. Hollywood had reached its low point in total feature film production, and competition from European production was steadily rising. Most importantly, the studio era model of systematic and tightly managed production appeared entirely erased from Hollywood practice. CLEOPATRA's initial director, Rouben Mamoulian, who had been established as one of the greats of the classic Hollywood era, summed up the entire problem of the post-studio era's free-lance system and the deterioration of a clear chain-of-command in Hollywood production. Shooting the film on location in Rome with the producer Walter Wanger, Mamoulian quickly developed a response to suggestions by Wanger: "You didn't hire me—Skouras (the production chief at Fox), Adler, and Screiber did."[64] Eventually, however, Mamoulian was dismissed as the film's director and replaced by Joseph L. Mankiewicz, thus creating more chaos on the set.

As the production process veered out of control, so, too, did the picture's expenses. The final negative cost exceeded $40 million. Even though the picture's gross rental revenue was on a par with the big roadshows of the late 1950s, including THE TEN COMMANDMENTS (1956), THE BRIDGE ON THE RIVER KWAI (1957), SOUTH PACIFIC (1958), and BEN-HUR (1959), Fox came nowhere near recovering its enormous investment in the film. Relatively good business in the domestic market, coupled with satisfactory earnings abroad, simply could not cover the staggering production costs.[65] As one Hollywood pundit put it, "Don't send a movie critic to review it, send a CPA."[66]

For some observers, the misadventure summed up everything bad about moviemaking in America *circa* 1963. CLEOPATRA was not just a movie that had spun out of control; rather, it was emblematic of the breakdown of an entire production process that historically had been well planned, systematic, and accountable. As an aftermath to the CLEOPATRA affair, 20th Century-Fox filed a $50 million lawsuit in 1964 against Richard Burton and Elizabeth Taylor on grounds that their "deportment" had been injurious to the production.[67] The suit was later dropped, but the following year Fox fired its head of production, Spyros Skouras, on whose watch CLEOPATRA had been produced.[68]

20th Century-Fox, however, rebounded mightily in 1965 when THE SOUND OF MUSIC became a sensational hit. Banking on THE SOUND OF MUSIC formula, the family-run studio controlled by the Zanucks then went on to produce two lavish and expensive musicals, DOCTOR DOLITTLE (1967) and STAR! (1968). The films recorded staggering losses, estimated at $11 million and over $15 million, respectively. Fox posted an overall loss of $36.8 million in 1969.[69] By the end of 1970, the Zanucks found themselves having to answer for company losses that were approaching $80 million. An intense battle among stockholders ensued, ending in the confirmation of Dennis Stanfill, a Naval Academy graduate and a former Rhodes scholar, to reorganize the company in 1970.[70]

COLUMBIA PICTURES

Of the Hollywood majors, only 20th Century-Fox and Columbia Pictures actually survived the decade without merging with or being bought out by a larger corporation. Of the two, Columbia Pictures had a much happier fate during the 1960s. A group of European investors made a takeover attempt in 1966 immediately after Gulf + Western acquired Paramount. That move, however, was blocked by the Federal Communications Commission (FCC). The regulators argued that since Columbia held financial interests in both radio and television broadcasting, there were sufficient grounds to prohibit foreign interests from investing in the company. Columbia was able to remain under the financial control of the Schneider family—father Abe and his sons, Stanley and Bert.[71]

Columbia's successes during the 1960s were the envy of the other majors. The company produced big money-making films in England, including LAWRENCE OF ARABIA (1962), A MAN FOR ALL SEASONS (1966), and OLIVER! (1968). Columbia scored well at the box office with vehicles for Sidney Poitier—TO SIR, WITH LOVE (1967), IN THE HEAT OF THE NIGHT (1967), and GUESS WHO'S COMING TO DINNER (1967). Columbia also found an off-beat success with IN COLD BLOOD (1967), a bleak and unrelenting portrayal of murder in the American heartland, and it picked up a veritable gold mine with its agreement to distribute EASY RIDER in 1969.[72] Columbia made huge earnings on the Barbra Streisand musical FUNNY GIRL in 1968, after Paramount had dropped the project and in the same year that Fox's big budget musical, STAR!, bombed.[73]

The Transformation of Hollywood

Gulf + Western's buyout of Paramount in 1966 was a catalyst that propelled the entire motion picture industry into new directions. TransAmerica Corporation bought out United Artists the following year. Once it had acquired 87 percent of United Artists stock, TransAmerica's management swiftly and efficiently diversified the company toward its own spin on the leisure market by buying up restaurant chains, motels, bowling alleys, and service stations.[74] During the early 1960s, United Artists had pursued excellent film production projects in Great Britain, including TOM JONES (1963), A SHOT IN THE DARK (1964), the Beatles' film A HARD DAY'S NIGHT (1964), and the James Bond series.[75] TransAmerica's directors wisely kept the highly successful and stable management team of Arthur Krim and Robert Benjamin in charge of production through the remainder of the 1960s. In 1969 the pair brought in yet another box-office and critical success with MIDNIGHT COWBOY, which earned the Academy Award for best picture that year.[76]

In 1967, Warner Bros. merged with the Seven Arts entertainment corporation of Toronto, Canada.[77] Seven Arts was initially interested in Warner's film library for the purpose of distributing and exploiting older films for television. In 1969, Warner Bros.-Seven Arts was acquired by Kinney National Services Corporation, which was headed by Steven Ross. Kinney manufactured and sold shoes, managed parking lots, and operated car rental agencies as well as a chain of funeral homes.[78] Warner Bros.-Seven Arts was the corporation's second major acquisition in the entertainment business, following the purchase of the Ashley Famous Agency from longtime show business entrepreneur Ted Ashley. Kinney then acquired *Mad* magazine for its entertainment division, dropped the Seven Arts from the Warner corporate name, and placed Ted Ashley in charge of movie production. He found immediate success with the popular "rockumentary" *Woodstock* (1970), which was produced cheaply and garnered excellent box-office earnings.[79]

Metro-Goldwyn-Mayer (MGM) entered the year 1969 under the presidency of Louis J. Polk, whose primary backers among stockholders were Edgar J. Bronfman (Seagrams Distillery) and the Time-Life magazine group. Soon, a second bidding faction, led by Las Vegas financier Kirk Kerkorian, whose wealth was primarily in airlines and hotels, moved on the studio. Kerkorian won the competition for control. Polk was ousted, and James T. Aubrey, his replacement, was hired from CBS Television. Aubrey moved quickly to redirect MGM's activities. To the chagrin of many Hollywood insiders, among whom he became known as "the Smiling Cobra," Aubrey promptly canceled fifteen feature film projects and moved ahead in selling off motion-picture industry branches of MGM, as well as the back lot, props, and the music library. The profits were poured into Kerkorian's MGM Grand Hotel and Casino development in Las Vegas.[80] Kerkorian's acquisition of MGM was the one instance of a buyout of one of Hollywood's "majors" during the 1960s that resulted in a de-emphasis of motion-picture production in favor of other leisure-based investments.[81]

THE EFFECTS ON HOLLYWOOD

Assessing the effect of the buyouts, *Variety* columnist Thomas M. Pryor concluded: "So far the congloms haven't brought any new ideas to the making and distributing of motion pictures."[82] The conglomerates did bring a "new anchor" of financial stability for the motion-picture industry, as the insightful independent producer Joseph E. Levine noted.[83] The New York-based Levine, who had pioneered co-productions with Europe, experienced the stability firsthand. In the summer of 1968 his small but prosperous Embassy films had been bought out by AVCO, a manufacturer of defense and aerospace equipment.[84] Indeed, the highly successful and resourceful film producer Frank Yablans argued that the movie industry began to "grow up" only when the major studios were incorporated into the larger business structures of the conglomerate corporations that acquired them.[85]

Hollywood majors continued to find financial backing from the banks they had relied on historically, especially Chase Manhattan and the Bank of America.[86] Nonetheless, while the sources of capital did not change abruptly, the financial strength of the conglomerates that took over the Hollywood companies assured a stable program of motion-picture production and substantially increased the borrowing power of the studios.[87] The British journal *The Economist*, which devoted nearly an entire issue in 1972 to an analysis of the effects, concluded that the large corporations' takeovers of the Hollywood majors saved the American feature film industry. Only with that fiscal stability and financial clout could Hollywood have survived and recovered from its economic depression of 1969–1971.[88] Film historian Garth Jowett, taking measure of Hollywood several years later, reached the same conclusion.[89]

Many critical voices were raised over the buyouts from within the Hollywood creative community. Young film director George Lucas expressed a view that would be echoed frequently: "The studios are corporations now and the men who run them are bureaucrats. They know as much about making movies as a banker does."[90] Veteran actress Katharine Hepburn noted that legendary moguls, like Sam Goldwyn, Louis B. Mayer, and Harry Cohn, "wanted to make money, too, but they had a romantic attitude toward the people who made movies and the movies themselves."[91] That argument was taken up by William Fadiman in his 1973 book, *Hollywood Now*. The Hollywood moguls were "monsters and pirates and bastards right to the bottom of their feet," he wrote, "but they *loved* movies, and they protected the people who worked for them."[92] Such opinions aside, the mergers and takeovers in Hollywood during the late 1960s stabilized studio finances and quickly set feature film production in the United States back on a promising financial course.

Hollywood bent but did not break during the 1960s. The entire feature film industry in the United States teetered briefly, but did not topple. From a low of just over 140 features produced in 1963, the number climbed back to 230 by the end of the 1960s. By the mid 1970s that number exceeded 300, equaling once again the volume of production in the mid 1950s.[93] There might be romantic motives for adoring Hollywood's colorful and legendary moguls of the past and preferring them to the new "suits" who had earned MBAs from such prestigious programs as Harvard and the Wharton School at the University of Pennsylvania. The historic truth, however, is more prosaic: corporate America saved Hollywood in the late 1960s and provided the motion picture industry the wherewithal and acumen for growth and prosperity during the 1970s and 1980s.

3

The Runaway Audience
and the Changing World
of Movie Exhibition

Audiences

To paraphrase 20th Century-Fox producer Jerry Wald, Hollywood's real problem in the 1960s was not so much "runaway production" as it was the "runaway audience."[1] A high point for movie attendance in the United States was reached in 1946 when an average of 90 million admissions to movie theaters were recorded weekly,[2] constituting a record 75 percent of the estimated "potential audience" nationwide.[3] During the next ten years, however, average weekly attendance dropped rapidly: 1956 figures set weekly movie theater audience figures at 46 million;[4] four years later, in 1960, that figure was 40 million; attendance plummeted to 20 million by 1970.[5]

The steadily shrinking movie theater audience in the United States was caused by the impact of television accompanied by changing demographics and lifestyles. A few media historians, such as Douglas Gomery, correctly argue that "the rapid innovation of over-the-air television took place . . . after the initiation of the decline in attendance at motion picture theaters."[6] The claim is statistically correct, but it is misleading. Movie theater attendance began to decline from its 1946 peak before television became widely available in the United States. Nonetheless, television was a primary cause of the subsequent decline in film attendance.

Across the United States, the spread of television was uneven. Where television first became available movie attendance declined most quickly. Whenever an additional broadcast channel was added in any market, the decline in movie theater attendance accelerated immediately and spread the most rapidly.[7]

While television took away a substantial portion of the audience from motion-picture theaters, it did not necessarily mean that great numbers in the American population were necessarily losing interest in seeing motion pictures. Over time it became clear that Americans still wanted to see movies but were quite satisfied to view them at home on the small screen of a television set. That was central to America's changing film culture during the 1960s. For example, when THE BRIDGE ON THE RIVER KWAI (1957) was shown on ABC Television in September 1966 it drew an estimated audience of 60 million. Consistently throughout the 1960s, a national, prime-time broadcast of a feature film by a major network did exceptionally well, even though comparatively few equaled the draw of an "event" film like THE BRIDGE ON THE RIVER KWAI. Neither the small screen and poor sound of the average television set, nor the periodic commercial interruptions, compromised a film's entertainment value enough to prevent large audiences from watching and enjoying nearly any kind of movie on television.[8]

THE ERODING MOVIE THEATER BUSINESS

Throughout the 1950s and the 1960s, the spread of television had a clear and devastating impact on the business of motion-picture theater ownership and the profitability of the entire exhibition sector of the American movie industry. The erosion of the movie theater audience in the United States, however, was attributable to factors that went well beyond the advent and rapid spread of television across the nation.

In 1946, the Census Bureau predicted that the population of the United States would reach 163 million only by the year 2000. Instead, because of the unexpected and unprecedented number of births in the United States between 1948 and 1955, that figure was reached forty years earlier, in 1960. Moreover, the post–World War II "baby boom" was reflected in rapidly changing American folkways and lifestyles. As late as the

Older, downtown movie theaters might occasionally still draw crowds—like this one at a 1968 film premiere in Detroit, but generally they faced declining audiences and closures during the 1960s. This particular theater building was soon converted into a parking structure.

World War II period, 15 percent of American women reached the age of thirty having never been married. By 1960, that percentage had fallen below 7 percent [9] According to one interpretation, these statistics document that young Americans in the post-World War II era were expressing their preference for "the psychic benefits of having children over other forms of consumption."[10] That argument, however, is problematic because it claims too much insight into deep and complex human motives as based on raw statistics. A more modest conclusion holds that the social and cultural consequences of rapidly rising marriage and birth rates in the United States during the postwar period determined the remarkable shifts in where much of America's middle-class population lived and how that population would spend its leisure time during the 1960s.

America's marriage and baby booms fueled the unprecedented growth of the nation's suburbs. By 1960, nine of the nation's fifteen largest urban areas had suburban majorities. During the 1960s, 95 percent of the growth in metropolitan areas in the United States occurred in suburban populations.[11] In addition to television, these burgeoning suburban populations had a continually increasing variety of leisure-time diversions available to them—outdoor sports, parks for recreational use, swimming pools, tennis courts, golf courses, bowling alleys and other indoor recreation centers, organized sports like little leagues, school athletics, country clubs, campgrounds, resorts, and automobile travel on new super-highways. While television was the most prominent direct competitor to the movie theater for America's leisure time and leisure spending, the motion-picture industry confronted a variety of activities that were expanding exponentially during the 1950s and 1960s.[12]

Movie theaters, moreover, were in a terrible position to try to follow middle-class America's exodus from the cities to the suburbs. Suburban land values rose quickly. Since the major Hollywood companies were prevented by federal antitrust decisions from owning movie theaters, the burden for expansion of cinemas to the suburbs was left largely to independent owners of the new theater chains.[13] With suburbanization came changing patterns of life within America's cities. Increasingly, "downtown" business districts were abandoned after business hours, and impoverished neighborhoods grew up around them. The growing suburbs were overwhelmingly white; only minuscule increases in the number of African American suburbanites occurred throughout the 1960s.[14]

Many movie theaters in American cities dated back to the 1920s and were palatial in size. Significant numbers of those houses would be converted to other uses or abandoned entirely during the 1960s. Indeed, the impact of eroding movie theater attendance and the growth of the suburbs produced clear racial effects in the exhibition sector of the American motion-picture industry. The decade began with a struggle by African Americans to integrate movie theaters in cities throughout the South, where they had previously been relegated by "Jim Crow" practices to the balcony seats; the 1960s ended with substantial numbers of urban movie theaters located in or near the central business districts of major cities all across the United States drawing nearly all-black audiences.[15] This fact reflected the continuing social realities of the 1960s that effectively separated the races in the United States geographically, even as rapid legal progress was made against segregation. In Hollywood production, however, it also meant that even if the audience was clearly delineated by race, there would nonetheless be a new receptiveness to black talent and themes in feature production, ranging from the film adaptation of Lorraine Hansberry's drama A RAISIN IN THE SUN (1961, Daniel Petrie), to the dark satire of PUTNEY SWOPE (1969, Robert Downey).

A new receptiveness in Hollywood to African American themes and talent was reflected in the screen adaptation of Lorraine Hansberry's A RAISIN IN THE SUN (1962, with Sidney Poitier; directed by Daniel Petrie).

THE PRODUCTION INDUSTRY RESPONDS

In its initial response to the advent of television and the decline of the movie theater audience, Hollywood tried to win back audiences with techniques that exploited the movie theater's capacity to offer superior picture and sound to those of television. Large-screen formats, such as CinemaScope, 3-D, VistaVision, Todd A-O, and Cinerama, were introduced. Some of the innovations flopped, such as 3-D, while others, like 70mm widescreen, continued to be favorably received throughout the 1960s. There were many problems with the technologies, and retrofitting movie theaters to exploit them were costly. The real problem, however, was that the films produced in the new formats still relied on Hollywood's classic story formulas, sentiments, and themes.[16]

The impact of television, changing demographics, and the ways in which America's middle-class families spent their leisure time not only decreased the numbers of people who went to movie theaters, but also radically altered the composition of the remaining audience. "Today people go to see a movie; they no longer go to the movies," said Robert Evans, the young, newly hired production chief at Paramount, in 1967. "The theater audience for movies had narrowed dramatically and had become increasingly selective," he added.[17] By the late 1960s entire segments of the potential moviegoing audience had been lost to the industry. For example, the only studio still making films aimed solely at children was Disney.

At the beginning of the 1960s many in the industry were arguing that "family films" were finished. By the end of the decade, industry pundits claimed that features aimed at the "family" market could no longer attract the adolescents and young adults who had become the mainstay of the movie theater box office; furthermore, such features actually increased the risk of alienating that adolescent and young adult audience from the habit of moviegoing.[18] More than just a decline in the number of moviegoers and a segmentation of the audience was happening during the late 1960s. Films that appealed to one niche were not just ignored by other portions of the potential audience, but were frequently condemned by them. The cultural polarization of the late 1960s was challenging and potentially destructive for an industry so market-driven as the Hollywood feature film.

As early as 1961, *Variety* had begun publishing obituaries for the Hollywood happy ending: "The sicko ones are making for box office health more readily than the happier movies."[19] As youth and distinct ethnic subcultures began demanding specific representation of themselves and their alternative values in feature films, Hollywood's celebration of the idea of the American population as a "melting pot" deteriorated in the second half of the 1960s.[20] European art films made considerable headway in the American market throughout the 1960s as well, catering to audiences primarily in urban areas and college towns. The art film audience was self-defined as better educated, more sophisticated, and more cosmopolitan in its tastes than the adherents of mainstream feature films, and it constituted a niche market entirely distinct from the more traditional moviegoing audience upon which classic Hollywood had depended.[21]

The art film audience was symptomatic of the growing differentiation and segmentation of the traditional mass audience for movies during the 1960s. By 1966, when the film critic Stanley Kauffmann published an article identifying what he called the "film generation," motion pictures were emerging as a flash point in American society's cultural wars and generational conflicts.[22] As the first wave of baby boomers reached the age of eighteen in 1966, their coming of age as moviegoers was simultaneously being greeted and spurred on by an increasing number of film festivals, college courses about film, and the writings of "serious" film critics, such as Andrew Sarris, Pauline Kael, and Stanley Kauffmann.[23]

Much of the mainstream establishment in Hollywood, of course, appeared intent on resisting the potential emerging changes in American film culture. Confronted with growing evidence of the success of "art cinemas" and of the foreign films shown in them, for example, Jerry Lewis testily asserted that there were "only twenty sophisticates in the world" and that he wasn't interested in making movies for them.[24] Katharine Hepburn excoriated the pretensions of "arty" features made by European directors, castigating in particular the enigmatic final scene in BLOW-UP (1966, Michelangelo Antonioni) in which the protagonist picks up an imaginary ball and tosses it to two mimes playing tennis: "There's no bunk in our pictures—unlike in BLOW-UP we play tennis *with* the ball."[25]

As art houses made inroads into the exhibition sector of the industry, especially on the East and West coasts, foreign films gained a following during the 1960s that was duplicated neither before nor after that decade. The provocative question for producers in the United States, however, was whether the film generation was truly being drawn toward forms of the art film—which were more sophisticated and mature in theme as well as being "cutting edge" aesthetically—or whether the emerging American film culture was better represented through a blending of modified Hollywood formulas served up with more sensationalistic effects. Between the appeal of art film and traditional Hollywood fare, the low-budget films of Roger Corman, producer/director at American International Pictures, best defined the directions in which feature films were going after the mid 1960s. Adolescents and young adults who had been raised in the American suburbs of the late 1950s and early 1960s favored eclectic and slightly rebellious films, ranging from horror and softcore sex movies to action-adventure films populated with characters whose screen presence invariably expressed some measure of alienation and existential *angst*.[26]

Year by year, throughout the 1960s, the demographics of movie theater attendance in the United States shifted toward younger, unmarried people.[27] The decrease in movie attendance among middle-aged Americans was steady, but among middle-aged women the drop was even more abrupt and deeper. By the beginning of the 1960s, movie theaters all over the country were closing during the daytime as the audience for "matinees," traditionally composed almost entirely of females, disappeared.[28] Women had been a majority of filmgoers in the United States from the end of the World War I to the 1960s. During the 1960s, as the total audience for theatrical films in the United States declined, the remaining audience was decidedly younger and increasingly male. That prompted producers and distributors to abandon such genres as romances and bioepics. By the late1960s, the young, male movie audience for movies appeared to be most interested in stories and characters challenging their own sense of adolescent boredom and their parents' conventional values. Moreover, and perhaps most interestingly, these elements also appealed to the tastes of educated sophisticates living in metropolitan areas who were becoming more vocal in their criticism of American society and culture during the late 1960s. They identified at a more intellectual level with the visceral and emotional rebellion of restless, alienated young suburbanites.

Exhibition

It could be argued that the major Hollywood companies had actually been well served by having been forced by the government during the 1950s to divest themselves of the motion-picture theaters they owned. Although the exhibition sector remained a major part of the industry during the 1960s, it was far more troubled than the production branch of American cinema. In 1965, the U.S. Department of Commerce estimated that movie theaters still accounted for over 90 percent of the total capital investment in the industry, with much of that expenditure in old and decrepit buildings in undesirable locations. Operating costs remained relatively high for movie theater owners while their average annual profits tottered at a trifling average of just 3 percent nationwide throughout the 1960s.[29]

Movie theater owners had to confront the irony that the same Hollywood companies forced by the government to sell off their movie theaters were able to increase their control over the distribution of feature films during the 1960s. Facing dwindling audience demand for their movies, the Hollywood majors cut back on the number of productions; since there was less product available, the distributor could exert greater control over it. The increasing dominance over smaller inventories allowed the major distributors to introduce the so-called "floor figure" as a common basis for rentals to movie theater operators. This system, which gave the distributor a guaranteed rental per film plus 10 percent of a film's actual attendance, replaced the historic rental system called the "house nut" that had been based solely on actual attendance. As a result, film distribution earnings steadily grew at the cost of the exhibitors.[30]

The American film culture being fashioned during the 1960s was largely unfavorable to exhibitor interests. The exhibition sector experienced extraordinarily rough financial times and business conditions during the decade: they were caught between rapidly changing demographics; often bound to choose between making substantial capital investments in older theaters located in the inner cities or selling the properties at a loss (or even abandoning them altogether); and they were squeezed financially by feature film distribution now monopolized by the Hollywood majors.

DRIVE-INS

The first "outdoor movie theater" was opened in 1933 by a New Jersey chemical manufacturer and accommodated 400 automobiles.[31] This new movie exhibition idea, however, did not catch on immediately. At the time, the United States was still in the throes of the Great Depression, and the ensuing years of World War II did not prove conducive to an appreciable growth in the number of drive-ins. After the war, however, America's changing demographics, expanding automobile culture, growing middle class, and burgeoning suburbs supported the swelling of drive-in theaters. In 1945, there still were fewer than 300 drive-ins nationwide. By 1956, that number exploded to 4,500. During the same period, roughly 4,200 indoor theaters in the United States had closed,[32] which suggests an almost one-for-one replacement of "hard-top" theaters (industry term) by drive-ins. While numerically valid, the statistic was deceptive and easily open to misinterpretation. In fact, few drive-ins were the equivalent of a standard indoor movie theater. They accommodated far fewer patrons on average, and they were open only for several months of the year in many parts of the United States. A disproportionate number of drive-ins built in the late 1940s and the early 1950s were in small town or semi-rural locations. Only late in the 1950s did the number of drive-ins near the booming suburbs accelerate. In hindsight, moreover, the expansion of drive-ins to locations in or near the suburbs appears, in most instances, to have occurred too late to fully capitalize on population shifts throughout most of the United States.

Suburban drive-in theaters constituted an especially good business investment so long as they were located at the fringes of developing areas where land could still be purchased relatively inexpensively.[33] In most places, however, land values had already risen so high by the suburban real estate boom that building drive-ins in ideal locales was rendered financially impossible. The number of drive-ins peaked just prior to the end of the 1950s, when they briefly accounted for nearly one-third of the movie admissions nationwide. The potential for their further development, however, was to be seriously compromised by a variety of factors in the 1960s.[34]

The peak of just over 6,000 drive-in movie theaters was reached in 1958.[35] After that, the number began to decline in direct proportion to the increasing demand for suburban property and its rising cost.[36] During the 1960s, drive-ins constituted a significantly larger portion of the total number of movie screens in the Southeast and the Midwest than anywhere else in the nation. A 1967 government survey established that the highest proportion of drive-ins to conventional movie theaters was 41 percent in Alabama; while the lowest, in New York state, was 15 percent. Still, there was no easy or simple formula by which to arrive at the relationship of drive-ins to enclosed movie theaters.

Mel Wintmen of the General Cinema Theater chain observed at the end of the 1960s, "the future of the drive-ins is in the past."

Montana, the most sparsely populated (per capita) of the continental states at the time, for example, had a drive-in to indoor theater ratio of 30 percent. Exactly the same ratio was found in densely populated Massachusetts. Fast-growing California, with a lifestyle emblematic of American automobile culture and suburbia, however, had only 223 drive-ins out of its 971 movie theaters, which at 23 percent was a lower ratio than in either Montana or Massachusetts.[37]

Even when they had accounted for roughly half of the nation's screens at the end of the 1950s, drive-ins never fully captured the idea of moviegoing for most Americans. They provided a second-class movie experience, even though more and more drive-ins began showing first-run movies during the 1960s.[38] The projected image was usually noticeably inferior to a movie theater; audio—tinny, piped-in sound from small speakers placed on or just inside the vehicle's window—was always inferior. Inclement weather was another problem. Viewers were subject to cold or heat, and even with mild temperature conditions unexpected thunder or wind storms could ruin a night at the drive-in. In some locations alongside major highways, lights and noise were bothersome.

There were definitely appealing aspects of the drive-ins: teenagers could talk with their friends during the movie, or make out, and small children could sleep in the back seat while mom and dad watched a movie and saved on the cost of a baby-sitter. Still, the aesthetic experience and the entertainment value of watching a movie at a drive-in was severely compromised for nearly everyone. Mel Wintmen, executive vice president of the General Cinema Theater chain, summed it up in a decidedly insightful malapropism at the very end of the 1960s: "The future of the drive-ins is in the past."[39]

THE MULTIPLEX

In August 1960, *Variety* reported that twenty-five cinemas were operating as shopping center hardtops nationwide. The same article profiled two especially successful shopping center cinemas, one in Miami Beach, Florida, and the other in Bergen, New Jersey.[40] A year later, *Box Office* concluded, "A new star in the motion picture firmament is the shopping center theater," and added "drive-ins require too much land area."[41] As climbing land values in the suburbs made opening new drive-ins prohibitively expensive, and the wrecker's ball demolished deteriorating or abandoned old theaters in America's inner cities, smaller and more cost-efficient "multiplex" cinemas began spreading.

The shift toward this new type of movie theater put a growing number of movie screens closer to where suburban audiences lived and shopped, and promoted a restructuring of exhibition that become more profitable. In 1963, Stanley H. Durwood of Kansas City, Missouri, pioneered a major shift in movie theater construction when he opened a cinema in a shopping center that consisted of two small theaters served by a single projection booth, thus saving significantly on labor and projection costs.[42] From this innovation, Durwood built AMC Entertainment, Inc., into one of America's largest-grossing theater chains over the next two decades, ultimately operating 218 theaters with more than 2,700 screens in the United States and a handful of foreign countries.[43]

Stanley H. Durwood, the founder of the multiplex cinema, at a Kansas City shopping center in the 1960s.

The ubiquitous, multiplying multiplex.

In the struggling exhibition sector of the American motion picture business in the 1960s, Durwood's fundamental concept of the multiple-unit indoor theater was quickly accepted as the model for innovation in movie theater design and a blueprint for future development.[44] Multiplex cinemas afforded to their owners obvious commercial advantages as compared to single-screen movie houses that operated with traditional projection practices. While older movie theaters and drive-ins were closing in record numbers by the mid 1960s, multiplex cinemas were opening with greatly reduced per-screen capital investment and the added promise of significantly lower labor costs for operation.[45]

By January 1966, the *Hollywood Reporter* could report that the construction of over five hundred new cinemas, nearly all of them suburban multiplexes, was being planned across the United States for the coming year alone. At the same time, the Theater Owners Association (TOA), the trade organization of the nation's movie theater owners, was issuing dire warnings about the potential for "overbuilding" screen capacity, even at the most desirable of suburban locations.[46] While many economic and demographic indicators pointed toward dwindling profitability overall for theatrical exhibitors of movies, specific multiplexes in particular surburban markets immediately proved to be excellent investments.

Commonly, such cinemas were built with cinder block in simple rectangles in complexes containing from two to eight separate theaters that normally ranged in size from a hundred to three hundred seats each. They were staffed by a minimum number of employees, increasingly younger in age, who could handle the entire business—from selling tickets, to providing refreshments, to starting the projection system, to cleaning out refuse left under seats.[47] For nearly all of the new multiplexes, location in or near a shopping center was imperative. During the late 1960s the presence of a multiplex cinema was becoming so increasingly attractive for nearly any major shopping center in the United States as to be considered a commercial necessity. The "foot traffic" through the mall could only increase with the opening of a cinema, since some of the people had come there primarily to see a movie. Parents might leave children at the movies for a couple of hours while they shopped. Large shopping center parking lots afforded moviegoers free and accessible parking, and since many multiplex cinemas were open after the major stores in the shopping center closed, they essentially extended the use of the center later into the night. As a result of the rise of the suburban shopping center multiplex, weekday movie matinees began to return to regions of the country from which they had disappeared. By the late 1960s, other retail merchants in many shopping centers actually began subsidizing movie theaters in order to have the centers open for longer hours.[48]

Based on the model of the shopping center multiplexes, renovation of selected older urban theaters into multiscreen houses commenced toward the end of the 1960s, especially along the eastern seaboard. In Boston, Massachusetts, for example, the large student-aged population prompted the Sack's chain of theaters to revive its in-city exhibition. Sack's "Cheri," a three-plex, opened in autumn of 1968 as the world's first self-proclaimed "drive-up." The "Cheri" provided an on-premises garage with parking for a thousand vehicles, which constituted an equivalent in the downtown business district to the copious free parking offered at suburban malls. The Sack's chain considered this amenity an absolute necessity to make the concept of the drive-up financially viable.[49]

New Operators and New Operations

As the type of movie theater was changing, so, too, theater ownership was becoming concentrated in the hands of new entrepreneurs. General Cinema and National Cinema Corporation rose to prominence in the exhibition sector. General Cinema epitomized the new theater owner of the 1960s, accounting for a chain of over 200 cinemas by 1970, almost all of which were in shopping centers and in new buildings. General Cinema pioneered a form of niche diversification for its operations. Branching out into the ownership of soft-drink bottling plants, they held a considerable investment in a tertiary business that provided one of the staples of the increasingly profitable movie theater concession business. This model then became typical for movie theaters.[50]

While rising profits were earned from concessions, however, an old and venerable profession in the exhibition sector of the movie industry swiftly faded. In the early 1960s, the heavily unionized group of motion picture projectionists were forced nationwide to agree on having one operator, rather than two, in the booth for a 35mm feature. Prior to that time, when so many large theater chains had been owned by the wealthy Hollywood majors, the unions had been able to win favorable terms of employment for projectionists. Through those years, the requirement that every theater projection booth have a projectionist and an assistant had been standard. That practice could be justified for training purposes and quality control, or condemned as union feather-bedding. Regardless, a combination of factors during the 1960s effectively doomed the practice, and the trend toward multiscreen cinemas and smaller seating capacities per screen quickly eroded the projectionists' position. In right-to-work states, primarily in the South and parts of the Midwest and Rocky Mountain regions, the profession of projectionist was all but eliminated by the end of the 1960s. Elsewhere, the specialized profession retained little power, even when its members kept up their union affiliation. Given the enormously changed demographics of the moviegoing audience by the late 1960s, then, the most typical ingredients for exhibitor success became a combination of shopping center locations, multiscreen operations, free shopping center parking (or the "drive-up" concept), limited seating per screen, projection automation, and the elimination of projectionists from the payroll.[51]

As mentioned earlier, Hollywood producers beginning in the early 1950s had tried to win back their declining audiences with widescreen innovations and 3-D. They even tried presenting several features in "Aromarama" or in the competing "Smell-O-Vision" system, where audiences experienced naturalistic odors pumped in and sucked out of the theater.[52] 3-D and such other gimmicks quickly fell by the wayside. Widescreen formats prevailed, but there were only several hundred "first-tier" theaters nationwide that were capable of presenting films in 70mm.[53]

Along with technical schemes intended to draw audiences to the theaters, marketing ploys were developed to elevate the prestige of the moviegoer's experience. The reserved-seat "roadshow" movies survived until the late 1960s, when they fared poorly with the adolescent and young adult audience that had come to dominate the demographics of America's moviegoing public.[54] Box-office disasters for two big-budget roadshow musicals produced by 20th Century-Fox—DOCTOR DOLITTLE (1967) and STAR! (1968)—effectively ended the practice of imitating stage theaters and other performance events with the advanced sale of reserved seat tickets for specific showings of large-scale, big-budget movies.[55]

Mainstream motion-picture exhibition in the United States by the late 1960s was beset by a fundamental irony: just as widescreen and surround-sound innovations were reaching technical perfection after a decade of missteps, exhibitors were bringing audiences to cinder-block spaces with one- to two-hundred seats and using projectors with special compensators that showed a sharp but small image on a screen that often was no further than thirty feet from the projection booth.[56] Critics complained about the transition to smaller theater spaces and smaller screens, claiming the magic and myth of motion pictures were being dealt a fatal blow by the multiplexes.[57] Almost all of America's great, single-screen movie palaces were gone, and along with them the ushers and usherettes, as well as nearly every other amenity that had characterized moviegoing in America's larger cities from the 1920s well into the 1950s. The exhibition aesthetic that emerged during the 1960s was defined entirely by functionality and commercial efficiency.

By the end of the 1960s, the theatrical exhibition of motion pictures succeeded to the extent that movies were now being shown where much of the audience was—in the suburbs. Increasingly, this meant that the exhibition of movies had come to be tied in with other diversions, such as shopping, that appealed to the adolescent or young adult moviegoer with disposable income. One film historian goes so far as to conclude that the multiplex put an end to people over thirty-five going to the movies.[58] It is equally plausible to argue that people over thirty-five had ceased going to the movies in significant numbers before the mutliplexes arose as a logical consequence of the suburbanization of so much of the American population.

THE ACADEMY AWARD CEREMONIES

"That's what I like about our industry"—proclaimed master of ceremonies Bob Hope, in opening the Academy Award presentations for the year 1961—"the big moment for

Hollywood movies comes to you from Santa Monica on television."[59] Indeed, in 1960 the annual Academy Award ceremonies had been moved from Hollywood's aging Pantages Theater to the Civic Center in the seaside community of Santa Monica, located due west of Los Angeles. By then, a national television audience of nearly 80 million throughout the United States was guaranteed to tune in to the annual Oscar presentation ceremonies. That figure would remain relatively constant throughout the decade—even as the actual audience for motion pictures in America's theaters was cut in half over the course of the 1960s. Moreover, with the international distribution of the taped Academy Award show for television broadcast in other countries, the "Oscar" ceremonies became a global event.[60] As the broadcast became a reliably popular and staple television entertainment event, the very medium that had contributed so heavily to undermining the mass appeal of theatrical movies to American audiences began serving as the primary new vehicle for exploiting Hollywood celebrity and exposing the artistry of the movies to a mass audience worldwide.

Arthur Freed had taken over producing the Academy Awards in 1959. Four years later, Freed would be named the president of the Academy of Motion Picture Arts and Sciences. Bob Hope, who served as master of ceremonies for the majority of the shows during the 1960s, received the Academy's first Gold Medal of recognition in 1966.[61] Indeed, both Freed and Hope were significant figures in the lessening of tensions between the motion picture industry and television broadcasting. Hope had never been greatly popular on radio, but via the movies he emerged in the 1950s as a great success on television. Freed took the mastery of spectacular staging he had learned at the MGM film studios to television during the 1950s and then repackaged this showmanship during the 1960s to celebrate and promote movies worldwide through the Academy Award ceremonies.

The honors, to Freed and to Hope, reflected the Academy's appreciation for their contributions to the event that had become the centerpiece of the Academy's existence by the 1960s. Neither of their contributions, however, was without controversy. The show itself inevitably reflected ongoing tensions between the motion-picture industry establishment and the television broadcasting industry, which even the abundant talents of Freed and Hope could not overcome. One especially nasty editorial published in a Los Angeles newspaper criticized the 1961 Awards ceremony as being covered "like a news event" and ridiculed the entertainment value of the program, calling it "worthy of being put on in a high school gymnasium."[62] An industry trade journal, *The Film Bulletin*, railed against master of ceremonies Bob Hope's sarcasm at the expense of the movie industry: "Don't continue to misuse the greatest billboard in the world," it cried. The Awards ceremony for 1961 ran 134 minutes, and even the producers agreed that it was too long.[63]

In response to widespread criticism of his performance the previous year, Hope was dropped by the Academy from his master of ceremonies role for the 35th (1962) Academy Awards. Frank Sinatra took over for him in 1962, and Jack Lemmon filled the role in 1963. Hope was restored as the master of ceremonies for the 37th Academy Awards, which took place on April 5, 1965. By then, the television show itself was being developed more in the direction of an elegant entertainment spectacle. Joe Pasternak, who had taken over as producer, insisted on having fountains built on stage for the ceremonies over the vehement opposition of ABC's Dick Dunlap, who thought that their trickling waters would prove to be too loud and distracting.[64] The following year, the Kodak Corporation assumed sole sponsorship of both the television and radio

Longtime host Bob Hope straightens his bow tie for television cameras at the 40th Academy Awards ceremony honoring films for the year 1967. The ceremonies were postponed for two days in April 1968 following the assassination of Martin Luther King, Jr.

broadcasts of the ceremonies. Since Kodak, the world's largest manufacturer of camera films, had a central and natural relationship to the motion-picture industry, many Hollywood observers deemed this move both appropriate and long overdue. In the mid 1960s, movie industry insiders were still very critical of an Oscar show that was interrupted by advertisements for toothpaste and sundry other products.[65] In 1966, the Awards were telecast in color for the first time. The following year, the distinction between "black-and-white" and "color" categories for motion picture camera achievement was finally dropped, merging them into a single award for cinematography.[66] The 41st Award ceremonies were postponed for two days following the assassination of Martin Luther King, Jr. The telecast won praise for restraint and dignity in the aftermath of this tragedy.[67]

Major changes occurred the following year. The ceremonies were moved from Santa Monica to the new Dorothy Chandler Pavilion at the County Music Center in downtown Los Angeles. Although this location was not geographically in "Hollywood," it was more stately than a setting two blocks from a pier and a ferris wheel. The show's starting time was moved up to 6:30 PST (9:30 P.M. on the East Coast), and the dress code was relaxed to permit men to wear tuxedos, instead of tails. Deciding to rework the show, the Academy's new president, Gregory Peck, limited Bob Hope to a brief appearance and turned the presentations over to ten personalities who were dubbed "Friends of Oscar": they were Ingrid Bergman, Diahann Carroll, Tony Curtis, Jane Fonda, Burt

Lancaster, Walter Matthau, Sidney Poitier, Frank Sinatra, Rosalind Russell, and Natalie Wood.[68] Hope was back as the solo master of ceremonies for the 42nd Academy Awards for the year 1969.

THE ART HOUSES AND THE NEW YORK FILM FESTIVAL

During the 1960s, a mass audience could still be drawn to movie theaters by exceptional roadshow movies and still remained fascinated with the allure of Hollywood celebrity and glamour, especially through the televised Academy Awards. However, an entirely different niche audience was being cultivated simultaneously by some movie exhibitors in the United States.

In the late 1950s, a distinct portion of the American audience began to exhibit an interest in foreign films. This breakthrough for foreign movies at the box office occurred in 1958 and not with the release of a film by one of the great European auteur directors; rather, it came with the American distribution of AND GOD CREATED WOMAN, starring Brigitte Bardot (1957, directed by her then-husband, Roger Vadim), which earned more than $4 million in the United States.[69] A wave of European art films, directed by such notables as Alain Resnais, François Truffaut, Jean-Luc Godard, Federico Fellini, Michelangelo Antonioni, and Ingmar Bergman, followed quickly. By the early 1960s, labeling a cinema an "art house," or promoting a movie by calling it "New Wave" could translate into considerable box-office profits for niche exhibitors in the United States.[70]

Movie theaters called art houses sprang up during the early 1960s, quickly accounting for over 500 screens nationwide.[71] Such movie theaters were often converted older theaters or other older buildings in larger cities and college towns.[72] The art houses, to a large extent, defined themselves by not showing mainstream Hollywood movies. Their programs were targeted at a young audience, but not adolescents. The rising number of young adults in the population, and changing social and cultural conditions, meant increasing numbers were continuing beyond their high school graduation to some form of post-secondary education. They formed the main demographic of art house audiences.

Art cinemas were distinctive in concept. They might feature an espresso bar in the lobby in lieu of a popcorn machine, for example. They were disproportionately located in the Northeast, on the West Coast, and in either large cities or smaller towns populated by significant numbers of college students. Their audiences tended to be focused in their tastes, often to the extent that devotees of the art house cinemas did not necessarily patronize other movie theaters showing mainstream Hollywood movies. The 1960s was the great decade of growth for the art house. By the 1970s, the long and steady growth was over, although a considerable number of art houses would survive well into the future showing a very identifiable mix of foreign films and low-budget American features labeled "independent."[73]

Along with the developing art house film culture of the 1960s came the rise of the film festival in America. The major festival linked inextricably with the growing import of European art films to the United States—the New York Film Festival—began on September 1, 1963, and opened to sold-out houses in the 2,300 seat Philharmonic Hall at the new Lincoln Center on Manhattan's West Side. Immediately, the New York Film Festival established itself as the premier gateway into U.S. distribution for foreign films.[74] Throughout the 1960s, the New York Film Festival (NYFF) would remain the most important vehicle for introducing American audiences to foreign films. In this regard, the Festival played a central role in advancing the importance of foreign films in

Some older neighborhood movie theaters, like the Charles in lower Manhattan (ca. 1962),
reinvented themselves as "art houses" and scheduled evenings of avant-garde fare.

American cinema culture and added impetus to the growing number of art cinemas
nationwide. The NYFF was significant in the rising culture that asserted the art film as
a distinct and clearly superior form of cinema that could be distinguished definitively
from Hollywood commercialism. As the critic Robert Gessner wrote in the *Saturday
Review* in 1964: "The second season of the Lincoln Center Film Festival reminded New
Yorkers once again what most urban Americans realize, namely the most imaginative
and intelligent film, is likely to come from abroad."[75]

Under the directorship of Richard Roud and Amos Vogel the Festival advanced a concept of film that conscientiously contrasted the global interest in "serious film" to
Hollywood's notion of movies as entertainment for mass audiences.[76] In 1965, regular
seminars on aesthetics and criticism, organized by the renowned film historian Arthur
Knight of the University of Southern California, were added to the NYFF schedule and
became a continuing feature.[77] Festival organizers and promoters understood that the
timing of its founding, and the earliest years of its success, coincided chronologically with
a rapidly shifting cultural scene predicated on the emergence of the "film generation." As
Amos Vogel asserted in 1965, "Films have finally arrived in international cultural circles
among the young people. There is much more excitement about films than about legitimate theatre. For young people [film] is their art—*the* twentieth-century art form."[78]

4

The Waning Production Code and the Rise of the Ratings System

The Production Code and Threats of Censorship

The popularity of many foreign films in the United States, the growth of the art houses, and the appearance of such vehicles promoting a new film culture as the New York Film Festival occurred early in the decade that would witness the most extensive shift in film content in the history of the American motion picture. The widely perceived "mature content" of many foreign films, especially their approach to sex and eroticism, revealed the burden of Hollywood's long established "Production Code" and posed a direct challenge to the kind of movies that the Hollywood majors had been producing.[1]

The motion-picture industry's Production Code had been established in 1930 by the major Hollywood studios in order to avoid threats of government-imposed censorship. The majors agreed that any feature film they produced and/or distributed had to earn the "Seal of Approval." Such a seal was awarded based on adherence to a set of guidelines largely concerned with how sex and criminality were treated in a film.[2] During the 1930s and 1940s, relatively few features produced in Hollywood skirted the Code, but by the early 1950s the Code began to be challenged on occasion. Even before foreign films made inroads at the box office in the United States, United Artists released THE MOON IS BLUE (1953, Otto Preminger) without obtaining a seal of approval. Tellingly, even without the seal, and although it was condemned by the Roman Catholic Church's Legion of Decency, THE MOON IS BLUE was a financial success.[3]

Indeed, many observers within the movie industry believed that the attention and publicity brought to the film by the decision to release it without a seal of approval actually helped its business significantly at the box office.[4] Another direct challenge to the Code occurred when financially ailing RKO-Pathé released THE FRENCH LINE (1954), starring Jane Russell. The Catholic Legion of Decency condemned this movie too, meaning that practicing Roman Catholics viewed it only under the onus of committing a mortal sin. RKO-Pathé apparently was unconcerned, however, carrying on an advertising campaign that brazenly referred to the film's 3-D photography and the lead actress's ample bosom: "THE FRENCH LINE will knock out both your eyes."[5]

A few years later, SPLENDOR IN THE GRASS (1961, Elia Kazan), starring Natalie Wood and Warren Beatty, was released with a seal of approval, even though the script ran directly counter to the Code: it dealt with the story of two young lovers who paid no price for their sexual indiscretion and who suffered emotionally by having denied their sexual impulses.[6] Clearly, the administrators of the Production Code were beginning to bend their interpretations in order to try to accommodate changing times and market conditions for the movie industry. John Wayne dismissed SPLENDOR IN THE GRASS as "too disgusting for discussion,"[7] but by then few American adults appeared to agree. The erosion of the Production Code was evident, and numerous Hollywood releases were decidedly more adult in the way in which they treated sex and references to it.

Natalie Wood and Warren Beatty play out a theme directly contradictory to the Hollywood Production Code in Elia Kazan's SPLENDOR IN THE GRASS (1961).

In the spring of 1961, Eric Johnston, the head of the Motion Picture Association of America (MPAA), which administered the Code, suggested for the first time that his organization might be willing to consider dropping it entirely in favor of the introduction of some sort of voluntary classification system for movies.[8] When Johnston's signal was interpreted as a green light by a production company run by the Mirisch brothers to attack the Production Code directly, the major production companies elected to publicly defend both the Code and the seal, even though there was widespread sentiment among the management of the Hollywood majors that the Code and the seal were outdated.[9] Their defense was underscored by the official position taken by exhibitors, a branch of the industry the Hollywood majors no longer controlled directly. At the end of 1961, the independent Theater Owners Association of America (TOA) went on record to reject any form of self-classification or rating of movies by producers. TOA preferred continuation of the Code and the seal to any rating scheme that theater owners would be expected to enforce at the box office. For the time being, the notion of scuttling Hollywood's Production Code was dead in the water.[10]

Nonetheless, simple continuation of the Code and the seal was becoming increasingly problematic. Foreign film imports were gaining at America's box offices; since they were not produced or distributed by the Hollywood majors, they circulated freely without the seal. Movies from France, Great Britain, and Italy, such as THE LOVERS (1958, Louis Malle), ROOM AT THE TOP (1959, Jack Clayton), HIROSHIMA, MON AMOUR (1959, Alain Resnais), A BOUT DE SOUFFLE (BREATHLESS, 1959, Jean-Luc Godard), L'AVVENTURA (1960, Michelangelo Antonioni), and LA DOLCE VITA (1960, Federico Fellini), were all sexually daring compared to contemporary Hollywood releases.[11] These films sometimes faced censorship problems, but they represented the fictionalized treatment of sex in ways considered more mature, complex, and sophisticated than anything permitted by the Hollywood Code. Their success pointed to a market for movies with adult treatment of sexuality and occasional nude scenes that could not be seen at home on television in the United States. Nonetheless, it was just as these foreign movies began showing in movie theaters in America's hinterlands, that calls for local censorship of movies in general increased in many parts of the nation.[12] That, in turn, rekindled the American film industry's deepest and most long-standing fear (which dated back to the 1920s and which the Production Code had been intended all along to circumvent)—that local ordinances restricting motion pictures would be upheld by the courts, creating havoc for movie exhibition nationwide. By the mid 1960s, in fact, many local American newspapers began refusing to print advertisements for movies that they considered too provocative or suggestive.[13]

Still under the control of Geoffrey Spurlock, whose tenure had begun in 1932, the actual administration of the seal of approval was thought to have remained largely rigid and wedded to the past. Many observers within the Hollywood industry believed that a real shift in the Code's policy was discernable only with the release of THE PAWNBROKER (1965). The film contained nudity in a scene of an encounter between the protagonist and a neighborhood prostitute who comes to his pawnshop desperately seeking money for her boyfriend. Even more surprising than the issuance of a seal of approval for THE PAWNBROKER from Geoffrey Spurlock's office, however, was the Catholic Film Office's revision of a rare "C" rating ("condemned") to a rating of "A-3" ("morally unobjectionable for adults") after a mere two feet of film were cut from one scene. The tandem of events indicated that cultural shifts were finally being acknowl-

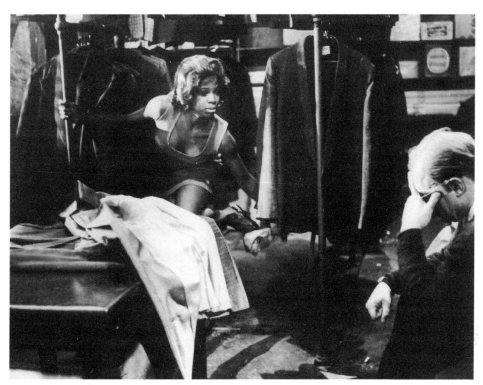

THE PAWNBROKER (1965) *challenged the Hollywood Production Code with scenes that included nudity. Lead character Rod Steiger as a pawnshop owner in an encounter with a prostitute shown here.*

edged in the very quarters that had been holding Hollywood films hostage to what many people regarded as entirely outmoded and puritanical standards.

The entire issue of control over movie content, after all, involved complex assessments as to what the public wanted or would tolerate, what parts of society would object to changes in Hollywood's traditional standards, and just how to proceed most efficaciously on behalf of an industry for which image and popular approval were vital. The principle source of protest against the "dubious morality" of Hollywood films during the late 1950s and the early 1960s came from agencies of the Roman Catholic Church, which frequently judged movies by standards that appeared to be rigid. In 1963, for example, the Church's Legion of Decency saddled both CLEOPATRA and IRMA LA DOUCE with a "B" rating (meaning "morally unacceptable, in part, for all").[14] The revision of the Church's rating for THE PAWNBROKER in 1965, then, marked a decided shift toward greater lenience in the official Catholic ratings. It was followed closely by a similar decision on WHO'S AFRAID OF VIRGINIA WOOLF? (1966, Mike Nichols), which broke the Code's standard on language. The movie contained eleven "goddamns," seven "bastards," a "screw you," a "hump the hostess," "up yours," and a reference to "monkey nipples." Initially denied approval by Spurlock, who was backed in his decision by the new MPAA President Jack Valenti, the seal of approval was actually granted after the film was cleared by the National Catholic Office of Motion Pictures (NCOMP). As a member of that office's staff wrote, "I can see little moral harm that will come from the use of vulgar language. Shock and disgust are not moral evils in themselves." More conservative Catholics, however, found this decision shocking and disgusting. Public protests occurred in many cities where the film played. At one of them, a devout parishioner carried a placard demanding the Catholic Church's hierarchy to "Get Rid of the N.C.O.M.Petents."[15]

Jack Valenti and the Ratings System

In 1966, Jack Valenti was chosen to succeed Eric Johnston as president of the movie industry's primary trade organization, the Motion Picture Association of America (MPAA). MCA/Universal Pictures President Lew Wasserman, a prominent Democrat, had reviewed a list of President Lyndon Johnson's White House staff and selected Valenti, a presidential aide, because of his extensive background in advertising and public relations. After Wasserman secured the endorsement of the heads of the other major

Presidential aide Jack Valenti in the White House with Lyndon Johnson shortly before Hollywood called him to head the Motion Picture Association of America.

Hollywood studios, the job as Johnston's replacement was offered to Valenti. He took over at the MPAA just as debate over the industry-wide Production Code was coming to a head. Prior to Valenti's arrival, the Code had been streamlined in order to make approval of scripts easier and to adjust the seal of approval decisions modestly in the direction of America's changing mores and attitudes toward sex and violence. These modest reforms, however, did not resolve the tensions between the continued existence of a Production Code in Hollywood, the vastly changed audience for motion pictures, and evidence of the broader society's changing values. While one industry insider argued that of Valenti's duties as president of the MPAA, only about 5 percent were concerned with the Code, it was in this arena that Valenti's leadership was held to be most critical in the public eye.[16] In fact, Valenti faced his first real challenge in his new job when BLOW-UP (1966, Michelangelo Antonioni) was denied a seal of approval for release by Metro-Goldwyn-Mayer (MGM). The studio, in order to skirt the Code and the board's decision, decided to proceed and distribute the film anyway through one of its subsidiaries called Premier Productions.[17]

Among all the major Hollywood studios, MGM had most strongly supported the Code historically. Their decision to proceed was enhanced by the fact that the film's director was an internationally acclaimed film artist. MGM had entered negotiations to secure approval under a new, reformed category called "SMA" (Suggested for Mature

In BLOW-UP (1966), the photographer played by David Hemmings romped with two teenage "birds" in a scene that showed pubic hair. The stunning box-office success of this film in the U.S. essentially broke the Hollywood Production Code and led to the MPAA's ratings system.

Audiences) by initially agreeing to two cuts from the movie—the main character's erotic tussling with two teenage girls that revealed a glimpse of pubic hair, and a brief sequence of his watching his neighbors' lovemaking. Antonioni, however, vociferously objected to this compromise. Even after its premiere in the United States in December 1966, however, MGM was looking for ways to gain a seal of approval for BLOW-UP in order to fully legitimize its release, and Production Code officials were still working with the studio. In the first six weeks of its release as a "premier picture" without the seal, however, BLOW-UP enjoyed extraordinarily good box-office business, and MGM decided to drop the matter. The entire BLOW-UP incident demonstrated to most observers that the Hollywood Production Code and the seal of approval had, in essence, become irrelevant.[18]

VIOLENCE ON THE BIG SCREEN

The related issue of graphic violence depicted on the screen heated up not long after the release of BLOW-UP, when BONNIE AND CLYDE (1967, Arthur Penn) received Geoffrey Spurlock's blessing and a seal of approval.[19] At the time, widespread debate in the mainstream press and in public policy circles over the film's violence fed growing public concern over the content of movies, television, and magazines. That same year, President Lyndon B. Johnson appointed a "National Commission on Obscenity and Pornography" to assess the situation and to report to the nation.[20] Valenti, Johnson's former aide, immediately wired the president on behalf of the MPAA to praise his decision and to pledge Hollywood's full support to the Commission.[21] Many in Hollywood trusted that Valenti's links to Johnson would help assure a Commission favorable to the industry's interests. Others, however, like the conservative Hollywood feature columnist Abe Greenberg, found neither Valenti's commitment, nor LBJ's commission, promising. "We are delighted with Valenti's strong language in which he excoriated pornography and violence in movies," wrote Greenberg. "But what, we feel constrained to ask, does Mr. Valenti plan to do about it."[22]

Valenti's position, as reconstructed from the record, consisted of carefully negotiating a moderate posture of apparent compromise. He recognized that a changing society had created new audience tastes. At the same time, he quickly became a prime mover in advancing the idea that Hollywood producers must move cautiously toward exploring new ground. Finally, whatever position the MPAA took, Valenti recognized that the issue was ultimately in the hands of the courts—the branch of government over which the movie industry had little or no influence and could not control.

Hollywood faced complicated issues. First Amendment protections had been extended tentatively to the motion-picture industry only in the early 1950s, but film was still bounded by restrictions that did not apply to print media. Additionally, the legal situation was especially threatening to the movie industry because court decisions being made in similar cases in different jurisdictions during the mid 1960s were not at all consistent. In 1966, for example, one federal court, deciding on a challenge by Columbia Pictures to the practices of the State of Kansas Film Review Board (whose existence dated back to 1917), held that actions by state review boards were unconstitutional.[23] Immediately after that decision, however, another federal court ruling in a similar case involving a Texas movie exhibitor and a local government (*Interstate Circuit v. The City of Dallas*) upheld the right of the states or of municipalities to classify films and, hence, to regulate their exhibition.[24] The Kansas decision encouraged those who sought more liberalized practices. The Dallas decision was applauded by those who sought to impose

Blood squibs enhanced pictorial realism, and the amplified sound of gunshots contributed to graphic scenes of violence that were the subject of controversy upon the release of BONNIE AND CLYDE.

stricter legal restraints on what might be seen in America's movie theaters and by whom.

1968 proved a decisive year on the issue. It began with the state of Maryland banning any showing of a sexually explicit movie from Sweden, I AM CURIOUS (YELLOW) (1967, Vilgot Sjoman), even though it was playing to large audiences in many other states at the time, including ones bordering Maryland.[25] Not long after, a Washington, D.C. movie theater owner and his employees were convicted under the city's new anti-obscenity law for showing sexually explicit films. As those defendants were being sentenced in the nation's capital, the municipality of Salt Lake City, Utah, passed a similar ordinance. At the same time, a city court judge in Detroit, Michigan, found several Wayne State University students guilty of showing films by political radical Wendi Tsen that portrayed what was judged "obscene" material.

In late spring of 1968, the United States Supreme Court declared in *Ginsberg v. City of New York* that state and city ordinances which drew a clear legal distinction between what motion-picture materials adults and minors could see in places open to the public were constitutional and enforceable.[26] In the wake of that decision, the *Boston Globe* newspaper launched an editorial campaign to encourage the commonwealth of Massachusetts to pass a law banning promotional trailers for films that might contain sexually explicit scenes from showing in movie theaters. The newspaper's argument for such a restriction was predicated on the notion that "family audiences" who came to a given theater to see a specific film would be oblivious to what coming attractions might

*Eroticism in I AM CURIOUS (YELLOW) (Sweden, Vilgot Sjoman, 1967) heated up debate
over obscenity laws after its U.S. release in 1968.*

be presented before the feature film; hence, they could be blindsided by material the
parents might consider offensive or improper for their children.

There were calls rising in many quarters for control of movie content. At the same
time, other Americans were arguing that Hollywood was still lagging far behind
European countries in bringing adult materials to the screen, and that Hollywood stood
to lose what was left of the college-aged audience. Many of the films drawing public out-
rage were not Hollywood features, although legal decisions about them established a
judicial context in which the mainstream feature film industry had to operate. As the
audience for movies was increasingly narrowing to an age group in their late teens and
early twenties, the entire Hollywood movie industry was confronted with the acute need
to tread a thin line through a morass of claims and counter claims regarding what kind
of standards—and, hence, what kind of movies—were best for society. Ultimately, it was
the changing demographics of the audience for movies that would be most telling on
what direction the standards took. One internal staff report, prepared in 1968 for MPAA
executives, concluded that "parents of elementary and junior high school children do not
pay much attention to films and are not greatly concerned with them."[27]

THE RATINGS SYSTEM

The ultimate and definitive position taken up by Valenti on behalf of the MPAA in 1968
was to distinguish between "sexual explicitness" and "violence" as offensive materials.

"When so many critics complain about violence on film," he argued, "I don't think that they realize the impact of thirty minutes on the Huntley-Brinkley [NBC television] newscast—and that's real violence."[28] In the midst of nightly coverage from combat zones in the Vietnam War, evening network broadcasts often carried graphic and bloody scenes of violence. Certainly, Valenti's logic helped to compartmentalize graphic sexuality as distinct from graphic violence. Not long after, Valenti refined his argument publicly when testifying before the Presidential Commission on Obscenity and Pornography. He argued that conflict was "the essence of drama." Sexually explicit material, however, he labeled as "trash" during the same hearings.[29]

Press releases and testimony were not the primary avenues through which Valenti was working. Not long after he became president of the MPAA in 1966, he began lining up support from the National Association of Theater Owners (NATO) for Hollywood to abandon its Production Code in favor of a ratings system for movies.[30] Indeed, Valenti's role in effectively lobbying the theater owners as a group to change their position on a ratings system was likely his greatest accomplishment as MPAA president during the 1960s. The support of exhibitors across America was crucial because any ratings system would shift the burden of enforcement from the people producing movies to owners and managers of movie theaters. Compliance with ratings would be implemented by listing them in local newspaper ads and by maintaining that admission to certain movies would be controlled and restricted at the box office. The question of how successful theater owners were perceived to be by the surrounding community in publicizing and enforcing the ratings was key to the rating scheme's success.[31] The ratings system, clearly, did not prohibit a producer from making any particular kind of film. At the same time, however, Valenti was increasing his appeals to producers not to abuse the newly won freedoms that would come from dropping the Production Code in favor of a ratings system.[32] If the MPAA spokesperson who had described Valenti's responsibilities as being only 5 percent devoted to matters having to do with the Production Code was correct, then that 5 percent was awfully, awfully large indeed.

The MPAA's new ratings system was actually modeled on one that had been in place for years in Great Britain. All films produced and/or distributed by the MPAA companies were to carry a rating of suitability: "G" (for general audiences); "M" (for mature viewers; later changed to "PG," for parental guidance); "R" (for films restricted to minors unless accompanied by an adult); or "X" (no one under 17 admitted; changed to "NC-17" nearly three decades later). Over the years, the rating designations would go through several permutations and a number of variations. At first, even the rating "X" was respectable: several highly regarded films, including THE DAMNED (1969, Luchino Visconti), the Oscar-winning MIDNIGHT COWBOY (1969, John Schlesinger), and A CLOCKWORK ORANGE (1971, Stanley Kubrick), carried that rating. Only during the 1970s did exhibition of hard-core pornographic films, and the media's attention to that phenomenon, turn "X" into a stigma.

Officially announced on October 7, 1968, the MPAA's motion-picture ratings system took effect on November 1 of that year. The ratings did not eradicate debate over movie content, of course, but the system provided excellent public relations for the movie industry and was widely accepted by the public. Hollywood appeared to be doing something proactive and positive about what sorts of movies America's youth would be seeing. For producers and distributors the solution was especially advantageous. Productions could proceed unimpeded and earn a rating—that could, moreover, be appealed or modified— while the actual burden of responsibility for enforcement of the system was left in the hands of movie theater owners. To further please Hollywood producers, with the single exception of one owner of a major movie theater chain, Walter Reade of New York City, the nation's exhibitors lined up solidly in support of the scheme.

Across the country, movie theater owners recognized that such a system could be highly useful for them as well. The ratings system was voluntary, not statutory, which meant that individual theater owners could decide how rigorously the ratings system was to be enforced in their specific theaters. The ratings system was, after all, industry policy, not law. In essence, any individual theater was left in a position to assess its own sense of community standards in booking features and permitting audiences to see them. Nonetheless, the ratings appeared highly responsible and constructive to most citizens, many of whom likely did not understand that they were voluntary, not statutory, and that their enforcement was left entirely to the discretion of the movie theater owners.

In the MPAA's ratings system, Hollywood had found a method of operation to accommodate the sexual revolution, a rapidly changing culture, and the shifting demographics of its audiences while appearing to act protectively toward what many citizens considered the larger interests of American society and the common good. Nonetheless, some people, both inside the movie industry and out, were still critical of the decision to replace the moribund Production Code with ratings. The new system posed some hurdles for producers, since the economic viability of a movie could hinge on whether it received an "R" or a "PG": for example, an "R" rating might kill the box-office potential for drawing people younger than seventeen. Some producers argued that the MPAA's rating board was dominated, especially in its earliest years, by pseudo-psychologists who tended to exaggerate the effects on children and adolescents of such genres as horror movies, and to rate such pictures accordingly.[33] Others claimed that the ratings system stood to penalize nearly any emotionally or aesthetically complex movie and would only further reinforce Hollywood's tendencies toward producing films based on safe and conventional stories and formulas.[34] Some critics even maintained that the ratings system would prove more restrictive than any limitations the government could have imposed and sustained constitutionally, since they believed that legal challenges to such actions by government eventually would be struck down by the courts.[35]

The Hollywood Production Code and the system that required each release by one of the major to studios to obtain a seal of approval was replaced by the ratings system. The solution was neither perfect nor could it please everyone. Taken on the whole over many years, however, the ratings system proved a comparatively effective scheme for relieving pressure on the American motion-picture production industry and preventing movies and their producers from becoming tied up in convoluted litigation and court cases that could drag on for years.

5

The Camera Eye

The Triumph of Color

Synchronized sound was introduced to the silent movies in 1927 and promptly swept across the motion-picture production industry. Just as silent films were accompanied by music from the earliest years, techniques for coloring or tinting motion-picture film existed as well. Yet color motion-picture film coexisted with black-and-white film for decades without making a sudden and sweeping takeover of feature film production. The Technicolor Company was founded in 1917, and experimentation in color motion picture film processes made great progress through the 1930s. Not until after World War II, however, did Eastman Kodak introduce new film stocks with color sensitive emulsions that were considerably less expensive and easier to use than anything that Technicolor had available.

Feature film production in black and white remained the norm even after Kodak's new stocks were placed on the market and consumer demand began to reduce the cost of shooting a feature in color. There was no immediate response by the American motion picture industry to shift feature film production to color, and there was no discernible audience demand for the industry to do so.

The number of feature films in color, as compared to the number produced in black and white, rose in Hollywood during the early 1950s—from only 12 percent in 1947 to nearly 50 percent in 1954. Interestingly, however, the number of movies produced in color actually declined between 1955 and 1957 before starting to increase again.[1] In 1958, recognizing that feature film production appeared to be divided rather equally between black and white and color, the Academy of Motion Picture Arts and Sciences began awarding separate Oscars each year for achievement in cinematography in the two different categories. The practice lasted almost a decade, abandoned only in 1967 when the color feature film was recognized by the Academy as having established an unchallenged dominance over black and white.[2] What caused that change in just eight years and accounted for the complete triumph of color film over black and white is an interesting story.

The color film stock for cameras that became the industry standard in the United States during the 1950s and 1960s was manufactured by Eastman Kodak. Introduced in 1953, the product line of negative color camera film (numbered by Kodak as a series, 5250, 5251, and 5254) underwent major advancements in the years 1959, 1962, and 1968, respectively. Each of those improvements provided more film speed with no increase in graininess. Because the image dye absorbed less and less green light at each step of its development, the naturalness of the film's color reproduction was substantially improved. Eastman Kodak remained dominant in supplying camera film for Hollywood throughout the 1960s, with no real challenge to its market saturation until the mid 1970s in the form of competition from Fuji of Japan.[3] Kodak's increased film speeds and superior color balance processes were clearly technological advances, although some critics argued that a certain visual richness that occurred in the three-strip Technicolor process was lost with the new Kodak camera stocks.

In conjunction with its advancements in negative (or "camera") film during the 1960s, Kodak made parallel progress in its color positive (or "print") films. Kodak's improvement of these films meant greater sharpness of line in the picture and accounted for truer and more balanced colors in prints that were struck for release to movie theaters. The Eastman color stocks developed in the 1950s were inexpensive and highly usable under varying light conditions. They produced prints, however, that were subject to fading, which remained the case until the introduction of a color reversal printing process in the 1970s. Throughout the 1960s, then, the techniques for making prints of a color film remained problematic and resulted in color fading that eventually became evident. Despite such problems, progress in color motion-picture technology during the late 1950s and early 1960s can be accurately summarized as significant. The increased speed and improved color rendition of Kodak's color negative film stock, in particular, was extraordinarily important to cinematographers and directors. Their improved ability to control the quality of the image when shooting color, and the greater tolerance of the film stock to accommodate various lighting conditions, were clearly positive factors that justified Hollywood's shift to color production.[4]

Production trends in vogue by the early 1960s—the tendency to move outside to film in all seasons, to film on real locations, and to use less elaborate artificial lighting—were underscored by the advancement of color film stocks.[5] What audiences saw on the screen was also vastly improved at the very end of the 1960s by the introduction of liquid gate printing. This laboratory process consisted of completely immersing the final answer print—from which duplicate copies of the film would be made for distribution to the theaters—into a transparent liquid of nearly the same refractive visual index as the clear emulsion and acetate base of the answer print itself. This liquid immersion filled in all the small scratches or abrasions on the answer print's surface, providing for a brighter, clearer, and richer picture to fill the screen.[6]

However, color did not become the standard of Hollywood feature film production because of the aesthetic choices of directors and cinematographers, or because of improving film stocks and laboratory processes. The shift was abruptly accelerated, and then almost immediately brought to closure, by the introduction of color television in the United States in 1963. The advent of color television destined the black-and-white feature film to virtual extinction in the United States. Hollywood was well along the way of being convinced that television constituted such a large potential market for films that future features produced in black and white would be increasingly difficult to sell to broadcasters. With the arrival of color television, it was promptly assumed that audiences in the future would expect virtually all feature films in color.[7] Hollywood's wholesale shift to color production, then, was essentially a producers' decision based on commercial assessments of future markets.

Initially, Hollywood cinematographers did not necessarily favor this shift, even though it was commonly acknowledged by the mid 1960s that color film stock was as easy, or even easier, to work with than black and white. The central issue was not so much a matter of the viability and ease of working with color film. Many established cinematographers, having developed a keen eye for what they considered the purer photographic elements of black-and-white cinematography and its challenges, preferred that medium aesthetically. In many ways, the cinematographer actually had to work harder and more creatively with light to separate the visual planes and to create an illusion of depth through shadow when working in black and white.[8] Given their attention to craftsmanship, and given the elaborate photographic traditions that had grown up over the decades for manipulating and managing light for black-and-white production, most Hollywood cinematographers would have preferred a continuation of black-and-white features. The move to color was essentially a producers' preference that resulted in the virtual elimination of anyone in the United States being able to choose to do a major feature film in black and white by the end of the 1960s. In other film-producing countries, the option remained open much longer.

The change in the United States occurred quickly. WHO'S AFRAID OF VIRGINIA WOOLF? (1966) and IN COLD BLOOD (1967) were unusual, after all, but hardly unique as black-and-white features, whereas Peter Bogdanovich's 1971 black-and-white feature, THE LAST PICTURE SHOW, was considered by both critics and industry pundits as an anomaly and an eccentric throwback to an earlier Hollywood era.

The precarious financial state of the feature film industry in the early 1960s fueled the impulse to move quickly in the transition to color. As theater attendance was steadily declining, Hollywood had to take the television market for feature films seriously, and had to look for any avenue through which production costs might be kept down. Many a producer could argue plausibly that a shift to color production actually would help keep feature films on target for their scheduled completion dates.[9] Color cinematography was easier to handle in many ways than black and white because it often required fewer and simpler lighting setups. And, while some cinematographers preferred black and white for aesthetic reasons, others, especially younger ones just entering the craft in the 1960s, quickly embraced color. They considered color production a natural and logical extension of an aesthetic that coincided with tendencies in Hollywood toward greater authenticity in shooting on location and greater naturalism in lighting design for filming both on location and on sets. Hollywood's long-standing view that color was desirable only for comedies, romances, and musicals was undergoing challenge. Long known among cinematographers for its sense of artificiality, escapism, and lightweight genres, color suddenly became perceived in the mid 1960s among Hollywood cinematographers as a key for opening up an enormously enriched sense of cinematic naturalism.[10]

Reflex Cameras and a Changing Visual Aesthetic

Cinematography itself was changed considerably during the 1960s by advancements in camera design that had begun in the preceding decade. The development of the reflex camera during the 1950s, and its perfection in the early 1960s, had a major impact on Hollywood feature film production. Reflex cameras permitted operators to see and focus their shots directly through the lens, rather than through a viewfinder. Since the use of the reflex camera permitted a camera operator to be able to follow an entire shot through its varying focal lengths, it provided far better control over the picture and its composition. Furthermore, the importance of the reflex camera was linked with the ascendancy of color film to its domination of feature film production in the United States by the late 1960s. Black-and-white film had offered considerable depth of field that functioned to keep the different planes of both the foreground and the background simultaneously in focus. Color cinematography had to rely much more heavily on focus pulling (changing the focus during the course of a shot to force the viewer's attention to a different plane) because color film did not render distinctions inherently in the same way as black-and-white film.

Among other things, the reflex system made the widespread use of the zoom lens possible. Such shots now could be followed by looking directly through the camera lens, enabling directors and their cinematographers to more easily call upon a wider range of focal lengths. The capacity to control the spatial relationships of humans to objects within the frame was greatly enhanced as well. Reflex cameras encouraged exploitation of a vast new range of visual possibilities through the use of different lenses and through moving shots in which focus had to be continuously adjusted.[11]

The design of the first truly practical zoom lens, with a ratio of 10:1, is credited to the Frenchman Pierre Angenieux.[12] The Angenieux lens, which was already widely in use in Europe in the early 1960s, drew Hollywood's attention only in 1965, with the release of DARLING (John Schlesinger), a British production that received Academy Award nominations for best picture and best director. For the next several years, the zoom lens was used extensively in Hollywood features and was well established in nearly every director of photography's arsenal by decade's end, although some critics soon complained the technique was overused and considered it a gimmick.[13]

The foremost companies in manufacturing and advancing the technology of reflex cameras were Arriflex of Germany, the Mitchell Company of Los Angeles, and the relatively small Cinema Products Company started by engineer Ed DiGiulio in the early 1950s. In 1967, Mitchell managed to gain temporary advantage over its competitors with the introduction of its new line of "BNCR" cameras, which quickly became standard in Hollywood. In addition to a reflex lens design, the BNCRs featured specially treated glass at the front of the unit that acted as a noise control and rendered the camera's operation substantially quieter than its competitors.[14]

Widescreen and Ratio

Other changes in the visual aesthetics of Hollywood during the 1960s were driven by the motion picture industry's struggle to come to terms with its own introduction of widescreen technologies during the previous decade. The 1960s began with widespread uncertainty and extensive professional debate in Hollywood over just how best to exploit widescreen formats.[15] Standard Hollywood widescreen during the 1950s utilized 35mm camera film that was printed to create images in CinemaScope or VistaVision that were spread out along a horizontally widened visual plane. Producing the look of a greatly elongated rectangular image that was radically different from the small "squared picture" that the viewer saw on television became a main impulse for adopting widescreen in feature films intended for theatrical release. Since directors, cinematographers, and editors found that widescreen productions tended to have a static quality visually, the primary question by the early 1960s was to what other end and purpose could widescreen be applied. Widescreen made montage sequences difficult and rendered those that called for rapidly dissolving images practically impossible. Fundamentally, the human eye had far greater difficulty adjusting to and tolerating quick editing and cut-aways presented in widescreen.[16]

Until the early 1950s, nearly all 35mm films were projected in an aspect ratio of 1.33:1, sometimes called "Academy aperture," meaning that the rectangular frame length was 1 1/3 times wider than its height.[17] The new widescreen formats, however, provided an elongated image that expanded the on-screen space both left and right. With CinemaScope the screen had an aspect ratio of 2.55:1, which was soon modified to 2.35:1 and called "Full Scope." The difference between conventional 35mm film shot for academy aperture and widescreen had to do almost entirely with the width of the projected image, for there was little difference between them with regard to depth of field. The only discernible distinction in the widescreen formats that the average viewer might detect was a slight reduction in depth perspective for interior shots.[18] At the end of the 1950s, a compromise aspect ratio for feature films of 1:85:1 (1:66:1 in Europe) had become widely standardized and was normally called "standard widescreen." Full Scope, with its 2.35:1 aspect ratio, was limited to a handful of historical spectaculars and war movies: THE GUNS OF NAVARONE (1961), LAWRENCE OF ARABIA (1962), THE LONGEST DAY (1962), DOCTOR ZHIVAGO (1965)—and such musical extravaganzas as MY FAIR LADY (1964) and THE SOUND OF MUSIC (1965). The theatrical presentation of such features presented one set of challenges, while the transfer of the widescreen formats to video for broadcast on television presented far more complicated ones. The introduction of a "letter-boxing" system permitted the transfer to video to maintain the appearance of the original aspect ratio of the widescreen theatrical release by diminishing the height of the video image that would be shown on television. Serious questions remained about the wisdom of pursuing widescreen formats much further because of the inherent diminution of the aesthetic experience of watching on television movies originally shot in widescreen formats.[19]

Aspect ratio, however, was not the only problem with transferring a motion picture to video for transmission on television. Film has twenty-four frames per second, whereas standard American video (NTSC standard) has thirty frames per second (technically. 29.9 fps). Because of these differences in fps, any transfer of film to video results in what is called a "field drop," meaning that every four frames of film must be extended to cover five frames of video. The televising of any film, then, must distort the original aspect ratio so that the picture will be squarer (less elongated) on the television screen, and there must also be a warping of the temporal pace of any film when it is shown on television.[20]

The issue of the aspect ratio for which a film is shot is further complicated because it is never an absolute indicator of how any film is actually exhibited and seen. The filmmaker's choice of screen format is important in shaping the viewer's aesthetic experience so long as the picture is actually seen in the specific ratio for which it was made, but it is rarely a visual element over which the filmmaker has any real control. Not only are all feature films substantially altered by transferring them to video and also by telecasting them for the small screen, but they inevitably are subject to being projected in different aspect ratios depending on the different theaters in which they have been shown.

Although 3-D had failed to catch on and was abandoned in the 1950s,[21] indicating that moviegoers were not necessarily interested in greatly increased depth perspective in the picture, Hollywood's interest continued in processes that greatly increased the picture that viewers could see on the screen peripherally. Nonetheless, the ascendancy of special processes for feature releases was a phenomenon of the 1950s, not the 1960s. Taken together, the CinemaScope, RegalScope, SuperScope, Technirama, and VistaVision widescreen processes accounted for 102 Hollywood productions in 1957, dropping to forty-seven just three years later in 1960. Cinerama, first introduced in 1952 and used for feature production a decade later, was a complicated system that rendered films into aspect ratios of 2.71:1 to 2:77:1. Cinerama initially used a complicated three-camera system for filming and, likewise, required three projectors for exhibition. This process was converted to a single-camera system only in 1966, although some critics argued that it was no longer really "Cinerama" anymore.[22] A much simpler competing system called "Ultra-Panavision" was made available in 1964. The visual impression of artificially curving otherwise square objects—a fundamental problem with the Cinerama technique—disturbed both critics and moviegoers. The controversy and criticism over this distortion was not stilled by the highly accomplished 2001: A SPACE ODYSSEY (1968, Stanley Kubrick), which might have been an ideal vehicle for this "look."[23] After 1968, all of the processes had been replaced by the vastly superior, simpler, and less expensive anamorphic lens system developed by the Panavision Corporation.[24]

Panavision and a Changing Hollywood

The Panavision company was at the center of the changing "look" of feature films during the 1960s by providing the Hollywood industry with less expensive alternatives to the various widescreen and 70mm production processes that the major studios pioneered during the 1950s. A comparatively small, upstart company, Panavision was founded in 1953 by Robert Gottschalk for the purpose of manufacturing anamorphic projection lenses. By 1958, a series of 35mm anamorphic lenses converting any standard 35mm image into an aspect ratio of 2:35:1 were marketed by Panavision under the brand name "Auto Panatar" and were competing with the CinemaScope process owned by 20th Century-Fox.[25] Moreover, Panavision lenses could accomplish this conversion with no risk of distortion to the image. By contrast, the faces of persons filmed at a distance of ten feet or less appeared to "bulge out" horizontally in CinemaScope.[26] The variable prismatic lens invented by Gottschalk in 1960 enabled Panavision's 35mm anamorphic process to considerably reduce the distortion inherent in all the other competing widescreen processes. It did so, moreover, with such success that even 20th Century-Fox, which had invested so heavily in its own widescreen equipment and processes, eventually adopted the Panavision lenses.[27]

Throughout the 1960s, Panavision built up its array of anamorphic lenses, introducing new telephoto focal lengths one after another and earning for this fledgling company a distinct place at the center of cinematographic research and development.[28] The optical system invented by Panavision also gave producers flexibility, since it permitted the printing of any 35mm film in a 70mm release print. This meant that widescreen prints could be circulated for the purpose of roadshow exhibition in movie theaters that could accommodate them, while, at the same time, conventional 35mm prints could be released to the thousands of theaters not equipped specifically for widescreen, or used for the comparatively inexpensive process of transfer to videotape for broadcast on television.

With its superior lenses that delivered increasingly clear and undistorted images, Panavision rose during the 1960s as the unchallenged supplier of professional camera packages to the motion-picture production industry in the United States. Using Mitchell camera bodies outfitted with Panavision's superior lenses, and operating solely as a

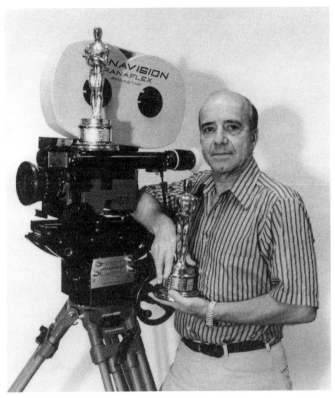

Robert Gottschalk, founder and president of the Panavision Corporation, which developed innovative lenses to improve cinema images.

rental house that served the increasingly free-lance production system of Hollywood, the company became legendary in its success.[29] At the very end of the 1960s, Panavision introduced a versatile camera called the "Panaflex" that could be converted easily from its studio configuration to a lightweight, hand-held version. The Panaflex, first used in THE SUGARLAND EXPRESS (1974, Steven Spielberg), quickly became standard in the feature film industry.[30]

Influences and Changes

The look of the American feature film changed substantially during the 1960s. The picture seen on screens in theaters widened, and color production doomed features in black and white. Nonetheless, the perception of depth within the image changed little, and myriad attempts to introduce peripheral and wraparound screen images were not well received. The 1960s witnessed innovations in cinematography, especially during the last few years of the decade, made possible by new cameras, lenses, and film stocks, as well as the challenge of filling a wider screen. The application of new technologies, and inventive approaches to them, however, finally depended on the artistic initiative of individual directors of photography, and were anchored by the interpersonal relationships formed within the feature film production process. The emerging free-lance system of production, where staffs were increasingly formed film by film, inspired much risk-taking. Individual film directors and directors of photography sought each other out and worked together in a new symbiosis that went far beyond the more traditional relationships that had resulted from studio assignments.

Classic Hollywood had harnessed photography to the imperative of storytelling. The visual look of a film was to support the structure and underlying dramatic motives of the story. During the 1960s, various cinematographers began exercising greater creativity in interpreting the visual material of their films. Vilmos Zsigmond, who was director of photography for THE TIME TRAVELERS (1964, Ib Melchior), THE NAME OF THE GAME IS KILL (1968, Gunnar Hellstrom), and FUTZ (1969, Tom O'Horgan), and moved on during the 1970s to industry prominence with DELIVERANCE (1972, John Boorman) and THE LONG GOODBYE (1973, Robert Altman), as well as work with Michael Cimino, Brian DePalma, and Martin Scorsese, summed up his aesthetic approaches and those of many other directors of photography who shot their first feature during the 1960s: "We live in a world of feelings, and it is the responsibility of the cinematographer to give visual form to the feelings that express the director's intent." He concluded, "We are like painters."[31]

INFLUENCES FROM NEW YORK AND EUROPE

The influence of East Coast directors of photography on Hollywood cinematography was becoming increasingly evident by the mid 1960s. Generally, New York filmmakers did not use nearly as many lights or as much equipment as their counterparts in southern California, and they veered away much earlier from well-lit studio sets and backlots.[32] British, French, and Italian filmmakers had likewise utilized location filming in the late 1940s. That was well before Hollywood copied the example of moving a production outdoors and onto actual locations and filming sequences with available light.

Many observers believed that location shooting was necessarily less expensive than studio or back lot filming and assumed that the New York and European cinematographers moved to location filming primarily for budgetary reasons. The reality was far more complex. For example, the control compromised by moving out of the studio could substantially increase the time needed for a feature's shooting schedule because of the more complicated setups involved. Moreover, the expense of location shooting depended on such variables as transporting and supporting cast and crew: Any truly informative cost analysis for a production had to calculate lodging and meal expenses against the cost of studio rental. The challenge of lighting and sound could considerably increase the budgets of films being done on location. One would think that available light was free of cost for a production shot on location,[33] but in fact it was much harder to maintain consistency in the light levels from shot to shot under such circumstances. In the studio, control over lighting and sound elements was predictable and reliable. Thus, more natural and simpler lighting did not necessarily mean less expensive production costs.[34]

Conrad Hall, one of the most accomplished cinematographers of the 1960s, insisted that he could use less lighting on IN COLD BLOOD (1967) because he had enough money in the production budget to do so: "I used the precise light in every situation. Instead of using two lights to do one job, I used one light . . . which makes it simpler and better . . . but also more costly because additional set-ups are required."[35] Location shooting and natural lighting became favored because they rendered aesthetic values in a production that were perceived to be more authentic. Such authenticity appealed to the look pre-

The "New York style" of cinematography used in THE HUSTLER *(1961) starring Paul Newman, was pioneered by Eugen Shuftan, a German-born veteran director of photography.*

ferred by the more sophisticated viewers and critics of the 1960s, while satiating aesthetic desires of a more independent breed of 1960s directors and cinematographers.

Although he had emigrated from Germany in the 1930s, Eugen Shuftan pioneered the "New York School" of cinematography in THE HUSTLER (1961). He earned an Academy Award for black-and-white cinematography that year. There were earlier avant-garde and European styles that were similar. Additionally, the very low-budget, experimental, and independent American feature by John Cassavetes, SHADOWS (1959), deeply impressed some Hollywood camera professionals. But it was Shuftan's stark, gritty, and realistic look in THE HUSTLER that got Hollywood's attention.[36] James Wong Howe, who began working in Hollywood in 1919, had pioneered hand-held cinematography on features, and served as the director of photography for HUD (1963, Martin Ritt), was one example. Howe integrated many techniques of the New York School into his superlative camera work on HUD, tending toward sharper contrasts than was traditional in the Hollywood style for this movie set in Texas. The results were considered a high point of accomplishment in black-and-white photography on the eve of its virtual elimination from feature production in the United States. Winning the Academy Award for cinematography (black and white) for HUD, Howe had achieved an extraordinary control over his stark images that served the film by helping to visually subdue some of the screenplay's pretentious allusions to ancient Greek tragedy.

In direct opposition to the stark and naturalistic visual aesthetics that were copied from the New York cinematographers, Hollywood cinematography right after mid-decade also took inspiration from European films that used very long lenses to cover staged dramatic action, as pioneered by the French director Claude Lelouch in A MAN AND A WOMAN (1966). This highly formalistic innovation drew a great deal of critical acclaim in the United States and was seen as a cinematographic breakthrough. Several other features produced in France and directed by Lelouch inspired the appearance of lighting that used heavy lens diffusion, which scatters white light over the entire image and gives the picture an almost ethereal look. The use of such lighting was advanced in Hollywood with THE GRADUATE (1967, directed by Mike Nichols, with cinematography by Robert Surtees) and GOODBYE COLUMBUS (1969, directed by Larry Peerce, with cinematography by Gerald Hirschfeld).[37] In both films the overall visual look conveys the mood of the picture as interpreted from the protagonist's point of view. This idea of such a visual design had been pioneered in expressionist films produced in Germany during the 1920s, many of which were considered self-consciously artistic. The same notion had previously appeared in Hollywood, however, primarily in specific genres, such as *film noir*. In the late 1960s, by contrast, such an aesthetic that intentionally drew attention to the cinematography was pushed to the forefront and became a recognizable tendency in some mainstream Hollywood productions.

Still, much of the most accomplished cinematography of the 1960s did not rely on the use of new lenses, or the sustained presentation of a gritty realism, or even the purposeful manipulation of lighting and film stocks to achieve "looks" that departed from a standard, polished visual surface that classic Hollywood had perfected. Frederick A. (Freddie) Young's work on one of the most highly regarded cinematographic triumphs of the decade, LAWRENCE OF ARABIA (1962), was a case in point. Young used the widescreen so that the vastness, harshness, and subtlety of the desert itself "seemed to be the star," observed Natalie Frederik.[38] Young's stunning desert photography and his skilled sense of composition, along with the pacing of the film's editing, contributed to the viewer's sense of the heat, loneliness, and harshness of the desert locales. Young carried his mastery of an especially rich elaboration on classic cinematography into DOCTOR ZHIVAGO (1965). There he handled the vast, snow-swept reaches of Siberia with the same deftness he had brought to the desert in LAWRENCE OF ARABIA. DOCTOR ZHIVAGO, too, was a feast of light and color, and it also spanned photographic perspective ranging from lush to stark. Young became a master of epics that utilized new technological processes for the full aesthetic exploitation of widescreen, and which used that format's aspect ratio to the fullest. Young continued those feats into the next decade with RYAN'S DAUGHTER (1970).[39]

During the 1960s the masterful widescreen cinematography of LAWRENCE OF ARABIA and DOCTOR ZHIVAGO was equaled only by the cinematography of Pasquale De Santis for ROMEO AND JULIET (1968, produced and directed by Franco Zeffirelli). These three films showcased cinematography that was highly crafted in its own right—without entailing any specific visual innovation—with aesthetic characteristics that were absolutely essential to the overall accomplishment of each of the movies.

INNOVATION IN FEATURE FILM CINEMATOGRAPHY

Along with the New York School influences, the European influences, and the accomplishment of exploiting widescreen to masterful cinematography, American feature films

Widescreen cinematography at its best—as Frederick A. Young, director of photography for LAWRENCE OF ARABIA (1962), evokes the vastness and the harshness of the desert.

of the 1960s displayed an eclectic array of cinematographic innovations and styles. Some of the innovations came from new talent in the ranks of directors of photography, but others were the work of longtime Hollywood professionals. Robert Surtees, a well-traveled veteran of the studio system who had begun his career during the silent movie era, was one of the best examples of the versatility, breadth, and creativity of Hollywood directors of photography during the 1960s. His initial cinematographic triumph in the 1960s was reflected in the Academy Award he received in the color category for MY FAIR LADY (1964). Filming this musical extravaganza required numerous and complicated setups in classic Hollywood key-light style for the various production numbers. The challenge to Surtees reached an apex when veteran director George Cukor demanded pristine, shadowless photography on the "Ascot scene," meaning that Surtees had to put up hundreds of lamps and color balance them just for this one scene.[40]

His accomplishments on MY FAIR LADY made Surtees a natural candidate for director of photography on 20th Century-Fox's production of DOCTOR DOLITTLE (1967). This lavish, $27 million musical was characterized by its sharp and clear high-key photography. After the DOCTOR DOLITTLE project, which was filmed in England, Surtees went back to Los Angeles as director of photography on a low-budget feature, THE GRADUATE (1967). Director Mike Nichols instructed Surtees that the film needed to have a subjective look that would reflect the way that things might appear in the confused mind of the protagonist. Shifting from the demands of classical key lighting on MY FAIR LADY and DOCTOR DOLITTLE, Surtees addressed this challenge, in part, by shooting much of THE GRADUATE with photographic compositions that concentrated a viewer's attention on the central action in scenes. This was done by placing static objects in the foreground of an inordinate number of his compositions, or by filling in the side areas of the screen with shadows.[41]

Surtees and Nichols collaborated in experiments with lenses, using techniques already well established in the British and French cinemas. For example, Benjamin (played by Dustin Hoffman) is seen from a very long focal distance appearing to be running hard and pumping his knees in the air but "getting nowhere," which conveys a fundamental idea about the character. In time, many critics would come to look upon such shots as clichéd, but when they first appeared in American features they were considered aesthetically ambitious. The visual choice of such shots underscored the movie's theme of alienation. Even more subtly, Surtees relied on even longer lenses throughout the movie to give the impression of Benjamin looking off into space, which created an existential underpinning for the character's situation—conveying visually a sense of the protagonist's isolation that otherwise would have been missing. Further drawing attention to the cinematography in a wholly unconventional manner, Surtees selected a wide angle lens to use at the movie's first real turning point—when Benjamin tells Elaine that he has been sleeping with her mother.[42] The very short focal length and very broad field of view from the lens exaggerates depth in the visual field and the figures near the camera.

Surtees experimented freely as well with the protagonist's point of view in scenes where Benjamin is driving the Los Angeles freeways in his sports car. Surtees tied down an Arriflex camera in the trunk space and devised a system where the actor, Dustin Hoffman, could activate the filming as he drove along the freeways and streets of Los Angeles. In yet another scene, Surtees used a hidden camera with an extremely long 500mm lens to film "hippies" on the Sunset Strip outside the Whiskey à Go-Go club as Hoffman and his co-star, Katharine Ross (playing Elaine Robinson), rush along the sidewalk to enter a striptease club. The actors' dialogue for this scene was picked up by wireless microphones concealed in their clothing. This was location shooting with a vengeance, as far removed as possible from the studio tradition, and as accomplished as the highly controlled musical sequences that had defined much of Surtees's previous career as a Hollywood director of photography.[43]

Surtees stands as one of the decade's premier innovators in cinematography. Right alongside him, however, was a newcomer, Conrad Hall, a graduate of the Film School at the University of Southern California. Surtees had worked his way through the old studio system, whereas Hall from the earliest years of his Hollywood career was never reticent about attributing his feel for film, and the priority that he gave to finding a different "look" for each film he shot, to the influence of his favorite USC professor, Slavko Vorkapich. Indeed, Hall's professional career as a cinematographer actually began when he sold one of his USC class projects, *Sea Theme*, to television.[44]

Not long after that, Hall shot his first feature as director of photography, THE WILD SEED (1965), which was produced for less than $300,000. He continued to shoot films, but his big breakthrough came with the attention given by both critics and industry professionals to his work on IN COLD BLOOD (1967, Richard Brooks). Hall brought to this film an unusual, but absolutely appropriate style that he himself described as "just beyond documentary."[45] Shooting with anamorphic lenses in black and white, Hall rendered the small town department stores and bus stations of Kansas, where IN COLD BLOOD was shot on location, into a truly disturbing and disorienting series of bleak and alienating images derived from the most banal of mid-American settings. Moreover, Hall

Conrad Hall's exquisite black-and-white cinematography was seen in IN COLD BLOOD
(1966). He described it as "just beyond documentary."

manipulated the same shooting techniques to push the reveries and fantasies of one of
the killers, Perry Smith, to nightmarish and hallucinatory extremes.[46] Despite the film's
accomplished cinematography, however, a number of critics complained that IN COLD
BLOOD suffered from being "tricked up" by fancy editing. The review in *Time* magazine
specifically complained that in instances when the flashy dissolves caused a bus to
become a moving train, or when a prostitute was metamorphosed into one of the protagonists' mothers, the results were excessive and actually undermined the photography.[47]

THE GRADUATE and IN COLD BLOOD were Academy Award nominees in cinematography in 1967, and both lost out to the work of Burnett Guffey, director of photography on BONNIE AND CLYDE. Like Robert Surtees, Guffey began his Hollywood
career during the 1920s. Like THE GRADUATE and IN COLD BLOOD, BONNIE AND
CLYDE marked strong new directions for the visual aesthetic to be pursued in major feature films in the last several years of the 1960s. The slow-motion killing of Bonnie and
Clyde at the end of the movie anchored a stylized visual formalism in the Hollywood feature. That formalism was symptomatic of a new willingness to draw attention to a
movie's artfulness and artificiality, which apparently did not alienate viewers. Arthur
Penn's direction and Guffey's cinematography combined to establish just how far innovation might be pushed in a mainstream feature film that went on to enjoy enormous
box-office success.[48]

Another exemplar of versatility in the period was the director of photography Haskell
Wexler. He earned an Academy Award for cinematography (black and white) for WHO'S

Haskell Wexler, on the right with a pipe in his mouth, moved easily from documentary shooting to feature cinematography and directing. He is seen here on the set for his own movie, MEDIUM COOL *(1961).*

AFRAID OF VIRGINIA WOOLF? (1966). Under the direction of Mike Nichols (who had worked in theater but was directing his first movie), Wexler turned the play into a "photographic marvel."[49] Although Wexler was not a repeat Oscar winner in cinematography the following year, he directed photography for the best picture Oscar-winner, IN THE HEAT OF THE NIGHT (1967, Norman Jewison). For this color film Wexler basically used a classic Hollywood key-light approach that he shot as if it were a black-and-white production. Wexler softened the overall look of the movie by introducing bounce-light into nearly all the scenes; the technique noticeably softened the delineation of objects and figures in the image. This use of such fill light started a distinctive trend in Hollywood cinematography that was immediately influential and widely copied.[50]

More importantly, Jewison and Wexler teamed the following year on THE THOMAS CROWN AFFAIR (1968), starring Steve McQueen and Faye Dunaway. Filmed almost entirely on location at Wexler's insistence, all the robbery scenes were done in documentary style. In addition to relying on hand-held cameras and allowing normal pedestrian and automobile traffic to pass through the location, Wexler had multiple cameras filming at once to get matching action. Such innovative camera techniques, and the coverage that was provided by them, actually determined the decision made in the final editing of THE THOMAS CROWN AFFAIR to present several different images of an action being shown at once on a divided screen. By presenting these related actions in a scene simultaneously, rather than in linear sequences, fundamental ideas about narrative and

editing were being overtly manipulated. It could be argued that by indulging this technique, which many critics called a gimmick, the final version was drastically displaced
from Wexler's original intention of filming the action so as to put emphasis on its feeling
of authenticity.[51]

The late 1960s gave rise to a concept of cinematography in the mainstream American
cinema where self-conscious attention to camera movement, angle, and presence was
significantly increased over the steadier, smoother, and more consistently lighted visual
style that had previously characterized Hollywood feature films. Documentary techniques, never considered acceptable in fiction films before, became widely appreciated.
In Hollywood's classic era, the films of individual studios had distinct and recognizable
visual styles, but by the late 1960s individual directors of photography were becoming
identified by their own particular approaches. Wexler expanded on the ideas he had pioneered in the two films he made with Jewison in his own low-budget feature, MEDIUM
COOL (1969), which he directed and photographed. He composed the entire movie
largely with low-angle shots, distorted perspectives, and unusual compositions and framing to evoke visual tension on the screen throughout the movie.[52]

By the end of the decade, directors of photography had become increasingly adventuresome and idiosyncratic in their choices of angles and lenses. Such imaginative creativity was fully accepted in Hollywood by 1969 when Laszlo Kovacs used the "fish-eye"
lens that distorted the image noticeably for the hallucinatory "drug trip" sequences in
EASY RIDER (1969, Dennis Hopper). Kovaks also used handheld shots to show moun-
tains and deserts, which was highly problematic because the Mitchell camera bodies he
had to use weighed between eighty and one hundred pounds each.[53]

The 1960s saw the rise of manipulating exposures and the processing of film in ways
that went beyond what had ever been acceptable in studio era. In many instances, such
cinematographic experimentation was aided and abetted by the attitudes and the
demands of new, young directors. When young Francis Ford Coppola saw the test
footage for his first major feature, YOU'RE A BIG BOY NOW (1966), he declared that the
photography was "too good."[54] Translating Coppola's complaint, the movie's director of
photography, New York-based Andrew Laszlo, began experimenting to reduce the sharp
and polished "Hollywood" look of this film. In some instances, Laszlo pushed his camera
film a full three stops, all the way up to an effective ASA of 400, for his shots in a department store under available light, although the standard, established ASA for the Kodak
color negative camera stock that Laszlo was using was only 100.[55] His experimentation on
YOU'RE A BIG BOY NOW with a cinematographic design intended to undermine the slick
and polished surface look given by standard Hollywood three-point lighting that keyed on
the main performers was a beginning point for Laszlo to become in the 1970s and 1980s
one of the great masters of filming with low light levels for major feature films.[56]

Indeed, as color replaced black-and-white film for features, directors and cinematographers began to increasingly experiment with underexposing 35mm Kodak color
negative. Some of them ordered their laboratories to force the development and printing of the film, which tended to give the image deeper and more saturated colors.[57]
Other directors of photography who wanted their colors to appear more washed out—
pushing the "look" of a production back toward the visual values and contrasts of black
and white—did exactly the opposite: they overexposed the color negative camera film
and had the laboratory print it "down."[58] The notion of tampering with the film stock and
manipulating the laboratory process by design was widely accepted by Hollywood professionals at the end of the 1960s.

Throughout the decade, cinematographers increasingly defined their own careers by the particular look they could bring to a feature film. They worked along the thin line of an expanding film aesthetic that accepted as its premise a fundamental paradox. As Andy Laszlo phrased it, "In cinematography you try to be authentic and at the same time you are trying to be theatrical."[59]

On THEY SHOOT HORSES, DON'T THEY? (1969), director of photography Philip Lathrop ordered the camera film to be shot underexposed and then had it developed "over" in the laboratory. As a result, the entire movie was given a grainy visual quality and a distinctive purplish-brown hue. That same year, Conrad Hall overexposed his camera film for BUTCH CASSIDY AND THE SUNDANCE KID. He then had it printed "down," reducing the color density and saturation to move the film along a visual spectrum that brought its look closer to black and white.[60]

NEW FIGURES, NEW DIRECTIONS

William A. (Billy) Fraker was another new director of photography to emerge during the late 1960s. He felt himself fortunate to do have done his first major feature, ROSEMARY'S BABY (1968), with director Roman Polanski, who was a new arrival in the United States from Poland. In his recollections of that experience, Fraker frequently refers to a scene where Rosemary's neighbor, played by Ruth Gordon, is sitting on the edge of a bed and talking on the phone. Polanski kept directing Fraker to move the camera to the left to establish the setup position for the beginning of the shot. "Now, by doing this," said Fraker of Polanski, "he began to cut Ruth off at the doorjamb. He cut her in half. Then he said: 'Stop the camera; this is it!' I looked through and all you can see is just part of her, but your hear her talking on the telephone. I said: 'You can't see her.' Roman said: 'Exactly, exactly.'"[61] Such willingness to break the conventions of classic Hollywood framing by drawing viewer attention to the camera and its unusual position was yet another example of the new visual aesthetic that was making serious inroads in Hollywood feature film production before the end of the 1960s.

Fraker's next film was BULLITT (1968, Peter Yates). Although Fraker won the National Society of Film Critics Award in cinematography for his work,[62] BULLITT was not even nominated for an Academy Award in that category. Already thought of as one of Hollywood's foremost location cinematographers, Fraker brought to perfection the techniques for achieving a seminal rendering of an action sequence in a major feature film. The critic and film teacher Ken Dancyger described the legendary car chase through San Francisco's streets that begins with Bullitt (played by Steve McQueen) being followed by two hit men and ended with Bullitt pursuing them: "The crispness of the cinematography provides a depth of field that beautifies this sequence." Dancyger added, "It's the choreography of the chase rather than the implications of its outcome (that the two men will die) that captivates our attention."[63] BULLITT, then, provides yet another example of one of the bigger box-office successes of the American cinema in the late 1960s utilizing formalistic techniques of cinematography that draw attention to themselves far more than they serve to advance the movie's story, contrary to what Hollywood's classic style had demanded.[64]

With an approach entirely unrelated to Fraker's, ICE STATION ZEBRA (1968) established a stunning visual environment. The veteran Hollywood cinematographer Daniel Fapp met two challenges: lighting for mood and effect in the confined and claustrophobic interior of a nuclear submarine, and demonstrating himself equally adept in his real-

In ICE STATION ZEBRA *(1968) Daniel Fapp, director of photography, created a stunning visual environment.*

istic visualization of the storm-lashed arctic weather station that eventually became the focal point of the movie's action.[65] In the free-lance environment of the New Hollywood that was taking full shape by the late 1960s, moreover, Fapp was able to shop in a relatively open market for creative assistance. For shots from the point of view of pilots, as Soviet jets raced in low altitude over the ice, Fapp enlisted the specialized artistic and technical services of John Stephens, who had been responsible for the race car drivers' point of view shots in GRAND PRIX (1967) and was becoming known as a specialist for this sort of photography.[66]

Rounding out the 1960s

By the time the American Society of Cinematographers (ASC) celebrated its fiftieth anniversary in January 1969, their members' craft had been substantially elevated in significance and creative independence in the American feature film during the preceding nine years.[67] The director of photography's new-found influence over production was being displayed throughout Hollywood. Philip Lathrop, for example, was able to convince the producers of THEY SHOOT HORSES, DON'T THEY? to do the picture, which was set in the 1930s, in anamorphic Panavision to capitalize on the form's elongated frame. "You can get a close-up of a character, while, at the same time, including the context of his environment within the frame," he argued. "The same close-up shot in a normal format would show very little in back of his character."[68]

Collaborating with the film's director, Sydney Pollack, Lathrop conceived shooting the entire movie in a fundamentally daring approach to camera movement. At times, his lens literally collides head-on with beams of light coming from overhead lamps. Throughout the movie, the camera keeps chasing after dancers. The sailor's death at the end of the film is in slow-motion, complementing the film's prologue where a young boy witnesses the shooting of a white stallion. The look that Lathrop brought to the film defines its overall aesthetic in ways that make it distinct as well as definitive in its interpretation of the 1930s period when it is set.[69]

As directors of photography were becoming more influential, career paths and potential remuneration opening up to them by the end of the 1960s surpassed anything that
had been available in the tightly unionized environment they had worked under in the
studio system. Several directors of photography who were to become prominent during
the 1970s, including John A. Alonzo, Vilmos Zsigmond, Gordon Willis, and Laszlo
Kovacs, were all able to launch their careers by being hired first on non-union jobs by
the producer/director of low-budget features, Roger Corman. As the director of photography on EASY RIDER in 1969, Kovacs was credited by many with completely uprooting and displacing the classic Hollywood idea of the invisible camera. According to
Joseph McBride of *Variety*, Kovacs used the camera "aggressively, almost as a weapon,
in the assault on the old school conventions."[70] It would be an exaggeration to claim that
Kovacs gained star celebrity from his work, but many critics were more than willing to
acknowledge that his cinematography on EASY RIDER was as notable as the script or the
acting in the movie.[71] Yet, without discounting the changing role of directors of photography by the end of the 1960s, it was Laszlo Kovacs who reemphasized for observers that
the cinematographer was still trying to get inside the director's mind in order to translate the director's vision into images.[72]

The new cinematography could be interpreted as underscoring the increased attention to the auteurist intent of individual directors, while at the same time the telling of
the film's story remained the dominant intention of the cinematographer. Whatever
experiments, innovations, and daring techniques the cinematographer might attempt,
the result still had to provide a look and feel that supported the central dramatic idea of
the movie. Yet what was meant by the very term "dramatic idea" in American feature
film production was changing. Hollywood filmmaking shifted away in the 1960s from
the classic cinema's regard for screenplays as the dramatic center, moving more toward
treating scripts as blueprints for telling a story visually. By the end of the 1960s, many
more movie stories were being "told" through the self-conscious use of shot selection,
camera placement, exaggerated lenses, and nontraditional lighting than had been the
case in classic Hollywood, where dialogue and character development were privileged
and preferred.

During the 1960s, actors and actresses were being called on to base their characters
more fully in subjective forces and motives. Scripts were becoming sparser in dialogue.
Cinematography in the American feature film had taken a giant step away from its classic role of seamlessly recording well-lit dramatic action and narrative discourse. The
American feature film had entered an era of greater visual innovation and self-indulgence that would not be reversed.

6

The Cutter's Room

From the late 1920s, Hollywood's traditional ways of editing feature films had developed in harmony with the primacy accorded to dialogue and story line. In its fundamental approach to both the spatial displacement and the screen direction of moving and stationary objects from shot to shot, all such classic editing emphasized the concept of continuity. According to the continuity principle of editing, scenes opened with an establishing shot that took in the entire space and then cut from this large master to shots within the scene that were selected to maintain a strong sense of matching action throughout. In addition to constructing and defining film space, continuity editing was vital to controlling a movie's manipulation of story time and sequencing. Shots were timed and ordered according to how they advanced the story, its logic, and its emotions; hence, the duration of any shot had little or no intrinsic aesthetic integrity in its own right. Continuity editing assumed that the narrative flow of the story was always primary. All shots included should contribute to a sense of matching action and logical progression of either the plot or of a character's development. "Extraneous" shots that did not advance the story were excluded.

In this classic Hollywood editing system, the role of an editor was to ensure that each and every sequence in a film built to its own dramatic climax.[1] Rules pertaining to editing were rigid and sacrosanct: standard fast rhythm, or pacing, was expected in comedies; by contrast, love and human interest stories were paced slowly.[2] Dede Allen, one of the great innovative film editors of the 1960s, recalled having been taught the editing craft at Columbia Pictures at the end of the 1940s in an entirely formulaic manner: "You always cut from a master to a closer shot, and then you go over-the-shoulder to close-ups."[3] Indeed, editors in the Hollywood studio system were basically considered "mechanics" who were not expected to contribute ideas or innovations in their cutting of a motion picture.[4] Theirs was a craft bound by a tradition that adhered strictly to established rules and conventions. Interestingly, it was practically the only field in the motion-picture industry under the studio system to which women had nearly equal access to work professionally.

Influence and Change

Because the narrative flow of a movie was considered of central importance in traditional Hollywood editing, any challenges to the narrative conventions of movie-making necessarily provided a rationale for new editing techniques. Insofar as European "art films" of the late 1950s began to shift attention from the primacy of the story to emphasis on the formal relationship of the director to visual material and formal characteristics of a film, seeds of challenge to the traditional conventions of continuity film editing were being sown. One of the first techniques to disappear from these European art films was the traditional reliance on the dissolve and the fade as standard devices used to indicate the passage of time or to introduce a change of location.[5] By the end of the 1950s, a full-blown challenge to the conventional assumptions and guidelines for the editing of narrative films was apparent in a number of European features: "When the French New Wave decided that people no longer had to walk in and out of doors that was an important change."[6]

In French director Jean-Luc Godard's influential feature BREATHLESS (1959) there was no concern for the time-honored geography of cutting. There would be a cut, for example, from Jean-Paul Belmondo staring at a gun in his hotel room to him walking on a street across town without any establishing shot.[7] Not only was the notion abandoned of establishing places clearly before any action might occur in them, but BREATHLESS contained jump cuts—a technique that had been strictly taboo for Hollywood editors. Such jarring cuts, which draw attention to themselves visually because they appear to leave out a portion of a sequence and jump abruptly from one image to another of the same person or object, were the antithesis of continuity editing. In favor of trying to construct a film according to its own internal rhythm and formalistic aesthetic, jump cutting and other New Wave editing techniques challenged the long-standing Hollywood practice of remaining faithful to the narrative purpose of the story line.[8]

Beyond shaking the concept of continuity editing, Godard and other French directors, including Alain Resnais, François Truffaut, and Claude Chabrol, also introduced various unconventional ways of breaking the narrative flow of their films. Such devices drew attention to distinctive cinematic elements that might be considered as distracting attention from the story. Quickly, such innovations caught on internationally. The 1963 Academy Award winner for best picture, TOM JONES (produced in Great Britain), contained freeze frames and suspended action of the sort that would not have been seen in a major feature film prior to the 1960s. Most importantly, such devices drew self-conscious attention to the artifice of the motion picture itself. They fundamentally challenged illusions of dramatic continuity that Hollywood had favored since the late 1920s. Much as the British production TOM JONES copied and popularized editing devices that had been pioneered by French New Wave films, earlier British films edited by Tony Gibbs—LOOK BACK IN ANGER (1959) and THE LONELINESS OF THE LONG DISTANCE RUNNER (1962)—violated the principles of continuity editing and called attention to the cutting. With the release in the United States not long after of four other British films all directed by Richard Lester—two *Beatles* movies, A HARD DAY'S NIGHT (1964) and HELP! (1965), along with THE KNACK (1965) and A FUNNY THING HAPPENED ON THE WAY TO THE FORUM (1966)—even mainstream Hollywood editing began embracing these new techniques.[9]

By the mid 1960s, Hollywood film editing in general had begun using far shorter shots than had been traditional, resulting in a quickened narrative pace.[10] This shift was immediately noticeable and controversial. Many critics began to complain that such editing was undermining the traditional narrative strength of Hollywood movies. Even those critics and industry professionals who were basically sympathetic to the changes, such as the veteran film editor Ralph Rosenblum, still thought that the new techniques

Jump cuts, fast- and slow-motion, and other cleverness in Richard Lester's A HARD DAY'S NIGHT, starring the Beatles, influenced a spirit of innovation in Hollywood feature film editing.

were being overused: "Since the Beatles, editing has become flamboyant solely for its own sake or to cover deficiencies in writing and directing." Rosenblum added, "When the editing of the film is the only memorable quality, the film most likely is forgettable."[11] Others, however, saw in these new approaches to editing a meaningful and valuable shift toward fuller exploitation of the motion-picture aesthetic. Many of the editors were also influenced and inspired by the cutting that they were seeing on television, as well as by editing found in the experimental films made by such avant-garde artists as Bruce Conner and Kenneth Anger.[12]

New Ideas and New Editors

In a painstaking and highly valuable study, British film critic and historian Barry Salt analyzed average shot lengths in American feature films for various chronological periods beginning with the silent era. Salt concluded that between 1958 and 1963 the average shot length (ASL) decreased from 11 seconds to 9.3 seconds. Between 1963 and 1969, the ASL decreased further to 7.7 seconds. By the end of the 1960s, the average shot length was barely two-thirds what it had been just a decade before. During the late 1960s, then, American feature films had reached the shortest average shot length in their history since the silent movies of the 1920s.[13] Salt's study provides empirical evidence to support what was widely *felt* about feature film editing during the 1960s—that the pace and rhythm of feature films accelerated notably during the decade. Shorter shots, edited one right after the other as straight cuts, were in vogue. Fades and dissolves had been widely abandoned as transition elements from scene to scene in favor of abrupt cuts, and the self-conscious use of jarring cinematic effects became an accepted part of the editing lexicon in mainstream feature film production.[14]

Underlying these changing approaches to editing were many forces, one of which was the latitude given to editors by a number of first-time directors during the mid 1960s.[15] It also has been claimed that the revolution in film editing during the 1960s was fueled in part by the introduction of new technologies and procedures, such as the flatbed and the tape splicer.[16] The flatbed, however, likely had less impact on feature film editing during the 1960s than has been claimed. Throughout the decade, Hollywood editors continued to prefer the upright Moviola for the cutting of features, even though its use entailed higher labor costs because an assistant to the editor was always required to rewind each shot.[17] The shift by film processing laboratories to print-ing frameline markers and arrowheads on workprints, on the other hand, had a major impact on the editing profession. This fairly simple and very important advancement allowed editors to distinguish between frames in a dark sequence of a film much more easily and precisely.[18]

Another technological development during the 1960s permitted the editor to divide a widescreen frame, allowing for the presentation of multiple images simultaneously. Pioneered in THE BOSTON STRANGLER and CHARLY (both 1968 releases), split screen techniques presented parallel action, a device that was taken to its fullest in the feature-length "rockumentary" WOODSTOCK (1970).[19] Such split screen experiments, although intrinsically interesting as adventures in image making, remained a footnote to the his-tory of feature film editing. More important than any changes in equipment or technol-ogy, and beyond the unusual gimmickry of the divided screen, a fundamentally new conceptual approach to the editing of feature films emerged during the 1960s, best exemplified by the work of Dede Allen.

DEDE ALLEN   In 1950, Dede Allen was working as an assistant cutter in the editing department at Columbia Pictures in Los Angeles. One day she crossed a union picket line at the studio, drawing unwanted attention to herself and provoking a good deal of animosity. Because of this incident she soon decided to quit her job and leave the West Coast for New York City, where she settled and married a documentarian named Stephen Fleischman who worked with ABC-News.[20]

By the late 1960s, Allen was at the very center of the revolutionary changes in the editing of feature films. So isolated was she from the West Coast scene that the editors guild of the International Alliance of Theatrical and Stage Employees (IATSE) refused to accept her as a member until 1978, which meant that up until that year she could not work in Hollywood unless a studio that wanted to hire her was also willing to employ a union editor to work alongside her. Effectively ostracized from the Hollywood main-stream and living in what was considered for a time during the mid 1960s as the more adventurous film production scene of New York City, Allen gained the opportunity to become the seminal figure in changing how American movies were edited. That began when director Robert Rossen invited her to edit THE HUSTLER in 1961.[21]

An ambitious black-and-white feature that challenged the best of the French New Wave films, and featuring cinematography by the German-born veteran Eugen Shuftan,

Film editor Dede Allen.

THE HUSTLER provided Allen an extraordinary chance to demonstrate her talent. As she recalls, Rossen was "very, very strong" on narrative. However, he helped her understand from the beginning that the movie was not about playing pool. Rather, as her editing would have to make clear, the movie was about people and about character.[22] In her ensuing conversations with Rossen, Allen began to realize that the events in the story did not necessarily have to be arranged in any kind of conventional continuity. The story elements might be moved around and rearranged in the editing process so that even if the story line became less clear because of her editorial decisions, the essence of what was being revealed about the protagonist's character would be strengthened. Being able to concentrate on the idea that THE HUSTLER was about character provided Allen a different dynamic for her cutting, once she accepted that the story could be of subsidiary importance.[23]

On THE HUSTLER Allen also had the opportunity to pioneer a kind of subcontracting of a specialized segment of the movie's editing. Such an arrangement would have been highly unusual, if not impossible, under the studio system, but the practice was to become increasingly common for features during the early 1960s. Allen asked Evan Lottman to work strictly on the pool game montages. He brought to those sequences a unique creative vision and interpretation of them. Instead of sticking to the fast-paced montage techniques that classic Hollywood editing had perfected or sequencing them in linear fashion, Lottman elected to render the images more abstract and associational. These new techniques allowed him to build emotionally on the competition between the two pool players, instead of telling the story of their rivalry. At times, Lottman even superimposed three images upon one another simultaneously.[24]

THE HUSTLER was an accomplished film that focused positive attention on Allen as its editor. As a result, she was hired to cut Elia Kazan's AMERICA, AMERICA (1963). Allen's editing helped contribute to the documentary feel of this feature film, which was shot in stark black and white by Haskell Wexler. By the mid-1960s, Allen had built her reputation in the industry as a highly skilled editor.

Allen's most forceful impact on the American cinema, however, occured when she collaborated with director Arthur Penn on BONNIE AND CLYDE (1967). This film marked a turning point in the editing of feature films that sent reverberations through the entire American cinema. Based on a screenplay by two magazine writers, Robert Benton and David Newman, BONNIE AND CLYDE was originally intended as a project to be directed by one of the prominent figures of the French New Wave, either François Truffaut or Jean-Luc Godard. The services of those directors could not be engaged, however, and the assignment shifted instead to Penn, a veteran director of drama for television who had just completed an offbeat feature, MICKEY ONE (1965), produced by and starring Warren Beatty. Penn displayed a distinct auteurist approach to all his work, and Beatty intended to produce BONNIE AND CLYDE as a quasi-art film. From the outset, Penn wanted the movie to incorporate the free intercutting of time and space, to use both slow and accelerated motion, and to display visual puns in the style of Truffaut as well as alternating moments of comedy and violence reminiscent of Godard.[25]

Considered a fairly innovative editor already, Allen was further empowered by Penn's constant encouragement to go further. She recalled, "I broke all my own rigid cutting rules about story, character, and how a scene plays."[26] The kinds of radical editing choices with which she had only toyed in THE HUSTLER were now given free reign in BONNIE AND CLYDE. Many of the action scenes in the film were edited from the point of view of the protagonist, Clyde Barrow, with close-ups of him often intercut with whatever he was seeing. So frequently does the film's action play as if perceived through his eyes that a pervasive subjectivity comes to dominate the tone of the film as the viewer increasingly identifies with Clyde.[27] The pace of the cutting was so carefully thought out, in fact, that the editing style itself finally reinforced a thematic unity throughout the film.

Several of the movie's scenes are remarkable and memorable because of the editing. For example, the killing of Bonnie and Clyde at the end of the film, when they are ambushed by the police, is polished artistry. Without the extraordinarily careful layering of the visuals and the sound, Allen's fast cutting could have easily resulted in a confused and jumbled scene. In an earlier scene, Allen had established her innovative approach to editing the picture and the sound. She elected to continue the frenetic pace of a shoot-out as characters tumbled into a getaway car, screaming and crying. The voice dialogue here was used by Allen to overlap the intercuts so that the sequence remained cohesive and especially terrifying.

Establishing shots were ignored throughout BONNIE AND CLYDE in favor of entering scenes with angle shots and close-ups. Even though these so-called "energy cuts" that Allen pioneered would soon be found nearly everywhere from Hollywood features to television commercials, initial reaction was much less positive. Veteran professionals in the Hollywood establishment judged BONNIE AND CLYDE to be poorly cut. "You mean," the producer Jack Warner asked Arthur Penn in amazement and disgust when he saw a first rough cut of the film, "that you're going to fade out and cut in?"[28] At one point dur-

The editing on Bonnie and Clyde *(1967) by Dede Allen emphasized unconventional pacing to render a new form of visual storytelling.*

ing the production, in fact, Warner wanted to fire Allen. He believed her editing style broke too many rules and conventions and was worried that her choices might leave the movie's audience "mistaking the bad guys for the good guys!"[29] In this regard, Warner's fears were telling! The studio executive's comment showed his fundamental misunderstanding of the basic theme of the movie—that it was intended to evoke sympathy toward the main characters.

The revolution in editing technique and style that Allen pioneered with Bonnie and Clyde was essential to Arthur Penn's directorial vision and to Warren Beatty's concept of the film, which he labeled "American New Wave." Although Allen's tendency toward fast cutting was copied widely almost immediately, in most instances such cutting was done without the clear artistic intent and purpose that she had sustained throughout Bonnie and Clyde. Imitators would frequently take from her example only the notion of stunningly short shots put together at a frenetic pace, whereas Allen's path-breaking work wove substance and style in a virtuoso display of innovative and unconventional pacing to render a fundamentally new form of visual storytelling.

Ralph Rosenblum For a short time in the mid and late 1960s, the motion-picture industry's leading feature film editors were working primarily in New York City. Dede Allen was there, of course, along with a trio of her highly successful proteges, Jerry Greenburg, Richie Marks, and Stephen Rotter; all were well established as editors of feature films before the end of the decade. Allen always maintained that there really was no "New York School" of editing, and certainly no "Dede Allen School" either. The work of Allen and her three former assistants should more accurately be ascribed the "Arthur Penn School," she joked, because Penn invariably shot so much footage that Allen was always justified in bringing more people on board as assistants to work on his films.[30]

In addition to Allen and her three former apprentices, Ralph Rosenblum was established in New York City. Although Rosenblum never worked on an Arthur Penn film, he was, along with Allen, one of the major forces in changing the way a feature film was edited and altering the perception in the industry of the creative role of an editor. Rosenblum edited two entirely different films—THE PAWNBROKER (1965, Sidney Lumet) and A THOUSAND CLOWNS (1965, Fred Coe)—that drew widespread attention and admiration in the industry.

From the opening of THE PAWNBROKER, Rosenblum's editing establishes an innovative dynamic between past and present, introducing a strong, underlying subjectivity to his handling of visual material. Following the opening sequence in which two children are seen in slow motion, running through high grass and stirring up butterflies they are trying to catch, the film cuts to a zoom in on Solomon Nazerman dozing in a lawn chair in a suburban yard outside New York City. This opening provides a prelude to the visual motif sustained throughout the film as its protagonist, an elderly Jewish survivor of the Holocaust, shifts back and forth in his mind between the present and the past. Worried that traditional flashback techniques would not suffice to deliver the story's emotional power, screenwriters Morton Fine and David Friedkin urged Rosenblum to be innovative and daring in his editing.

Influenced both by the French feature HIROSHIMA, MON AMOUR (1959, Alain Resnais)[31] and a French film adaptation of Ambrose Bierce's short story AN OCCURRENCE AT OWL CREEK BRIDGE (1955, Robert Enrico),[32] Rosenblum worked from a basic conceptual strategy that permitted each of the many flashbacks in THE PAWNBROKER to be as fast-paced and disruptive as possible. In fact, these periodic disruptions become all the more compelling and noticeable because the movie in general depends heavily on relatively long takes and the rhythm in its dialogue scenes relies on a highly conventionalized, "reverse-angle" editing that shifts back and forth between the characters who are speaking. Typical of the aesthetic shift established in feature film editing during the second half of the decade, Rosenblum's unusual and dynamic pacing of THE PAWNBROKER depended heavily on his limited use of editing techniques that departed from convention. From a basic premise of how editing style might convey subjectivity by suggesting entry into the protagonist's mind, Rosenblum's radical departures from classic editing style are reserved for a handful of sequences in the movie where the protagonist is abruptly thrust back into his recollections of incidents that occurred during his incarceration in the Nazi extermination camps. These are visually disturbing and visceral because they rip apart the movie's narrative flow in ways that had not been seen before in an American feature film. The flashback sequences are intended to show the protagonist's memories and present in a uniquely powerful visual manner the continuing malaise and torment that he feels about them. These dissonant and unsettling flashbacks work artistically precisely because they let the viewer get into the character's psyche.[33]

Rosenblum used several editing devices to underscore the mood of each flashback sequence. Among them was the "flutter cut," an editing technique in which very short clips of film from different scenes are cut together to create a visual staccato. In one such sequence the character Nazerman is watching New York street hoodlums beat a

Ralph Rosenblum's editing on Sidney Lumet's THE PAWNBROKER *(1964) intensified flashback scenes that haunt the protagonist (played by Rod Steiger).*

young man who attempts to flee them by climbing a fence. The old man's memories are brought in directly by flutter cutting short bits of him in close-up, years earlier, witnessing some of the brutality perpetrated by his Nazi captors.[34] The emotional stakes of such radical editing techniques are heightened by Rosenblum's judicious use of such sequences and by an underlying psychological frustration to which the editing sometimes refers by associating viscerally powerful cuts with scenes related to sexuality. The latter occurs, for instance, in the scene where a desperate local prostitute enters the pawnshop and offers sex to Nazerman. The flutter cut flashes back to his memories of the sexual humiliation of a Jewish woman at the hands of Nazi death camp guards.

In his work on THE PAWNBROKER, Rosenblum imitated devices from several French films of the preceding decade, but he also extended them. Like Dede Allen, Rosenblum broke editing conventions and rules. More importantly, and like her also, his innovations shifted editing away from its traditional reliance on telling a story to the creation of a new and permeating subjectivity in the feature film.

A THOUSAND CLOWNS, also edited by Rosenblum, was an entirely different sort of film. Light-hearted in spirit and liberated in its mood, it opens with a title sequence consisting of random shots of New York City crowds heading to work, intercut with a middle-aged man and a boy riding bicycles. This immediately establishes bicycle riding as a guiding visual force in the film. Throughout the movie, Jason Robards and Barbara Harris are seen riding around Manhattan on a bicycle-for-two. Rosenblum put together shots in an entirely painterly manner, liberally mixing in stock footage of New York City streets and buildings to create a buoyant mood.[35] He repeatedly let go of the film's narrative logic in favor of a more rhythmic composition.

According to Rosenblum, the single most important element that shaped his approach to editing this film was his knowledge of, and love for, music.[36] While working closely with screenwriter Herb Gardner, Rosenblum demanded that the sound track was laid in before he cut the visuals. With A THOUSAND CLOWNS, Rosenblum started the habit of putting a scratch score to every film to establish a basic rhythm. As a result, his editorial choices came to be so fundamentally driven by the music that he soon stopped looking at the script entirely when editing any movie.[37] Rosenblum had departed fully from the classic Hollywood editing model, in which the script was of supreme importance and the editor's primary virtue was adherence to the story line and its logical advancement. Rosenblum's approach created no agreed-upon strategy for editing, however, even among his coterie of editors in New York City. Richie Marks, for example, went on record as saying that he found cutting to music altogether distracting. Marks approached his own work from exactly the opposite perspective, arguing that there was always what he called an "internal rhythm" to the visuals themselves and that it was the editor's job to discover that rhythm solely in the images of a movie without regard to the sound.[38]

Nonetheless, Rosenblum's impact on film editing was substantial enough to support the argument that, along with Dede Allen, he had dramatically altered the ways in which most film editors would work in the future. Of A THOUSAND CLOWNS and his subsequent films, it could truly be said that the producer, the director, and the screenwriter got back from Rosenblum a new film, and ostensibly a far superior one. By the end of the 1960s, Rosenblum's reputation was so well established across the motion-picture industry that when he took footage of TAKE THE MONEY AND RUN (1969), the first feature that Woody Allen directed, and salvaged a respectable comedy from an impending disaster, few of his fellow professionals were surprised.[39]

GEORGE TOMASINI   Dede Allen, Ralph Rosenblum, and the others in the New York School were seminal figures in film editing during the 1960s and their work established them as major influences on the American feature film. Among other film editors who blazed new trails during the early 1960s was Hollywood veteran George Tomasini, who began editing for the director Alfred Hitchcock with REAR WINDOW (1954). Tomasini's most important work with Hitchcock was the memorable shower scene in PSYCHO (1960). Its aesthetic and dramatic accomplishment was achieved largely through the editor's skill. The completed forty-five second sequence that Hitchcock originally storyboarded was compiled by Tomasini from footage shot over several days that utilized a total of seventy different camera setups.[40] From that mass of footage, Tomasini selected sixty different shots,[41] some of them very short, through which he elected to rely heavily on the techniques of "associative editing." Film cuts were made less jarring to the eye by the editor's choices of clustering images that are similar in shape. For example, Tomasini takes a slow zoom-in on Janet Leigh to the extreme close up on the iris of her eye and then cuts to a close up of the circular tub drain with whorls of water. Because the cut goes from one circular image to another—from the eye of a live human being to the drain taking away the running water—the visual transition is smooth and the two shots are associated to suggest visually that her life is "draining away."[42]

Critics David Bordwell and Kristin Thompson have argued convincingly that the editing defines the fascinating and revolutionary aesthetic of the shower murder in PSYCHO.[43] This aesthetic is achieved through an increased exploitation of editing to build

Janet Leigh in the shower scene from PSYCHO (1960, Alfred Hitchcock). Editing by George Tomasini built tension and suspense.

tension and suspense. Even more broadly, however, Alfred Hitchcock's ability to survive and prosper as a popular filmmaker during the 1960s reflects his ability as a filmmaker to adjust to a new rhythm and sensibility, which was mastered by his editor, George Tomasini.[44] The attention that Hitchcock gave personally to storyboarding scenes in all his movies was well known. As his chosen editor, Tomasini was more than a craftsman who simply followed the director's drawings. It was Tomasini, for example, who had to choose the exact place for making each cut, and, as the editor, he had to continually adjust and tailor the cutting to create a rhythm that interpreted Hitchcock's overall vision. The conceptual framework for how a scene was to work visually was the director's choice, but its actual execution on the screen was in the hands of his editor.

Moreover, the editing in Hitchcock's features of the 1960s did not merely follow the leads of other movies, but was instead at the cutting edge of change. Along with the generally conventional editing in THE BIRDS (1963), and the relatively slow pace of almost the entire film, there are several absolutely stunning sequences of birds attacking, as well as selective instances of jump cuts. The first mass attack by crows occurs in the schoolyard during schoolgirl Cathy Brenner's birthday party. It is first set up with shots of the birds assembling on the playground's jungle gym. Then there is a jump cut as Mrs. Brenner brings her daughter's cake out of the schoolhouse and onto the playground.

When the birds attack, Melanie Daniels (Tippi Hedren) leads the children in a run for safety, away from the school and the birds. With the children running toward the camera in a traveling shot that moves from left to right, the birds dive down and peck

*A storyboard from THE BIRDS reflects Alfred Hitchcock's
careful preparation for shooting a film.*

away at their victims, and some of the birds become entangled in the children's hair. This
relatively long, continuous tracking shot is interrupted by very brief shots (some as short
as a second and a half) of the birds diving. Relying on the visual impact of these very
brief shots, Tomasini heightens the emotional impact by cutting them into the tracking
shot to produce a strong, visceral sense of physical assault and disruption.[45]

Tomasini also uses three jump cuts in THE BIRDS in the sequence when Mrs.
Brenner discovers farmer Dan pecked to death in the bedroom of his modest home.
Such radical editing devices work so well in Tomasini's overall editing strategy because
he relied on them so sparingly. The economic use of bursts of nontraditional, sensational
editing in the midst of a more conventional narrative pacing based on the principles of
classic continuity was displayed in the final film that Tomasini completed before his
death, MARNIE (1964, Alfred Hitchcock). The veteran editor again exploited short shots
effectively because of his willingness to juxtapose them into sequences that also contained relatively long takes and to use them judiciously.

A still from the famous chase sequence in THE BIRDS *(1963).*

ANNE COATES   On the other side of the Atlantic, Anne Coates edited LAWRENCE OF ARABIA (1962). Hired by the film's producer and director David Lean, who had originally established himself in the British cinema as a film editor, Coates readily acknowledged that she approached LAWRENCE OF ARABIA under the strong influence of the French New Wave films she was seeing at the time. Coates was already familiar with a couple of the American features edited in the new style at the beginning of the 1960s that completely abandoned dissolves and fades in favor of direct cuts.[46] Her work on LAWRENCE OF ARABIA was very much emblematic of the extraordinarily close symbiosis between Hollywood and the British film industry during the 1960s, especially during the early years of the decade. When LAWRENCE OF ARABIA was released, Coates was among the talented citizens of the United Kingdom who became a pillar in filmmaking circles within the mainstream of the American industry. Coates won the Academy Award for editing, and LAWRENCE OF ARABIA continues to win accolades for its brilliant pacing as well as for Coates's specific editorial choices.

One of the most famous scenes attributed to the editing occurs when Peter O'Toole blows out a match and the editing cuts to a glorious orange sunrise on the desert. That cut was called for in Robert Bolt's screenplay, but it was editor Coates who precisely timed the exact moment to make it.[47]

Coates recalled that about the time that she was working on LAWRENCE OF ARABIA she picked up a classic textbook on editing written by Karel Reisz, a formidable figure of the British cinema, only to discover that she was "doing it all wrong." Reisz's guidelines were "full of rules and regulations, such as counting frames after someone speaks."

These were rigid and mechanical guidelines to which neither she, nor George Tomasini, nor Dede Allen, nor Ralph Rosenblum, had continued to conform to during the 1960s.[48] Each of them contributed truly remarkable and revolutionary new directions in feature film editing.

Recalling years later in an interview that direct cuts were used "just to do [LAWRENCE OF ARABIA] in a different dramatic way," Coates added: "In the script it said dissolve, but I'd been to the French cinema quite a bit, and they were doing a lot of direct cutting. [By then] opticals were becoming old-fashioned."[49] Even though the next film that Coates edited, BECKET (1964), was cut in a more conventional and theatrical manner, she still found opportunities to exhibit her creativity. In one scene with horses and men on a beach Coates used cuts to capture the drama of the moment without worrying about continuity and without regard for matching specific horses and their mounts from shot to shot.[50]

Toward the End of the Decade

By the late 1960s, new directions in feature film editing were well established at the very center of a changing American cinema that found itself scrambling to adjust feature films to the tastes of an audience composed increasingly of moviegoers in late adolescence and young adulthood. The increased creative power of editors and the unique bonds that were developing between specific editors and film directors in the new freelance atmosphere of Hollywood reinforced and further promoted these changes.

1967 saw not only the brilliance of Dede Allen's groundbreaking work on BONNIE AND CLYDE, but also the innovations undertaken in the editing of THE GRADUATE, which followed exactly the preconceptions of director Mike Nichols. The film's editor, Sam O'Steen, had established his relationship to Nichols two years earlier when O'Steen—who had been an assistant editor for a decade—was given the opportunity to edit his first feature, WHO'S AFRAID OF VIRGINIA WOOLF? (1966). Then, with THE GRADUATE, both Nichols and O'Steen had an opportunity to push their collaboration in the direction of a more innovative editing style. For example, one sequence in the film begins with the recent college graduate Benjamin (Dustin Hoffman) floating on an air mattress in his parents' swimming pool. As he leaves the pool to walk back into their house, the scene cuts smoothly to a room at the hotel where Benjamin is meeting an older woman, a friend of his parents named Mrs. Robinson (Anne Bancroft) for clandestine sex. Over the next couple of minutes through continuous editing the scenes shift back and forth between his parents' home pool and Benjamin's mental projections of his meetings with Mrs. Robinson. As he takes a forward, lunging stroke in the pool in one elegantly smooth edit, the shot transitions to him coming down on top of his lover in the hotel bed. This associational montage displays adeptness of the editing technique and reinforces the inner sense of Benjamin's feelings of alienation and ambivalence toward his relationship with Mrs. Robinson. Moreover, the editing of this sequence draws out Oedipal dimensions that Hollywood melodramas, like those of Douglas Sirk (MAGNIFICENT OBSESSION, 1954; WRITTEN ON THE WIND, 1957; or IMITATION OF LIFE, 1959) or Nicholas Ray (REBEL WITHOUT A CAUSE, 1955, or BIGGER THAN LIFE, 1956), where they would only have been obliquely implied.[51]

By 1968, increased effort and emphasis was being placed on post-production in Hollywood features.[52] Experimentation was widespread and a fundamental change in the pacing in narrative films had been accepted by the industry. This was true of both big budget, mainstream Hollywood productions as well as lower budget ones, like American International Pictures' WILD IN THE STREETS (1968). Edited by Fred Feitshans and Eve Newman, the movie was made riveting by its pacing and street scenes of young people battling with police, edited to look like television news footage. It was nominated for an Academy Award for editing.

The most compelling street footage of 1968, however, appeared in an entirely contrived sequence, with nary a hint of documentary feel about it—the car chase through the streets of San Francisco in BULLITT, created from footage shot over a period of nearly five weeks. Billy Fraker, the cinematographer for the film, attributed the success of the chase sequence primarily to the work of the editor, Frank Keller.[53] At the time, Keller was credited with cutting the piece in such a superb manner that he made the city of San Francisco a "character" in the film.[54]

The film's producers thought so highly of Keller's work, in fact, that they decided to premiere the entire chase scene alone on the popular *Ed Sullivan Show* on CBS television before the movie opened in theaters. They believed that the sequence was not only strong enough to stand on its own, but that its exposure on television would attract viewers because they would want to see the chase sequence on the big screen in movie theaters.[55] The most complimentary assessment of Keller's work, however, was found in industry gossip maintaining that his editing had saved BULLITT, just as editor Ralph

A still from the renowned car chase on San Francisco streets in BULLITT *(1968), edited by Frank Keller.*

Rosenblum was credited with saving Woody Allen's TAKE THE MONEY AND RUN (and also William Friedkin's THE NIGHT THEY RAIDED MINSKY'S, 1968). Indeed, by the end of the 1960s, regard for the editor's pivotal role in the making of a successful feature was greater than at any prior time in the history of the American cinema.[56]

By 1968, new talent and innovation were being widely encouraged in feature film editing. New techniques and risk-taking became increasingly common as the traditional emphasis on story and continuity gave way to a freer, faster, and more dynamic editing style. The new editing style, however, was not always received well critically. A review in *Variety* faulted Roy Lovejoy for his editing choices in 2001: A SPACE ODYSSEY (1968), claiming "shots are cut abruptly and without clear purpose."[57] Moreover, industry partisans of continuity editing objected to the ways in which story development appeared to be sacrificed to visual sensations. Nonetheless, subsequent criticism has tended to recognize the editing as the film's greatest aesthetic accomplishment. Ken Dancyger declared, "2001: A SPACE ODYSSEY is so memorable and so significant specifically because of the innovative ways in which real time and film time become totally altered in it, along with the innovative ways in which long and short shots are juxtaposed."[58]

Innovations in film editing that manipulated time and space radically continued in 1969 with Donn Cambern's work on EASY RIDER. At several points in the film there is visual foreshadowing of future events, which Cambern called "very subliminal." In fact, they appear on the screen so quickly as to not permit the viewer to focus on them. For example, toward the end of the movie when Billy and Wyatt (Dennis Hopper and Peter Fonda) are looking at photographs in a bordello, there is a sudden, short burst of a motorcycle burning, anticipating their murder on the highway several minutes later at the end of the film. Cambern also experimented throughout the film with bursts of several frames of film between scenes, creating a pulsating, underlying tempo and tension in the movie.[59]

The strong alternative theme and techniques of Sam Peckinpah's experimental western THE WILD BUNCH (1969) made it a fitting showcase for innovative editing. Thomas Lombardo, the film's editor, not only broke one of the final, remaining "rules" of editing by cutting directly into slow-motion shots, he also set a record for the number of sepa-

A futuristic scene from 2001: A SPACE ODYSSEY (1968).

Sam Peckinpah's THE WILD BUNCH *(1969) contained the greatest number of shots of any feature produced through the 1960s. Film editor Thomas Lombardo created a series of fast-paced montages, sometimes cutting directly to slow motion to enhance effects.*

rate shots in a feature film with 3,624.[60] Even though THE WILD BUNCH was in Panavision 70—the widescreen release format that had effectively replaced CinemaScope—Lombardo cut the movie as if it were in 16mm and paid no special attention to the wide screen. Creating one fast-paced montage after another, Lombardo underscored what was to become regarded as Peckinpah's distinctive and dynamic style of directing. With his radical treatment of time within nearly every scene, Lombardo pushed the revolution in American feature film editing farther than any of his colleagues. THE WILD BUNCH was established at the end of the 1960s as the epitome of fast-paced editing in a narrative film.[61]

The changes in editing style that culminated in the late 1960s were based on a range of innovative and experimental approaches that came from various sources. After the 1960s, departures from editing strictures deemed necessary for story continuity were not only accepted practice, but had become an industry norm. Central to the new cinema was a radical shift from the narrow imperatives of visual continuity, permitting the editor to draw the viewer's attention directly to a film's visuals through fast-paced editing and the use of such techniques as the freeze-frame and slow motion. Furthermore, innovations through editing created conditions for the acceptance that pacing could vary to follow an appropriate rhythm in each individual film.

7

Sound and Music

The Historical Primacy of Dialogue Sound

The coming of synchronous sound to the motion pictures in 1927 with THE JAZZ SINGER introduced a new aesthetic based on the relationship of the visual picture to the soundtrack. Many critics have argued that its arrival prompted Hollywood to abruptly shift feature film production toward models taken from stage and away from the more expressive visual creativity that had developed in silent cinema during its "golden years" from 1923 to 1928. During the earliest years of the "talkies," such critics argued, motion pictures developed an over-reliance on dialogue and voice-over, as filmmakers struggled with rudimentary, and often problematic, technologies for recording sound onto film.[1]

Synchronous sound was immediately accepted in both popular and critical circles as a natural progression of the motion-picture medium, whereby picture and sound combine to form a new entity that shifts the aesthetic experience of the film viewer from a separated "I see" and "I hear" toward a more complete sensory synthesis that can be described as "I feel; I experience."[2] Nonetheless, audiences almost never put film sound to the same tests of verisimilitude as the picture. Movie sound is more easily accepted as stylized and abstract than what is seen on the screen. Aside from voice dialogue, such sound elements of a film as music, effects, and noise are inevitably left open to a great deal of creative latitude and inventiveness.[3]

The primary purpose of sound in the classic Hollywood movie was narrative. As a result, dialogue established an unshakable primacy that drove picture editing in the vast majority of American feature films.[4] As innovations in film editing broke down the long-established tradition of narrative logic in movie storytelling during the 1960s, motion-picture sound was free to undergo adaptations to new demands. It would be incorrect, however, to argue that either the aesthetics or the technologies of motion-picture sound kept pace with the revolutionary changes occurring in picture editing and the tempo of visual pacing of movies during the 1960s. Hollywood sound work during the decade remained a craft widely considered subsidiary to the main elements of production. The term "sound designer," which conveys the notion of an artistic talent responsible for the overall aural texture of a film, and which places that activity on the same level with other creative decision makers, like editors, only came into use in Hollywood at the end of the 1970s,[5] when "Sound Montage and Design" was credited to Walter Murch for his work on APOCALYPSE NOW (1979).[6]

The 1950s and Widescreen

Throughout the 1950s and into the early 1960s, improvements in motion-picture sound quality were closely associated with the experimentation being done with widescreen formats. For one thing, the physical space on the actual film print for optically printed sound was greatly increased with the larger film widths.[7] More importantly, in 1952 Cinerama introduced the techniques of "point source" sound, which soon became considered an absolute necessity to accompany any large screen projection.[8] The sheer size of the widescreen formats created new challenges for creating convincingly mixed sound tracks.

Producer Michael Todd's "Todd A-O" process was introduced in the musical film OKLAHOMA! (1955). Although voice dialogue continued to be recorded in the traditional, single-channel method in this process, both the music and the sound effects were recorded stereophonically on an elaborate system featuring a mixing console that required five engineers to operate. "Todd A-O" was used initially for music only, driving five speakers placed behind the screen and several additional surround speakers located throughout theaters that were retrofitted for this new sound technology.

The most important innovations with regard to widescreen sound during the 1950s were being wedded to the techniques used to "pinpoint" the source of a sound by having it smoothly follow the sound-source as it moved on the screen. This concept required rapid changes in sound recording techniques, as well as advances in printing sound optically on film. The overall effectiveness of pinpointing the source of sound relied on the quality and the placement of speakers in movie theaters. The declining fortunes of the exhibition sector of the American cinema during the late 1950s and throughout the 1960s, however, made the quality of in-house sound systems in movie theaters all across the United States a vexing issue that severely compromised the advancement of motion-picture sound.[9]

Specific Problems

Changes in sound technology and processes during the1960s proved difficult to introduce and apply broadly across the industry. Sometimes, such advances created more problems for motion-picture sound technicians than they solved. As a result, motion-picture sound processes advanced during the 1960s by fits and starts; there were surprisingly few innovations that produced unqualified successes. For example, it proved easier and more efficient to do many kinds of refined sound mixes on optical film than on the new, multitrack recording systems. Magnetic tape was vastly superior for recording and editing music on audio tape. But it is easy to overlook how complicated this superior sound recording system might be in instances where sound had to be simultaneously synthesized with and matched to picture. For instance, in a scene where a couple exits from a loud house party into a fairly quiet garden, it proved quite challenging to balance the sound level of the couple's dialogue in the relatively quiet garden with receding party noises. In such a situation, new recording processes slowed down the sound mixing work on a film while providing little or no advantage in audio quality over the older system.[10]

In fact, the use of three- and five-microphone, multitrack sound recording on movie sets and locations had generally given way by 1968 to the older, simpler, monaural techniques that Hollywood had traditionally used. This "throwback" was caused by a simple and very practical pressure: acceptable sound could be recorded and mixed on less expensive equipment and with far less labor expense with the older, monaural system. A number of other factors influenced the retreat to monaural sound recording. The increased preference for shooting "on location," rather than in a studio or on a set, lent itself to simpler sound recording techniques. The impulse to favor simpler sound techniques over newer innovations was also promoted by the increased flexibility in filming brought on by the use of newer, lightweight, handheld cameras and the increased popularity among cinematographers of zoom lenses and dolly shots. Industry-wide, feature film editors strongly favored single-channel recording over stereophonic recording because the older system allowed them greater latitude for handling a range of camera angles, actor movements, and visual transitions. Problematic "sound jumps" created by multitrack recordings during the editing of scenes were easily avoided by simply sticking with the monaural recording system.[11]

While motion-picture industry sound professionals displayed reluctance to adopt some new techniques, substantial numbers of motion-picture exhibitors were unwilling and/or unable to make the necessary capital investment to bring sound systems in their theaters up to new standards of recording, mixing, and reproduction. Stephen Handzo, a leading expert on the history of motion-picture sound, attributes the cause of the slow pace of theater improvement in the United States during the 1960s all the way back to the Supreme Court's consent decree of 1948 that prohibited the Hollywood majors from continuing to directly own movie theaters. That decree, according to Handzo, limited investment by theater owners in new technology and speakers. Along with the serious problems in the exhibition sector caused by plummeting theater attendance, attempts to keep up with the new sound processes were simply impossible during the 1960s. Although the Ampex company successfully designed a special equalizer, relay, and switching system to make Todd A-O's six-track magnetic sound compatible with existing sound systems in older theaters, many problems still remained. Lack of substantial capital to invest in upgrading older theaters slowed the introduction of innovations.[12] For example, even though the physicist Ray Dolby was well along in his experiments to reduce noise and to balance sound effectively on four channels by the late 1960s, his system did not reach movie theaters until more than a decade later. It was only with STAR WARS (1977) that Dolby sound was established as truly successful for theatrical releases. Moreover, even after Dolby sound was finally introduced, the system was often used only for music, with dialogue still coming from a single central channel.[13]

First-run houses in major metropolitan areas offered audiences magnificent, 70mm magnetic multitrack stereo sound, and sometimes Cinerama sound was even better. During the 1960s, however, such instances were never the norm of the moviegoing experience. Movie sound could have been far superior to what the average moviegoer was actually hearing in movie theaters, but it was not. As Handzo wryly noted, and with only a small measure of exaggeration, across the United States by 1970 "there was a better sound system in the average American teenager's bedroom than in the neighborhood theater!"[14]

THE NAGRA, ADR, AND FOLEY TECHNIQUES

The 1960s proved a frustrating decade for advancements in motion-picture sound mixing and for the improvement of sound systems in most movie theaters across America. Nonetheless, there were positive changes in motion-picture sound recording technology that became widely and quickly accepted as industry standards. At the end of the 1950s,

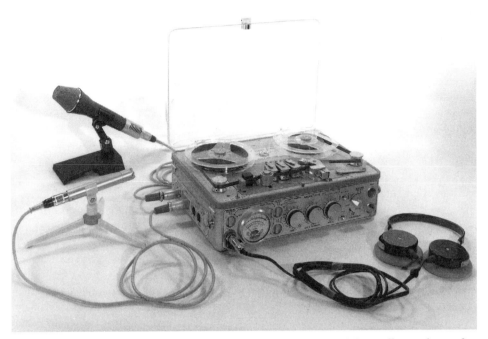

The Nagra III, manufactured in Switzerland, became standard for Hollywood sound recordings by the early 1960s.

the Nagra III, a reel-to-reel magnetic tape recorder cabled to a camera by a sync pulse, was introduced by a Swiss manufacturer. It soon became established as the recording equipment of preference for Hollywood feature production as well as for most documentary film work in the United States.[15] The Nagra's recordings on quarter-inch magnetic tape produced good fidelity and offered the mixer considerable latitude in using sound. Furthermore, Nagra recording equipment was lightweight and portable, very sturdy, highly reliable, and operated with cheap C-batteries—all of which permitted the Nagra to be used effectively for either studio or location filming.[16]

The Nagra III was state-of-the-art in 1960 and proved extraordinarily reliable and effective throughout the ensuing decade.[17] Equally important to motion-picture sound during the decade were advances in automatic dialogue replacement (ADR) techniques. In the ADR system, picture and sound are interlocked on tape machines that can be run forward and backward easily and reliably. If an actor has flubbed a line, for example, the tape is reversed and the line simply spoken again by the actor. The sound recordist can then make a notation, re-record a word or a sentence, and lay them in during the mix; differences between the original recording and portions re-recorded are imperceptible. "Looping," yet another, even more common form of ADR, is done during the post-production stage of filmmaking. Actors and actresses are called into a sound studio after principal photography on a film has been completed in order to record portions of dialogue for insertion into a motion picture's soundtrack.

These ADR techniques greatly enhanced the ability of the sound recordist to cover what dialogue sound was needed for any scene without necessarily demanding an entire new take on a set or a location. Because of the dramatic increase in location filming during the 1960s, reliable automatic dialogue replacement techniques became much more important than they had been in the past. Voices compromised during actual filming could be replaced adeptly while retaining the "atmospherics" created by ambient and extraneous sounds.[18]

ADR advances developed hand-in-hand with improvements in looping and dubbing techniques. As the global commerce in motion pictures increased during the 1960s, the post-synchronization sound techniques needed for dubbing the voices of a film into different languages became increasingly more sophisticated and polished. The main economic impact fell, of course, on the distribution sector of the motion-picture business, but production processes were impacted as well. Films such as the "Spaghetti Westerns" of director Sergio Leone (e.g., A FISTFUL OF DOLLARS, 1964, and THE GOOD, THE BAD, AND THE UGLY, 1966) could be shot by allowing international casts to say practically anything they wanted during actual filming and then relying on post-synchronized dialogue for the final version of the film that would appear in theaters. In all such instances, of course, the entire range of ADR, looping, and post-synchronization techniques for dialogue sound was being advanced and perfected.[19]

The work for Hollywood's so-called "Foley artists" grew exponentially during the 1960s. Theirs was a highly specialized skill within a system that had been originally created to cleverly imitate sounds in the studio that would be added to the movie track during post-production. Developed by Jack Foley at Universal Pictures at the end of the 1940s, this system found relatively limited use during the 1950s. At the beginning of the 1960s, in fact, there were only six Foley artists working regularly in Hollywood. That situation changed radically as filming moved away from the controlled environments of Hollywood studios and backlots. By increasingly going on location in the streets or in nature, feature filmmakers fueled the need for Foley artists to create sounds in post-production that had not been recorded during the actual shooting. Whether the needed sound was the pounding of horses' hooves, the layering of crowd noise to make fifty people sound like 50,000, or the pounding of the Malibu surf recorded in the middle of the night matched to a couple strolling and talking on the beach at midday, Foley sound techniques added enormously to the flexibility and aesthetic range of movie soundtracks in the 1960s. It became commonplace for sound recordists to record some "wild" sound coincidental to the sound that was recorded during the actual filming at nearly every location. Audio reels full of wild sound became the stuff from which elaborate mixes could be made. Thus, a rich layering and sweetening of the soundtrack was accomplished by adding in sounds recorded at a location that were extra to what had been recorded during the actual take of a scene.[20]

A Changing Aesthetic for Motion-Picture Sound

The advancement of ADR, looping, and Foley techniques, all of which increased the effectiveness of adding sound to scenes in postproduction, meshed exceptionally well with Hollywood's new preference for location filming during the 1960s. Location shooting often relied on sound manipulation in the mixing room, where movie sound tended to be deliberately mixed and equalized "big," primarily by compression. Soundtracks were increasingly being pushed from an aesthetic of naturalism toward a more artificially crafted and manipulated motion-picture sound design. If the sound recorded in a scene was not considered sufficient, post-production sound technicians commonly called in Foley experts to increase the "bigness" of the sound by layering in added tracks from other sources to those actually recorded during filming. Improved technologies were an important factor in the shift to more consciously manipulated tracks that uprooted and broke with the long-standing traditions of classic motion-picture sound "realism."[21]

Equally important to advances in the techniques and technology of motion-picture sound during the 1960s was the development of a creative environment that encouraged experimentation. The collapse of the Hollywood studio system contributed to a production atmosphere in which more artistic decisions were being made by individual directors and editors in direct consultation with sound technicians. For example, the 1960s began with a new emphasis to create perspective and subjectivity in movies by the manipulation of sound.[22] Such shifting was initially well presented in the soundtrack for SPARTACUS (1960), the direction of which Stanley Kubrick had taken over from Anthony Mann when the latter was dismissed from the production. Frank Warner, the picture's sound supervisor, later recalled that Kubrick pointed out to him how sound might be shifted and controlled so as to focus the viewer's attention in the frame somewhere other than at its visual center. Hence, Warner experimented with this notion throughout the film by utilizing sound to introduce elements of subjectivity, and to emphasize the central character's point of view. When Spartacus is waiting in his underground cell to fight a gladiator in the arena, the viewer hears from above the background sounds of one of Spartacus's friends fighting. The sound structure of the scene contributes directly to the viewer's curiosity as to what Spartacus is really thinking about. Such aural tactics achieve a primary aesthetic of evoking a sense of a character's subjectivity in juxtaposition to the highly realistic context of other ambient sound in the scene.[23] This technique of shifting of the viewer's attention by the use of sound from a source not seen in the picture gained momentum during the 1960s. Off-screen sound was experimented with successfully, for example, in LAWRENCE OF ARABIA (1962). The approach of planes to drop bombs on a desert camp is first suggested by a rumble coming from the right side of the screen. Lawrence and another officer abruptly look off-screen right as their dialogue identifies the sound.[24]

By the late 1960s, overlapping dialogue sound, in which a voice from the next scene begins on the track just before the visual end of the scene that precedes it, was no longer uncommon. As part of the shifting aesthetic that permitted the formal characteristics of a feature film's construction to be more evident to the viewer, sound was increasingly used in ways that Hollywood previously had considered too jarring.

Nearly all the experimentation in motion-picture sound aesthetics during the 1960s was closely related to innovations in editing. The increased willingness to manipulate movie sound in ways that were noticeable to viewers paralleled the increased willingness of editors to draw attention to visual cuts and to disruptions in the established continuity principles of classic scene making. Sometimes, the close relationship between innovations in editing and in sound was the result of a single artistic vision that united the two. Pioneering film editor Dede Allen always worked closely with the film's post-production sound people, coordinating her own artistic choices in the editing with the spots in a film where sound was being crafted in new ways. Dialogue lines might be laid on top of one another in the final editing, or strung together without pauses that had actually been recorded during a take.[25] A terrifying sense of violence was heightened throughout BONNIE AND CLYDE (1967), for example, by making the sound of gunshots extra loud. After the film was released, it was reported that projectionists all around the world, unaware of this intention, would try to lower the sound volume at those moments, believing that the exaggerated sound of the shots was a mistake on the optical track of the print they were showing.[26]

Such innovations in sound were piecemeal and incremental, but they pointed consistently to an increased flexibility in manipulating the soundtrack, primarily in order to heighten the subjective mode of feature films. In THE GRADUATE (1967), mismatching sound techniques were present in several scenes shot at extremely long distances but in which the dialogue between the characters was heard as distinctly as if they were being photographed close to the foreground of the picture. This technique was a formalistic adaptation to many scenes in the film shot with lenses of very long focal length, where subjects were seen by the movie viewer as if at a great distance. Hence, the aesthetic of sound realism had to be abandoned in a number of dialogue situations. Such mismatched sound, moreover, contributed to an approach throughout the movie that subtly reinforced the protagonist's sense of alienation and estrangement from his surroundings. This willingness to mismatch sound to picture was conceptually integral to shooting much of THE GRADUATE in focal lengths that provided distinctively "artistic" visual shots, unlike any the naked eye can actually see. Hitherto, such mismatching of sound to picture had rarely been found in Hollywood features, although "art directors," such as the Japanese filmmaker Akira Kurosawa, had used the device extensively.[27] In addition, the overlapping of dialogue between scenes—permitting the voice from the next scene to begin before the scene pictured has actually changed—was pioneered in CITIZEN KANE (1941) but had been used rarely for a quarter of a century until it abruptly came into vogue in Hollywood between 1966 and 1970.[28]

Film editor Dede Allen pumped up the volume when Warren Beatty pumped the lead in BONNIE AND CLYDE (1967).

Taken overall, however, the initiatives and advances in motion-picture sound were relatively modest during the 1960s. New technological innovations were tried, but monaural sound recording continued to prevail. The Dolby system was invented but not yet integrated into motion-picture production and exhibition. There were distinct innovations in post-production sound mixing spurred on by the adventuresome Hollywood directors and technicians of the decade. Still, even their experimentation was often compromised by the lack of improvement in sound systems in many American movie theaters. What most moviegoers actually heard at the average showing of a film throughout the 1960s remained severely compromised by inadequate investment in, and advancement of, actual theater sound systems.

Music in Film

As the Hollywood studio system collapsed, all the major studios terminated their contracts with their musicians by 1958.[29] Like all the other professions and crafts in film production, film musician and film composer were becoming free-lance occupations. Hollywood studios cut back drastically on the number of people under contract for music services, usually continuing to employ only a head of the music department and a skeletal staff of supervisors.[30] The end of "in-house" orchestras and of studio contracts with individual composers increased the presence of free-lance work in Hollywood and the importance of directors in making myriad artistic decisions about their films—what kind of music was put to a film, how it was to be used, and where it was placed would never again be the same.[31] The 1960s was the decade in which the types of music that might acceptably accompany feature films changed entirely: "In the studio age," noted Ethan Mordden, "a universal tendency toward romantically symphonic accompaniment [had] made the score to one film sound much like the score to another. A slight infusion of jazz had widened the possibilities of film scoring during the 1950s, but it was during the 1960s that the idea prevailed that a unique film needs a unique sound that translates its characters and setting into music was truly explored."[32]

While changes in cinematography and editing had resulted in new directions that overlapped only during the last several years of the 1960s, substantial transformations in film music occurred earlier. Film music anticipated and had flourished alongside the phenomenal growth of the American popular music industry during the late 1950s and the early 1960s. Between 1954 and 1960 the value of domestic retail record sales in the United States rose from $182 million to over $521 million.[33] This nearly threefold increase in less than six years reflected both the expanding variety of music available to listening audiences in the United States and the demographic fact that the growing audience for popular music was composed primarily of the rapidly increasing number of adolescents and young adults in the American population.[34] The demographics and tastes of this new audience for recorded music, of course, anticipated the changing audience profile of moviegoers that would become evident by the mid 1960s. As a result of the increased demand by young listeners for recorded music, the number of production employees in the recording industry in the United States more than doubled between 1960 and 1969, from 8,200 to 17,500.[35]

Of course, there had been movies prior to the 1960s, such as BLACKBOARD JUNGLE (1955, Richard Brooks) and ROCK, ROCK, ROCK! (1956, Will Price), that brought rock 'n roll to the screen. Those two features were aimed at too narrow an audience demo-graphic, however, and were still considered marginal to the Hollywood mainstream. The rock music in THE GIRL CAN'T HELP IT (1956, Frank Tashlin), starring Tom Ewell and Jayne Mansfield, was an exception. The scoring for these films was considered highly unusual and proved to be well ahead of its time. It would take the full-fledged cultural changes of the mid and late 1960s to turn rock music into a highly desirable resource for movie scoring for major Hollywood features. Most film music remained highly formu-laic and predictable well into the late 1950s, even though jazz influences entered the movies in scores by Alex North (A STREETCAR NAMED DESIRE, 1951, Elia Kazan) and Elmer Bernstein (THE MAN WITH THE GOLDEN ARM, 1955, Otto Preminger). These innovations, however, remained essentially subliminal (meaning they did not necessar-ily dominate a movie's soundtrack to the extent of taking over and driving the film), or were still considered inappropriate for major features until 1958. Then, the jazz sound was modified and fully integrated into the industry's mainstream expectation of a movie sound. That modification, in part, shifted jazz away from its African American origins to a "lighter, whiter" sound that could be thought of as appealing to a far wider audience. That change occurred, moreover, not with a feature film, *per se*, but rather with Henry Mancini's theme for the television series *Peter Gunn*. Hired to compose the series' music by director Blake Edwards, who had known Mancini's wife professionally for a number of years, Manicini and Edwards launched a collaboration that was to greatly influence the entire course of Hollywood movie music into the mid 1960s.

HENRY MANCINI   The *Peter Gunn* theme was a blend of jazz and pop music that pointed Mancini toward becoming the great transitional figure in movie music between the late 1950s and mid 1960s, as well as being the most important professional figure in exploring the overlap between music written for television and music written for the movies. With Edwards directing and Mancini composing the music, the pair collabo-rated on a string of influential feature films in the early 1960s, including BREAKFAST AT TIFFANY'S (1961), EXPERIMENT IN TERROR (1962), DAYS OF WINE AND ROSES (1962), THE PINK PANTHER (1963) and its sequels, and THE GREAT RACE (1965). Mancini may not have been considered the equal of many of the great classic "screen composers," and his scoring was limited to a relatively narrow range of comedies and romantic dramas (he did not compose effectively for westerns or epics, for example), but his impact on Hollywood music as a whole was enormous.

In what was becoming the free-lance work world of Hollywood, where loosely cou-pled professional ties predominated, the teamwork of Edwards and Mancini provided a model for creative collaboration.[36] With his 1961 score for BREAKFAST AT TIFFANY'S, Mancini truly established himself as the eminent composer of film music for the early part of the 1960s. As the critic Ethan Mordden observed, "one couldn't imagine these tunes, in these orchestrations, making do in any other film: 'Moon River,' 'Latin Golightly,' 'Something for Cat,' 'Hubcaps and Tail Lights,' 'The Big Heist.'"[37] With these songs, as well as with his overall arrangement of the music for BREAKFAST AT TIFFANY'S, Mancini radically challenged the entire idea that movie music should pro-vide background and exist as a secondary and relatively formulaic accompaniment to the picture and dialogue. Mancini wanted his music to be conspicuous; he was at the fore-front of shifting the aesthetic of motion-picture music in Hollywood toward this con-cept.[38] Mancini's impact in demonstrating that the times were truly changing for Hollywood movie music was evidenced when BREAKFAST AT TIFFANY'S lapped up the

Henry Mancini (seen here between Beatles Paul McCartney and John Lennon) con-
tributed greatly to making popular music a distinct artistic element of cinema.

film industry's approval by winning the Academy Award for best original score. His winning of this particular category with a score that was entirely jazz/pop-oriented, and
beating out traditional powerhouse Hollywood composers that year, including Miklos
Rozsa (EL CID) and Elmer Bernstein (SUMMER AND SMOKE), marked the beginning of
a new era for movie music in the United States.

Mancini won Academy Awards for best song two consecutive years: 1961, for "Moon
River" from BREAKFAST AT TIFFANY'S, and 1962, for the title song from DAYS OF WINE
AND ROSES. Both tunes became best-selling recordings. They were not, however, his
greatest hits: probably no piece of music composed by Mancini surpassed the worldwide
popularity of his instrumental theme for THE PINK PANTHER (1964), which one giddy
critic claimed had become more recognizable to American ears than "The Star Spangled
Banner." When he composed this theme, the animated pink panther that appears in the
film's opening credits had not yet been created. The zany ways in which the panther's
movements matched the music turned out to have been anticipated entirely in Mancini's
imagination.[39]

Summing up the transition out of the classic tradition of Hollywood music and scoring to the decidedly lighter sound that he brought to motion pictures, Mancini
remarked, "The melodic approach is still valid, the Tchaikovsky-like melody is still
wanted and needed, but the treatment of the melody has to be different—in keeping
with the times." Mancini brought a distinctively fresh and appealing sound to film scoring that was in step with the changing instrumentation and recording techniques of the

1960s.[40] As Mike Greene, president of the National Academy of Recording Arts and Sciences, said in eulogizing the composer in 1994, "Mancini brought to the pop music world a new level of genius. Long before the rest of the world took notice Henry Mancini envisioned the truly symbiotic relationship between music, film, and people."[41] Although one of Mancini's singular strengths was his belief in the aesthetics of a lighter "pop" sound for movie scoring, he nonetheless maintained that music should never be used as a cover for weaknesses in the picture's cinematography, editing, or the cast's performances. To Mancini, film music was a distinct artistic element in its own right.[42]

BERNARD HERRMANN   The team of director Alfred Hitchcock and composer Bernard Herrmann was similarly innovative and influential in the early 1960s. Herrmann was no Hollywood newcomer, having started his career in movie scoring with CITIZEN KANE (1941). Nonetheless, in 1960 the veteran Herrmann proved ready and willing to embrace innovation and to strike out in new directions. He composed a chilling and haunting score for PSYCHO (1960) that was performed solely by an orchestral string section. Indeed, Herrmann's scoring choice prevailed over Hitchcock's instinct about the film's music. Because of Herrmann, PSYCHO left a legacy that guided the composing of music for movie thrillers for several decades.[43] In its overall influence on the American feature film industry, the impact of the veteran Herrmann's creativeness in scoring PSYCHO very much paralleled the impact of the editing work by the veteran George Tomasini on the same film.[44]

The Hitchcock-Herrmann collaboration pushed further in experimentation with THE BIRDS (1963). Taking the radical step of omitting background music entirely, and working in close consultation with a German avant-gardist named Remi Gassman, Herrmann fashioned a soundtrack entirely from recorded bird sounds mixed with sounds generated by a computer. It was a triumph of technique that depended largely on Herrmann's willingness to fundamentally rethink the nature of movie scoring, and to turn entirely to artificially generated sound.[45] Even such singularly innovative partnerships as Hitchcock and Herrmann working in the increasingly free-lance environment of Hollywood in the mid 1960s, however, did not always prevail. Strong objections from the producer, Universal Pictures, forced Hitchcock to abandon Herrmann's dark and brooding score for TORN CURTAIN (1966) in favor of lighter music that most critics later concluded added absolutely nothing to the mood and tension of the movie.[46]

Still, Herrmann's experimentation on THE BIRDS reflected an increased willingness in Hollywood to radically alter the soundtrack in feature films, and to work with far less music than had been the past norm. After THE BIRDS, all kinds of experimentation in soundtrack scoring became acceptable, including practically eliminating a music score altogether in favor of a provocative mix of sounds. John Frankenheimer's SEVEN DAYS IN MAY (1964), for example, had a music score that lasted less than ten minutes, when most movies were still accompanied by compositions stretching for an hour or more.[47] MAROONED (1969, John Sturges) had no standard music at all. An extremely realistic widescreen production about a NASA accident in space, MAROONED utilized a minimalist sound design executed by Arthur Piantadosi. Piantadosi took a Nagra quarter-inch tape recorder home with him to record his experiments of plucking strings on a piano, then played the tape backwards and looped the sounds. Piantadosi was recognized when *High Fidelity* magazine chose the MAROONED soundtrack as its "score of the year" for 1969.[48]

Bernard Herrmann's chilling score for Psycho *(1960, with Janet Leigh, pictured) used only string instruments, notably the screeching, birdlike violins for the shower murder.*

The Expanding World of Movie Music

Changes in movie music were linked directly to changes in the tastes of teenage Americans in the 1950s and 1960s, and those changes in taste were also related to race. Historically, jazz constituted one of the great African American contributions to the culture of the United States. Henry Mancini succeeded in "whitening" the tone and rhythm of jazz, of course, much as Carl Perkins and Elvis Presley led the way to drawing white audiences in the 1950s to rock 'n roll, which many people, especially in the South, had called "race music." The origins of both jazz and rock 'n roll among African Americans meant that the sound associated with "Black music" experienced rising acceptance in the mainstream American recording industry, as well as in Hollywood, during the 1960s. Many new musical talents were nurtured and provided breakthrough opportunities, including African Americans.

Veteran great Duke Ellington won even wider recognition after scoring ANATOMY OF A MURDER (1959), but the true breakthrough for African American composers in Hollywood came with Quincy Jones's stunning work on THE PAWNBROKER (1965). In 1967, Jones did the music for both IN THE HEAT OF THE NIGHT and IN COLD BLOOD. Although his theme for IN THE HEAT OF THE NIGHT gained more popularity with the mass audience, critics devoted more attention to his work on IN COLD BLOOD, in which he pushed farthest the infusing of a jazz score with a deeply disquieting musical idiom.[49]

The score by Quincy Jones for IN COLD BLOOD included a section played backward to accompany a scene where two drifters (Robert Blake, left, and Scott Wilson) approach a farmhouse.

Jones, as a new Hollywood composer in the 1960s, demonstrated great flexibility and openness to experimentation, but he also displayed a capacity to let go of any posture of preciousness toward his own artistic creations when the situation demanded. For example, when Richard Brooks, the director of IN COLD BLOOD, disliked a section of Jones's score, Brooks instructed the sound mixer, Jack Solomon, to simply leave it out. Solomon, however, played Jones's composition backwards on the tape and decided to use the music in this way to accompany a scene where two drifters approach the farmhouse of their victims. Brooks was delighted with the results, as was Jones.[50]

By 1965, the earnings of recording companies in the United States had grown exponentially, and ancillary enterprises of these companies had expanded rapidly. By that time, free-lance composers were scoring two-thirds of the motion pictures produced by Hollywood.[51] The increase in television work, the number of recording sessions, and advertising meant more musicians working for more money. Earnings in 1967 for musicians from television jingles *alone* topped $400,000, and earnings for musicians performing on the soundtracks for films being produced for television totaled more than $3.8 million, outdistancing the earnings from work on feature films for theatrical release by nearly $800,000.[52]

The great boom in the record industry, along with the great challenge to standardized tastes and traditions brought on by the counterculture in the late 1960s, introduced the practice of many movies being scored not by composers but by others using "found" music. 2001: A SPACE ODYSSEY (1968) was typical of this trend. The film was essentially scored by relying on director Stanley Kubrick's record collection and his idiosyncratic tastes. Indeed, the threat of "found music" entirely replacing original composition and scoring in motion-picture soundtracks was thought to be real, at least briefly. The mood and style of American movie music was being opened up rapidly, and no one could quite predict just which direction the new phenomenon would take. Younger, emerging motion-picture directors, in particular, evinced attitudes toward music that were decidedly eclectic, and which willfully courted all sorts of innovations in film music. Francis Ford Coppola, one of the first film school graduates to break into Hollywood as a director, created his first high-budget studio feature, YOU'RE A BIG BOY NOW (1966), with a genuine musical feeling. It was paced like a "scopiotone," a genre of very short movies produced briefly in France during the 1950s that were essentially precursors to music videos of the 1980s; scopiotones were shown as accompaniments to jukebox music and had provided the first directorial opportunities for several French New Wave directors.[53]

The importance of folk music in the social protest movements of the 1960s, along with the identification of rock music with the American counterculture, meant that the growing movie audience of young adults was primed to hear those kinds of music on movie soundtracks. In the second half of the 1960s, increased emphasis on unique music for a specific film encouraged a turn to pop music groups for scoring films. Hollywood hired rock musicians to create new music for a film, or they acquired the rights to previously recorded music.[54] The scoring for THE GRADUATE (1967), for example, consisted of songs by Paul Simon and Art Garfunkel that lent a distinctive underpinning to the film's offbeat story line. Nonetheless, although the Simon and Garfunkel "sound" was new and different, it was used conventionally. Just track, for example, the lyrics of "The Sound of Silence" through the movie: its essential purpose remained strongly narrative, precisely as in classic Hollywood scoring. The entirely different sound given to BONNIE AND CLYDE by the bluegrass, banjo-picking of musicians Lester Flatt and Earl Scruggs may have been even more unique and distinctive, as compared to the conventions of classic Hollywood scoring, but the music was still used primarily to provide transitions in time and place and, thereby, to move the narrative forward.[55]

By 1969, as Hollywood was trying—sometimes with decidedly limited success—to exploit the youth market, more and more features were being produced in which the

Director Stanley Kubrick's selection of "found music" from his record collection, including the theme from Richard Strauss's Also sprach Zarathustra, *replaced compositions and scoring with great effect in* 2001: A SPACE ODYSSEY.

music soundtrack was not only essential, but could also be said to dictate the shape and structure of the film: examples include ALICE'S RESTAURANT (1969, Arthur Penn), ZABRISKIE POINT (1970, Michelangelo Antonioni), and EASY RIDER (1969, Dennis Hopper).[56] EASY RIDER, specifically, presented a compilation of rock songs by different groups and individuals that were central to the entire dramatic dynamic of this "road movie." The hit album marketed from the songs used in EASY RIDER inaugurated a record-oriented trend in movie soundtracks, providing possibilities to the producers of a film for large financial earnings on their investment in the movie and in the music rights they had acquired for it.[57]

Even films that featured complex plots and dialogue, like MIDNIGHT COWBOY (1969, John Schlesinger), made room to simply let the music take over. Typical of this tendency was the bicycle ride of Paul Newman (with Katharine Ross at times) in BUTCH CASSIDY AND THE SUNDANCE KID, accompanied by what some considered to be a wholly anachronistic song for the scene—"Raindrops Keep Fallin' on My Head." When Burt Bacharach earned an Academy Award for his original score for the movie, the recognition marked the Hollywood establishment's final and definitive embrace of the new directions in scoring for films that had begun with Henry Mancini's consecutive Oscars in 1961 and 1962.[58]

NEW FACES

In addition to new kinds of scoring by the likes of Quincy Jones, Simon and Garfunkel, and Flatt and Scruggs—each of whom forcefully brought to movie scoring authentic, indigenous forms of American music—Hollywood experienced an accelerated increase of foreign composers who became prominent in scoring for American feature films during the 1960s. Historically, Hollywood had had a long and well-established tradition of immigrants becoming major Hollywood composers, such as Erich Wolfgang Korngold, Max Steiner, Franz Waxman, Miklos Rozsa, and Dimitri Tiomkin, but during the mid 1960s the industry experienced a new burst of foreign-born film composers.

The British composer John Barry, for example, created a highly marketable theme for the James Bond series, beginning with DR. NO (1962), which quickly led to the high point of the Bond series' musical influence with GOLDFINGER (1964). That film's memorable title song was composed by Barry with lyrics by Anthony Newley and Leslie Bricusse and sung over the opening credits by Shirley Bassey; it became a hit single record as well. In an entirely different genre, Barry composed the music for BORN FREE (1966), which was produced in the United Kingdom by Sam Joffee and Paul Radin for Columbia. Barry worked with the lyricist Don Black to score this appealing animal film that was shot entirely in Kenya and which earned him an Academy Award for best original score that year.

Moving from his native Argentina, by way of France, Lalo Schifrin marked his debut in Hollywood with THE CINCINNATI KID (1965, Norman Jewison). Two years later he won wide acclaim for his scoring of COOL HAND LUKE (1967, Stuart Rosenberg). In counterpoint to protagonist Paul Newman's performance as a silent man and existential antihero, Schifrin's music becomes a character in the film.

Another composer, Michel Legrand, was discovered by Hollywood after the success of his scoring of the French production, THE UMBRELLAS OF CHERBOURG (1964, Jacques Demy,), which was a wholly unpredictable, all-singing musical set primarily in a dress shop and at an Esso service station in the French provinces. This offbeat international success, which pays homage to Hollywood musicals while maintaining its distinctive Gallic flair, drew the American motion-picture industry's immediate attention. Soon, Legrand was composing for Hollywood, and he successfully remained a major figure in motion-picture music throughout the 1960s even though his score for ICE STATION ZEBRA (1968) was panned mercilessly by critics.[59]

Another important Hollywood newcomer who had a tremendous impact on film scoring during the 1960s was American-born Jerry Goldsmith. From the beginning of his career, Goldsmith was willing to take risks and to compose against the grain of the movie's story. He did the music for two movies starring Sidney Poitier, LILIES OF THE FIELD (1963) and A PATCH OF BLUE (1965), as well as scoring John Frankenheimer's SECONDS (1966), a disturbing psychological drama with an exceptionally downbeat ending, to which Goldsmith counterpointed an orderly and serene score. Goldsmith's greatest triumph during the 1960s, however, was his pulsating symphonic score for PLANET OF THE APES (1968, Franklin J. Schaffner). The score won him wide critical acclaim as well as lavish praise from movie industry executives. Goldsmith's music was regarded as an absolutely necessary element of the movie and crucial to the box-office success of Schaffner's relatively bizarre fantasy.[60]

Among other composers whose careers were flourishing during the 1960s was Frank DeVol, who scored SEND ME NO FLOWERS (1964, Norman Jewison), CAT BALLOU (1965, Elliot Silverstein), THE GLASS BOTTOM BOAT (1966, Frank Tashlin), HAPPENING (1967, Elliot Silverstein), and GUESS WHO'S COMING TO DINNER (1967, Stanley Kramer). By contrast, John Williams, who began his Hollywood apprenticeship in the 1950s and became a major figure in Hollywood musical scoring during the 1970s (when THE POSEIDON ADVENTURE, THE TOWERING INFERNO, and JAWS established him as the musical "master of disaster"), made only a modest impact on film music in the 1960s with his scores for GIDGET GOES TO ROME (1963, Paul Wendkos), THE KILLERS (1964, Don Siegel), and VALLEY OF THE DOLLS (1967, Mark Robson).[61]

Musical Changes of the 1960s: A Summary

A more traditional movie music sound tried to flourish alongside innovation at the end of the 1960s, but the bell had tolled for tradition. Elmer Bernstein sustained his professional success in Hollywood throughout the decade, winning, for example, the Academy Award for original score for THOROUGHLY MODERN MILLIE (1967) over notably less traditional nominees, but this award could best be interpreted as the old guard establishment's recognition of a score decidedly in contrast to the new trend in movie music. The professional fate of nearly all the other veteran Hollywood composers who stuck to traditional motion-picture scoring was decidedly compromised. It was no secret among Hollywood insiders, for example, that by 1968 Alex North, who only a few years earlier was still regarded as one of the industry's composing giants (SPARTACUS, 1960; CLEOPATRA, 1963; WHO'S AFRAID OF VIRGINIA WOOLF? 1966) was being passed over entirely by producers as they sought a newer and more commercial sound. Before the end of the 1960s, it was clear that there was literally no work left in Hollywood for the likes of Max Steiner or Miklos Rozsa. Even Bernard Herrmann looked for greener fields by relocating to London, where he ended up working on low-budget horror pictures

Elmer Bernstein, Academy Award winner in 1967 for best original music score (for
THOROUGHLY MODERN MILLIE) *was the rare exception for studio composers of the*
1950s: His career continued to thrive in the 1960s.

until 1975, when Martin Scorsese summoned Herrmann to score what would be the
composer's final film, TAXI DRIVER (1976).[62]

During the 1960s, the musical palette for scoring American feature films was radically enlarged and altered. The transformation was aesthetic, fueled by the rapidly
changing audience tastes for popular music in the United States. A great deal of popular American music at the end of the decade was pulsating and jarring. The decade's
transformation of American popular music could be traced easily by contrasting the
soundtrack from Michael Wadleigh's documentary WOODSTOCK (1970), based on the
1969 music festival, to cute and melodic ditties, such as Patti Page's "How Much Is That
Doggie in the Window?" or Doris Day's "Que Sera, Sera" ("What Will Be, Will Be"), that
had topped the popular music charts barely a decade earlier. By the late 1960s, adolescents and young adults who constituted what Stanley Kauffmann described as "the film
generation" had clearly imprinted their tastes on movie music. The implications of this
shift in taste were not lost upon the conglomerates that were taking control of

Hollywood studios at the same time and absorbing them into their integrated "leisure divisions." Hollywood's new approach to film music, moreover, fit well with the conglomerate's intention of making film production an anchor of their broader business forays into truly diversified leisure markets. The new approaches to movie music aimed at spin-offs from soundtracks for the recording industry and for soundtrack albums loomed as major new sources of revenue that effectively exploited the tastes of those adolescents and young adults who constituted the "film generation."

8

The Twilight of the Goddesses: Hollywood Actresses in the 1960s

From its inception at the end of World War I, the Hollywood "star system" was predicated on packaging talent in ways that increased the likelihood for producers and distributors to maximize the opportunity for market control by promoting a movie on the basis of its stars and their celebrity status. Over the decades, the presence of star players in a movie would reliably attract audiences into movie theaters. The serious dislocations for production and the eroding audience in the theatrical exhibition sector confronting the American feature film industry by the early 1960s at first was interpreted as heightening the stakes for presenting established stars to audiences. For a time at the very beginning of the decade, the movie industry invested greater hopes in the effectiveness of "star power."

Hollywood stardom itself, of course, was based on assumptions not clearly defined about a particular kind of screen presence. The cinema in the United States had never developed the traditions of Great Britain and Europe, where actors and actresses crossed easily back and forth between stage and screen. Hollywood thespians normally had far less formal acting training than their counterparts on the other side of the Atlantic. Indeed, an actor's capacity to transform into new and different characters had arguably been less important in Hollywood than the capacity of a screen player to fit into type. Central to an effective screen portrayal was the physical image on screen, which evoked an audience response that appeared to be based heavily on anticipation and the easy recognition of identifiable traits.[1]

During the 1960s, actresses in particular found that it was very difficult to navigate the murky waters of sustained success in Hollywood. It remains a challenging question to what extent this situation was caused by the changing motion-picture production environment, the changing tastes of the audiences, or the values of the counterculture that flourished among college-age adults during the final few years of the decade. Moreover, it is difficult to avoid the conclusion that the challenges confronted by major American screen actresses must have had something to do with changing attitudes toward women, their work, their sexuality, and their place in American society during the decade.

By the late 1960s, a woman's right to sexual pleasure was more widely acknowledged, at least among the younger generation of Americans, and was facilitated by the relatively commonplace availability and use of the birth control pill. This fact in itself, however, did not mean that the "sexual revolution" was truly about sexual equality for women. The sexual revolution constituted a demonstrable shift in behavioral mores that did not necessarily redefine gender roles. Moreover, the more politicized forms of protest of the late 1960s were not inherently based on greatly altered concepts of masculinity and femininity. Women were active in the ranks of the civil rights movement, the antiwar movement, and other counterculture causes, yet all of these movements were led by men. Feminism as a movement had not yet become a major factor in American society. In fact, the rhetoric of protest, from the 1968 sanitation workers strike in Memphis, Tennessee—led by Martin Luther King, Jr., right before his assassination—to the exhortations of the Chicago Seven, to the confrontational style of the Black Panthers, to activism in the antiwar movement, was decidedly traditional. The picketing city sanitation employees in Memphis carried placards proclaiming "I Am a Man!," and other political protesters on the left in the 1960s, as distinguished from flower children, assumed public postures of toughness and militancy.[2]

The central historical questions of just how much, with whom, and how quickly attitudes and perceptions toward gender evolved in America during the 1960s are impossible to unravel. Betty Friedan's *The Feminine Mystique,* published in 1963, challenged stereotypes of femininity and questioned the concept of "proper roles" for women in society. Nonetheless, even those who read Friedan and agreed with her were still inclined toward a reasonable interpretation of her book as a forum on consciousness as a matter of personal change, rather than one setting a clear feminist political agenda. It was not until 1971 that Germaine Greer's bestseller *The Female Eunuch,* by arguing precisely that the personal *was* political, shifted the concept of women's liberation clearly to a collective political action. Thus, it was left to a later period, after the 1960s, for the full thrust of feminism to emerge in America. For all its claims to liberation and radical transformation, the late 1960s was neither especially hospitable to women's claims for equality in society, nor did the era prove to be amenable to the screen careers of Hollywood actresses. Moreover, the social and cultural upheaval of the last several years of the 1960s raised questions about whether the fundamental ethos and social reality of the American counterculture was more about hedonistic self-indulgence, or about liberating all men and women. Aspects of the 1960s counterculture remained disturbingly close to the hindsight of the neo-conservative social critic Wendy Shalit, who argued that "any society that has declared war on embarrassment" is one that is essentially hostile to women. The cultural imperative to "do your own thing" and a widespread emphasis in society upon "letting it all hang out" might well be so interpreted.[3]

Screen stars and their roles convey powerful gender images. The demographics of an increasingly younger audience for movies is assumed to mean that a greater portion of that audience becomes interested in depictions of maleness and femininity because of their own concern with their emerging social roles as young men and women. Nonetheless, it can also be argued that even Hollywood stars who are cast by type are not necessarily being seen by movie viewers as standing in for gender roles in real life. The stars may be types whom audiences are inclined to interpret sociologically beyond the films in which they appear, but, more importantly, they function as precise dramatic personae, rather than as gender emblems in their actual screen playing. In addition, as with all phenomena of culture and their interpretation, even the most clearly defined stars and screen types still remain open to conflicting, and frequently contradictory, interpretations.

DORIS DAY   One female type that appeared set to survive the 1950s and move relatively unscathed into the early 1960s was the chaste and wholesome female image portrayed by Doris Day. With her box-office appeal still firmly in place, Day was in a position by 1961 to negotiate a multi-picture deal with Columbia Pictures that would utilize her husband, Marty Melcher, as producer for her films.[4] As Hollywood's outstanding female box-office draw in each year from 1962 to 1965,[5] Day was a success held to be based primarily on her physical looks. She was widely considered to personify a "girl next door" type, and this image was closely linked with cultural attitudes and conventions associated with the 1950s that continued through the first half of the next decade.[6]

Although Day's typical character can easily be dismissed as a stereotype of the 1950s virgin, her popularity and staying power in the movies suggests something more authentic and complex.[7] It is notable, moreover, that Day's box-office appeal through the early 1960s was global, which makes it at least somewhat problematic to maintain that her continuing effectiveness on screen was based solely on a shallow reflection of mainstream American cultural values in the period immediately following World War II.[8] As the critic Molly Haskell argues in her seminal study of female images in the movies, *From Reverence to Rape* (1974), there is "something here beneath the plot contrivances [of Day's movies], and something in Doris Day, that is truer to the American reality than most critics would like to admit." Her characters' virginity was less emblematic as an expression of middle-class values than it was a comedic device invariably integral to the obstacle course encountered by Day's characters. As Haskell observed further, many of Day's films could be interpreted plausibly as going against the grain of the 1950s' concept of motherhood, since in the majority of them her character's right not to be a mother is steadfastly asserted.

Day's strength was her singular interpretation of "naturalness," which she was able to reliably exploit over and over again. Day's was a calculated characterization that resulted not only in chaste portrayals, but which also counterpointed her character to Hollywood's other great female stereotype of the late 1950s—the sex goddess. Nowhere is this counterpoint more clear than in Day's performance in THE THRILL OF IT ALL! (1963), which satirizes a Marilyn Monroe look-alike who slithers out of a bubble bath to give a panting, nearly breathless, advertising pitch. Unimpressed, however, a group of soap company executives decide that they prefer Day's character's straightforward testimonial to how she got her children to wash with their product.[9]

Interestingly, although Day was number one on a list of Hollywood's "ten most profitable stars" for each of the years from 1960 to 1965, she did not even make the list for the years 1966 to 1970.[10] In her case, the "decade split" was absolutely clear. Moviegoers of the early 1960s adored her; those of the late 1960s did not. Turning increasingly to television work after 1965, Day managed to maintain a prominent place in the pantheon of American popular culture icons, appealing primarily to an older audience while becoming a prime target for ridicule by cultural critics and a substantial number of young adult moviegoers. After having left the big screen for the relative security of television, Day adjusted her on-screen image by playing the mother of an eighteen-year-old son in WITH SIX YOU GET EGGROLL (1968, produced by CBS television's feature film division).[11] Originally titled *There's a Man in Mommy's Bed*, the movie featured a rock music score by the Grass Roots and a script that had, as a *Variety* review noted some-

A maturing Doris Day (here with Brian Keith in With Six
You Get Eggroll*) modified her screen image and played a
role to fit the changing times in 1968.*

what incredulously, Day's character "bedding down" with her boyfriend (played by Brian Keith) before their marriage.[12]

MARILYN MONROE   The exact opposite of Doris Day's screen image was embodied in Marilyn Monroe, who reached the peak of her career in Some Like It Hot (1959), a well-crafted comedy directed by Billy Wilder. Over the next several years, however, her film career and her life unraveled. In The Misfits (1961, John Huston), the last film that Monroe completed, she co-starred with Clark Gable while working in a constant stupor from drugs and alcohol. The Misfits was a superbly shot (the director of photography was James Wong Howe) "anti-western" about the twilight of the American frontier that ends with a symbolic round-up of wild mustangs for slaughter. What could have been a strong and dark film is compromised by a verbose and glib screenplay by Arthur Miller (Monroe's husband at the time). The Misfits will be remembered primarily as the final screen appearance of two Hollywood legends, Monroe and Gable.

By the beginning of the 1960s, Marilyn Monroe appeared to many observers of the Hollywood scene as being burdened by her celebrity, and her reputation in the industry was becoming increasingly negative. Monroe, who had been considered difficult to work with for a number of years, was by then regarded as a disruptive individual on sets and as an irresponsible and unreliable talent. On June 8, 1962, after weeks of difficulties and

*Marilyn Monroe's last appearance on screen came in THE
MISFITS (1961).*

missed shooting days (she had shown up for only twelve of the thirty-five days for which
she had been on call), Monroe was fired from SOMETHING'S GOT TO GIVE, in which
she had been cast opposite Dean Martin. Two months later she was found dead in her
home. On orders from Police Chief William Parker, the Los Angeles County coroner
declared her death a suicide.[13]

In death, Monroe's image was to become tragic, fueled by consistent media attention,
speculation about her relationships with President John F. Kennedy and his bother,
Robert, as well as subsequent artistic exploitation of her by the artist Andy Warhol and
the writer Norman Mailer. While Monroe may not have been considered a great beauty
by the standards of other eras, her screen image during the 1950s had captured a sensuality that came to be considered iconic. She had been at her best in those roles in
which her characters toyed cleverly with the notion of the sultry dumb blond, with THE
SEVEN YEAR ITCH (1955) and SOME LIKE IT HOT (1959). Monroe remains a figure
largely definitive of the 1950s and the blossoming of the international influence of
American popular culture in the non-communist countries of the world. Her screen persona was developed during the 1950s and became emblematic of that decade because it

appealed to what many cultural historians recognized as America's fundamentally Puritan roots. Her vibrant and vivid image was fraught with contradictions. Primary among them was that her sexuality evoked deeper fears about our natures while simultaneously promising that sex could be innocent and without danger. The nude photo of Monroe that graced the pages of the first edition of *Playboy* magazine in 1953 can be seen as a beacon of sensuality anticipating the subsequent sexual revolution of the 1960s.[14]

After her death, Monroe was celebrated in ways having little to do directly with her films. Seen either as a symbol of 1950s tastes, or as a precursor of the sexual revolution, or as a "camp" icon, Monroe was quickly transformed into a subject of both adoration and satire that was quite unique, even in the emerging celebrity culture of the United States. In the process, fascination with her life and loves off-screen and a fixation with her photographic image in itself soon transcended any real consideration of even her successful roles on screen. Monroe was placed in an odd pantheon in which she was celebrated as an embodiment of American popular culture during the two decades following World War II and simultaneously portrayed as one of its most prominent victims. Ultimately, her image became a caricature much in the way that Elvis Presley's had after his death. Her influence on American screen actresses in the 1960s was largely to turn them away from the image that Monroe had crafted. Following Monroe's death, Hollywood screen stars tended to nourish screen personas that were psychologically far more complex than hers and visual appearances that were far less simplistically sensual.

JANET LEIGH AND JOANNE WOODWARD   Two actresses who had done extremely well during the 1950s, Janet Leigh and Joanne Woodward, both entered the 1960s as the spouses of Hollywood male stars of roughly equal prominence, Tony Curtis and Paul Newman. As Marion Crane in PSYCHO (1960, Alfred Hitchcock), Leigh earned a supporting actress Academy Award nomination for her character, who is stabbed to death sooner than halfway through the film. In this role, Leigh played in one of the great "turning point" films of cinema history, and also reached the apex of her own Hollywood career. She and Tony Curtis divorced in 1962 after a decade of marriage, and she married a stockbroker. Her remaining films in the 1960s were THE MANCHURIAN CANDIDATE (1963, John Frankenheimer), BYE, BYE BIRDIE (1963, George Sidney), AN AMERICAN DREAM (1966, Robert Gist), and HARPER (1966, Jack Smight).

In her most accomplished role among these, the thirty-six year-old Leigh was cast as an "oldster" alongside Dick Van Dyke in BYE BYE BIRDIE. They manage the career of a teen rock idol named Conrad Birdie, who performs a swivel-hipped send-up of an Elvis Presley-type rock singer. Leigh and Van Dyke are soon deeply engaged in plotting the pivotal event of the film, and of Birdie's life and career, by setting up a last kiss for Conrad with his middle-American sweetheart, played by Ann-Margret, before he departs for military service. While there was parody, of course, in describing Leigh as an oldster in her BYE BYE BIRDIE role, there was also a telling reality about the way in which Hollywood still perceived aging female screen talent. By her mid-thirties, an actress might well be considered past her prime. In contrast, Leigh's ex-husband, Tony Curtis, a year older than her, was still starring in major roles as late as 1968 with his portrayal of the confessed killer Albert de Salvo in THE BOSTON STRANGLER (directed by Richard Fleischer) and finding supporting parts into the 1980s.

Similarly, in 1963, when Joanne Woodward was thirty-three and honored at Graumann's Chinese Theater on Hollywood Boulevard with a ceremony during which

Joanne Woodward in RACHEL, RACHEL *(1968) directed by husband Paul Newman.*

she ritualistically placed her hand prints in wet cement, her movie acting career appeared to most pundits to already have passed its peak and to be headed for a normal decline in the Hollywood profession.[15] Never considered conventionally beautiful, Woodward had managed a difficult role in THE STRIPPER that same year, playing a part originally intended for Marilyn Monroe. To nearly everyone' surprise, however, Woodward marked a significant professional triumph five years later by playing a middle-aged woman trying to break out of her role as a small-town spinster in RACHEL, RACHEL (1968), directed by her husband, Paul Newman, whose own acting career was on the upswing (the couple's young daughter, Nell, was cast in the movie as well). Woodward garnered an Academy Award nomination for best actress even though many traditionalists in the industry dismissed the performance as a "character" portrayal. Other observers, however, recognized immediately the skill that Woodward displayed in handling this role. Her performance as a spinster school teacher trying to break out of the boredom and frustration of her life was seen by them as an example of stunning and mature acting because Woodward worked so hard and so successfully to keep her own distinctive, personal mannerisms tightly in check. In this sense, she was playing directly against the more glamorous persona of her earlier screen career that had been established during the 1950s.[16]

Woodward's career was believed to have peaked a decade earlier. In 1957 she won an Academy Award for best actress in THE THREE FACES OF EVE (Nunnally Johnson), and then played in two films, THE LONG, HOT SUMMER (1958, Martin Ritt) and, opposite Newman, in RALLY 'ROUND THE FLAG, BOYS! (1958, Leo McCarey). In RACHEL, RACHEL, Woodward marked her transformation into a more mature screen presence by demonstrating her adeptness at doing something that relatively few female stars in Hollywood history had managed up until that time. Nonetheless, Woodward's career from 1968 on provides a stunning contrast to Paul Newman's that was emblematic of the gender difference for acting talent in feature films. While her husband could plunge ahead, playing highly dynamic and active roles in COOL HAND LUKE (1967) and BUTCH CASSIDY AND THE SUNDANCE KID (1969), and parlaying his box-office and critical successes into increasing prominence as a major Hollywood star, Woodward's career had to be defined by screen roles reserved for "mature women" alongside occasional television work. Indeed, Newman would still be starring in a forceful, masculine role as late as 1981 in FORT APACHE, THE BRONX (Daniel Petrie), where he plays a tough cop with a lover who looks to be thirty years his junior. The disparate career tracks of this talented couple, in microcosm, summarize a simple and long-standing truism about acting in Hollywood: normally, the careers of male leads could endure as much as fifteen to twenty years longer than their female counterparts.

ELIZABETH TAYLOR   Among serious dramatic screen stars who had entered the decade of the 1960s at a high level of prominence and demand within the industry, only Elizabeth Taylor sustained a successful career throughout the entire decade. Janet Leigh, who had been nominated for a supporting actress Oscar for 1960, played in roles of declining importance after that, and Joanne Woodward regained prominence playing the role of a single, mature woman in a film produced and directed by her husband. Taylor's career, by contrast, was in the ascendancy, and survived the star's ill health, personal scandals, and even her starring role in that financial catastrophe, CLEOPATRA (1963).

In 1960, with the $750,000 salary that she had negotiated for her role in BUTTERFIELD 8, for which she won the first of her two Academy Awards for best actress during the 1960s, Taylor became the most important woman, with the most financial clout, in Hollywood.[17] Nonetheless, Taylor was star-crossed. In the early 1960s, she struggled to survive both serious illnesses and a very public scandal caused by her romance with co-star Richard Burton on the set of CLEOPATRA while she was still married to singer Eddie Fisher. As for her screen career, it was remarkable that she could rise professionally above the hostile criticism heaped on CLEOPATRA, even though she was widely faulted by the critics because of her emotional temperament and lazy work habits as having contributed to picture's runaway cost.[18] Taylor was closely and inexorably associated both with the star image and the production values that made CLEOPATRA a caricature of big-budget Hollywood run amok. In one especially biting article, the critic Sybil March linked the colossal financial failure of the film directly to the "vapid performance" by Taylor and pilloried the actress as "Hollywood's last orgasm."[19]

Yet, later in that same year, director Anthony Asquith wrote a compelling portrait praising Taylor's uncanny sense of rhythm and pause in all of her work.[20] Shortly thereafter Richard Schickel of *Time* magazine called Taylor Hollywood's last great star. In spite of the resonating sound of finality to his claim, he surely intended the comment as the

Elizabeth Taylor in her Academy Award-winning performance in WHO'S AFRAID OF
VIRGINIA WOOLF? *(1966).*

highest level of professional praise. Whether Taylor's career in the early and mid 1960s
really marked the end of a great era of screen playing or not, she personally demonstrated
a startling adaptation to the new circumstances of the industry and to changing audience
tastes. Taylor's greatest triumph of the 1960s came with her masterful performance in the
role of a highly negative character in WHO'S AFRAID OF VIRGINIA WOOLF? (1966). In
this film adaptation of Edward Albee's emotional stage play, Taylor broke the long-standing and traditional dictum of a female Hollywood star by drastically aging her face and
fattening her body to achieve a disheveled and slovenly look for the role of the middle-
aged harridan Martha. Inspired by the direction of Mike Nichols, Taylor, more importantly, transcended the mere physical appearance of the role by convincingly turning
herself into an angry, frustrated, screaming, and lewd professor's wife on screen.[21]
Through a combination of her own talent and daring on the one hand, and the changing
audience taste for movies in America on the other, Taylor won both critical acclaim and
an Academy Award for best actress. The film gained a considerable following among the
college-aged audience, who were defining a new demographic of moviegoers to which
Hollywood had to appeal. Hence, Taylor's character marked a turning point for major
Hollywood actresses to potentially play against type and to play against the physical
attractiveness and values of character classically associated with star roles.[22]

   Taylor led the way among major Hollywood actresses in successfully negotiating the
changing professional landscape for screen acting careers in the mid 1960s. She also led
the way for herself and for her fellow professionals by demanding and getting substan-

tial guaranteed salary commitments as well as positioning herself to play a prominent role in influencing the major decisions about a production. By the end of the 1960s Taylor's price per film had risen to $1.25 million and she was taken seriously, indeed, whenever she voiced her opinions concerning the packaging of production projects or actual artistic and technical decisions made on the set. Taylor was Hollywood's great female survivor of this turbulent decade that otherwise proved such an extraordinarily difficult and challenging one for female stars.[23]

NATALIE WOOD   The daughter of Hollywood set designer Nick Gurdin, Natalie Wood began her acting career as a child in 1945. By the early 1960s, Wood's adult career appeared headed on a steady upward course. Her work opposite Warren Beatty in SPLENDOR IN THE GRASS (1961) earned her an Academy Award nomination for best actress. That film was followed by WEST SIDE STORY (1961), a hit even though Wood's performance was not considered a strength by critics. During that same year, however, and immediately after her marriage to the actor Robert Wagner, she became involved in a dispute with Warner Bros. that led to the longest suspension—a full eighteen months—of any contract actor or actress in the history of Hollywood. Although the dispute was eventually resolved in Wood's favor, giving her the right to take on roles in films produced by entities other than Warner Bros., the suspension was costly to the development of her career and left many powerful men in the industry with feelings of resentment toward her.

Natalie Wood (right, with Rita Moreno) in WEST SIDE STORY *before her eighteen-month suspension by Warner Bros.*

Wood returned to the screen with the leading role in LOVE WITH THE PROPER STRANGER (1963). She played an Italian-American shop girl who becomes pregnant by a jazz musician (played by Steve McQueen) and elects to have a back-alley abortion rather than reveal the pregnancy to her parents. In a gritty production directed by Robert Mulligan, Wood gave one the strongest performances of her career. Given the naturalism of the film, which led many to place LOVE WITH THE PROPER STRANGER on the cutting edge of what they hoped would be Hollywood's new direction, and by having tackled an especially challenging role, Wood appeared ideally positioned to prosper in a Hollywood environment where the establishment was looking for new talent and concepts to rescue it from financial doldrums caused by a downturn in production.

For the next several years, Wood's versatility was readily acknowledged in an industry known for typecasting, and she became widely regarded as a rising star in the Hollywood firmament. Wood also was one of the few women acknowledged as a major player in the new Hollywood business environment, being recognized as a powerful talent who could routinely approve directors and co-stars on her projects. She suffered a major setback, however, in THIS PROPERTY IS CONDEMNED (1966, Sydney Pollack), which co-starred Robert Redford. Industry insiders believed that this adaptation of a Tennessee Williams play, with a screenplay co-authored by a young Francis Ford Coppola just out of graduate school at UCLA, and with cinematography by the veteran James Wong Howe, promised great critical and financial success. Those expectations were clearly dashed within a very short time of the movie's release. THIS PROPERTY IS CONDEMNED bombed at the box office and was panned by critics.

Objectively, Wood's career should have accommodated this setback relatively easy. Both men associated with the production, Pollack and Redford, continued their upward ascent in Hollywood unscathed. By contrast, from this single professional failure, and likely driven by a complex set of underlying circumstances and personal issues, Wood entered a period of a deep psychological depression that culminated in her attempted suicide toward the end of 1966. Although her suicide attempt was successfully kept secret for many years,[24] after the release of THIS PROPERTY IS CONDEMNED Wood simply disappeared from the screen until 1969. She reemerged in director/writer Paul Mazursky's attempt to capture the ethos of the sexual revolution and the attempts of suburbanites at being hip in the rollicking comedy, BOB & CAROL & TED & ALICE (1969).

AUDREY HEPBURN   "The chief characteristic of her skill," wrote critic Simon Brett of actress Audrey Hepburn, "is its apparent absence. The distinction between [her] and the character she is playing is almost impossible to draw, so completely does she identify with her." As a contract star at Paramount during the 1950s, Audrey Hepburn earned three Academy Award nominations that were followed by a fourth for BREAKFAST AT TIFFANY'S (1961). Playing Holly Golightly, an upscale Manhattan prostitute whose career is deftly disguised in the sweetened screen adaptation of the Truman Capote novel, Hepburn was aptly described as a cross between a grown-up Lolita and a teenaged Auntie Mame. Playing a party girl whose self-positing willfulness disguises her deeper insecurity marked the pinnacle of Audrey Hepburn's career. On the basis of her success in BREAKFAST AT TIFFANY'S, Hepburn was selected over Julie Andrews—who had created the role in the stage play on Broadway in the 1950s—to play Eliza Doolittle in the musical MY FAIR LADY (1964, George Cukor). Hepburn managed to negotiate a $1 million contract for her work on the film. Subsequently, however, many critics assessed her as "awkward" in the role.[25]

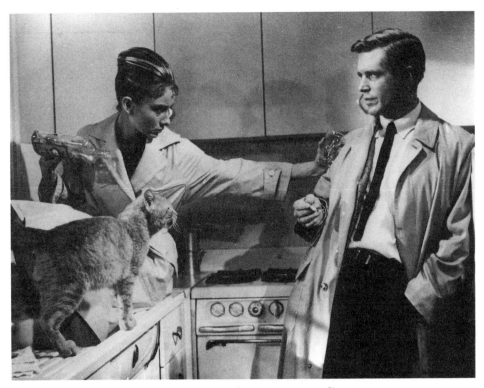

Audrey Hepburn (with co-stars "Cat" and George Peppard) in BREAKFAST AT TIFFANY'S *(1961).*

In retrospect, Hepburn's "Holly Golightly" character in BREAKFAST AT TIFFANY'S possessed a free-spiritedness and abandon that might have been seen as a precursor for the counterculture image of more independent-minded young women during the late 1960s. After MY FAIR LADY, however, Hepburn actually found Hollywood disarmingly disinterested in her as the second half of the 1960s brought the "film generation" into its wholesale takeover of audience demographics for theatrical releases. In 1969, Hepburn married an Italian psychiatrist and essentially put her acting career on hold for more than a decade. The complete slide of her career after the mid 1960s, followed by her personal choice to leave Hollywood entirely at the end of the decade, marks Hepburn as one among many actresses whose screen careers disintegrated in the late 1960s, either because of a rapidly changing culture or for personal reasons.

JULIE ANDREWS   The 1960s provided fleeting stardom for several unusually promising actresses whose careers fizzled nearly as quickly as they soared. Julie Andrews was one of them. Her career flourished at mid-decade only to flounder by decade's end. Andrews was described by industry insiders at the beginning of the 1960s to be "up for grabs in Hollywood, with absolutely no takers."[26] Although Warner Bros. passed on her for the lead in MY FAIR LADY, in which she had starred on Broadway, Andrews did THE AMERICANIZATION OF EMILY (1964, Arthur Hiller), and Disney Studios cast her for the lead in MARY POPPINS (1964). The former was a black comedy about a British war widow (Andrews) falling for a cowardly American marine (James Garner) who appears

Julie Andrews starring in THE SOUND OF MUSIC *(1965) and setting new standards for Hollywood "typecasting."*

far more dedicated to the pursuit of pleasure than he is to the idea of hitting the beaches in Normandy. The latter topped the scale for exuberance and memorable songs, with Andrews playing an Edwardian nanny. The enormous success of MARY POPPINS won Andrews not only an Academy Award for best actress, but the lead in THE SOUND OF MUSIC (1965) as well.

THE SOUND OF MUSIC won the Academy Award for best picture, and Andrews gained a nomination for best actress (she lost out in that category to Julie Christie, of DARLING). After her triumph in THE SOUND OF MUSIC, Andrews was at the peak of her career. Nonetheless, her triumph was brief, as she soon found herself to be a victim of Hollywood typecasting. Her rise to stardom had been little short of meteoric, and she had been well paid for her roles in both MARY POPPINS and THE SOUND OF MUSIC ($750,000 for each). However, the two pictures combined to place her in the apparently inescapable niche of saccharine sweetness and vapidity.[27] Moreover, it was not a case of her failing to recognize the problem. Andrews intentionally tried to play against this sweet image by taking the role of the fiancée of a scientist (Paul Newman) in TORN CURTAIN (1966, Alfred Hitchcock), a cold war spy thriller. She did a credible enough job, but that hardly sufficed to change Andrews' Hollywood image, or to redirect her screen career.[28] She was next cast as the friendly wife of a missionary in an adaptation of a James Michener novel, HAWAII (1966), and then played the lead as a young Kansas woman who arrives in New York City in search of spouse in THOROUGHLY MODERN MILLIE (1967, George Roy Hill). Returning to type with a vengeance, Andrews played this role to the hilt with every drop of sweetness and sunshine for which she was by then overly famous.[29]

Her career bubble burst quickly. Coming off THOROUGHLY MODERN MILLIE, Andrews headed directly to STAR! (1968), produced with the hope that it would be the equal of THE SOUND OF MUSIC. Instead, this ill-fated biopic musical directed by Robert Wise failed abysmally at the box office. The financial catastrophe of STAR! immediately labeled Andrews as "box-office poison." Within a year of being at the top of Hollywood stardom, her bankability plummeted. As if they had been lying in wait for her to falter, contemporary critics spared few negatives in describing her performance in STAR! As the failure of the film registered in Hollywood, columnist Joyce Haber asked rhetorically about Andrews' career, "is *she* still a star?"[30]

This single flop had come for her at precisely the wrong time. In a rapidly changing culture Andrews went within four years from being box-office gold, to being pigeon-holed as a stereotype, to enormous failure. STAR! bombed in a year that many industry insiders hoped would mark a return to traditional Hollywood production values that reestablished stardom once again as a guarantee for stunning profits. Andrews' career might have weathered the adversity of this one major failure much better in an era less charged with social and cultural unrest and defined less clearly by the demographics of a rapidly shifting audience for theatrical movies.

Only a handful of Hollywood careers have plummeted as quickly as Andrews'. Her story graphically illustrates the underside of the "free-lance" system that had replaced the reliance of studios on contract players. The only bright spot for Andrews at the end of the decade was personal: in 1969 she married director Blake Edwards. In 1981, Edwards produced and directed S.O.B., a bitter look back on the roller-coaster ride that his wife's acting career had taken in the mid and late 1960s. This savage portrayal of a Hollywood producer trying to save a floundering production by adding pornographic sex scenes had Andrews baring her breasts on screen. S.O.B., however, appeared to have been released ten years too late to have much real bite. Its satire was dated, and by the early 1980s audiences apparently cared little about the titillation of seeing Julie Andrews' bosom.[31]

MACLAINE, DUNAWAY, AND ROSS   Shirley MacLaine's promise in the early part of the 1960s (THE APARTMENT, 1960, and IRMA LA DOUCE, 1963) was not really built on and exploited during the rest of the decade. Throughout the 1960s MacLaine was perceived in the industry more as a "cartoon character" than a talented actress who could effectively satirize conventional culture. MacLaine's physical beauty was truly a veneer over a comedic chaos raging beneath its surface, but during the 1960s this persona was too easily interpreted by a considerable part of the audience as being inauthentic and deceptive. SWEET CHARITY (1968), which marked Bob Fosse's debut as a film director, nearly ended MacLaine's career. Playing a "taxi dancer" (someone paid to dance) with a heart of gold, much like her prostitute character in IRMA LA DOUCE, MacLaine was widely blamed in industry circles for the failure of this uneven and complex musical. Only in the mid 1970s did MacLaine manage to reemerge a Hollywood star by finding a new

Faye Dunaway, highly stylized as Bonnie Parker in BONNIE AND CLYDE, *and highly promising as a future female star in 1967.*

direction for herself as a mature and seasoned character and by gaining a great deal of publicity because of her "New Age" passion for channeling spirits. As a result, she successfully reinvented her screen career.[32]

Faye Dunaway's success in BONNIE AND CLYDE (1967), in which she had performed for $35,000, catapulted her abruptly into a position where she could demand $600,000 a film, which she received the following year for THE THOMAS CROWN AFFAIR. As Bonnie Parker, playing opposite Warren Beatty's Clyde Barrow, Dunaway brought a coolness to her interpretation of a character that marks the role as a turning point in the American cinema. As an amoral thrill-seeker whose detached exterior appears to cover a fragile and potentially sensitive inner-self, Dunaway created a stylized interpretation that proved to have an enduring impact on an emerging new type of female role.

Dunaway's ascendancy with BONNIE AND CLYDE and THE THOMAS CROWN AFFAIR, however, marked her in Hollywood at the end of the 1960s as only a tentative star. In the eyes of the industry, she remained far too problematic as a box-office draw. Audiences might appreciate her, but producers could not quite fathom why, and, hence, were reluctant to count on audiences necessarily wanting to continue to see her. For the time, Dunaway's image as a sort of updated Bette Davis character, essentially tough and just a little bit nasty, was accepted only begrudgingly by the Hollywood establishment and, even then, only to a limited degree.[33] Only with her success in CHINATOWN (1974), in which she found a role that fit nearly perfectly her screen persona of the tough exterior hiding a more complex and fragile inner-self, did Faye

Dunaway regain the prominence that she had briefly held in 1967–1968 and stake an unchallenged claim on stardom.[34]

Katharine Ross, who had played with mediocre success in four films prior to THE GRADUATE (1967), appeared poised to become a major female star after it. Over the next two years, however, Ross proved reluctant to accept any of the many movie projects that were offered to her. In the estimation of some Hollywood observers, she was being overly cautious and choosy. Then she played between Paul Newman and Robert Redford in BUTCH CASSIDY AND THE SUNDANCE KID (1969), which seemed to rekindle her promising career. This offbeat hit, however, was carried largely by the performances of her two male co-stars, whose "buddy" antics created a screen legend. Her performance in the movie surely was satisfactory, even if most critics focused on the stellar play of Newman and Redford. Still, whatever promise Ross's career had right after BUTCH CASSIDY AND THE SUNDANCE KID was not developed for both professional and personal reasons. Ross virtually disappeared from the Hollywood scene following that movie. Even though she was offered a number of major roles at the time, Ross turned down every one of them. The veteran Los Angeles movie critic Charles Champlin eventually was able to observe and to report the comparatively startling news for the movie industry that Ross actually had decided that she preferred stage work to movie acting, and that she was more content acting at small playhouses around Los Angeles than in making major features for the big screen.[35] Her personal life also may have interfered with her career, as the *Newsweek* columnist and movie critic Joe Morgenstern suggested. Through most of the 1970s, with her film career effectively on hold, Katharine Ross was living with Conrad Hall, the director of photography whom she had met while filming BUTCH CASSIDY AND THE SUNDANCE KID.[36] Whatever the reasons for her decision, Ross was one enormously promising female lead in Hollywood at the end of the 1960s who essentially turned her back on playing in Hollywood movies.

JANE FONDA   By the late 1960s, Shirley MacLaine, Faye Dunaway, and Katharine Ross had each displayed flashes of promise for stardom. Despite their several distinct successes, however, their prominence was not realized until much later in their careers, if at all. In contrast, the two women who emerged as the top actresses of the American cinema right at the end 1960s, Jane Fonda and Barbra Streisand, both positioned themselves for stunning and sustained success throughout the 1970s. They were entirely different types: Jane, the daughter of screen legend Henry Fonda, had remarkably delicate hands and a slightly affected Vassar accent; Barbra was pure Brooklyn, through and through.

Jane Fonda entered movie acting at the end of the 1950s with a golden name and great promise. In 1962, the critic Stanley Kauffmann had written of her, "I have now seen Miss Fonda in three films. In all of them she gives performances that are not only fundamentally different from one another but are conceived without acting cliché and executed with skill."[37] Kauffmann's enthusiasm for these three films, however, was bracketed by a career that had begun with a disastrous first film, TALL STORY (1959), in which Fonda played a cheerleader opposite Anthony Perkins, and by THE CHAPMAN REPORT (1962), a misguided and unsuccessful feature. Indeed, her performance in THE CHAPMAN REPORT was considered so inept that the *Harvard Lampoon* named her the worst actress of the year. Coming off this debacle, the middle years of the 1960s did not prove especially favorable for Fonda.

In 1967, however, she recovered a good deal of critical acclaim by playing opposite Robert Redford in an adaptation of a Neil Simon romantic comedy, BAREFOOT IN THE

Jane Fonda transformed her "personality starlet" image into a mature and complicated screen presence in THEY SHOOT HORSES, DON'T THEY? (1969).

PARK. She followed that appearance by playing an intergalactic ingenue in her husband Roger Vadim's BARBARELLA (1968), based on a sometimes truly zany script by Terry Southern, but which, as a whole, drew a decidedly mixed response. Many critics felt that Fonda was playing only a relatively simplified and cartoon-like character. BAREFOOT IN THE PARK and BARBARELLA were successful in their own ways, but both movies left many critics pondering whether Fonda was better suited for "stupid cupid" roles (as in the former), or potentially best exploited as a "sexpot" (as in the latter). At the end of 1967, a year that marked a genuine turning point in the American cinema, there was no assurance as to what direction Jane Fonda's screen persona and acting career might follow and sustain.[38]

A considerable body of critical opinion continued to write her off as a weak female stereotype until her stellar performance in THEY SHOOT HORSES, DON'T THEY? (1969) firmly anchored her career.[39] In this movie about desperate men and women trying to win prize money in dance marathons during the Great Depression of the 1930s, Fonda was applauded for her sensitive and insightful interpretation of that era's psychology. Under

Sydney Pollack's direction, Fonda would often appear to be looking directly at people but without focusing on them. She created a character that was held together and sustained throughout the movie by a consistent inner logic that also effectively communicated a larger sense of malaise.[40] With her role in THEY SHOOT HORSES, DON'T THEY?, Fonda was transformed immediately from a "personality starlet" into an accomplished "character actor."[41] At the end of the 1960s, it was difficult to ignore the interpretation that the sudden maturity and sharpness seen in her performance in THEY SHOOT HORSES, DON'T THEY? marked an on-screen parallel to Fonda's own off-screen transformation into a politically conscious, activist figure. As the 1970s dawned, Fonda was positioned perfectly to capitalize on that success and to enter the heyday of her career.

BARBRA STREISAND   In 1968, Joanne Woodward successfully revived her career with a stellar performance as a lonely spinster in RACHEL, RACHEL. That same year, Katherine Hepburn also returned to the screen in THE LION IN WINTER (officially listed as a British production). Both Woodward and Hepburn were nominated for Academy Awards as best actress. Woodward finished as a runner-up in the voting, while Hepburn shared that year's Academy Award with a Hollywood newcomer named Barbra Streisand.

Barbra Streisand as Fanny Brice in FUNNY GIRL (1968).

Streisand debuted on Broadway in 1962 at nineteen in I CAN GET IT FOR YOU WHOLESALE. Four years later, having swept Broadway and having completed two specials for television, she came to Hollywood with $35 million worth of movie musicals lined up for her before she had ever faced a camera.[42] Streisand arrived in town just as Hollywood was turning to lavish musicals in the mid 1960s in a desperate attempt to win back a disappearing mass audience.[43] Although she fit none of the classic models of the Hollywood star, she triumphed immediately. The critic Sidney Skolsky suggested that Streisand's instant success was emblematic of how truly low the Hollywood industry had declined in the mid 1960s, implying that only an industry in dire crisis could have fallen back upon her problematic looks and talents.[44] By contrast, however, Tom Ramage argued that Streisand's performance in a pedestrian musical like FUNNY GIRL (1968) was the sole reason the film could rise above sentimentality and mediocrity. Her talents were great, he maintained, and her screen presence was truly effective.[45]

By the time she worked on HELLO DOLLY! (1969), Streisand was not only earning $1 million dollars per film, but was contractually guaranteed a percentage of the movie's gross earnings worldwide. The 1960s ended without Streisand having the opportunity to show her versatility for the dramatic, or to fully exercise her importance as a powerful figure in the entertainment business. Nonetheless, she had established herself by the end of the 1960s as Hollywood's most important female screen discovery of the decade. Fonda and Streisand positioned themselves to become central figures in Hollywood during the next few years. Both of their careers marked successes that were not entirely predictable by classic Hollywood standards. Changing audience demographics, along with the changing tastes that were spawned by the counterculture in America, marked the late 1960s as a pivotal era for a substantive transformation of the character types who prevailed in American feature films. The more traditional Hollywood "types" found dwindling response. The stakes for an acting career had gotten higher with the demise of contract playing, and, as a result, both startling career triumphs and abrupt eclipses of a given star's popularity became more common among Hollywood leads.

Fonda's screen presence evolved into a portrayal of savvy and sensitive women who transcended the fragility and dependency that often characterized that screen type in the past. In this regard, Fonda's personal political commitment and her opposition to the Vietnam War likely contributed positively to the public's perception of the roles she took on screen, especially among moviegoers of college age. Streisand, whose persona combined a basic pleasantness with a touch of zaniness, was, by contrast, able to carry genre and period pictures. She was an actress of plain looks who could still play successfully opposite the most highly photogenic of male leads, while her singing voice gave her a versatility that was rare and widely admired.

9

Male Domination of the Hollywood Screen

On every Hollywood front, and for nearly every major screen talent, the 1960s proved to be far more agreeable to male actors. In particular, the years from 1967 through 1969 marked the appearance of several male talents who would remain prominent Hollywood screen figures for the next two decades. Throughout the 1960s, veteran star actors became increasingly prominent as producers, and, in a number of instances, shifted their talent and careers to film directing. Even when they did not take on those roles, major stars were gaining influence over the artistic choices made on specific projects in which they were involved. Interestingly, that form of artistic power was enjoyed as well by at least a few actresses by the mid 1960s.

Male screen-acting style was modified generally during the decade, but the real changes were found in the expanding range of roles available to male leads, and the new types of actors who might successfully be chosen to fill them. As the characters in American feature films played by the major male stars shifted toward darker, more complex, and "antiheroic" types, the essence of who were acceptable male leads, and the characteristics and values they represented, was altered perceptibly.

Most subtly, the standard characterization of "masculinity" in American movies shifted. Rugged, individual, and aggressive male types still found work as Hollywood leads, but a set of more tentative and reflective character types emerged during the 1960s to share the American screen with them. Among the male Hollywood leads of the decade whose screen personas best reflected these shifts, although in varying ways and to different degrees, were Paul Newman, Robert Redford, Warren Beatty, and Steve McQueen. All four were conventionally handsome men by Hollywood standards. Their roles during the 1960s gently displaced and modestly reshaped the most standardized image of the male star, which had been honed for decades and carried over from Hollywood's classic era. Subsequently, it was the rise to stardom of Dustin Hoffman that completely shattered the classic Hollywood image of the male star and opened the way for others, including Gene Hackman. Both Hoffman and Hackman would have been limited by the standards of classic Hollywood to the category of character actor.

Until Dustin Hoffman's success turned the prior Hollywood conception of a leading man upside down, the transformation of the male screen image during the 1960s was largely carried on the shoulders of four stars. The essence of screen characterization that

Warren Beatty had perfected by the late 1960s was based on a persona that displayed an essential sense of bewilderment, much as Robert Redford's essential character was rooted in pensiveness, and Paul Newman's in a an abiding intelligence and insightfulness. In contrast to these three, Steve McQueen's essential character emerged as anchored in a kind of brutishness that likely would not have sustained Hollywood stardom in any earlier epoch of the American cinema.[1]

PAUL NEWMAN   By the end of the 1960s, Paul Newman and his wife, the actress Joanne Woodward, chose to live much of the time in the East at their estate in Connecticut. Nonetheless, Newman was at the peak of his influence and success in mainstream Hollywood. Widely regarded as one of the industry's most accomplished talents, he successfully combined work as an actor, a director, and a producer. As an actor, his career breakthrough occurred when he played the lead role in SOMEBODY UP THERE LIKES ME (1956), a movie version of the life of the boxer Rocky Graziano. Some critics recognized in Newman, when compared to Marlon Brando, a more defensive method actor who was successful in modifying the rough screen caricature of the American proletarian that Brando had pioneered in ON THE WATERFRONT (1954). Brando established the Hollywood benchmark of a formulaic model for such portrayals. As Brando faded from screen prominence during the 1960s, and as changes in audience expectations shifted toward more subtle, sophisticated, and multi-dimensional depictions of working class characters, it was Newman who became widely regarded as the master of the muted and subtle versions of such roles, invariably handling them with a finesse that Brando appeared incapable of sustaining.[2]

Starring as a pool shooter named "Fast Eddie" who challenges the legendary "Minnesota Fats" for great stakes in THE HUSTLER (1961), Newman created one of his most renowned proletarian characters. Under the direction of Robert Rossen, Newman's Fast Eddie displayed a psychological fragility and a tentativeness beneath his rough veneer that was surprisingly touching and effective—despite his flashes of abusiveness toward women.[3] Much like a great number of the screen characters whom he played in a manner that consistently displayed complexity, Newman was known personally across the movie industry as a particularly reflective and thoughtful professional. That in itself conflicted with the tendency of Hollywood moguls during the studio era to regard their male contract players as "handsome, wayward, slightly backward children."[4] With Newman, there could be absolutely no confusing his intelligence and sensitivity with any such a stereotype. He was deeply interested in really understanding the motivations of his characters, as well as the meanings of their actions, and he was inevitably analytical in interpreting the impact of specific scenes and how they played in the overall structure of a film, while always being concerned about the quality of the dialogue in any particular screenplay. Newman became recognized as *the* sensitive and thinking method actor, and he was widely considered to personify a "new breed" of screen lover for the 1960s.[5]

In the early 1960s Newman founded a production company in partnership with the director Martin Ritt that they called "Jodell." Newman also participated publicly in political and social movements, being active in both the anti-nuclear ("Ban the Bomb") protests of the era as well as the civil rights movement.[6] Additionally, Newman was a box-office sensation. While many acting careers ended abruptly and others faded away during the turbulent years of the 1960s, Newman finished every year between 1962 and 1969 (with the exception of 1965) on the top ten list of American actors at the box office.[7]

Paul Newman (shown propped up by George Kennedy) played an endearing antihero in COOL HAND LUKE *(1967).*

Newman's three most memorable films from the 1960s, when method acting could be said to have blended imperceptibly into the mainstream of American cinema style,[8] were HUD (1963), COOL HAND LUKE (1967), and BUTCH CASSIDY AND THE SUNDANCE KID (1969).

As the hard drinking son of a Texas cattleman in HUD, Newman chases women with the same relentlessness with which he leads his family's defiance of the government's order to slaughter their herd to prevent the spread of hoof-and-mouth disease. Directed by Newman's production partner, Martin Ritt, HUD provided Newman a vehicle through which he could sustain a brilliant performance that could have been compromised by the screenplay's pretentious allusions to Greek tragedy.

Five years later, in COOL HAND LUKE, Newman created one of the most distinct and enduring screen characters of the decade. In this caustic satire of prison life and chain gangs in the Deep South, Luke becomes a hero to his fellow prisoners. Newman plays Luke with precision, crossing back and forth between his character's hard-bitten surface and his deeper, nearly Christ-like inner self in this parable of a rebel who crosses the law. Luke, who is arrested for knocking the tops off parking meters when he is drunk, is first loved by his fellow prisoners. Over the course of the film, however, his inmate disciples reject him. In the process, Luke becomes an endearing antihero facing down a brutal and capricious authority represented by the prison system and the warden.[9] In the screenplay, Newman's fictional character is pitted against a region, the South, which becomes a handy scapegoat for evil. In this sense, the screenplay may be considered flawed by many critics, but Newman leaves no doubt with the viewer about his capacity to play Luke with a sense of emotional range and balance that is truly admirable. With this role, Newman firmly established himself as one of the American moviegoer's favorite symbols of the rebel in the late 1960s.[10]

By that time, the Hollywood establishment regarded Newman off screen as a confident and self-positing individual who had reached the height of achievement within the industry. Newman was named producer of the year (by the Producers Guild of America) for RACHEL, RACHEL (1968) and was chosen by the New York Film Critics as director of the year for the same film. At the same time, he had become one of the handful of Hollywood talents who could demand and get over a million dollars for a movie performance.[11]

Capping his enormously successful rise during the 1960s, Newman was paired with Robert Redford in BUTCH CASSIDY AND THE SUNDANCE KID (1969). The film's packaging might be regarded as the epitome of deal-making and financing for the "New Hollywood." Put together by David Begelman and Freddie Fields—two former agents at MCA who had formed their own company, Creative Management Associates, to capitalize on the changing situation in producing—the pairing of Newman and Redford proved a goldmine for the two producers, and for the two stars as well.[12] In this outrageously funny "western" that many critics lampooned for having the slimmest of plots, Newman and Redford act as ideal foils. The film's pacing is superb under the direction of George Roy Hill, and the parrying of dialogue between Newman and Redford is especially excellent. One of Hollywood's wittiest westerns, BUTCH CASSIDY AND THE SUNDANCE KID was a critical and box-office triumph that pointed clearly into the next decade as a model for successful production formulas.

The premise of the movie itself, while set in the American West, parodies François Truffaut's "New Wave" classic JULES ET JIM (1962) with its suggestions of a *ménage à trois* romance populated by two close male friends and a somewhat neutral female placed between them. Given the subsequent professional success of the two male stars, it is easy to overlook the fact that the film marked a decided character shift for Newman, as well as a genuine turning point in Robert Redford's career. Up until then, Redford had appeared in ten films, five of which had been abysmal failures.[13] On the eve of the 1970s, Begelman and Fields of Creative Management Associates had provided the motion-picture industry a stunning example of how to bring together the right two actors who could carry a picture that likely would have foundered with nearly any other talent.

ROBERT REDFORD   As a result of BUTCH CASSIDY AND THE SUNDANCE KID, Robert Redford was abruptly catapulted from the precarious position of an on-again, off-again male lead into a dominant Hollywood star.[14] Redford's own production of DOWNHILL RACER (1969, Michael Ritchie) may have been admired by motion-picture industry insiders for his relative success in making an inherently risky project, but it was his role as the "Sundance Kid" that redirected his career. In DOWNHILL RACER, Redford permitted himself to play a decidedly unlikeable, selfish, and emotionally cold character. DOWNHILL RACER was set in the rarified world of competitive skiing, which was a problematic factor that many industry pundits feared would prove disastrous for the film's box-office appeal. The movie was successful enough to provide a clear indication of the kind of independent-minded production projects with which Redford would become increasingly identified in the future.[15]

Robert Redford, flanking Katharine Ross and Paul Newman in BUTCH CASSIDY AND THE SUNDANCE KID *(1969), moved easily between high-profile and low-budget films.*

The box-office triumph of BUTCH CASSIDY AND THE SUNDANCE KID, alongside the respect earned by the high-risk DOWNHILL RACER, anchored Redford as a Hollywood insider who could move easily between "big budget production packages" and riskier, more independent film projects. In an environment of changing audiences, further characterized by fluctuating tastes among the audience members, Newman and Redford were among the few actors to have a truly solid grasp on stardom as the 1960s ended. The disenchantment with traditional star types, though widespread, clearly was not universally devastating. Both Newman and Redford were handsome and photogenic. In physiognomy, at least, they resembled many classic Hollywood male leads. What was different about them, what distinguished them from male leads in classic Hollywood features, was the intelligence conveyed by their screen personae.[16]

WARREN BEATTY   After being a hit in his Broadway stage debut, Warren Beatty was lured away from the stage to the movies. Beatty's screen acting career was reasonably well launched with SPLENDOR IN THE GRASS (1961, Elia Kazan), though his co-star, Natalie Wood, received more critical praise for the film. *Time* magazine appraised Beatty: "With a facial and vocal suggestion of Montgomery Clift, and the mannerisms of James Dean, [Beatty] is the latest incumbent in the line of arrogant, attractive, hostile, moody, self-confident, bright, defensive, stuttering, self-seeking, and extremely talented

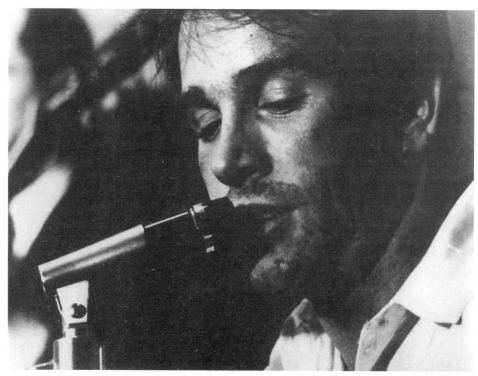

Existential angst, American style: Warren Beatty in MICKEY ONE (1965).

actors who become myths before they are thirty."[17] Even while working on his first film, Beatty proved perceptive enough to foresee that a radically changing film industry would extensively transform Hollywood over the course of the next several years.[18] He decided not to act immediately on those insights. Instead, he adopted a stance of caution during a period when the industry was in turmoil and the production of features was declining. In 1963 production reached an all-time low: between 1962 and 1964 Beatty elected not to appear in movies.

Beatty's reappearance was hardly an unmitigated success. During the filming of LILITH (1964) Beatty's alleged behavior on the set—reputedly never speaking to his costar, Jean Seberg, during the entire filming—gained him much ill will. Moreover, Beatty's personal life at the time became easy fodder for the gossip columnists, a situation that much of establishment Hollywood still considered risky for a star's career. When actress Leslie Caron's husband, Peter Hall, charged her with adultery and named Beatty as co-respondent, Beatty paid all the court costs for Caron's London divorce.[19] Still more disconcerting for his career, however, was criticism of Beatty's frequently inarticulate speech before the cameras in LILITH. On the set, other actors and the technicians nicknamed him "Whisperin' Jack Smith." Indeed, his problems with articulation were joked about widely among industry professionals: "Tell him it's a talkie," became a Hollywood tag line for Beatty. Many in the industry considered his poor vocal delivery a serious problem that could cripple his acting career, although that never happened.[20]

1965 could have been a disastrous year for Beatty's career; before it was over, he had rebounded from both personal and professional criticism by co-producing and starring in a decidedly off-beat film, MICKEY ONE, that drew an inordinate amount of interest and attention. Teaming with Arthur Penn in what was considered to be the most "European" and artistic of that great director's movies, Beatty portrayed a successful nightclub comedian plagued psychologically by some vague past deed. While it is not clear whether Mickey is trying to escape the Mafia, his own conscience, or the repressive indifference of contemporary American society, Beatty's performance of a man living at the very edge of his own psychological and moral means is enormously compelling and effective. There are few scenes in the history of the American cinema, for example, that are as truly disquieting as when Beatty is auditioned in a silent, darkened auditorium, straining and struggling with himself as he looks out into its dark emptiness.[21] With its existential underpinning—Arthur Penn described Beatty's character as being "guilty of not being innocent"—MICKEY ONE marked a turning point for Beatty, and he became a dominant Hollywood figure for the second half of the 1960s.[22]

The major step in that transformation of Beatty, from an interesting talent willing to work against the industry's grain into one of Hollywood's major players, was the production on which he began development in 1964, completed and released in 1967, BONNIE AND CLYDE. LILITH and MICKEY ONE were both provocative films, and each one gained a good deal of positive critical acclaim, but neither sufficed to establish Beatty fully as either a major Hollywood star or as a prominent producer. Before the unexpected, runaway success of BONNIE AND CLYDE, in fact, some Hollywood pundits were still dismissing Beatty as "the male counterpart of a Hollywood starlet."[23] His acting as Clyde Barrow earned Beatty an Academy Award nomination, but, more importantly, his producing the film with Warner Bros. financing (after both Columbia and United Artists had turned it down), and his success in convincing distributors to take it, established him as a pivotal figure in the rapidly changing Hollywood scene. Beatty had put together a package that gave to the world an unlikely screen hit that marked a real "turning point" for the Hollywood feature film in the late 1960s.[24]

STEVE McQUEEN Some critics initially dismissed Steve McQueen as a "method cowboy" after he moved from television's *Wanted: Dead or Alive* to his first feature film in 1959, NEVER SO FEW (with Frank Sinatra).[25] Next, McQueen was brilliantly cast in THE MAGNIFICENT SEVEN (1960), a western directed by John Sturges and based on the Japanese director Akira Kurosawa's THE SEVEN SAMURAI (1954).[26] Two years later, McQueen shone brilliantly in THE GREAT ESCAPE (1962), also directed by Sturges. As his character took shape in that film as a rebel, McQueen was being widely written about as the 1960s' successor to James Dean and Marlon Brando.[27] He displayed his increasing versatility by playing a carefree jazz musician opposite Natalie Wood in LOVE WITH THE PROPER STRANGER (1963). By 1965, when he starred as a poker shark in THE CINCINNATI KID, McQueen had achieved a distinct plateau of Hollywood success. For the remainder of the decade he was a number one box-office draw, holding a position of popularity with adolescent audiences that was unchallenged by any other male movie star and was truly paralleled among that audience only by the popularity of a handful of prominent rock musicians.[28]

In 1966, McQueen's own company co-produced THE SAND PEBBLES with director Robert Wise's production company. The movie is set in China during the 1920s and McQueen plays the member of an American gunboat crew wrestling with the moral imperatives of imperialism. Among audiences, the script was easily interpreted as a parable for the growing military intervention of the United States in Vietnam after

Steve McQueen with Jacqueline Bisset in BULLITT *(1968).*

President Lyndon B. Johnson had successfully won congressional approval for the Gulf of Tonkin Resolution to escalate the war. In his role as Jake Holman, McQueen proved extraordinarily convincing and demonstrated the range of his acting. "One cannot imagine an old-fashioned star, or anyone but McQueen [in the role]," wrote Ethan Mordden, adding that "his heroism awes us because it must be built upon the established McQueen archetype of the selfish, loser slob."[29] Similarly, in the next several years, McQueen honed in on the elemental toughness of his characters while branching out into different directions. In BULLITT (1967) he did his own stunts, while in THE THOMAS CROWN AFFAIR (1968) he managed to convey an extraordinary level of eroticism in a contrived chess game he played opposite Faye Dunaway.[30] McQueen's star status remained unsullied through the decade.

GENE HACKMAN   Much as BONNIE AND CLYDE was a turning point for Warren Beatty's career, the same film essentially launched Gene Hackman's ascent toward Hollywood stardom, which he achieved with THE FRENCH CONNECTION (1971, William Friedkin). Hackman was previously a character actor in supporting roles for several features, including LILITH with Beatty. Hackman's pivotal role in BONNIE AND CLYDE, however, was praised at the time by the popular newspaper critic Sidney Skolsky as having brought out the best in Beatty and his co-star, Faye Dunaway. In even wider critical circles, it was agreed that Bonnie and Clyde succeeded to a great extent because of the numerous scenes in which Hackman effectively keyed the two stars' performances.[31] Critical hindsight has reinforced this line of interpretation, seeing in

Hackman's performance a significant element of the film's effectiveness. Even at the time, the Hollywood industry responded favorably to Hackman's display of talent in the film. By 1969 he had appeared in six other features, and in the process he mastered the transition from supporting player to star.[32]

Hackman's overnight popularity was predicated on a kind of audience acceptance that likely would not have existed in previous eras. In studio-era Hollywood, an actor with Hackman's looks and physique almost assuredly would have been relegated permanently to character parts. Hackman noted that he did not believe even in the late 1960s that American feature films had yet "overcome the good looking hero." He attributed his Hollywood success to his capacity to convincingly play, and look, the part of a number of different "middle American types."[33] Hackman was not conventionally handsome, nor could he be said to possess the forlorn charm of that other great acting discovery of 1967, Dustin Hoffman. Nonetheless, his acting talent and screen persona were considered just the right combination for the "New Hollywood."[34] Michael Ritchie, who directed Hackman in DOWNHILL RACER (1969), was not alone in emphatically labeling Hackman as America's best actor.[35] In an environment where screen presence was often regarded with suspicion and not necessarily assumed to be dependent on genuine acting talent, Hackman established himself by the end of the 1960s as a formidable and highly respected leading man in Hollywood.[36]

DUSTIN HOFFMAN   Even more impressive than Hackman's Hollywood breakthrough was Dustin Hoffman's. Indeed, he stands as the single most distinctive turning-point figure in the transformation of the Hollywood male star in the 1960s. Hoffman was a struggling actor doing stage plays and occasional commercials. His total previous screen experience was limited to a forty-five second appearance in a forgettable feature film, THE TIGER MAKES OUT, when director Mike Nichols, who had seen him perform in an off-Broadway play, spied him on the street and invited him to audition for the role of Benjamin in THE GRADUATE.[37] The year before, Nichols had directed the highly successful film version of Edward Albee's hit play, WHO'S AFRAID OF VIRGINIA WOOLF? (1966). That success placed Nichols in an excellent position to be trusted by producers to bring the inexperienced Hoffman to the screen as a new type of antihero.

Hoffman's performance as Benjamin in THE GRADUATE hit Hollywood like a bombshell. Although the actor subsequently described himself as playing "just another alienated man" and tended to dismiss the uniqueness of his portrayal, most critics disagreed. Bosley Crowther, the venerable critic at the *New York Times* who officially retired from writing film criticism at the end of 1967, dubbed Hoffman "a marvelous young actor . . . like no one else."[38] Hoffman, who appeared to possess none of the characteristics of a classic Hollywood leading man, and who was considerably older than the character whom he was playing, was a success that the industry establishment could not immediately fathom. Along with the box-office triumph of THE GRADUATE, the popularity of GOODBYE COLUMBUS (1969, Larry Peerce) and IF (1969, a British import directed by Lindsay Anderson), which also lacked established stars in leading roles, confounded the Hollywood establishment.[39]

Hollywood producers did not know what to make of such a new "type," and it was far from clear at the time as to just what long-term impact the surprise success of Hoffman in THE GRADUATE would have on American feature film production. Indeed, in the early spring of 1968 when Hoffman was notified officially of his nomination for an Academy Award for best actor for his work in THE GRADUATE, he was officially jobless and receiv-

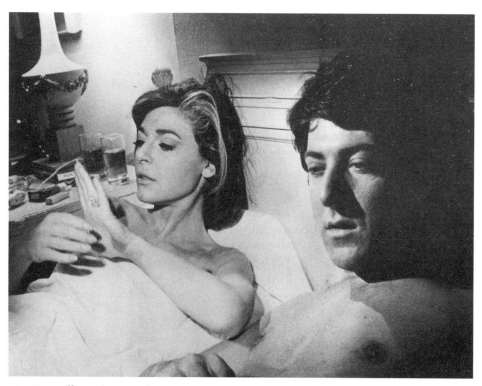

Dustin Hoffman (seen with Anne Bancroft in THE GRADUATE, *1967) went against the advice of* GRADUATE *director Mike Nichols to play seedy Ratso Rizzo in* MIDNIGHT COWBOY *(1969).*

ing unemployment benefits. Nonetheless, most industry observers recognized that Hoffman's stellar performance as Benjamin pointed not only toward future roles and acting triumphs for him personally, but coincided as well with a new era in Hollywood features for men whose looks were less than ideal. Lee Marvin, James Coburn, and Walter Matthau, for example, whose careers in features had begun much earlier, came into increasing demand for lead roles by the mid 1960s.[40] In this environment, actors such as Jack Nicholson, Donald Sutherland, and Gene Wilder were suddenly transformed from being regarded as marginal performers to being sought-after leads.

As a newcomer to a lead role in a feature, Hoffman had been paid a mere $17,000 for his landmark work in THE GRADUATE. Two years later, in MIDNIGHT COWBOY (1969), Hoffman received over $250,000.[41] Mike Nichols, who had cast him for THE GRADUATE and who briefly became his would-be professional mentor, tried to dissuade Hoffman from accepting the role of Ratso Rizzo in MIDNIGHT COWBOY. Nichols considered this character irredeemably unattractive. He also warned Hoffman that he was likely to come off badly in the film because he would be playing alongside the muscular and handsome Jon Voight, who had already been cast to play the Texas cowboy, Joe Buck.[42] When MIDNIGHT COWBOY was released, however, with its controversial "X" rating and its squalid portrayal of a seedy midtown New York City milieu, its box-office success indicated just how far the standards of profitable Hollywood filmmaking had been stretched beyond the traditional conventions. Remarkably, Hoffman managed to submerge himself entirely into a set of mannerisms and physical characteristics for Ratso that displayed his great acting range. What a far cry this role was from that of a clean-cut, college graduate who was socially awkward and vaguely alienated from the upper-middle-class values of his parents. Both Hoffman and Voight received Academy Award nominations for the best actor category for 1969. While neither won, both were clearly geared for major Hollywood stardom in the coming decade.

SIDNEY POITIER   The early years of the 1960s had witnessed the continuing prominence of many actors who had established themselves during the 1950s as pillars of classic Hollywood presence and type. Through a combination of their own aging and the audience demands of a changing culture, however, few of these actors could truly sustain star careers through the 1960s. As the older and more traditional type of male actor faded from the Hollywood scene, newer talent tended to bring characters with either a rougher edge or a more pensive personality to Hollywood's increasing portrayals of male independence and cunning. As more movies were produced emphasizing character over story, a wider range of character types found their way to movie stardom as well. By the last few years of the 1960s, the public's taste for Hollywood actors sometimes appeared to favor characters that were exactly the opposite of the traditional Hollywood hero. There were numerous exceptions to this trend, of course, but the most salient among them was Sidney Poitier, who continued to be cast, well into the late 1960s, directly against the changing *zeitgeist* of audience taste. There was absolutely nothing about his characters or the way that he portrayed them that fit the "end of the decade" vogue of the antihero.[43] Nonetheless, by the end of the 1960s, Hollywood's only major star who was African American had become the highest paid actor in the world.[44]

The son of Jamaican parents, Poitier was raised in Miami and had played his first role in Hollywood, a small part, in 1949. Ironically, his exceptional career path had actually been made easier because Poitier originally failed the standard Hollywood "Negro Actors" audition due to his slight West Indian accent. Denied many of the subordinate and stereotypical roles that studio-era Hollywood offered to blacks, his career took a more quirky, but also much more successful path. Ten years after failing his Hollywood audition, Poitier was paired with Tony Curtis in THE DEFIANT ONES (1958), a message film by Stanley Kramer about two escaped convicts, one white and one black, fleeing a manhunt together through the swamps. This role garnered Poitier a best actor nomination at the Berlin International Film Festival. He did not win the award, but his nomination gave a tremendous boost to his career, and this international attention was duly acknowledged in Hollywood. Five years later, Poitier did indeed capture a best actor award at the Berlin Film Festival for his performance in LILIES OF THE FIELD (1963), for which he also won an Academy Award.

Although he was not an activist, it is difficult to discuss Poitier's Hollywood career in the 1960s without reference to the civil rights movement and its triumphs in ending segregation in public accommodations and in securing voting rights in states throughout the South. During this period, Poitier was cast neither in films with political themes nor in Hollywood features that dealt directly with the civil rights movement and the legal end of segregation. Placed against the complex background of racial progress, racial unrest, and racial awareness that characterized the 1960s, Poitier's Hollywood acting career during these years is difficult to assess. His roles and his career could be praised or criticized from the point of view of a set of ideological stances, of course, but a truly balanced appraisal of his screen roles and their place in American society is more difficult.

Sidney Poitier was American cinema's most popular male lead in 1967 (seen here from
IN THE HEAT OF THE NIGHT).

In 1967, the critic Hollis Alpert unflinchingly described Poitier as being as archetypal in his roles as Gary Cooper was in his. Whether in A PATCH OF BLUE (1965, Guy Green), TO SIR, WITH LOVE (1967, James Clavell), GUESS WHO'S COMING TO DINNER (1967, Stanley Kramer), or IN THE HEAT OF THE NIGHT (1967, Norman Jewison), Poitier invariably was the masterful, restrained, wholly proper, and desexualized hero.[45] In appearance and in conduct his characters were always impeccable. Poitier played a schoolmaster whose patience with unruly pupils verged on saintliness in TO SIR, WITH LOVE. He was an expert homicide detective from Philadelphia, Pennsylvania, who carried out some stunning sleuthing in deepest Mississippi in IN THE HEAT OF THE NIGHT. His character in GUESS WHO'S COMING TO DINNER was not merely a successful medical doctor, but also a Nobel Prize laureate. These remarkably enlightened heroes were extreme, but what so many critics found especially disturbing about Poitier's roles during the 1960s was the completely desexualized nature of all of these portrayals. As Clifford Mason wrote describing Poitier's character in A PATCH OF BLUE: "He's a Samaritan who befriends a blind white girl and successfully takes her away from her corrupt prostitute mother, but who never once gives even an inkling that he might be thinking about making love to her." In such roles, Mason concluded crassly, Poitier was serving simply as Hollywood's "showcase nigger."[46]

Whatever similar ideological or more general cultural critiques might be aimed at his roles, however, these showcase characters turned out to be perfect for Poitier as an actor. He was the first African American to win best actor at an International Film

Festival; the first to be "cemented" on the Walk of Stars at Grauman's Chinese Theater in Hollywood; and the first that the Hollywood establishment accepted as a mainstream producer, star, and screenwriter (THE LOVE OF IVY).[47] Poitier won the American Jewish Committee's award for his contributions to human relations in 1965. The public selected him as the most popular film star in America in 1968 (beating out the 1966 and 1967 winner, Julie Andrews) in the annual vote conducted by the *Motion Picture Herald*,[48] and movie theater owners all across the United States, on the basis of counting their revenues from his films, selected Poitier as their "Star of the Year" for 1967 and 1968.

The phenomenon of Sidney Poitier's acting success can easily be perceived as a product of 1960s Hollywood's liberal good intentions, or could be ridiculed as the crass exploitation of a pleasant male stereotype by producers during an era of new consciousness about race in America. Writing in the 1980s, two decades after the fact, however, critic and historian Terry Christensen reached an admirably balanced and benign interpretation: "Sidney Poitier was ridiculed for playing cuddly, acceptable blacks in . . . 1960s films, yet his screen presence surely helped prepare white audiences for integration. He also helped create an audience for virtually all black films."[49] Beyond film industry politics, and beyond the commentary generated by social and cultural pundits at the time, however, there was a simple truth: Sidney Poitier executed the kinds of roles that could easily have belonged to actors in classic Hollywood twenty or thirty years earlier. His popularity with moviegoing audiences, moreover, demonstrated that alongside the shifting tastes in the 1960s large portions of the mass audience still adored a cinema of sentimentality and were willing to support such movies and their stars. By the late 1960s, Poitier stood for an older way of conceiving and making films that hearkened back to Hollywood's classic era because he still was limited by perceptions of what audiences would accept of an African American star. Poitier's roles in the mid and late1960s may best be understood by comparison to the female star, Julie Andrews, with whom he competed neck-and-neck in "star popularity contests" and "box-office draw" during these years. The popularity and on-screen success of both Poitier and Andrews was defined to a large extent by their capacity to sustain roles effectively that many film critics considered dated.

The Comic As Auteur

Sidney Poitier played roles that appealed to what many critics in the late 1960s were describing as a "throwback" sensibility to the sentimentality and heroism of classic Hollywood films. His characters cut against the grain of underlying alienation and estrangement that was at the core of the antihero role featured in a number of increasingly popular movies at the end of the decade. Another Hollywood figure who similarly, and far more willfully, resisted the trends of the 1960s was the exceptionally versatile comedian and filmmaker, Jerry Lewis. Early in the 1960s, when European art films were gaining widespread critical attention in the United States, when runaway production was threatening the Hollywood production industry, and when an eroding American audience for theatrical releases was causing confusion at the major studios about what films to finance, Lewis continued to press forward as a producer/director/actor with a consistent agenda: 1) cater to kids and the family trade; 2) keep production costs down; 3) go all out to promote each new film.[50]

Along with producing, directing, and promoting his own films for a market that the rest of the American motion-picture industry had practically abandoned, Lewis also blazed a path for himself as a gadfly critic of Hollywood. In 1963, the year that marked a low point for the number of American feature films produced, Lewis lambasted Hollywood as "disorganized and disunited" and contrasted this disarray to the $180 million his films had grossed from 1958 to 1963.[51] Lewis never wavered in maintaining that the European "art film" would prove of fleeting importance, pointing out that he personally would never lower himself to begin to try to make movies that pandered to what he called "the twenty sophisticates in the world." He also faulted what he perceived as the growing cult of Hollywood celebrity to expose movie stars to the public in a "pedestrian atmosphere" that was unflattering, and which he claimed was killing the "beautiful illusion" upon which the classic appeal of Hollywood stars had been built.[52] For a time, Lewis appeared to be the only person in Hollywood saying what many of the industry's veterans must have been thinking about the changes to which their industry had to adjust in the early 1960s.

Interestingly and ironically, however, it was during the 1960s that Jerry Lewis came to be far more appreciated both by critics and audiences in Great Britain and France than he was in the United States. In his native country, his films were routinely dismissed by industry insiders and critics alike as lowbrow and retrograde. By contrast, the *London Times* celebrated Lewis in January 1965 as "the only real old-style star in the world, doing two films a year, regular as clockwork, which make money . . . and he's the one unmistakable comic genius in the great tradition of the silents."[53] An article by the respected British critic John Russell Taylor in the prestigious journal *Sight and Sound* offered an even more precise, analytical praise of Lewis's work: "[In his films] there is a fantastic proliferation of mute and incoherent responses to one basic stimulus . . . [and] an entirely personal way of mangling English, with nouns turning into verbs, verbs into adjectives, and notions twisting, turning, dividing, and reforming."[54] France's film critics nearly unanimously selected Lewis best director for THE NUTTY PROFESSOR (1964).

In an industry where directors perennially struggled for a semblance of control over their work, Lewis was a unique phenomenon. In 1960, for example, he produced, directed, and starred in THE BELLBOY, which he insisted on performing essentially mute. The next year he produced, directed, and starred in THE LADIES' MAN (1961), which featured him breaking up the set of a television show and dancing a tango with tough guy character actor George Raft. All this was captured with sweeping camera movements that were immediately praised and copied by two French New Wave directors, Jean-Luc Godard and Julien Temple. A vintage Jerry Lewis comedy, THE LADIES' MAN had a story line about a Hollywood boarding house for aspiring actresses where the newly hired house boy, Herbert Herbert (played by Lewis and with a character name apparently spoofing *Lolita*), turns out to be a unrelenting misogynist. With each of these comedies, Lewis demonstrated convincingly to the entire industry that he was that rare performer who was "perfectly able to get better results under his own direction than under anyone else's."[55]

Still, Lewis's zany satires of life in industrialized America, his depictions of screwball characters, and the frenetic energy of his comedy were not appreciated by American reviewers and critics. While the British and the French applauded his artistry, Lewis's recognition as a Hollywood genius initially came neither from critics nor from produc-

The comic as auteur: producer, director, writer, actor Jerry Lewis (seen here in THE DISORDERLY ORDERLY *1963).*

ers, but rather from the technical side of the movie industry. Early in the 1960s, camera engineers and other technicians began visiting Lewis's sets to study his specially built cameras and their related equipment. In 1965, in acknowledgment of an array of initiatives that Lewis had pioneered in photography, sound, music recording, and directing, he was invited to deliver the keynote address at the annual conference of SMPTE (the Society of Motion Picture and Television Engineers).[56] By that time, nearly everyone in Hollywood had to acknowledge the value of the closed-circuit video system that Lewis had designed to enable directors to watch a scene that had just been filmed by replaying a tape that ran concurrently with the motion-picture camera. The ability of the director to look at a scene right after filming it, rather than waiting at least twenty-four hours for the dailies to come back from the laboratory where they had been processed and printed, permitted immediate decisions on changes in blocking and lighting, as well as camera position and movement.[57] Soon, the closed-circuit videotape system Lewis used on his sets would become an industry standard. In recognition of its importance Lewis received in 1966 the first Award for Technical Achievement ever presented by one of Hollywood's major equipment suppliers, the Alan Gordon Company.[58]

Nonetheless, the mid and late 1960s proved an exceedingly difficult period for Lewis. In 1965, he dropped his long-standing working relationship with Paramount after wrangling with the studio over artistic control of several of his films. He teamed with Columbia Pictures instead, although that relationship would never prove as fruitful as the one with Paramount. Lewis planned to open a chain of franchised cinemas to show family-oriented fare, but that never came to fruition. In spite of the technical awards and recognition for his on-set innovations, and aside from the fact that he began teaching occasional courses in the prestigious School of Film at the University of Southern California, it was not until 1970, with WHICH WAY TO THE FRONT?, that Lewis again equaled the level of his creative work of the early 1960s.[59] Soon after, however, in 1972 he quit producing and directing films, apparently frustrated by his inability to secure financing for a film set during the Holocaust that he was calling THE DAY THE CLOWN CRIED.

MEL BROOKS AND WOODY ALLEN

Two other comics like Lewis, both of whom emerged in the second half of the 1960s onto the feature film scene, were to become significant as writer/director/players in their own films—Woody Allen and Mel Brooks. Both men started their careers in television, where they had worked for the legendary genius of television comedy, Sid Caesar. After leaving Caesar's staff, Mel Brooks had a brief writing stint for Jerry Lewis at Paramount. Allen, when he quit television, first turned his interests to writing for the stage and later gravitated into movie production, but did not relocate to the West Coast.

Brooks was finally given the opportunity to write and direct his own first feature, THE PRODUCERS (1968). The movie's improbable script was based on the premise of a conniving producer and his accountant who set out to fleece wealthy widows by luring them to invest in a Broadway musical. Their scheme is to put on a production so dreadful and outrageous (a musical tribute to Adolf Hitler) that it must close immediately, leaving the producers with the opportunity to abscond with the investors' money. Many of the scenes in this film were nearly as outrageous as the idea for the Broadway musical itself, culminating in a grand production number, "Springtime for Hitler," that amounted to a wild, excessive, and memorable parody of musical and theatrical entertainment itself. Although the movie faced considerable problems financially because it was saddled by a very poor distribution plan, THE PRODUCERS nonetheless earned Brooks an Academy Award for best story and screenplay (written directly for the screen). That industry recognition, in turn, was enough to enable Brooks to move on next to producing and writing a movie version of THE TWELVE CHAIRS (1970) that was followed by a box-office hit, BLAZING SADDLES (1974). With his capacity to combine writing, directing, and acting, Brooks carved a niche for himself as a Hollywood auteur, a term which he once interestingly defined for a magazine interviewer as "someone who gets an idea which is usually rooted to his basic philosophy of life."[60]

Meanwhile, Woody Allen would become during the 1970s and the 1980s the foremost model of the relatively independent filmmaker, working consistently through a variety of genres with highly successful productions made on relatively modest budgets. Allen had previous screenplay credits in the 1960s (WHAT'S NEW PUSSYCAT, 1965, and CASINO ROYALE, 1967), but directed his first feature, TAKE THE MONEY AND RUN, only in 1969. Before the production could be completed and the film released, however, "New Hollywood" met "Old Hollywood." The first editor lined up for the film was a West Coast veteran who expected to be told exactly how to cut the movie. When the footage turned over to him proved too confusing and daunting, he quit, and the editing assignment for the film was given to Ralph Rosenblum in New York City. Rosenblum carefully rearranged the footage that had been shot according to Allen's zany wit, rather than following the conventions of allowing for all the coverage needed to effectively edit each scene. At the time, a number of industry pundits credited Rosenblum with "saving" the film, concluding that Allen's initial foray into directing had proven a highly problematic initiation to the craft.[61] Although Allen's tale of Virgil Starkwell's criminal career did not measure up to the sophisticated mood and structure of his later features, it was sufficiently funny to garner him a deal with United Artists for three future pictures that were to be produced by the team of Jack Rollins and Charles H. Joffe. The groundwork for Allen's subsequent highly successful and highly idiosyncratic career as writer/director/actor was set.

10

The Establishment Judges:
Academy Awards for
Best Picture

The Academy and the Industry Establishment

Founded in 1919, the Academy of Motion Picture Arts and Sciences quickly became a core institution of the Hollywood establishment. While the Academy had many functions, after World War II its primary responsibility was to distribute awards of merit.[1] For nearly two decades, the Academy Awards for achievement in motion pictures, which had originated in the late 1920s, were chosen by a panel of ten governors of the Academy and presented at annual ceremonies attended primarily by industry professionals. In 1946, however, participation in the selection process was greatly expanded so that nearly all guild and union members in the motion-picture industry might have some role in the nominations. Under these new rules, which remained unchanged through the 1960s, voting was by category (e.g., cinematographers voting for the awards for cinematography, editors for the awards in editing), and all of the roughly three thousand Academy members were eligible to vote on best picture for each year.[2]

With the spread of television during the 1950s and the 1960s, the annual telecast of the Academy Awards ceremonies increasingly became a centerpiece in the promotion of specific movies and the American cinema in general. In addition, as the Hollywood studio system declined through the 1950s, a financial and professional advantage accrued to individual producers, actors and actresses, and production personnel who received an Academy award, or, in some instances, just a nomination. By the early 1960s, industry insiders estimated the expected increase in gross earnings for any movie selected as best picture to be in the range of $1 million to $5 million. In the growing free-lance production environment of Hollywood, Academy Awards translated directly into increased leverage for the recipients to favorably negotiate future deals.[3]

During the 1960s, some complaints in Hollywood about the politics of the Academy Awards referred back to the 1950s and the federal government's anti-communist investigations of Hollywood. Rumors were widely spread across the industry, for example, that both EXODUS (1960, Otto Preminger) and SPARTACUS (1960, Stanley Kubrick) were passed over for nominations in the best picture category because the screenplays had been written by Dalton Trumbo, who had earlier been blacklisted and briefly imprisoned for his unwillingness to cooperate with the House Un-American Activities Committee of the U. S. Congress. Of greater concern among industry professionals during the 1960s, however, was the perception that nominations and the Academy's voting were becoming increasingly influenced by the concerted public relations campaigns undertaken on behalf of specific movies and their talent. The nomination of THE ALAMO for best picture in 1960, for instance, was widely attributed to the blitz of advertising in the entertainment trade papers on its behalf.[4]

While some critics regarded the Oscars as emblematic of Hollywood's fundamentally shallow commercialism, other Hollywood insiders countered that the "Academy types" were living in an "ivory tower," and that they were unable to exploit the full potential of either the Academy Awards themselves or the televised ceremonies at which they were presented each year. For an industry that underwent a significant downturn in production in the early 1960s, and in which confusion abounded over cinema's changing audience and how to appeal to it, the matter of how the Academy Awards should be handled and how the ceremonies should be produced for television became flash points for debate. Bitter articles and editorials in the industry trade papers gave play to those debates.

Nonetheless, throughout the 1960s, the Academy Awards presentation lumbered along without major changes. Although the assumed politics surrounding the nominations and selections for the Oscars continued to be hotly debated by Hollywood pundits, and the format and length of the award ceremonies were perennially criticized, no true attack upon the Academy occurred. It was among the many "establishments" in American society that drew unfriendly fire as the culture wars erupted nationwide in the late 1960s, only to survive its detractors relatively unscathed. Thus, although it would be highly problematic to interpret what the award of each specific Oscar meant during any specific era, including the 1960s, the selection of the best picture for each year was indicative of what the Hollywood "establishment" considered to be the cinema's highest achievement of the previous year.

Best Picture, 1960–1969

The Academy's selection for best picture for 1960 was THE APARTMENT, co-written by I. A. L. Diamond and Billy Wilder, the movie's director. This comedy followed the same pair's highly successful SOME LIKE IT HOT (1959). The protagonist of THE APARTMENT, C. C. "Bud" Baxter, is an insurance company clerk played by Jack Lemmon, who lends his apartment to several adulterous bosses for their amorous liaisons. Shirley MacLaine played an elevator operator in Baxter's building, and Fred MacMurray was the most obnoxious of Lemmon's bosses. THE APARTMENT was the last black-and-white movie to win the Academy Award for best picture for over thirty years, until SCHINDLER'S LIST (1993).

In many ways, THE APARTMENT was a vintage Hollywood comedy: witty, wordy, fast-paced, and highly polished. At the same time, however, it was considered updated and daringly hip. As the British film critic Derek Monsey wrote, "Some people may find THE APARTMENT sordid and immoral. It is. It's meant to be. It's also funny and pathetic and the funniest soursweet comedy Hollywood has made in years."[5] It was rare for a comedy to stand up so well across a number of the major nomination categories for the Academy

Jack Lemmon in THE APARTMENT *(1960), Billy Wilder's best picture winner and the last black-and-white film to win the award until 1993.*

Awards, but THE APARTMENT did. It was an exception, however, precisely because its underlying and unrelenting moral bleakness meshed with the sardonic and pessimistic mood that a great many films would cultivate later in the 1960s.

THE APARTMENT was produced in the standard medium of classic Hollywood cinema, black-and-white film, but its trenchant portrayal of the emptiness of middle-class American life and values was "late sixties" to the core. The film was nominated in several categories, including directing, writing (directly for the screen), cinematography, art direction and editing. Jack Lemmon and Shirley MacLaine were nominated for best actor and best actress, respectively. Although neither of them won an Oscar, both were awarded the British equivalents of the Academy Awards for their performances.

Walter Mirisch, the film's producer, was a model for Hollywood's new breed who were becoming dominant in the business during the 1960s. Building on his strong personal ties throughout the industry, Mirisch and his brothers, Harold and Marvin, were running a firm in the late 1950s that provided business and legal services to independent producers. The Mirisches specialized in arranging financing, distribution, and marketing for films. They worked with many studios, but their primary focus was a contractual relationship with United Artists, the Hollywood studio that had pioneered financing pictures by dealing directly with the creative forces who made them.[6] That arrangement worked for over sixty features during the 1960s.

Mirisch repeated his role as the producer of the Academy Award's selection for best picture with WEST SIDE STORY (1961, Robert Wise). With a book by Arthur Laurents based on *Romeo and Juliet*, music by Leonard Bernstein, and lyrics by Stephen Sondheim, Jerome Robbins directed and choreographed the musical during its long run on Broadway. Initially, Robbins was also hired to direct the movie, but less than a month into rehearsals United Artists demanded that he move aside for Hollywood veteran Robert Wise. Robbins stayed on long enough to direct several of the musical numbers, but was then sacked altogether. In typical fashion for a changing and increasingly freelance Hollywood, Robbins remained in the credits as co-director. Wise, who began his career editing CITIZEN KANE (1941, Orson Welles), eventually was given complete creative control over WEST SIDE STORY and was credited as a co-producer.[7] Still, even when the directorial issues had been ironed out, many industry pundits considered the casting for the movie weak. Natalie Wood, hardly known for her singing voice, played the lead as Maria, with three males—Richard Beymer, Russ Tamblyn, and George Chakiris, none of whom was considered a major star—as major characters among the rival teenage gangs in New York City on which the story focuses. All fared extremely well with the critics.[8]

A scene from WEST SIDE STORY *(best picture, 1961), directed by Robert Wise.*

WEST SIDE STORY opens with helicopter shots of Manhattan's soaring skyline as the camera gradually moves closer toward the street in a tenement neighborhood, where the sounds of staccato finger-snapping draw the viewer into the menacing neighborhood being fought over by rival gangs called the Sharks and the Jets. Shot on location on the streets of the West 60s in Manhattan, where condemned buildings were about to be razed for the construction of Lincoln Center, the film had a decidedly gritty look. WEST SIDE STORY captured Oscars in ten categories, but its commercial prospects for enormous earnings were considered to have been compromised. Advance "roadshow" sales for the film registered over $250,000 in the five largest cities of the United States,[9] but the picture was over two-and-a-half hours long and was considered an extremely high risk for foreign distribution.

Into the early 1960s, Hollywood pundits in general continued to fear that nearly any musical film was a potential disaster with audiences abroad. Wise had further increased the distributor's risk by insisting on having the songs in WEST SIDE STORY subtitled, rather than having the numbers dubbed into foreign languages and sung by singers who were already well known in their own countries.[10] Musicals had a reputation in Hollywood of faring poorly in markets overseas largely because it was believed that foreign viewers had trouble following a story line conveyed largely by lyrics that were sung in American English. Wise's persistence and ultimate victory with using subtitles showed the influence that a director now had in the American feature film industry. Moreover, Wise's insistence on gambling on foreign audiences accepting songs in the original American English paid off and marked a turning point in the industry's attitude toward musicals and their prospects for large earnings abroad. WEST SIDE STORY was a runaway success internationally; the film even played one of the major screens in Paris, the Georges V Cinema, for a record 218 weeks (just over four years).[11] In addition, the domestic box-office success of the film was still so phenomenal into the middle of the decade that in 1966 Mirisch turned down an offer from NBC of over $3 million for a single telecast of the picture.[12]

Both THE APARTMENT and WEST SIDE STORY contained elements that were considered daring for the time, but neither of them could be considered a landmark film. By contrast, the Academy's selection for best picture for 1962 was a landmark production. Co-produced by Sam Spiegel and David Lean, who had also been production partners for THE BRIDGE ON THE RIVER KWAI (1957), LAWRENCE OF ARABIA had complete financial backing and a distribution deal with Columbia Pictures, although the production company of record was listed as Horizon Pictures, Ltd. of Great Britain. Three years in the making and with a production cost of more than $15 million (originally budgeted in the $7 million to $9 million range), LAWRENCE OF ARABIA, based on British playwright Robert Bolt's first film script, was by far the most ambitious and expensive project with which Columbia Pictures had ever been involved.[13] Columbia claimed that it had not even reached the break-even point on its expenses until 1965, nearly a full three years after the film's theatrical premiere. In this reckoning, however, Columbia's bookkeeping was disguising the steady stream of company earnings for those three years generated through its distribution fees.

LAWRENCE OF ARABIA was a solid box-office success, even though the film received decidedly mixed reviews from a number of major American critics when it was first released. The *New York Times* initially labeled it a "camel opera," although later, at Academy Awards time, the paper published a second review that was more positive.[14] Much of the criticism that greeted the film was based on the fact that it was constructed as a vast spectacle that many people thought simplified the protagonist's character and his career.[15]

While LAWRENCE OF ARABIA disappointed a number of mainstream critics in the early 1960s, it nonetheless left decidedly strong and positive impressions on at least two younger viewers who would mature into prominent American filmmakers. Steven Spielberg, who was fifteen years old when the movie premiered, later recalled, "LAWRENCE OF ARABIA was the first film I saw that made me want to be a movie-maker." Martin Scorsese, five years older than Spielberg, continually refers back to his first viewing of the film, repeatedly praising it as "one of the great cinema experiences."[16] In 1998, when the American Film Institute assembled its list of the "One Hundred Greatest American Movies" as determined by the votes of fifteen hundred leaders from the American film community, LAWRENCE OF ARABIA finished fifth overall, placing it in the highest position of any feature released during the 1960s. With its best picture selection for 1962, the Academy actually appeared to get ahead of the cultural curve for a change.

Although produced in Great Britain, LAWRENCE OF ARABIA was classified as "American" by the Academy. The following year's best picture, TOM JONES (1963, produced and directed by Tony Richardson), by contrast, marked the first time since 1948 that a film formally classified as British won the award. Based on Henry Fielding's eighteenth-century novel, TOM JONES presented to its audiences a lusty, rollicking, and uninhibited romp. At the time, a popular cartoon in the *New Yorker* depicted a man asking his psychiatrist, "What's my problem? TOM JONES depressed me."

Released three years after the Federal Drug Administration in the United States approved an oral contraceptive commonly known as the Birth Control Pill,[17] and just as the emergent contemporary lifestyle described by the phrase "Swinging London" was becoming identifiable internationally, TOM JONES was openly sensual, celebrating sexuality in a lighthearted and upbeat manner in ways that Hollywood production had not yet approached. Joyce Redman's sexual predilections in the role of a merry seductress openly preferring younger men, for example, foreshadowed by a half-decade her Hollywood counterpart in the character of the predatory and sullen Mrs. Robinson in THE GRADUATE (1967).[18]

Tony Richardson's direction brought to TOM JONES a playfulness that grew directly out of the willingness of the French New Wave to draw self-conscious attention to the filmmaking process. Many of these were old-time movie devices, of course, that dated back to the silent era. The French New Wave, however, had reintroduced and highlighted them for the purposes of self-conscious fun and as self-reflexive devices within the parameters of the European "art film's" inquiry into the deeper nature of the cinema experience itself.[19] Tom, for example, carefully places his hat over the camera lens before making love, and the movie freely uses subtitles, asides by actors to the audience, freeze frames, and jump cuts, which classic Hollywood had strictly avoided.

TOM JONES appeared at the right moment to challenge traditional sexual mores and pretensions, doing so in a manner that found broad support in the audience through genuine wit and pervasive good spirit. Even with a cast that included Albert Finney, Susannah York, Hugh Griffith, and Diane Cilento, the film had been produced for under $1 million. Released by United Artists, its enormous box-office success occasioned a new flood of American investment into British production. For Tony Richardson, however, TOM JONES proved his only major hit as a director with the American mass audience. Over time, the influence of the film, too, proved almost

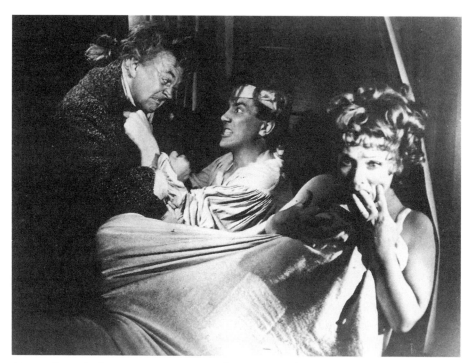

Scenes from the lusty romp TOM JONES *(best picture for 1963), directed by Tony Richardson.*

entirely as an icon of cultural change and attitudes toward sex in the early 1960s, rather than heralding new directions in cinematic art.

By contrast to the modest budget of TOM JONES, the next year's best picture, MY FAIR LADY, directed by Hollywood veteran George Cukor and starring Audrey Hepburn, was a $17 million production that no one ever would accuse of displaying either new aesthetic or cultural directions. With this role Hepburn became Hollywood's second actress to be paid over $1 million dollars for a picture (Elizabeth Taylor was the first), even though she couldn't manage a satisfactory Cockney accent and a singer named Marni Nixon had to perform all her songs, which Hepburn lip-synced. Julie Andrews won the best actress award that year for her lead in MARY POPPINS, whereas Audrey Hepburn was not even nominated for MY FAIR LADY. That may have registered as personal vindication for Andrews, who had created the role of Eliza Doolittle in the stage version that played on Broadway, but for the executives at Warner Bros., who turned her down for the movie version, her Academy Award could not have mattered less. MY FAIR LADY earned record grosses for its "roadshow" sales at 150 movie theaters across the United States,[20] and had reported $46 million in earnings worldwide by the end of its first year in distribution.[21] Premiering in a year during which the Beatles first toured the United States, conquering teenage audiences everywhere they went, it is easy to overlook that many American adolescents liked MY FAIR LADY, too. The film's opening in Hollywood, for example, was greeted by crowds of screaming teenagers police estimated to exceed 15,000 on the sidewalk outside the Egyptian Theater.

The following year's best picture was another musical, THE SOUND OF MUSIC (1965), produced and directed by Robert Wise, whose success with WEST SIDE STORY in 1961 had clearly rekindled the industry's interests in movie versions of hit Broadway shows. Once THE SOUND OF MUSIC premiered on screen, the publicity department of 20th Century-Fox started touting it confidently as "the most popular film ever made," which indeed it was until being displaced from that ranking in the late 1970s.[22] It grossed $11 million more than MY FAIR LADY in its first year,[23] and, better yet, had cost less than half as much to produce.[24] THE SOUND OF MUSIC fared well with reviewers for local newspapers[25] and even with a few national critics, most notably Bosley Crowther and Judith Crist, who treated the film well in general while lavishing praise on Andrews, who lost out in her bid that year for a repeat Oscar as best actress. Crowther's and Crist's positive critical assessments, however, were overshadowed by the opinions of most national critics who ridiculed THE SOUND OF MUSIC as being shallow to the point of mindlessness. The *Saturday Review* criticized its "lukewarm liberalism that seeks to transform a modest tribute to "Edelweiss" into a stirring anti-Nazi song of protest."[26] Notably, even that "lukewarm liberalism" apparently was enough to cause THE SOUND OF MUSIC to fail in only one major film market in the world—West Germany.[27] Germans, however, weren't the only ones who did not like the film.[28] Stanley Kauffmann complained that he should be given a special award "for sitting through this Rodgers and Hammerstein atrocity, so studiously saccharine that one feels that one has fallen into the hold of a tanker bringing molasses from the Caribbean."[29] More surprisingly, perhaps, John E. Fitzgerald of the National Catholic Film Office concluded, "While the story is as joyous and wholesome as anyone could want, the plot of this Austrian torte is as full of holes as a Swiss cheese."[30]

The other musical of the decade that took a best picture Academy Award was OLIVER! (1968). While hardly drawing the negative criticism that greeted THE SOUND OF MUSIC, OLIVER! achieved only modest box-office success. Long in the planning,[31] OLIVER! was yet another of those productions, essentially British in its cast, crew, and

Julie Andrews singing about her favorite things in THE SOUND OF MUSIC *(best picture for 1965), directed by Robert Wise.*

production venue, that was financed by and produced for Columbia Pictures in conjunction with Highland Films, Ltd.

Two years earlier, A MAN FOR ALL SEASONS (1966), another Columbia-Highland production, won the Academy's best picture award. With a screenplay by Robert Bolt, who won that year's award for best screenplay based on material from another medium, the film was based on the life of Sir Thomas More, the devout Catholic who resigned from the service of King Henry VIII of England rather than assist the king in violating the Church's authority by marrying Anne Boleyn. Produced for a budget of under $2 million, A MAN FOR ALL SEASONS was shot at Shepperton Studios near London and had neither the swashbuckling action, nor the adventuresome heroes typically found in Hollywood historical epics. It was based on what the critic Philip K. Scheuer described as the best drama written for the stage in English during the 1960s,[32] and could be said to have beaten out the movie version of what was arguably the best drama written for the American stage during the 1960s, Edward Albee's *Who's Afraid of Virginia Woolf?* A MAN FOR ALL SEASONS was a serious drama with a cast devoid of Hollywood "names": the lead was played by British stage actor Paul Scofield, who won a best actor award for what was his first film role. During the entire decade of the 1960s, it was most likely that A MAN FOR ALL SEASONS benefited more at the box office from its Academy Award for best picture than did any other winner. The film had decidedly modest earnings across the United States, but business picked up markedly after its selection by the Academy.[33]

An even greater surprise to both pundits and the public, however, was the Academy's best picture selection for 1967. The award ceremonies that year were postponed for two days following the assassination of the Reverend Dr. Martin Luther King, Jr., and took place on April 10, 1968. The Academy's voting had resulted, as it turned out quite poignantly, in a best picture award for IN THE HEAT OF THE NIGHT (directed by Norman Jewison and produced by Walter Mirisch). The film concerned an African American detective from Philadelphia, Pennsylvania, who ends up solving a murder in a Mississippi town by working with the local white sheriff. Starring Sidney Poitier and Rod Steiger, with a haunting theme song performed by Ray Charles, and filmed on location in Sparta, Illinois (not Sparta, Mississippi), the film was based on a classically strong script by Sterling Silliphant, who won the writing award that year. IN THE HEAT OF THE NIGHT, which dealt with the relationship between two people who did not wish to be involved with each other, beat out two films that year that each had enormous appeal to the emerging young audience, BONNIE AND CLYDE and THE GRADUATE, as well as a second film that year starring Poitier, who played a highly successful physician engaged to marry a white woman in GUESS WHO'S COMING TO DINNER.

The best picture selection for 1969, by contrast, was MIDNIGHT COWBOY, a gritty drama set at the margins of life in contemporary New York City. Earlier in the decade, a script reader at United Artists had evaluated the novel by Leo Herlihy on which MIDNIGHT COWBOY was based and recommended against its adaptation for the screen

Dustin Hoffman and Jon Voight in MIDNIGHT COWBOY *(best picture for 1969), directed by John Schlesinger.*

"because the action goes steadily downhill."[34] By the very end of the 1960s, however, the script was perceived as eminently producable precisely because it was aimed at an audience receptive to its highly negative portrayal of disintegrating urban life in America and the hopeless situation and abject alienation of the movie's main characters. The film was directed by John Schlesinger, whose inventive and saucy DARLING (1965), starring Julie Christie, had been produced in Great Britain and nominated for a best picture Academy Award.

Joe Buck, played by Jon Voight, travels from Texas to New York believing that he will find women ready and willing to pay him for his sexual services. There he meets a street character named Ratso Rizzo (Dustin Hoffman), who strikes up an acquaintance with Buck and promptly tries to con him. The two eventually become friends, however, and the remainder of film explores their unlikely relationship until Ratso becomes so ill that Joe must steal money to take him on an escapist bus trip to Florida.

Branded with the scarlet letter "X" in the new MPAA ratings system, MIDNIGHT COWBOY nonetheless encountered absolutely no difficulties at the box office. In fact the "X" subsequently was changed to an "R" rating in 1971 without a single frame being cut from the film. By 1969, the film's "downer" story, gritty New York milieu, and raw attitudes toward sexuality were widely and easily accepted among both critics and the moviegoing public. Writing in the *New York Post*, Archer Winsten summarized mainstream critical response to the movie: "MIDNIGHT COWBOY is the kind of solid work that stays superbly in one piece, a statement about our time and people that doesn't have to stand back and orate."[35] Despite having given the film its "X" rating, the MPAA, the motion-picture industry's trade organization, selected MIDNIGHT COWBOY as the official entry of the United States to the Berlin Film Festival. The International Catholic Film Office also gave MIDNIGHT COWBOY its imprimatur by labeling it the movie of 1969, stating that it offered viewers "the best articulation of man's problem from a Christian viewpoint."[36]

The Academy Awards' Best Pictures: A Summary

With the Academy's best picture choices for the decade, the Hollywood establishment left a valuable record of self-perception within the industry. The 1960s began with the naming of THE APARTMENT, the last black-and-white feature selected as best picture for more than thirty years. It was a wry script, set in mid-town New York City amid a world of businessmen morally adrift. The 1960s ended with the selection of MIDNIGHT COWBOY, a bleak descent into New York City's netherworld of drifters and losers at the margins of society and living in the midst of a crass and self-obsessed metropolis. THE APARTMENT was the best of Billy Wilder's films, capping his career as a director of often cynical movies that nonetheless sustained their humor. It reveals a flicker of the troubling discontent brewing beneath the surface of American materialism and success, whereas MIDNIGHT COWBOY is a troubling descent into the exploration of a wealthy society's dark underside. In between, the Academy's best picture selections bore witness to the unprecedented symbiosis and complicated production alliances between Hollywood and Great Britain that resulted in LAWRENCE OF ARABIA (1962), TOM JONES (1963), A MAN FOR ALL SEASONS (1966), and OLIVER! (1968).

Among the four musicals that won best picture awards during the decade, WEST SIDE STORY (1961) and OLIVER! (1968) shared a darker dramatic side, while MY FAIR LADY (1964) and THE SOUND OF MUSIC (1965) presented worlds full of light, color, and

Sidney Poitier in In the Heat of the Night *(best picture for 1967), directed by Norman Jewison.*

upbeat joy—even amid class repression and Nazi oppression, respectively. From one point of view, the 1960s could be perceived as the decade that saw the "last hurrah" for musical films based on Broadway hits and intended to appeal to a truly mass audience of all ages. In another sense, however, their production values pointed clearly toward the high concept films that would become centerpieces of the new Hollywood aesthetic that became fully articulated after the arrival of the "blockbuster" with Star Wars (1977).[37]

Lawrence of Arabia, with its brilliant cinematography and its extraordinary exploitation of widescreen aesthetics, was the most pictorial of the best picture selections for the decade. It was the one film that truly embraced an emerging emphasis on visual sensation and the visceral power of the screen, rather than relying primarily upon the conventions of classic Hollywood scripting. By contrast, the best picture of 1967, In the Heat of the Night, could be seen as a throwback to classic Hollywood movies that revealed, primarily through dialogue and classic development of character, a human relationship that strained plausibility, but which tugged at all the right emotions for the mass audience. This motion picture's selection by the voting members of the Academy can also be seen as coinciding with Hollywood's underlying political liberalism, which by the late 1960s had become fully reestablished as an accepted facet of the movie industry's facade. Whatever else it did to America culturally, the late 1960s created an atmosphere in which the film industry could leave behind the politics of fear that had spread throughout the community during the "Blacklist" era of the 1950s. By the end of the 1960s, Hollywood filmmaking was no longer a "conservative" undertaking in any normal use of the word.

11

Landmark Movies of the 1960s and the Cinema of Sensation

Landmark Movies

The concept of "landmark film" requires the identification of specific movies that became conspicuous to critics and audiences at the time of their release, or which, in historical hindsight, stand out from the more typical productions of an era. Some of the films discussed in this chapter may be categorized as turning points in feature film production on the relatively narrow grounds of their aesthetic and visual style, while others are set apart because of the place that they hold within the broad sweep of a changing American culture. Some of these movies are better known for the new potential they were perceived to offer to the motion-picture industry and to American cinematic art, rather than for any changes that they actually spawned. Some of them provoked attention during the 1960s, especially from major newspaper and magazine critics whose role in the nation's public discourse over appreciation of movies as an art form was on the rise, though they may have subsequently declined in significance over time. Others, by contrast, were underestimated or overlooked during the 1960s, but later grew in critical stature and recognition.

DAVID AND LISA   Judith Crist, one of the nation's leading movie critics in the early 1960s, identified DAVID AND LISA (1962, directed by Frank Perry and based on a screenplay by his spouse, Eleanor), as the best film of the year. In fact, it was the only movie produced in the United States that Crist included in her top ten list for that year. Crist's opinions were becoming increasingly important as she rose to prominence, writing for the *New York Herald-Tribune* and emerging as a putative rival to the veteran Bosley Crowther at the *New York Times*. National attention was also drawn to the movie when *Time* magazine declared DAVID AND LISA "the best U.S. movie released in 1962."[1]

Based on a published case history written by psychologist Dr. Isaac Rubin, DAVID AND LISA portrayed two alienated teenagers. Contemporary in its outlook on youth and the difficulties encountered by adolescents in an essentially stifling society, DAVID AND LISA was made as a low-budget, independent film entirely outside the Hollywood mainstream. In an era of declining fortunes for the motion-picture industry, DAVID AND LISA

A scene from the low-budget success, DAVID AND LISA *(1962), which leading film critic Judith Crist called "the best film of the year."*

instantly became emblematic for anyone who identified their hopes for the rebirth of the American cinema with alternative movie making. Even the *Los Angeles Times* editorialized that the motion-picture industry should take a critical look at itself because two hundred movies like DAVID AND LISA (at a per picture production cost of $110,000) could be produced for what had been spent alone on Hollywood's mega-failure, CLEOPATRA.[2]

Distributed by Continental, a branch business established by the maverick New York City movie theater proprietor Walter Reade, DAVID AND LISA was named best picture by a new director at the Venice Film Festival and swept the awards for best actor (Keir Dullea) and best actress (Janet Margolin) at the San Francisco Film Festival. It also managed to garner two Academy Award nominations (Frank Perry for best director and Eleanor Perry for best screenplay based on material from another medium). Along with its critical acclaim, DAVID AND LISA was profitable as well. After only six months in distribution, the movie's estimated gross exceeded $2.5 million.[3]

This profitability was largely the basis for its reputation in the early 1960s as "the most successful example to date of a new kind of American film, the low-budget picture shot outside the Hollywood factory system."[4] Its low cost and subsequent earnings were, of course, in its favor. More importantly, however, many critics recognized in DAVID AND LISA an alternative aesthetic that broke with the polished look of Hollywood features, and a dramatic development that revealed in its main characters a psychological depth that the industry's mainstream features could not duplicate. The greater emotional range and authenticity of these characters, along with the fact that they were played by unknowns, provided what many Americans appreciated as a kind of artistic maturity in DAVID AND LISA that reminded them of the best of the European "art films."[5] While a representative of United Artists weighed in with the assessment that Hollywood's major studios could not afford to make small pictures "because our overhead is too high," DAVID AND LISA nonetheless was the movie of the early 1960s that inspired devotees of art cinema to believe that an alternative model of production could shift the feature film industry in the United States in new directions, and that such a shift might eventually overtake and topple mainstream Hollywood.[6]

THE MANCHURIAN CANDIDATE   The year 1962 also saw the release of THE MAN-CHURIAN CANDIDATE, an important movie that came straight from the heart of main-stream Hollywood. Produced and played by well-established Hollywood talent, this film tantalized critics with what they perceived as its unique courageousness, for it chal-lenged directly many of the commonly held beliefs of cold war America. Indeed, the film satirized both the political right and left and gave ideologues on both sides plenty to be angry at. Its volatile reception ended abruptly, however, when it was pulled out of public exhibition immediately after the assassination of President John F. Kennedy on November 22, 1963. Over the years, THE MANCHURIAN CANDIDATE and its place in cinema history have been reassessed, and it has come to be acknowledged as a landmark feature of the early 1960s.

Based on a novel by Richard Condon, the film was co-produced by Frank Sinatra, who also starred in the role of a Korean War veteran named Major Ben Marco. Marco and members of his platoon had been prisoners of war in Korea. After returning home, Marco becomes plagued by nightmares that eventually suggest a Congressional Medal of Honor winner, Raymond Shaw (played by Laurence Harvey), has been brainwashed by Communist interrogators in Korea and programmed to kill fellow platoon members and eventually to assassinate the president of the United States. With Shaw's father-in-law (played by James Gregory) depicted as a ranting McCarthyite senator and his mother a sinister political meddler (played by Angela Lansbury), Shaw easily gains access to the inner-circles of the American government. The director, John Franken-heimer, who had relocated to Hollywood after directing a string of dramatic successes for television in New York, managed to deftly balance the elements of a searing political satire with a nail-biting thriller.

While critics generally liked THE MANCHURIAN CANDIDATE,[7] its production and release were trouble-ridden from the beginning. The head of United Artists, Arthur Krim—who also happened to be the national finance chairman of the Democratic Party—repeatedly expressed serious doubts about the script. Krim pressured for changes that would move the story away from its pivotal attention on a scheme to assas-sinate the president to safer dramatic ground. Sinatra, who was resisting the proposed changes and who had close personal ties to President Kennedy, had to obtain Kennedy's personal approval for the production to proceed using the script that Sinatra wanted. Even with the imprimatur of the president, however, THE MANCHURIAN CANDIDATE was still widely considered too controversial by almost everyone in the Hollywood estab-lishment, and condemned as downright inflammatory by many.[8] As soon as it premiered, the movie was blasted from both the political left and right. A Communist party publi-cation, *The People's World*, called THE MANCHURIAN CANDIDATE "the most vicious attempt yet to cash in on Soviet-American tensions" and labeled the movie "poison."[9] By

Pushing the envelope for political criticism, Frank Sinatra and Laurence Harvey played brainwashed soldiers in THE MANCHURIAN CANDIDATE (1962).

contrast, the syndicated Catholic film critic, William H. Mooring, lambasted it as undisguised left-wing propaganda.[10] A chapter of the American Legion in southern California declared the film was proof that communists again were infiltrating the movie industry and called for renewed investigations of Hollywood by the House Un-American Activities Committee (HUAC).[11] When THE MANCHURIAN CANDIDATE opened at one theater in Orange County, California, Communist party members found themselves picketing the movie alongside anticommunist extremists from the John Birch Society.[12]

Moreover, even before it was withdrawn from distribution following Kennedy's assassination, THE MANCHURIAN CANDIDATE had become embroiled in the kind of financial shenanigans that were becoming legend in Hollywood by the early 1960s. United Artists persistently listed the production at such a loss on its books that any revenues generated by its distribution for years to come would be owed to the studio and would not benefit the producers. The practice of keeping double sets of books and tallying revenues earned against production costs was as old as the film industry itself. Now that more films were owned by their producers, and not directly by the studios themselves, however, this kind of bookkeeping became increasingly problematic and a point of conflict between producers and the studios that were backing, or partially backing, a movie's production or distribution. Because of the controversy that arose with United Artists over profits, losses, and the keeping of the financial books for THE MANCHURIAN CANDIDATE, a frustrated and disgusted Sinatra refused for twenty-five years to re-release the movie, and it remained lost to the public. It was only upon its re-release in

1988 that THE MANCHURIAN CANDIDATE became widely heralded for having been far ahead of its time and critically applauded as a delicious black comedy mixing melodrama and satire.[13] So potent was the movie's critique of American society that the major national television networks considered it too controversial and decided to pass on telecasting it at the end of the 1980s, even though it had grossed over $3 million at theaters and earned an equal amount in video sales within a year of its reissue.[14] As one industry pundit remarked, THE MANCHURIAN CANDIDATE went from being a commercial failure to being applauded as a classic "without ever passing through success."[15]

Although its original run had been brief, the movie had a significant effect on the industry even during the 1960s. THE MANCHURIAN CANDIDATE, noted Douglas Brode, "changed Hollywood's notion of what audiences would accept in both the style and subject of a mass market film, blending a savage satire of politics in particular and America in general with suspense and romance."[16] Subsequently, over several decades, the Hollywood establishment came not only to tolerate the movie, but to embrace it. Whether this notable acceptance was based primarily on appreciation for its satire of conventional American life and cold war politics, or more on the way in which the Hollywood industry could in hindsight value the courage of the producers of THE MANCHURIAN CANDIDATE, was debatable. When the American Film Institute polled Hollywood insiders in 1998 to select the "One Hundred Greatest American Movies," THE MANCHURIAN CANDIDATE was among those listed.[17]

DR. STRANGELOVE   An even more popular send-up of the cold war mentality was a satirical comedy starring Peter Sellers, DR. STRANGELOVE, OR HOW I LEARNED TO STOP WORRYING AND LOVE THE BOMB (1964). Directed by Stanley Kubrick, who had expatriated himself from the United States and was working in Great Britain, the film was written by Kubrick and Peter George, based on the latter's novel and a script by Terry Southern. A dark satire ridiculing the American political consensus that supported cold war policies,[18] the movie is normally credited as a British production, but the question of attribution as to the movie's nation of production remains confused. Although actually produced in Great Britain, it was financed by Hollywood and the cast was largely American. In 1989, when the United States Library of Congress established its National Film Preservation Board charged with identifying and conserving the most important American films, the very first feature from the 1960s to be named to the Board's list was DR. STRANGELOVE.[19]

With its unrelenting spoof of military officers and political leaders of the United States and USSR, its "bewilderingly cynical and satirical point of view," and its array of characters, none of whom was completely sympathetic, DR. STRANGELOVE anticipated by several years the widespread disillusionment among student-aged Americans with cold war rhetoric and much of the military technology that had been spawned by it.[20] In 1964, however, establishment film critics were not necessarily amused. Bosley Crowther opined in the *New York Times*, "DR. STRANGELOVE is beyond any question the most shattering sick joke I've ever come across." He added, "It discredits and even holds contempt for our whole defense establishment, up to and even including the hypothetical commander-in-chief."[21]

The script's broad humor, along with Kubrick's uncanny skill for integrating the bizarre into an underlying and pervasive aesthetic of realism, pointed toward comedy and irreverence that delighted student-aged audiences. DR. STRANGELOVE brought what some critics labeled as "sick humor" directly into the mainstream of the American

Peter Sellers (rising up from the wheelchair) had three major roles in the darkest of cold war satires, DR. STRANGELOVE, OR HOW I LEARNED TO STOP WORRYING AND LOVE THE BOMB *(1963).*

commercial cinema,[22] while further bowing to adolescent tastes by using character names such as Jack D. Ripper, Merkin Muffley, and Dimitri Kissoff. From the movie's subtitle, *How I Learned to Stop Worrying and Love the Bomb* through many of its visual vignettes and its general humor, DR. STRANGELOVE paralleled the social satire of *Mad*, the popular magazine for adolescents and young adults founded during the 1950s. Nonetheless, DR. STRANGELOVE was a finely crafted movie that was deadly serious about the threat of a global nuclear war. The distinctiveness and the legacy of this landmark movie were embedded in an unusually compelling combination of parody and serious social criticism.[23] Two other films released in 1964, FAIL SAFE (Sidney Lumet) and SEVEN DAYS IN MAY (John Frankenheimer), also dealt with the cold war or the threat of nuclear holocaust, but neither of them so effectively marked the parameters within which Hollywood explored those topics in the 1960s as did THE MANCHURIAN CANDIDATE and DR. STRANGELOVE.

MICKEY ONE   In 1965, Warren Beatty produced and starred in MICKEY ONE, which was budgeted at under $1 million and initiated the collaboration between Beatty and director Arthur Penn. Judith Crist, who was by then securely established as one of the country's most prominent critics, first saw it during the 1965 New York Film Festival at Lincoln Center, the increasingly important annual showcase for "serious film," and exclaimed in print: "We've made it—or to shove chauvinism aside—an American film

that raises the New York Film Festival to new heights! MICKEY ONE is a brilliant, original screen work, visually exciting and intellectually satisfying."[24]

The uniqueness of MICKEY ONE defied description for many observers and critics,
but stylistically it was probably best characterized as a "strange combination of American
realism and French New Wave techniques."[25] With the protagonist's strong existentialist
yearnings, this enigmatic story of a night club entertainer trying to escape the forces of
evil, as well as his own psyche, had an unusual structure that relied on a melange of genres, including melodrama, comic vignettes, expressionist exaggeration, and fantasy, to
portray the protagonist's inner *angst*. MICKEY ONE came as close to being a pure art film
as any production that acquired mainstream Hollywood financing during the 1960s.[26]

Interestingly, in spite of its unusualness, MICKEY ONE was reviewed favorably in the
industry trade journals, including *Film Daily* and the *Motion Picture Herald*, but panned
in both the *New Yorker* and *Cue*, with the latter describing the movie as "terribly shallow and lost in the glitter of gaudy technique."[27] A disappointment at the box office,
MICKEY ONE was nonetheless highly regarded in its own day and remains a legendary
cult classic of the 1960s. Three decades after its completion, the director Martin
Scorsese was instrumental in restoring a 35mm print of the film for theatrical re-release.

FACES   During the 1960s, the best model in the American cinema for low-budget filmmaking, risk-taking, and innovation in feature film production pushed toward the edges
of what was recognized by serious critics as genuine "art film" was provided not by
Warren Beatty, but rather by the actor turned occasional auteur, John Cassavetes.
Moonlighting, in essence, to work on his own films alongside his major acting roles in
such mainstream Hollywood movies as THE DIRTY DOZEN (1967) and ROSEMARY'S
BABY (1968), Cassavetes toiled on highly independent production work with his spouse,
the actress Gena Rowlands, and his friends from the industry, all of whom essentially
volunteered their time to Cassavetes' films.

Cassavetes' first feature, SHADOWS (1959), cost less than $40,000 and was based on
an idea that had grown out of an exercise in an improvisation class that Cassavetes was
teaching at the time.[28] This ambitious and troubling tale about race in America, basically
shot with a handheld camera, was strongly influenced by the British "Free Cinema" of
the late 1950s, which emphasized nonfiction films documenting working-class lives.
Because the movie's action was unscripted and the performances entirely improvised,
editing was a Herculean task. Nonetheless, SHADOWS won the Critics Award at the 1960
Venice International Film Festival and established Cassavetes as a kind of "folk hero" to
American proponents of alternative, high-risk, low-budget features produced on a financial shoestring and which relied on self-distribution.[29]

In 1968, when the annual New York Film Festival had become established as the
showcase for serious American features that challenged mainstream Hollywood production, the movie that dominated the Festival was Cassavetes' FACES. That film was
crafted far more conventionally than the exceptionally experimental and improvisational
SHADOWS, which in some circles was regarded more an avant-garde film than an independent feature. Nonetheless, FACES faithfully expressed Cassavetes' concept of an
actor-oriented cinema in which cast members developed their own characterizations
through weeks of rehearsal that resulted in screen performances uniquely imbued with
a dynamic of spontaneity and faithfulness to life. Distributed by Walter Reade's
Continental Pictures, FACES was named by the New York Film Critics as runner-up for
best picture of the year (to THE LION IN WINTER), and Cassavetes was named runner-

Faces from John Cassavetes' FACES (1968), which expressed his concept of an actor-oriented cinema.

up to Paul Newman (RACHEL, RACHEL) as the year's best director. In addition to gaining the relatively predictable attention of film critics and film festival audiences, FACES garnered establishment Hollywood recognition in the form of three Academy Award nominations: Seymour Cassel for supporting actor; Lynn Carlin for supporting actress; and Cassavetes for best screenplay written directly for the screen.

FACES enjoyed a very good press response across a range of publications, fueled by the penchant of movie critics and other writers comparing it favorably to more mainstream feature films. A review in *Psychology Today* called it the American equivalent of LA DOLCE VITA (1960, Federico Fellini) while citing theories by neo-Marxist psychologist Erich Fromm to explain the kind of moral and spiritual malaise of the middle-class characters portrayed in the film. The magazine's reviewer credited Cassavetes' production with giving viewers an exceedingly honest portrait of "marriage as we know it" alongside its implied critique of capitalist society, which the magazine applauded.[30] *Playboy* magazine praised the way that Cassavetes stayed with his tormented and alienated characters: In its presentation of "the terrifying contemporary pattern of people living lies," the magazine proclaimed, "FACES digs far deeper than VIRGINIA WOOLF."[31] A review in *Film Bulletin* contended that FACES "bridges the gap" between MARTY (1955, Delbert Mann) and WHO'S AFRAID OF VIRGINIA WOOLF? (1966, Mike Nichols), "and then penetrates beyond, concentrating on successful, apparently happy people unwilling to admit to themselves the nothingness into which they have fallen."[32] The critic Deac Rossell maintained that FACES "shows the lives of Los Angeles suburbanites the

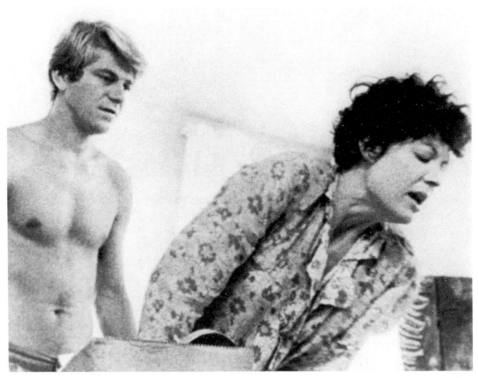

Seymour Cassell and Lynn Carlin in FACES *(1968), portraying the middle-class American dream turned into a "one night in L.A. nightmare." They received Academy Award nominations for supporting actor and actress, respectively.*

way THE GRADUATE should have,"[33] and C. Robert Jennings of the *Los Angeles Times* contrasted the directorial skills of John Cassavetes—whom he credited with conveying authenticity and poignancy in every single scene of FACES—to Mike Nichols, whom Jennings faulted for simply "creating behavior" throughout THE GRADUATE.[34] Ray Carey, ranging more broadly in order to define a framework within which he could explore the distinctiveness of the film, wrote that "American film critics take for granted that art is essentially a Faustian enterprise—a display of power, control, and under-standing. In a word, their conception of artistic performance is virtuosic." By contrast, Carey held the work of Cassavetes to be great precisely because of the director's capacity to "let go" and, thereby, to render an entirely different experience onto the screen.[35]

The sustained minimalist aesthetic in FACES challenged nearly all traditional ways of scripting and acting in the American feature film. Some commentators even called it "avant-garde" because of the film's many long takes and its slow pace. However, it is not correct to label FACES "avant garde" or "experimental." The film was a dramatization of incidents in the lives of fictional characters that had moorings in narrative practices of the post–World War II European cinema and reflected an approach close to the slow-paced studies of psychological alienation by the Italian director Michelangelo Antonioni in the late 1950s and early 1960s. The style of FACES also paralleled the observational impulse of one of the leading movements in 1960s documentary that appeared at the beginning of the decade with the arrival of cinéma verité and its American counterpart, "direct cinema." FACES stood as a real exception in feature production in the United States, prompting the critic Richard Schickel to write, "This is, I think, a great and courageous film in which Cassavetes has dared more than any American director in memory."[36]

MEDIUM COOL Like Cassavetes, Haskell Wexler was best known during the 1960s for earning his living by working on mainstream Hollywood productions. By the middle of the decade, he was well established as a director of photography on the industry's "A-list." In the process, however, Wexler began creating for himself a distinct and unusual professional path by moving easily back and forth from cinematographer on major Hollywood features to shooting documentaries. His level of comfort in bridging fiction and nonfiction was abundantly clear in MEDIUM COOL (1969), the first feature film that Wexler produced and directed. Critic Douglas Brode lauded MEDIUM COOL for weaving dramatic and documentary techniques together as well as any film since Roberto Rosselini's Italian neo-realist classic, ROME: OPEN CITY (1945).[37]

The protagonist in MEDIUM COOL is a television cameraman played by Robert Foster. His attitude toward his work is initially technical, but over the course of the film his perceptions are altered by his progressive realization of the ideological power and political complexity of the moving image. At the same time, probably no film, either fiction or nonfiction, better expresses the exceptionally raw political, generational, and racial tensions in American society at the end of the 1960s than MEDIUM COOL.

Haskell Wexler's MEDIUM COOL *(1969) integrated fictional scenes with documentary footage of the 1968 protest demonstrations in Chicago.*

Although set against the background of a major political party's convention and the street demonstrations by young people that broke out in response to it, the script of MEDIUM COOL was completed nearly a year before such actual events took place outside the Democratic National Convention in Chicago in August 1968.[38] In fact, documents subsequently obtained under the Federal Freedom of Information Act have verified that the production of MEDIUM COOL was under close surveillance from at least four different government agencies from its inception because of the suspected connections between the film's producers and radical protest groups.[39]

Contemporary movie critics generally applauded the point of view and values of MEDIUM COOL, typified by Deac Rossell's assessment of it as "a collage of politics and humaneness, produced with a technical excellence and inventiveness rarely found in any film."[40] Besides its technical polish and the integration of fictionalized street scenes with documentary footage of actual demonstrations in Chicago, MEDIUM COOL created unusual moments of social implication, such as the sequence when Foster's character and his soundman visit a group of black militants in a small apartment to interview them. The critic John Simon describes this as "perhaps the only instance in the American commercial film [of the 1960s] of racial tension caught root and branch on screen."[41]

In a manner unusual in the history of the American feature film, MEDIUM COOL reflected the vast complexity of how politics are simultaneously tangential, yet inextricably intertwined, with the lives of ordinary people. MEDIUM COOL, moreover, is full of complex sociological, political, and cinematic cross-references. At one point, John and Eileen (the woman he has fallen in love with) are watching French director's Jean-Luc Godard's CONTEMPT (1963) on television; the film is thematically critical of the commercialization of cinematic art and the Americanization of culture around the world. For most critics, such details added to the rich artistic and social texture that Wexler managed to weave throughout the film, although the critic John Simon found this instead to be a kind of "cineaste snobbery" that he considered inconsistent with the otherwise broad political and humanitarian values of the film.[42] More trenchantly, Stanley Kauffmann argued that "the fault of the film is that Wexler himself is caught in the same trap as his hero: in the sensual pleasure of shooting film, the ease of creating effects, and indulgence in them for their own sake." Kauffmann recognized what he believed an inherent contradiction in Wexler's attempt to criticize the nature of media representation in television by using another form of media representation, the feature film.[43]

Nonetheless, MEDIUM COOL has generally withstood the test of time. The critic Charles Champlin, who for many years wrote for the *Los Angeles Times,* summarized the accomplishment of this movie by comparing it to two of Hollywood's decidedly more popular films of 1969: "It is less clever than MIDNIGHT COWBOY and less indulgently personal and emotional than EASY RIDER, but it asks larger and more disturbing questions than either."[44] The overt political seriousness of MEDIUM COOL may have partially compromised its box-office popularity, even at a time when the interest of young people in politics was imagined to be at its height.[45] Paramount, moreover, marketed the movie ineptly, most likely holding back its best efforts with a film that was widely known across the industry to have been under such close governmental scrutiny during its production."[46] Because its box-office draw was comparatively weak, the influence of MEDIUM COOL on other Hollywood films and filmmakers at the time was substantially diminished. Nonetheless, it remains not only a landmark film of the late 1960s, but also a direct influence on such later features as NEWSFRONT (1978, Philip Noyce) and CIRCLE OF DECEIT (1981, Volker Schloendorff).[47]

Rebels of the Western and the Transformation of a Genre

In 1962, as the Hollywood feature film industry was approaching a nadir in production output, Kirk Douglas's company, Bryna, in association with David Lewis, produced a film for Universal entitled LONELY ARE THE BRAVE. Dalton Trumbo's screenplay for the movie was based on a novel by Edward Abbey that portrayed the plight of a Southwestern cowboy whose cherished way of life is being obliterated by the modern world. The action of the film focuses on Douglas, playing the lead character, getting arrested to join a friend who is in jail for aiding illegal Mexican immigrants. The pair break out of jail, but they are hunted down with helicopters by a technocratic posse led by a sheriff played by Walter Matthau.

Although the film was clearly about character, exploring the protagonist's dilemma as rooted in his sense of alienation from a changing modern world in which time-honored folkways are being destroyed, Universal Pictures handled the distribution and promotion of LONELY ARE THE BRAVE just as it would for a conventional western. The movie's unfortunate fate at the box office was sealed by the distributor's inability to recognize and exploit the correct demographics of the potential audience for it.[48]

The screenwriter for LONELY ARE THE BRAVE was Hollywood's best-known victim of the "Hollywood Blacklist," Dalton Trumbo. Douglas had essentially rehabilitated Trumbo two years earlier when he produced SPARTACUS with a screenplay by Trumbo that was acknowledged in the credits under the writer's real name. Nonetheless, what was most interesting about his script for LONELY ARE THE BRAVE was not the way in which the story might be interpreted from a leftist perspective on modernization, but rather how it reflected the shift in American feature films of the 1960s toward the exploration of character through themes of alienation and resistance to modern authority.[49] Along with John Huston's THE MISFITS (1961) and Sam Peckinpah's RIDE THE HIGH COUNTRY (1962), LONELY ARE THE BRAVE pushed the basic formulas of traditional westerns to reinterpret the western frontier West as a lost ideal. This initially modest shift, moreover, would finally give way at the very end of the 1960s to the distinctly defined genre of the "anti-westerns," exemplified by THE WILD BUNCH (1969), LITTLE BIG MAN (1970), and SOLDIER BLUE (1970).

The most commercially successful movie of the 1960s that played off the conventions of the classic western and simultaneously went beyond them was considerably lighter in tone. BUTCH CASSIDY AND THE SUNDANCE KID (1969, George Roy Hill) made great use of manipulation of its formal screen elements, intercutting black-and-white sequences with color footage and giving the final release print a greenish-gold tint. Stills and freeze-frames—along with the color changes—were utilized throughout this popular movie to underscore the director's romanticizing of his material.[50] Unlike BONNIE AND CLYDE, in which criminals were represented as existentially doomed victims of their own nature, however, Butch and the Sundance Kid were characters transformed by the screenplay from legendary renegades into unabashed "fun-heroes."[51] Starring Paul Newman and Robert Redford, BUTCH CASSIDY AND THE SUNDANCE KID helped define the male buddy film as a distinct sub-genre in the American cinema.[52]

Douglas Brode proclaimed the movie "the most charming western ever made,"[53] but its appeal ranged far beyond the beguiling performances of its two male stars. The deeper success of the film resided in its ability to satirize the myths of the movie western while still glorifying the men who presumably created them. BUTCH CASSIDY AND THE SUNDANCE KID may have given the western a new lease on life, but it did so only by uprooting entirely the structure and basic assumptions of the classic movie western.[54] BUTCH CASSIDY AND THE SUNDANCE KID can be seen as speaking directly to the contemporary American culture, circa 1969. As one critic noted, the movie fit both the cultural moment and the new, youthful audience: "BUTCH CASSIDY AND THE SUNDANCE KID constantly wants to have things both ways by being romantic *and* cynical simultaneously, which is essentially an adolescent desire."[55]

BUTCH CASSIDY AND THE SUNDANCE KID played with the myth of the American West in a manner that was both gentle and conservative. A send-up of Hollywood western formulas, it indulged in escapism that few, if any, classic westerns had ever attained. The tone was so light and airy that it frequently became ethereal. In the same year, Sam Peckinpah's THE WILD BUNCH (1969) carried the stylization of violence in the western farther than any American movie had done before. The critic Winfred Blevins proclaimed THE WILD BUNCH that film year's "wildest, raunchiest, goriest, most realistic, and most sordid." He also concluded that it was 1969's "most original, best acted, most dramatic, most impressive feature"[56] TRUE GRIT, released the same year and starring John Wayne, who won a best actor Oscar in his role as Rooster Cogburn, summed up the westerns of the past. THE WILD BUNCH presented a frantic embrace of a new set of rituals that revolutionized the place of the western film in the American cinema.

Some critics declared Peckinpah's accomplishments to be of the highest cinematic order. "Directorially, THE WILD BUNCH is comparable to nothing," wrote Joel Reisner, "excepting the work of Kurosawa, ever seen on the screen before. . . . It is as hair-splitting as it is hair raising."[57] Peckinpah, typically, filmed the bloody shootouts in his movie with six different cameras simultaneously, each of them running at a slightly different speed. Collaborating with the editor Louis Lombardo, they used slow motion to stylize violence in a manner that had only been trifled with (such as in the finale of BONNIE AND CLYDE) previously.[58] THE WILD BUNCH, like BONNIE AND CLYDE, made extensive use of the technical innovation of explosive "squibs" to simulate bullets striking victims. The visual effects were impressive, of course, as these exploding squibs—essentially wired plastic bags filled with red dye—made for enormously powerful moments of visual impact in color film. To a large extent, this widespread exploitation of graphic and bloody violence that began in the late 1960s could be seen as the logical consequence of new technologies and the fact that feature film production in the United States had crossed over entirely to color photography. The use of color cinematography for serious dramatic film supported directors in bringing more and more graphic violence to the screen.

Much of the controversy surrounding THE WILD BUNCH at the time, of course, had to do with the single issue of the movie's graphic representation of violence. The critic and historian Arthur Knight believed that Peckinpah was sincere in his intention to make a movie so "strong and stomach-churning and so detailed in its catalogue of horrors that all the attraction of violence for its own sake would disappear."[59] Joseph Morgenstern, however, editorialized in *Newsweek* that Peckinpah was not to be excused for the violence on the grounds of possible metaphorical intentions. Morgenstern argued that Peckninpah was proceeding on a fundamentally false premise if he believed that violence could be stylized artistically so that it became capable of commenting upon itself.[60] Diana Trilling, a literary critic, wrote in the *New Republic* that the movie was "devious," while the historians Leonard Quart and Albert Auster argued much later that

William Holden blasting away in Sam Peckinpah's THE WILD BUNCH *(1969), a land-mark in the cinema of sensation.*

the intellectual incoherence of THE WILD BUNCH and its resorting so frequently to graphic violence was symptomatic of many American films in the late 1960s, which they judged as "incapable of doing more than evoking an image of a world gone awry."[61] Several observers felt obliged to justify its gore by interpreting the film's story of the intrusion of the U.S. cavalry in the Mexican Revolution early in the century as a parable for the controversial U.S. military intervention taking place in Vietnam.[62]

Surely, this film marked a high point for the 1960s' emerging cinema of visceral screen effects, characterized as it was by an enormous advancement in the visual power that delivered carnage on the screen.[63] Whether or not the movie's story line might accurately be interpreted to parallel the U.S. military presence in Vietnam, or was reflective of the nation's loss of innocence after President John F. Kennedy's assassination in 1963, the thematic darkness of THE WILD BUNCH meshed with a pessimistic zeitgeist that characterized a number of the landmark movies in the late the 1960s. Peckinpah was widely seen as having pushed the traditional violence of frontier legend, which had always dominated Hollywood westerns, over the edge. In this sense alone, THE WILD BUNCH qualified as a landmark film: It held up a mirror to a dark and troubling side of the American myth of the West, while implicitly posing troubling questions about Hollywood's decades-long perpetuation of that myth. Undoubtedly, THE WILD BUNCH forced some members of its audiences to confront their own voyeuristic ambivalence toward its graphic horrors.[64]

1967: The Watershed Year

The year 1967 marked a turning point for the American cinema with three landmark movies, COOL HAND LUKE (Stuart Rosenberg), THE GRADUATE (Mike Nichols), and BONNIE AND CLYDE (Arthur Penn), each of which presented central characters who were identifiable to their audiences as antiheros. Their box-office success appeared to be based on the enormous appeal of each for audiences composed primarily of late adolescents and young adults. For this audience, the identification with the antiheros was assumed to be rooted in a widely shared sense of alienation from middle-class American society, the values of America's older generations, and the nation's economic, social, and political "establishment."

In COOL HAND LUKE, Paul Newman played a rebellious and self-destructive convict in a prison in the Deep South. Newman pushes Luke's character to the existential limit, until it becomes clear that the only choice left to Luke is either bowing to conformity or death. "You're gonna have to kill me," he tells a fellow inmate played by George Kennedy, who gives Luke a terrible beating. It's a boast that turns out to be prophetic. For, as the critic Richard Schickel wrote, in COOL HAND LUKE there is not a single instance of the standard Hollywood technique of trying to "glamorize the unglamorizable."[65] COOL HAND LUKE marked an accomplished interpretation of a character whose surface behavior could have been dismissed as simply flawed, but whose deeper dimensions emerge during the course of the film, with Newman's interpretation of Luke alternately funny, stalwart, submissive, defiant, pathetic, and, according to the critic Hollis Alpert, "finally, truly tragic."[66]

Newman's triumph in the film was significant, but, as the critic Charles Champlin argued, it was the movie as a whole that "proved that the term 'Hollywood' need not be a limiting definition."[67] In a nation experiencing an enormous pull of cultural change, and for an American cinema now forced to appeal to younger audiences, COOL HAND LUKE was emblematic of a shifting audience taste toward stories about individualists, malcontents, and rebels who steadfastly resisted the proprieties of respectable society. With its classic hero out of vogue, Hollywood seemed to be concocting its own version of the antihero out of a pastiche of underdog status, American individualism, and existential quest for identity and self-expression that lacked the deeper philosophic brooding found in its Western European cinematic counterpart.

Arrested for being drunk and decapitating parking meters around the square in a small southern town, Luke is reminiscent of the rebel heroes that Hollywood had been treating on and off since the mid 1950s—he is a veteran, and he is of the working class. Nonetheless, Luke's character typifies the cultural shift of the late 1960s in which a number of motion pictures accept such a flawed hero as his own victim. As Strother Martin, playing the prison's warden, intones, "What we got here is a failure to communicate." What this line really means, of course, is that Luke's resistance has taken on the characteristics of a passiveness that authority cannot manage. There is a muted quality to Luke that suggests a form of civil disobedience more than a raging anger against the establishment and its rules.

An entirely different sort of alienated character was Dustin Hoffman's Benjamin in Mike Nichols's film, THE GRADUATE. The son of affluent Californians, Benjamin returns to his parents' home right after his graduation from college and begins a sexual affair with a bored middle-aged woman (Anne Bancroft) who is married to one of his

Benjamin (Dustin Hoffman) saves his true love Elaine (Katharine Ross) from bourgeois life as the entrapped older generation looks on helplessly in THE GRADUATE *(1967).*

father's business partners. Subsequently, Benjamin falls in love with her daughter, Elaine (Katharine Ross). Nonetheless, Benjamin's disquietude with the world in which he finds himself is also held beneath the surface of his essentially placid character, and his anger with that world is eventually channeled into the action of a screwball comedy.

Although the screenplay was based on a Charles Webb novel that had been published in the 1950s, by the late 1960s America's burgeoning youth culture accepted the story as an ideal vehicle for expressing much of the shared resentment of substantial numbers of American young people against the affluent upper middle-class lifestyle in which they had grown up in suburbia.[68] The film's appeal to college-aged audiences, moreover, had a great deal to do with the soundtrack by Paul Simon and Art Garfunkel, which underscored Benjamin's point of view. The protagonist's subjectivity was conveyed by the repeated conventions of camera positioning and the film's editing, which some critics insisted were being overused. These "new stylistics" gave THE GRADUATE an exceptionally contemporary "look," even though, in the end, the movie's story could be regarded as an updated example of one of the most worn of Hollywood clichés—"love conquers all."[69] In the final sequence of THE GRADUATE, Benjamin pursues Elaine to a church where she is about to marry a medical student. He disrupts the ceremony, ostensibly saving her from a future life of dull conventionality in upper–middle-class comfort by blocking the doors of the church with a large cross and escaping with her on a city bus that coincidentally happens to be passing by. In its melange of satire and sentiment, and its unflinching identification with two sympathetic characters who are the college-aged children of affluent parents, THE GRADUATE became a "key alienation film" of the 1960s.[70]

Produced for just over $3 million,[71] THE GRADUATE broke house records for attendance in nearly 90 percent of the movie theaters where it played. Its success saved Joseph E. Levine's struggling production company Avco-Embassy from bankruptcy.[72] As *Variety* proclaimed, "THE GRADUATE spanned the generation gap, and Joe Levine has the profits to prove it."[73] Nonetheless, at least one audience survey indicated that THE GRADUATE did not so much span the generational divide—with 72 percent of the viewers being under the age of twenty-four, and 24 percent in the age group twenty-four to thirty, leaving only 4 percent over thirty years of age—as it focused on the widening differences in generational tastes.[74] How the younger generation perceived the movie was no better summarized than in a young woman's letter to the *Saturday Review* (July 1968): "[THE GRADUATE] speaks to us, a generation of young people who refuse to accept the plastics, extramarital sex, and booze given to us by our 'elders.' We, as Benjamin, want more than what many of our critics suspect; we want truth, with all its crudeness, shock, and beauty."[75] In keeping with the rhetoric of an antimaterialist zeitgeist that was sweeping over large numbers of young adults in America during the late 1960s, director Mike Nichols staunchly proclaimed to one campus audience that his movie was about "the Los Angelization of the world in which *things* take over a person's life."[76]

While one critic argued that there was nothing really new in THE GRADUATE "except Dustin Hoffman's face,"[77] another claimed that Nichols had provided the film with "the texture, if not the substance, of contemporaneity," and offered the opinion that the songs from the movie's soundtrack, like "Scarborough Fair" and "Mrs. Robinson," would symbolize the late 1960s for decades to come. The film's sexual frankness was fairly provocative for a mainstream Hollywood movie and meshed with the widespread "upheaval in American sexual mores" often referred to as the "sexual revolution" that was evident by the late 1960s.[78] THE GRADUATE reflected the generalized sense of alienation felt by great numbers of adolescents and young adults toward the entire value system of their parents' generation. That sense of alienation embraced, at least metaphorically, the kind of estrangement from society and the embrace of lawlessness embodied in 1967's other great landmark movie, BONNIE AND CLYDE.[79]

BONNIE AND CLYDE managed not only to capture the shifting mores, values, and attitudes of a substantial number of young adults who were its core audience, it also established more forcefully than nearly any other mainstream American feature film of the 1960s its distinct aesthetic principles and production values. When its release was pending, Warner Bros. concluded that the movie likely would do acceptable business only on what was called the "popcorn circuit," which consisted of theaters located in small and medium-sized towns and cities in the South and Midwest, where there were few other diversions than going to a movie each week. Warner Bros. was convinced the movie would have little appeal to audiences in what they considered the more sophisticated markets on the East and West Coasts or, for that matter, in nearly any of America's more populous urban areas. Initially, these projections by the Warner distribution staff appeared to be correct when BONNIE AND CLYDE was reviewed savagely in the *New York Times*.[80] Then, *Time* magazine dismissed BONNIE AND CLYDE as "sheer, tasteless aimlessness." In *Films in Review*, Page Cook attacked it as "dementia praecox of the most pointless sort" and opined that there is "*evil* in the tone of the writing, acting, and directing of this film."[81] Writing in the *Los Angeles Citizen-News*, Abe Greenberg summarized the bewilderment of much of the establishment press, and, by implication, of

The visual sexual innuendo and characters outside the law in Bonnie and Clyde *(1967, Faye Dunaway and Warren Beatty pictured) were seriously examined by Pauline Kael, a major voice among American film critics.*

an older generation of Americans: "They were the 'bad guys' who became 'good guys,' sort of Robin Hoods in the eyes of one segment of the public. Yet, none of this jells with the trail of death and destruction left by the Barrow gang. Therein lies the puzzlement— why did producer Warren Beatty 'humanize' these murderous characters and make the lawmen seem heavies."[82]

At a point in cultural time, however, when the generation gap in the United States appeared to widen daily, masses of young people were lining up to see Bonnie and Clyde all across the United States. In response to this phenomenal box-office draw, in fact, a number of critics felt compelled to reassess their initial opposition to the film. *Time* magazine's Stefan Kanter retracted his earlier criticism and, in a rare second review, declared Bonnie and Clyde as the best film of the year and "the sleeper of the decade."[83] In similar fashion, Joseph Morgenstern admitted that his own initial negative review of the movie in *Newsweek* had been "grossly unfair."[84]

One major critic who applauded Bonnie and Clyde from the beginning and who, in hindsight, appeared prescient in doing so, was Pauline Kael. By the mid 1960s, Kael was well established as a major voice among American film critics. She had become one of the first movie critics of the 1960s to collect and publish her critiques in books that sold well, giving those books catchy titles, such as *I Lost It at the Movies* (1965) and *Kiss,*

Kiss, Bang, Bang (1968). She blazed a career path that coincided with the "film gener-ation's" shifting interest away from traditional literature toward the movies, and Kael's reviews gained an authoritative cachet among serious devotees of the cinema. She was also the ascendant champion of sociological criticism of the movies, guiding her readers toward understanding movies as parables of contemporary social and political issues. It was Kael's discovery of an ideological message in BONNIE AND CLYDE that explained to many its appeal to audiences of young adults. "In 1967," she wrote, "the movie-makers know that the audience wants to believe—maybe even prefers to believe—that BONNIE AND CLYDE were guilty of crimes, all right, but that they were innocent in general; that is, naive and ignorant *compared with us.*"[85]

Subsequently, Kael would be echoed by countless others trying to grasp the signifi-cance of BONNIE AND CLYDE as a cultural turning point in the American cinema. Charles Marowitz, writing in the *Village Voice* at the end of 1967, enthused: "One can no longer consider the film as a film. It has transcended art to become a psychic conve-nience. It has gone beyond the pale of criticism to become the rarest of all things, an artifact that is both symptom and cause." Set in the early 1930s, BONNIE AND CLYDE alluded only peripherally to the failures of capitalism, dealing instead with the Great Depression in a highly stylized manner while managing to suggest vague connections to contemporary disquietude and protest in American society in the late 1960s. "A good deal of the picture's financial success," noted Marowitz, "was the fact that the late 1960s' audiences related to the rootless alienation of the film's milieu. Bonnie and Clyde are rebels without a cause . . . characters which the so-called 'youth movement' of the 1960s turned into campy pop culture heroes."[86] In its oblique references to injustice and repression, and in its more direct portrayal of its protagonists as victims, BONNIE AND CLYDE represented what some observers chose to label a shift in the entire social role of the Hollywood movie. "Today fewer and fewer films aim to distract," Jean-Louis Comolli argued. "They have become not a means of escape but a means of approaching a problem."[87] The problem that the film's director, Arthur Penn, thought he was address-ing was large—the question of repression and violence in American society. He com-pared the depression-era Southwest of his movie to the entire United States in the late 1960s, which he caricatured as "a church-going, highly moralistic, highly puritanical society, which has integrated and made a part of itself a kind of violence against other human beings, which, viewed from the outside, seems absolutely intolerable."[88]

As the *Los Angeles Citizen-News* commented, "Not since GONE WITH THE WIND has any film created such worldwide, intensive excitement as has been the case with Warner-Seven Arts' BONNIE AND CLYDE. A few other films [in history] have gained sim-ilar acclaim and box-office success, but none has started so many significant trends throughout the film world."[89] In its first year, BONNIE AND CLYDE grossed more than $40 million worldwide. This business success pointed clearly toward a formula combin-ing alienated outsider characters with action and graphic violence that would become a Hollywood staple for the next several decades.[90]

Other Landmark Films and Developments of the 1960s

EASY RIDER   The combination of the alienation theme and outsider characters, along with visual vignettes that were emblematic of America immediately following the social and cultural unrest that had peaked with the assassinations of Martin Luther King, Jr., and Robert Kennedy and the events of the Democratic National Convention in Chicago in 1968, merged in a challenging movie that elevated what might have been dismissed as a "biker flick" into a landmark movie of the late 1960s. With production costs just under $300,000 through principal photography,[91] Easy Rider became both a critical and a box-office success in 1969. Produced by Peter Fonda (the son of Henry and the brother of Jane) in conjunction with Bert Schneider (the son of longtime Columbia Picture Board Chairman Abe Schneider), and directed by Dennis Hopper (the son of Hollywood gossip columnist Hedda Hopper), the film's making and distribution was a collaborative effort of these children of the Hollywood establishment that challenged the establishment's fundamental concept of how to make successful movies, and what to make them about. Applauded at the Cannes Film Festival, where Hopper was honored with a jury award for best director of a "first film," and Peter Fonda shared a screenwriting award with co-author Terry Southern, Easy Rider promptly became a global symbol of what some commentators were hailing as the "New American Cinema."[92]

Peter Fonda claimed that when the idea for Easy Rider first formed (reportedly in a Toronto motel room), he compared the project in his own mind to The Searchers (1956, John Ford), in which John Wayne's character pursues a five-year odyssey to find and kill the Indian who had kidnaped his niece. Fonda saw the quest in Easy Rider differently, however, because "they're not looking for Natalie Wood (who played Wayne's

Peter Fonda (on the star-spangled cycle) compared his Easy Rider *(1969) project to John Ford's western* The Searchers *(1956), except that Fonda's characters "are looking for America and they're on choppers."*

niece in THE SEARCHERS), they're looking for America and they're on choppers."[93] With a narrative structure built on a journey east from Los Angeles toward a destination called Heaven, Florida, EASY RIDER has been said to bitterly observe the death of frontier America as part of its symbolism. Richard Schickel described the film's odyssey even more broadly as portraying "a desperate flight from the System" by essentially innocent individuals.

The success of EASY RIDER convinced many in the American motion-picture industry that young audiences did not care any more about lavish productions and thousands of extras. EASY RIDER appeared to mark the convergence of several directions in the contemporary American cinema. It challenged the traditional Hollywood model in favor of low-budget productions with small casts and expressed a highly personal creative vision, yet it was targeted with great success at the late adolescent and college-age audience. The characters played by Fonda, Hopper, and Nicholson were easily read as fictional outsiders whose rebelliousness reflected elements of a fundamental myth that was central to the counterculture of the late 1960s.[94] EASY RIDER was the first hit feature to truly integrate rock music into its entire story line, hence welding the enormous transformation of American music during the 1960s with the motion-picture industry's sudden discovery of the more youthful audience for theatrical motion pictures.

The film had lots of fallout and consequences in Hollywood. His comparatively brief role in EASY RIDER saved Nicholson's acting career and put him on the road to stardom. The movie's surprising box-office success sent the Hollywood industry scrambling to produce films presumed capable of imitating some element of its appeal, but the first wave of these productions were all were markedly unsuccessful—GETTING STRAIGHT (Robert Rush), THE REVOLUTIONARY (Paul Williams), and THE STRAW-BERRY STATEMENT (Stuart Hagmann), all 1970.[95] Given those failures, the film's runaway success in 1969 might be dismissed as a fleeting episode in Hollywood's history. However, many observers plausibly argue that EASY RIDER—even with the failure of immediate attempts to imitate it and to exploit the youth market by so doing—had a decided impact in the industry, opening doors for Hollywood production to many truly innovative talents who otherwise might not have been given a chance to direct features, such as Robert Altman, Hal Ashby, Peter Bogdanovich, and Bob Rafelson. More deeply, EASY RIDER convinced the industry that movie production for the future would have to be based largely on a search for formulas and aesthetics that could truly excite the core audience of moviegoers—now composed almost entirely of adolescents and young adults.

Alfred Hitchcock and the Emerging
Film Aesthetic of the 1960s

The situation in Hollywood by 1969 reflected changes in the American feature film that had to do both with the characters and contents of popular movies with a fundamentally new aesthetic that had been emerging throughout the decade. The broad sociological changes that influenced the types of characters and the kinds of film content toward which Hollywood had shifted could be reliably accounted for by reference to the youth culture that appeared in the United States in the second half of the decade. The new aesthetics that had arisen in the American feature film, however, could not be explained in the same way.

*Veteran director Alfred Hitchcock. The aesthetic of a cinema
of sensation was turned on by the shower scene in his film
PSYCHO (1960).*

The new aesthetic of a cinema of sensation neither emerged during the closing years
of the 1960s, nor was it pioneered during the turning point year for the American feature film in 1967. Instead, it made its first appearance in a movie released in 1960 that
was directed by a veteran Hollywood filmmaker, Alfred Hitchcock, who had started his
film career in his native Great Britain. At a time when lesser directors were taking over
their own films from an increasingly enfeebled studio system, Hitchcock did so in a
manner that pointed toward major changes in the aesthetics of the American feature
film. With PSYCHO (1960), Hitchcock established "a new perception of film" that was
rooted in the visceral manner in which the viewer was drawn into and held by a movie.[96]
As the French New Wave director François Truffaut remarked, PSYCHO "was oriented
toward a new generation of filmgoers" and was premised on an aesthetic that was fundamentally new.[97] PSYCHO has been called "the movie that cut movie history in half":
The precise moment at which that division occurs is in the famed motel shower scene
when Janet Leigh's character, Marion Crane, is stabbed to death.[98]

Vincent Canby wrote of PSYCHO nearly two decades after it premiered that with this
movie Hitchcock had achieved the first real instance of "pure film" in the American
commercial cinema. Canby explained that the shower scene uses the visual medium of
the motion picture to achieve an immediate effect upon the viewer that could not be
successfully conveyed by any other medium. The murder scene is constructed and ren-

dered for the primary purpose of sensation. PSYCHO breaks entirely from the demands of classical Hollywood film that placed a primacy on the narrative. It also bypassed the conventions of scripting characters as opposing forces that guided the viewer toward clearly empathizing with one of them. PSYCHO is "probably the best 'scare' film ever made and one in which there is not a single character to engage our sympathies . . . and not a single character who isn't expendable."[99]

In its own time, PSYCHO was certainly controversial. Initially, the film was burdened by misguided marketing attempts that hyped the idea that no one could be admitted to a showing anywhere once the movie had begun. In particular, this scheme created havoc at drive-ins all across America, but, in general, there arose a kind of carnival atmosphere around this movie, which deserved to be taken very seriously.[100] The stabbing scene in the shower was considered excessive and shocking in 1960 and it attracted negative commentary, as well as calls for its censure and possible prohibition. An unsigned review of PSYCHO published in *Esquire* in 1960 commented, "I'm against censorship on principle, but that killing in the shower makes me wonder. And not because of the nudity; I favor more nudity in film."[101] Six years later, in 1966, CBS-television canceled a planned national broadcast of the movie shortly after the kidnapping and murder of the daughter of U.S. Senator Charles Percy (R-Illinois).

At the time, however, most critical and industry attention was given to the film's unusual dramatic elements—such as the lead actress being murdered before the film was half over—rather than to the powerful new visual aesthetic that was created in the shower scene. The story line of PSYCHO was seen as subversive of the values that had been traditionally advanced in classic Hollywood movies, because the central idea of the film was that horror could come from the heart of an American family and could be perpetrated by a superficially harmless and likable character such as Norman Bates (Anthony Perkins).[102]

Nonetheless, PSYCHO was truly important aesthetically because the shower scene was shot and then edited so as to give the sequence a ragged edge that, in hindsight, could be assessed as "Stravinsky-like" in its impact on the modern American cinema.[103] In its thrusting and jabbing power, the sequence was for the American feature film in 1960 what the 1913 premiere of Igor Stravinsky's *Rite of Spring* had been for modern music and dance. Although there were no riots outside the cinemas in 1960, as there had been in 1913 outside the theater in Paris where *The Rite of Spring* premiered, PSYCHO nonetheless marked the arrival of what was to become the dominant motion-picture aesthetic of the late twentieth century. This aesthetic, honed and polished subsequently by Hollywood, constituted a cinema of sensation that emerged and grew up separately from the previously dominant "cinema of sentiment" that had characterized classic Hollywood production.

Three years after the release of PSYCHO, Hitchcock's THE BIRDS (1963) was innovative in its indulgence of the new, visceral, visual aesthetic the director had established with the shower sequence in 1960. In many ways, Hitchcock actually was experimenting more radically with sensation and form in this later movie, which is perhaps why it is artistically neither as successful, nor satisfying as PSYCHO. Complaints abounded in 1963 about THE BIRDS departing from the traditionally safe moorings of a strong story and well-drawn characters, but the dialectic that was emerging in THE BIRDS was actually rooted deeply in the tension between the aesthetics and pace of a conventional drama that was abruptly punctuated at several instances by the sudden intrusion of birds attacking humans. As a whole, THE BIRDS followed a slow pace with a considerable

Janet Leigh, intensely frightened, in PSYCHO. *Later, she would relax with a nice shower.*

number of long takes and an abundance of conventional, reverse-angle editing dominating its dramatic sequences. What was really going on in the film, however, is best understood as the awkward presence of two distinct aesthetics, uneasily juxtaposed to one another.

The conventions of a cinema of sentiment that relies on storyline and character clash directly in THE BIRDS in those several sequences of the movie that appeal solely to the viewer's appetite for sensation and visual effects. At the time, the reviewer for *Variety* pilloried the story line of THE BIRDS: "Beneath all of this elaborate featherbedlam, it's a Hitchcock-and-bull story that's essentially a fowl ball," but acknowledged the effects: "still it's an experience in a theatre [where] a kind of chemistry runs through an audience."[104] Similarly, an unsigned review in *Film Daily* complained about the "needless slowness and obviousness" of Evan Hunter's screenplay, but concluded that the movie was still carried to admirable and significant heights by "its compelling and unforgettable visuals."[105] Pauline Kael lambasted THE BIRDS as "pointless and incomprehensible."[106]

THE BIRDS marked the emerging attempt to redesign the fundamental structure of a feature film by distinguishing those parts of a movie that are dialogue-based and conventionally dramatic from other parts that consist of sensational visual action and effects. The film attempted, with only partial success, to reintegrate these disparate elements into an artistic whole. The real importance of this film in the history of the American cinema, however, was where it pointed, and not how fully it achieved its own goals when it was released and exhibited.

"Bond, James Bond"

Toward the end of 1961, two Hollywood partners, Albert "Cubby" Broccoli and Harry Saltzman, signed an agreement with United Artists to produce seven features that would be distributed by the studio. As specified in this deal, each of the films was to be set in an exotic locale with action and special effects that would make them desirable for theatrical showings, but not necessarily for the television market. The movies were to be based on a series of novels by Ian Fleming about an urbane British spy named James Bond.[107]

Well into the mid 1950s, American movies were still commonly described as studio films (denoting a Paramount style, an MGM musical, etc.), although innovations might occur from the visionary daring of auteurist directors (like Hitchcock) increasingly from the late 1950s onward. The James Bond series of films were an instance in which a new aesthetic was being crafted largely by the initiatives and vision of Broccoli and Saltzman. Along with their production staff, they fashioned a formula that included exotic locales, a new "Bond woman" to partner with James romantically in each new film, fantastic gadgetry that provided what the industry called "Bondian effects," and plot "bumps," as

Producers' formula I, James Bond style: exotic locales, visual effects, and superb art direction in THUNDERBALL *(1965).*

Producers' formula II, James Bond style: Beguiling sexuality (in GOLDFINGER, 1964).

Broccoli called them, that held together the self-contained action sequences that would supplant a traditional narrative structure in these movies.[108]

DR. NO (1962), the first of the Bond movies, starred Sean Connery (as Bond) and Ursula Andress, and immediately established the series as a glossy, high-tech blend of action, sex, and wit. FROM RUSSIA WITH LOVE (1963 and, like the first, directed by Terrance Young), the second film in the Bond series, was for many critics the best of the series during the 1960s—disarmingly witty and complex. The plot focuses on an international organization, SPECTRE, that conspires through the machinations of a grand chess master to harm cold war relations. FROM RUSSIA WITH LOVE manages to take a harsh look at conventions of the cold war mentality while portraying stunning visual vignettes, as in the cat-and-mouse game aboard the Orient Express.

At the same time, some of the Bond movies could be childishly naughty. GOLD-FINGER (1964, Guy Hamilton) bore a title destined to provoke adolescent jokes about wealthy gynecologists and left a legacy at which even the veteran ABC-television journalist and news commentator, Sam Donaldson, was still marveling thirty years later: "You gotta love any movie where the heroine is named Pussy Galore."[109] Number four in the series, THUNDERBALL (1965, Terrance Young), featured stunning underwater photography but was primarily distinguished by spectacular hardware that could produce special effects which seemed calculated primarily to awe teenage boys in the audience. Increasingly, such hardware would come to dominate the series.[110]

Through the 1960s, the Bond movies offered Hollywood a model for a slick entertainment package that deftly skirted what was left of Hollywood's disintegrating

Production Code. The Bond movies were all labeled "British productions," even though they were funded entirely from American sources and were quintessentially anchored in mainstream Hollywood culture. Nonetheless, they never entirely betrayed their British pedigree. Each of them had tongue-in-cheek humor, unique and clever gadgets, and international locales that always appeared genuinely sophisticated.[111] The Bond movies were ingenious hybrids of an increasingly internationalized popular culture industry where, in this instance, British production talent blended neatly with American producing and marketing skills. In essence, the Bond movies offered to Hollywood a model for a phenomenon of the screen basically unknown before the late 1960s but increasingly prominent in Hollywood after the late 1970s—the action blockbuster.[112] With their melange of high production values, sex, and action, and the parody of popular culture while at the same time advancing it, the highly successful Bond movies pointed to a more lasting vehicle for satisfying adolescent and young adult tastes than many of the similarly aimed self-conscious movies of the late 1960s.

The Cinema of Sensation Advanced

BULLITT   Along with two previous movies discussed as landmark films, BONNIE AND CLYDE (1967) and THE WILD BUNCH (1969), a third film helped define the aesthetics of the cinema of sensation established so forcefully in the American feature film. A thriller set in San Francisco, BULLITT (1968) had a plot that was neither more complicated nor more challenging than any conventional detective film. The title character, an idiosyncratic police lieutenant played by Steve McQueen, is enlisted through the San Francisco police department by a politician to be responsible for the safety of a gangster who has turned police witness and is hiding in town. BULLITT truly announces itself as a movie of sensation just minutes after the preliminaries are over, when a door is kicked open, shots are fired, a policeman is hit, and the informant blasted clean off his bed and into the wall behind him.[113] The importance of this scene in the plot is transcended entirely by the careful attention to cinematographic detail and to the soundtrack. Those effects come alive in the renowned automobile chase through the hilly streets of the city. At the time the film premiered, Richard Schickel wrote in *Life* magazine, "BULLITT is not, I think, a sensational movie—not in the colloquial usage of that term. But it is a movie of sensations. By this I mean that the director, Peter Yates, has aimed at making as palpable as possible those sensuous aspects of the physical world of a San Francisco cop working on a dangerous case."[114] More than two decades after the film's premiere, James Destro offered this altogether praiseful assessment of its place in the American cinema: "Director Peter Yates crafted a visual style in the late 1960s that is still being used in the 1980s."[115]

2001: A SPACE ODYSSEY   The appearance of Stanley Kubrick's 2001: A SPACE ODYSSEY (1968) marked yet another major movie of the 1960s funded and distributed by Hollywood (MGM) but filmed in Great Britain and released as a British production.[116] Like several other landmark films of the decade, it displeased many established film critics because its story and its characters did not measure up to their expectations of classic Hollywood narrative standards. Stanley Kauffmann condemned "Kubrick's feeble sense of narrative," claiming the film "even dulls our interest in [its] technical ingenuity."[117] The review in *Variety* faulted the film for "lacking dramatic appeal" and "conveying suspense only after the half-way mark."[118] The *Hollywood Reporter* complained that the movie's dialogue was minimal (it amounts to no more than forty minutes of the film's 140-minute running time).[119] Indeed, in what was written about the movie in newspapers and magazines across the country during 1968, it became evident that what was called the "elliptical narrative" of 2001 either bewildered or frustrated most movie critics.[120] Nonetheless, just like several other movies of the 1960s that were subject to similar negative commentary from the older generation of establishment critics, 2001 was considered spectacular by delighted audiences of late adolescents and young adults.[121]

Its departure from the traditions of highly structured narrative and dialogue did not harm its popularity. As film historian Ethan Mordden wrote, "Not everyone attended 2001, but just about everyone under thirty did, solemnizing the development of a youthful audience as the decisive element in a [Hollywood] film's success."[122] Called in and dispatched by the *New York Times* in an apparent effort to fathom how the critical community could be missing whatever these audiences of young people were digging in 2001, John Russell Taylor of the *London Times* concluded that young males were able to enjoy the "mechanical side" of the film and could embrace the entire movie as "a succession of thrilling appearances." Taylor ventured the opinion that this "new" audience was drawn to this kind of movie because they were so used to a cultural diet heavy on television and the comic strips.[123]

Finally, in a highly charged article published in an alternative newspaper in Los Angeles, Gene Youngblood, one of the era's leading proponents of experimentation in the cinema, articulated the notion that what he labeled "expanded cinema" had entered mainstream motion pictures with 2001.[124] A slew of negative reviews in 1968 repeatedly faulted 2001 for its lack of plot and weak characterization, but in hindsight at least one critic labeled it "the most influential movie" released between 1960 and the close of the twentieth century![125] Even at the time of its release, French New Wave director Jean-Luc Godard enthused over 2001, proclaiming that its very lack of a strong story in the conventional sense liberated the film entirely from formulaic scripting and "melodramatic machinations" of classic Hollywood.[126] If in 1968 2001: A SPACE ODYSSEY proved to be a "head-scratcher" for older audiences, it registered as a "mind-blower" for legions

One of the long scenes without dialogue in Stanley Kubrick's 2001: A SPACE ODYSSEY (1968). Dialogue occurs in less than half the running time of this film.

of younger moviegoers. The industry trade journal *Film Daily* found absolutely nothing "old style" in it,[127] and *Variety* described its real devotees as "quasi-hippies," bemoaning only the fact that this audience could not be counted on to buy tickets in advance for a movie, which had been a long-standing promotional ploy for any "roadshow" feature.[128]

Kubrick had been able to convince MGM to more than double the planned $4.5 million budget for 2001 to over $10 million.[129] Since 2001: A SPACE ODYSSEY was shot on Super Panavison 70mm, the use of the traditional methods of either blue-screen or of traveling matte techniques could not be employed for its special effects. Instead, Kubrick often placed actors in front of a highly reflective screen, with both the camera that is filming them and the projector that is creating imagery behind them sharing a similar position and the same viewpoint. The result was a brightened and highlighted live-action foreground set against an equally bright background.[130] Front projection had been pioneered only the year before in Roger Vadim's BARBARELLA, which had been filmed in Rome, Italy, at the Cinecittà studios.[131]

Visual effects were central to 2001, although at least one critic ventured the opinion that a substantial portion of the young people in the audience was less interested in the movie's masterful cinematography and front projection than in what drugs to ingest before going to see it. Moreover, the movie itself could be said to promote this spectatorial position, given that the character Dave's space journey during the last thirty minutes is blended by Kubrick into the abstract psychedelic and surrealistic imagery of the "Stargate Corridor" sequence that managed to simultaneously "blow away the pot-smoking audiences and make special effects history."[132] Nonetheless, the movie still was perceived in 1968 as being just abstract and avant-garde enough to prevent mainstream Hollywood producers from copying it immediately.[133]

The Cinema of Sensation: A Summary

By the end of the 1960s, the appeal through powerful visuals and the accelerated editing of them created a visceral aesthetic in the American feature film that found special resonance with much of the new, younger audience for theatrical movies. The demographic data available to the motion-picture industry, moreover, indicated that adolescent and young adult moviegoers did not necessarily have to appreciate such movies on the big screen. As a commercial calculation, it was extremely important for the industry to discover that these movies of sensation held their appeal on the small television screen as well. Indeed, the highest rated motion picture shown on American television during the entire decade of the 1960s was ABC's national telecast of FANTASTIC VOYAGE (1966, Richard Fleischer) on October 12, 1969.[134] The "New American Cinema" that was emerging by the end of the 1960s was based to large extent on a changing movie aesthetic that appealed to the senses primarily at the cost of classic character development and dramatic story. This cinema of sensation, moreover, was being added onto the traditional Hollywood repertoire of sentiment and spectacle, not replacing them.

The landmark movies and the cinema of sensation of the 1960s pointed most clearly toward expanding and readjusting the story formulas that had prevailed in the classic Hollywood cinema, rather than replacing them. Increasingly, characters in movies of the late 1960s inhabited fictional worlds that were more problematic and fraught with greater ambiguity than those worlds of Hollywood's more traditional heroes and heroines. Movies became faster-paced and more visually graphic (in every sense of the word). Most importantly, the audience for theatrical movies in the United States now consisted overwhelmingly of people under thirty, a demographic fact that increasingly defined the global audience for movies as well. The takeover of the Hollywood studios by large business conglomerates in the late 1960s, however, did not necessarily determine specific aesthetic choices for the industry's future. Nor was a blockbuster mentality established in Hollywood's boardrooms until more than a decade after those takeovers occurred. Indeed, at the end of the 1960s and the beginning of the 1970s, a surprising number of young directorial talents were nurtured in Hollywood and their relatively risky productions were supported.

Antiheroes, special effects, a growing cinema of sensation, outsider stories played in tawdry milieus, increasing mixtures of highly romantic and highly cynical portrayals in the same movie, and a more pessimistic thematic bent in feature films were all legacies of the 1960s. They were all clearly established by the end of the decade, but nowhere was the future of the American feature film clearly predetermined when the 1960s ended. At the beginning of the 1970s, the American feature film was entering a rich era of "a hundred flowers": youth movie formulas would be pursued; first-time directors would be given an opportunity to bring their auteurist visions to the screen; and old formulas were crafted to new demographics and sometimes reformulated to fit what appeared to be a new sociology, as with the "Blaxploitation" movies. Beyond all of this, Hollywood in the early seventies would navigate the turbulent waters of economic crisis, eventually emerging with a new range of creative possibilities, fundamentally with the aesthetic of a cinema of sensation well established in the way mainstream production was now conceived.

12

The Nonfiction Film

Richard M. Barsam

Historical, Theoretical, and Technological Origins

The American nonfiction film of the 1960s has both traditional and experimental roots.[1] Although 1960s' filmmakers continued to produce the traditional documentary film, it was in the development of direct cinema, an experimental departure from these roots, that the nonfiction film genre was revitalized. What, in the 1930s, John Grierson called "the documentary idea," namely the use of film for reality-based didactic purposes, yielded in the 1960s to direct cinema and the idea of a new cinematic realism. This realism was grounded in the exploration and use of film for its own sake. The new approach evolved more from aesthetic than social, political, or moral concerns, which constituted an astonishing phenomenon considering the documentary film tradition and the social transformation outside cinema that was taking shape during the decade.

The rebirth of the American nonfiction film in the 1960s was brought about by various factors: the Anglo-American nonfiction film tradition; the influences and achievements of nonfiction filmmaking in the post–World War II years; the beginnings of a stronger and more independent system of nonfiction film production and distribution; the emergence of television as a medium with serious potential for exhibition of nonfiction film; the experiments in the United States and abroad with cinematic forms seeking a free, direct expression of the realist impulse; and the technological developments that produced lightweight, mobile equipment.

Cinema became a leading art form during the 1960s in the United States and elsewhere, reflecting a political and aesthetic revolution and appealing to the sensibilities of a youthful generation. This generation understood, perhaps better than any before it (and certainly better than any previous American generation) the language and effect of cinema. The spirit of the new waves that helped to fashion a fresh European narrative film also helped to shape the contours of a new nonfiction film.

However, the American nonfiction film movement as a whole was neither radical nor even highly politicized. While social struggles had engaged the radical filmmakers of the 1930s, the filmmakers of the 1960s, most of whose values were material rather than social, shirked the social responsibility that had traditionally constituted the Griersonian ideal.[2] That ideal constituted a cinema with the sole purpose of advancing specific social and political ideologies. Nor was nonfiction film likely to reflect any unified social policy, for the history of the American nonfiction film outside the television networks has traditionally been the history of individual efforts, rather than, as in England, of group endeavors.[3] Thus, in their pursuit of a film ideal, American nonfiction filmmakers of the 1960s developed direct cinema, a new cinematic approach to recording and revealing what they saw and heard.

THE ORIGINS OF DIRECT CINEMA

Direct cinema, which was cinematically if not politically radical, represented both a break with the American tradition and a unification of the American with the various European nonfiction film traditions. The result was a rekindling of the power and a rebirth of the potential of the nonfiction film medium. While direct cinema did not replace entirely the other nonfiction styles, it was the most important achievement of the American nonfiction film during the 1960s. Direct cinema reaffirmed two theoretical aspects of the nonfiction film: that the genre contained within itself limitless possibilities for cinematic expression, and that all good nonfiction films take their shape from their subject matter. It now seems inevitable that such a departure from the norm would appear in the turbulent 1960s.

The origins of direct cinema are found in its avant-garde nature, in the realist impulse, in worldwide movements toward a new cinematic realism, and in the new developments in motion-picture technology. Direct cinema, distinctly American in its striving for a wholly native language of expression, represented a break with the rigid formulae and the pedantry of approaches that characterized the American nonfiction film tradition until that point. It was a catalyst in freeing American nonfiction filmmakers from the Griersonian mode, in sparking a resurgence of creativity in a genre that had become increasingly static, and in helping to satisfy what André Bazin called "our obsession with realism."[4] In responding to the realist impulse that had always been at the heart of their tradition, American nonfiction filmmakers continued to work as independent artists; as before, the American government (as patron) was largely unsympathetic to their efforts, and the large public audience routinely apathetic about their achievements.

DIRECT CINEMA AS AVANT-GARDE

The emergence of direct cinema in the late 1950s resulted in a cinematic form that literally and formally speaks for itself.[5] Like most avant-garde movements, its achievement was to awaken filmmakers and audiences alike to a new way of recording and revealing reality.[6] Direct cinema comprised a fairly cohesive group of filmmakers who shared goals, who had a clear sense of the challenges they were posing to the more dominant and conventional forms of the nonfiction film, and who produced a significant body of films. They undertook to explore reality, to record it as directly and as accurately as possible, to avoid conventional cinematic control of pro-filmic and filmic reality, and to strive for objectivity by avoiding preconception in shooting or manipulation in editing.[7]

In theory and achievement the most realistic cinema yet created, direct cinema gave new dimensions to what the French critic André Bazin labeled the "myth of total cinema." Direct cinema is both mirror and prism, as well as being both realistic and formalist, hence consisting of the improbable fusion of two modes of cinema that were, before its appearance, generally thought to be mutually exclusive. The development of direct cinema confirmed what film theorists had claimed all along: that cinema does not produce reality, but rather a model of reality. In striving for this cinematic form, the filmmaker's goal is to make something seamlessly convincing, not factually perfect. The filmmaker does not exercise total Griersonian control over all aspects to make a point, but instead relinquishes "some measure of control over some aspects of the filmmaking process and by doing so implicitly claims some degree of 'truthfulness' or 'believability' for that film."[8] Theorists will continue to inquire whether, in eschewing metaphor and pattern, these films can replace actual explorations of human feeling and experience and deserve to be called "true" or "accurate." In the beginning, realism was sought in a film's content; however, direct cinema, developing out of the factual and the formalist traditions, seeks realism in both form and content.

THE REALIST IMPULSE

The realist impulse, the desire to record life as it is, provides the roots for the major theories, production practices, and achievements of the American nonfiction film.[9] Humanity, humanism, and human concerns remain central to the history of nonfiction film, while ideologies of theory and interpretation come and go.[10] Even setting aside the social responsibility that John Grierson held to be cinema's principal mission, many films in the nonfiction film tradition are considered as "expert witnesses" to life. From the very beginning, realism was sought in a film's content; but, direct cinema, developing out of the factual and the formalist traditions, goes further in seeking realism in both form and content.

The factual film was born with Auguste and Louis Lumière and their short, unedited glimpses of actual life. Other early filmmakers—among them Burton Holmes, Cherry Kearton, Herbert Ponting, Emery and Ellsworth Kolb, Martin Johnson, and Lowell Thomas—were explorers interested chiefly in shooting footage of actual events or expeditions to exotic locales.[11] The most famous of these early documentarists was Robert Flaherty, an explorer and an artist, who, in NANOOK OF THE NORTH (1922) and MOANA: A ROMANCE OF THE GOLDEN AGE (1926), imposed fictional narrative on both factual and staged footage in a personal, poetic approach that holds a unique place in nonfiction film history.[12]

For nonfiction theorists and filmmakers alike, a primary emphasis has been on the development of cinematic realism out of that ineluctable area in which form and content coalesce. It is this dual, if not always balanced, concern with form and content, with what people see and how they see it, that helps to distinguish nonfiction film (and specifically direct cinema) from the more familiar fiction film. Nonfiction film is the art of representation, the art of presenting actual physical reality in a form that strives creatively to record and interpret the world and to be faithful to actuality without substantially altering the filmmaker's perceptions of it.

Direct cinema reaffirmed a classical principle of aesthetics, expressed in this double relation: 1) that the parts of the work of art are in keeping with each other and with the whole; and 2) that the alteration of any part will inevitably bring with it the alteration of the whole. These dual forces challenged filmmakers to use creative imagination in making up their own rules according to the nature of the subject being filmed. Filmmakers could discover their topic within the possibilities proposed by the medium, especially in the relationship of shooting to editing and in the freedom to construct a film that becomes their model of reality. What Susan Sontag observes about still photography also applies to cinematography: "Instead of just recording reality, photographs have become the norm for the way things appear to us, thereby changing the very idea of reality, and of realism."[13]

Direct cinema is self-reflexive cinema, cinema about the nature and process of cinema itself, calling the attention of the serious viewer to its form and language, as well as to the process of its making. The unity produced by this highly organic relationship results in a paradox: a unification of disparate, contrary, even opposing elements—what Samuel Taylor Coleridge defined as "unity in multiplicity."

European and American Backgrounds

The theoretical and practical origins of direct cinema are firmly rooted in the first page of nonfiction film history. Auguste and Louis Lumière called their short films *actualités*. To them, art was not an imitation of reality, but a direct, non-narrative record of actual people doing actual things. The essential triumph of the Lumière films and the secret of their simple beauty is what the critic, Dai Vaughan, calls their "harnessing of spontaneity."[14] After the Lumières, the factual film of both ordinary and extraordinary events grew in the hands of Thomas A. Edison and others, and movie audiences responded enthusiastically to films of war, travel, and exploration.[15]

But it was the Russian Dziga Vertov who laid the foundations for direct cinema. He used the term *kino-pravda* (film truth) to describe his approach:

> *Cinéma verité* is by Ciné-Eye and for Ciné-Eye but with the truth of its resources and possibilities. It is photographing people without make-up from angles that take them unaware, and getting them with the camera-eye at a moment when they are not acting and letting the camera strip their thoughts bare.[16]

Vertov was obsessed with the ability of his "film-eye" to show the truth on the screen through the direct and uncontrolled recording of life itself. Erik Barnouw observes of Vertov that "the emphasis—harking back to Lumière—was on action caught on the run, from any revealing vantage."[17] Vertov's masterpiece, The Man with the Movie Camera (1929), deliberately artificial in its conception, kaleidoscopic in its coverage, self-reflexive in its effect, and, in Barnouw's words, "dazzling in its ambiguity," suggests within these antinomies the nature of direct cinema. He is the father of direct cinema and the prophet of its potentialities.[18]

The American Robert Flaherty, like Vertov, wanted to capture reality as he saw it, trusting his own camera work completely. He eschewed *mise-en-scène* for what James Monaco aptly calls *trouve-en-scène*.[19] Unlike Vertov, he explored life, seeking a reality that also conformed to his vision. Flaherty's influence on direct cinema can be seen in his intuitive approach to the subjects he filmed; his reliance, in the later work, on the relationship between shooting and editing footage (and on editors other than himself)[20]; his influence on such direct cinema pioneers as Richard Leacock, his assistant cinematographer on Flaherty's last film, Louisiana Story (1948)[21]; and in his creation of a highly personal cinema concerned with human life.[22]

The next significant influences on direct cinema occurred in the postwar film movements of Italy, Britain, and France. Together, these constitute "the first efforts that were made to create a cinema that was not costly, that came closer to reality, and that was free

from slavery to technique."[23] Italian neo-realism developed naturally from the long history of realism in the Italian cinema, including the documentary films of the fascist
period.[24] In the late 1950s, the British filmmakers Lindsay Anderson, Karel Reisz, and
Tony Richardson formed the Free Cinema Group.[25] Following Vertov and the Italian
neo-realists, they turned their cameras on ordinary people and everyday life, and thus
had a small, but important influence on direct cinema.[26] In France, a similar striving for
a new cinematic realism in the nonfiction film was found in the work of Georges
Rouquier, Georges Franju, Jean Gremillon, Roger Leenhardt, Alain Resnais, Chris
Marker, Edgar Morin, Agnes Varda, and Jean Rouch, whose pioneering work had an
enormous influence on the development of cinéma verité.[27]

THE TECHNOLOGICAL ORIGINS OF DIRECT CINEMA

Once again in the history of cinema, technological developments preceded aesthetic
impulses. As Stephen Mamber observed, direct cinema "indicates a position the filmmaker takes in regard to the world he films."[28] Lightweight, portable equipment makes
possible the achievement of that position, which is both physical and ontological.[29]
Although direct cinema acknowledges the antipodal nature of our organic world, as well
as our perception of it, it remains as a fundamental simulation of reality and is thus
dependent on its technological tools for this achievement. Like all cinema, direct cinema fools the eye. The use of a specific choice of lens can give the illusion of spatial
depth. The use of straight editing respects the forward progression of time. The use of
associational cutting (in such devices as flashbacks and flash-forwards) evokes the mind's
ability to make inferences. The use of synchronous sound confirms other perceptions.

Technological developments made during World War II, in Hollywood and elsewhere, had a major influence on the "look" of direct cinema. The traditional "look" of
Hollywood films relied on 35mm cameras and fine grain film stock, as well as the
achievement of high studio production values.[30] The most famous American nonfiction
films had what James Monaco calls a "quasi-fictional, highly 'worked' quality."[31] During
World War II, however, the production of training, incentive, and combat films provided
a new use for lightweight, compact, durable 16mm cameras with improved lenses and
standardized, interchangeable parts. Unlike the Hollywood, "highly worked" image,
these cameras generally produced a black-and-white image that was sometimes shaky or
blurred as a result of handheld cinematography. The audience, however, perceived a
form of authenticity in these less-than-perfect cinematographic images. Most importantly, the camera was freed from the tripod. Although direct cinema rarely used the
handheld camera (preferring instead the shoulder-mounted camera), the widespread
perception of footage shot by portable cameras as real and believable was considerably
strengthened as television (also black and white at that time) emerged to accompany and
then mostly to replace the other black-and-white media (newsreels and newspaper photographs) as this country's principal source of visual news reporting in the 1950s.
General familiarity with these developments "might well have helped audiences to
accept similar qualities of verité style twenty years later, as well as giving verité films an
air of authenticity Hollywood films could not share."[32]

Advances in sound recording, also begun during World War II, were improved still
further in the mid 1950s with the development of a magnetic tape recorder capable of
synchronous sound, by around 1960, with the substitution in tape recorders of transistors for vacuum tubes. As Robert Allen observed, "the difficulties in shooting synchro-

nous sound on location stand out clearly in both neo-realist and traditional documentary films."[33] The use of transistors reduced the weight of the tape recorder from several hundred pounds to only twenty. The portable tape recorder offered the freedom to record actual synchronous sound; multi-track tape mixing equipment gave sound editors greater control over their material. Furthermore, as Monaco observes, "crystal synchronization provided the final necessary flexible link in this system, allowing cameraman and sound recordist to work independently, unhampered by the umbilical cord that used to unite recorder and camera."[34]

The "ideal" film became a possibility. It could be made anywhere, not just in the controlled studio environment; would require no more than available light, and thus avoid the theatrical look of much studio lighting; would have the option to record reality either in color or in "journalistic" black and white; and would record sound as it occurred in actuality, not as it was recreated in the studio. The early direct cinema pioneers preferred a lightweight, shoulder-mounted 16mm camera such as the Auricon, but also used the Arriflex or French Eclair-NPR, and employed a compact, lightweight sound recorder using 1/4" tape (usually a Nagra, Nagra Neo-Pilot, or Stellavox). To maintain sync with the camera, they used several devices, including a tiny radio transmitter and a method developed by Drew and Leacock that relied on a Bulova Accutron electronic watch.[35]

DIRECT CINEMA AND CINÉMA VERITÉ: A COMPARISON AND CONTRAST

American direct cinema emerged as a revolutionary development, with roots in a symbiotic combination of aesthetic influences, technological developments, and audience interests. Direct cinema is not only different from cinéma verité, but the term has replaced the more ambiguous cinéma verité in designating the synchronous recording of image and sound. It is therefore essential to an understanding of direct cinema—what it is and what it is not—to understand how it is similar to, and just how much it differs from, cinéma verité.

Cinéma verité, the principal French nonfiction mode of the 1960s and 1970s, represents an application of New Wave cinematography practices to real events rather than staged ones. In a manner characteristic of other French innovation in cinema, it evolved through an homage to cinema history. It fused Georges Méliès' adaptation of magical tricks to the cinema and the Lumières' fidelity to the cinematographic recording of actuality. To this paradoxical foundation, it added the conceptions of the camera as a catalyst; the filmmaker as an active participant behind and sometimes in front of the camera; the elimination of devices from fictional cinema; the shooting and recording of real events rather than staged ones; and a visual style that incorporated informality and spontaneity into its "look," including such unconventional "mistakes" as poor lighting and the optically violent movement of the camera, which was frequently handheld.[36] Overall, cinéma verité brought about a redefinition of film aesthetics.[37] In turn, this led to the development of a new self-reflexive cinema.[38]

The achievements of cinéma verité created audience and critical reactions so diverse that the term cinéma verité was applied to many innovative, experimental, or new developments in cinema after 1950, even if they had nothing in common with it.[39] Moreover, it was applied pejoratively to many cinematic techniques, like direct cinema, whose fresh or startling qualities disturbed the status quo.

The origins of cinéma verité, which Erik Barnouw recognized as a "catalyst cinema,"[40] included the divergent achievements of many filmmakers, including two Canadians,

Pierre Perrault and Wolf Koenig,[41] and three Frenchmen, Chris Marker, Mario Ruspoli, and Jacques Rozier.[42] Of the pioneers, the best known and perhaps most important is Jean Rouch, although his work is ancillary to the mainstream development of cinéma verité.[43] His films, which he labels as "ethnographic fiction," represent a genre of their own, even as they are relevant to this discussion of direct cinema.[44]

Rouch's influence is seen most clearly in CHRONICLE OF A SUMMER (CHRONIQUE D'UN ETÉ, 1961), co-produced with sociologist Edgar Morin and photographed by Michel Brault, who later participated in the development of cinéma direct, a Canadian form of cinéma verité. A feature-length film that consists mainly of interviews with Parisians (who were asked, "are you happy," and who answered with unpredictable and highly personal answers), it was subtitled *"une experience de cinéma verité,"* apparently in homage to Vertov.[45] With others who have experimented with the lightweight equipment and the direct approach, Rouch discovered the power of the camera to provoke people to behavior that was not typical of their everyday lives, and he saw in cinéma verité a means of liberating people from their limited selves.[46]

At the heart of the differences between cinéma verité and direct cinema is the ancient question of the "truth" of a work of art, its fidelity to reality. But, as Peter Graham wrote, the idea that either form achieves some absolute truth "is only a monumental red herring."[47] Both cinéma verité and direct cinema are ways of seeing, of understanding, and of conveying the filmmaker's perception of the world. Each filmmaker defines the truth according to his or her own convictions, sensibility, and experiences, within a cultural context. In practical terms, more often than not the "truth" is the truth that occurs to filmmakers during the moments of observing, shooting, and editing: not the truth, but a filmmaker's truth.[48]

Allied to the question of film truth is that of the filmmaker's approach. Erik Barnouw neatly summarizes the complex matter:

> The direct cinema documentarist took his camera to a situation of tension and waited hopefully for a crisis; the Rouch version of cinéma verité tried to precipitate one. The direct cinema artist aspired to invisibility; the Rouch cinéma verité artist was often an avowed participant. The direct cinema artist played the role of uninvolved bystander; the cinéma verité artist espoused that of provocateur.
>
> Direct cinema found its truth in events available to the camera. Cinéma verité was committed to a paradox: that artificial circumstances could bring hidden truth to the surface.[49]

Both approaches raise issues, such as the filmmaker's relationship to the material, the role of the camera, and the nature of the editing to be done. Theory may be contradicted by actual practice, however, for there are profound implications in the deceptively simple acts of picking up the camera at a particular time, of selecting and framing a shot, of starting to shoot—all involving the artist's judgement, the subjective selection and arrangement of details. The theoretical positions taken by many direct cinema and cinéma verité filmmakers are so dominated by conflicting notions of truth and conceptions of the medium that these positions constitute less a theory than a searching for one. There are, however, many points on which they agree, and these represent for us a useful, if incomplete touchstone.

Unlike the realist cinema advocated by the German critic and scholar Siegfried Kracauer,[50] which carries with it a comparative neglect of editing, cinéma verité and direct cinema are products which fuse fluid, informal cinematography and formalist editing. While editing is important to cinéma verité, it is the most important single element in direct cinema. Most likely, the direct cinema filmmaker both shoots and edits (as Frederick Wiseman so often does), or works closely in a highly collaborative arrangement (as in the example of Albert and David Maysles and their editors). In direct cinema it is the film editor—more clearly than the film editor of any other kind of cinema—who produces a model of reality. Charlotte Zwerin, editor of the Maysles' SALESMAN (1969) commented on the division of responsibilities between persons doing the shooting and those doing the editing:

> One of the really important contributions of an editor in a *verité* film arises from the fact that he only sees what is on the screen. The cameraman will tell you that a great deal of what he gets in shooting depends on his relationship to the subject, but whatever is happening between himself and the person he's shooting distorts the event for the cameraman; he can't see the scene in perspective. But the editor has the advantage of knowing that something either is or is not conveyed on the screen. His immediate reaction isn't blunted by any personal knowledge.[51]

Ellen Hovde, editor of the later Maysles' film GREY GARDENS (1975), believes that the editing of direct cinema "takes on the same importance as the camera work—and that camera work and editing combined are directing."[52] According to editor Patricia Jaffe, "the answer lies in allowing the viewer to experience what the film maker felt in the screening room . . . . In terms of editing, this often means cutting sequences very close to the way they were shot."[53] In Frederick Wiseman's films, for example, it is the editing that results in a well-defined structure and point of view. Different as these approaches to editing may be, all these filmmakers emphasize not only the importance, but even more clearly the primacy of editing over cinematography in direct cinema.

In direct cinema, the term "filmmaker" subsumes the functions denoted by the terms "director," "cameraman," "sound recorder," and "editor." These are neither obsolete functions, nor are they discrete functions in direct cinema; rather, they are each singular operations incorporated by the more comprehensive term "filmmaker," and denoting what Richard Leacock calls the "integrated process" of this new style of filmmaking.[54] Inherent in this process, according to Bazin, is the filmmaker's awareness of, and obligation to preserve, a deeper psychological reality, as well as the audience's freedom to choose from a variety of interpretations of reality.[55] Central to direct cinema is an ambiguity of equivalents that creates the illusion of reality itself. Direct cinema is a manifestation of time (more than space) in which memory and forgetting, objectivity and subjectivity, inevitably collide.

Cinéma verité and direct cinema share objectives and characteristics. Both are committed to reality in the form of a realistic observation of society, which constitutes an "essentially ethnographic orientation."[56] Clearly, direct cinema relies on the advantages produced by the use of lightweight equipment, the close relationship between shooting and editing, and producing a cinema that simultaneously brings the filmmaker and the audience closer to the subject. Nevertheless, cinéma verité and direct cinema were still fundamentally different approaches to creating cinematic reality. Cinéma verité film-makers position themselves to be participants in, and commentators on, the action they record, whereas direct cinema filmmakers always avoid narration and (with the excep-tion of the Maysles brothers) rarely appear as personae in their films.

The mutual impact of cinéma verité and direct cinema during the 1960s redefined con-ventional realist theory and practice for many nonfiction filmmakers.[57] For a nonfiction filmmaker working in the 1960s, itself a decade shaped by chaos and liberation, direct cin-ema represented a change from tradition, an opportunity to confront directly the social forces of the time, and a challenge to bring closer together cinematic art and its relation to reality. In the United States, direct cinema at first appeared to have completely trans-formed the realist nonfiction film tradition with the freedom and clarity of its approach.

AMERICAN DIRECT CINEMA: THE FILM AS HETEROCOSM

American direct cinema was a radical solution to the problem of cinematic reality, and one that severed the nonfiction film almost entirely from its backgrounds.[58] For the film-maker, there were two key events in this development: first was the replacement of the issue of social responsibility by that of the freedom of the artist to create film as hetero-cosm; second was a clear distinction between the process and product of nonfiction film-making, embodied in the uncontrolled nature of the profilmic process (lack of planning of the event to be filmed) followed by the controlled direct cinema product. Direct cin-ema is a disguised self-revelation, in which the filmmaker (either visible or invisible in the film) both expresses and conceals himself. Acknowledging the filmmaker as an artist reaf-firms a metaphor that for centuries equated the poet with God in his unique and most characteristic function. Direct cinema exists for its own sake as a self-contained universe of visual and aural images; we cannot demand that it be true to nature, only that it be true to itself. The heterocosmic analogue—the parallel between creating film and creating the universe—illuminates the process by which direct cinema is created, more than the prod-uct of that effort. Every important process in, or product of, direct cinema is a micro-cosm, a discrete and independent universe with its laws provided by the filmmaker.[59]

Direct cinema is the result of two predominant and related factors—the desire for a new cinematic realism (similar to the "new journalism" of such writers as Truman Capote and Tom Wolfe) and the development of equipment necessary to achieving that desire. Direct cinema uses whatever cinematic properties are necessary to record real-ity and then to re-present it. Although different filmmakers take different approaches to creating direct cinema, the basic desire is the same: to capture a carefully selected aspect of reality as directly as possible; to use lightweight, portable equipment in an informal attempt to break down the barriers between the filmmaker and the subject; to capture footage while events are happening, rather than to create footage in the studio; and to provide the viewer with the feeling of being there. To this end, direct cinema is unscripted and unrehearsed (although internal evidence in many films indicates some preparation); the camera work is intimate, increasing the direct relationship between the filmmaker–subject–viewer; the sound recording is direct and synchronous, often clouded by pickup of extraneous noises that contribute to the sense of reality; and the editing tends to be continuous, rather than discontinuous, striving for a chronological, rather than dramatic, presentation of events. For the filmmaker, this practice involves a direct observation of reality; for the viewer, this results in a direct perception of reality. In direct cinema, "sounds and images are therefore caught simultaneously and restituted in the same manner at the time of projection. But 'direct' designates also and above all the simultaneity of the shooting and of the event represented."[60]

There are several principal elements that distinguish direct cinema from other approaches to the nonfiction film: rejection of the nonfiction film tradition; uncontrolled filming of real people in real situations; rejection of traditional direction and script; creation of a model of reality that includes many types of ambiguity; spontaneous sense of the viewer's "being there"; primacy of observation over narration; use of lightweight, portable equipment; live sound recording; primacy of editing over long-take cinematography; and primacy of form over content. Although these characteristics overlap to some extent, each will be considered separately.

REJECTION OF THE NONFICTION FILM TRADITION

By advocating freedom instead of formulae, pioneers of direct cinema rejected the dominating influence of the Griersonian approach to the nonfiction film that had long been dominant in English-speaking countries. They also abandoned the traditional concerns and genres of the nonfiction film, some of which had become burdensome, especially as they appeared in dull educational, process, and training films. By introducing vibrant studies of people and institutions in its images of private and public life, direct cinema makes emotional demands on audiences that would have been unthinkable in nonfiction film before the 1960s. Direct cinema does not set out to define and solve problems, but instead explores the many interpretations inherent within any subject without the need to choose one or another. In its non-traditional aims and achievements, direct cinema "knowingly reaches for unattainable goals" in realistic filmmaking.[61]

With a belief in uncontrolled forms and with the equipment that made this possible, direct cinema eliminated re-takes, staging, large production crews, interviews, narration, explanatory titles, musical scores, special lighting, costumes, makeup, and montage—anything in fact that had traditionally characterized the filmmaker's control over the material. For these, direct cinema filmmakers substituted a self-control that acknowledged their limitations in re-presenting reality, and created a self-reflexive cinema that calls attention both to their style and to the real world that lay beyond their cinematic control.

UNCONTROLLED FILMING OF REAL PEOPLE IN REAL SITUATIONS

An uncontrolled process that fosters a direct relationship of the filmmaker to real people in real situations is the essential element in direct cinema.[62] This element, in turn, requires the filmmaker to choose between focusing the film on personalities or on social issues.[63] In the American direct cinema movement of the 1960s, films were made on personalities and social issues, as well as on personalities who themselves created social issues, and social issues that created personalities. Paradoxically, the "uncontrolled" direct cinema process resulted in a film product that revealed a great deal of control and common sense.[64]

Central to this control is the choice of the subject, who must possess the "spiritual energy" that D. A. Pennebaker insists is at the heart of these films.[65] No amount of camera work will create an interesting film about a dull person.[66] The elements of real people, filmed in real situations, doing real things, raise the corollary question of the validity of using archival footage in direct cinema.[67] The use of such footage, no matter how care-

fully selected, integrated, and explained, establishes a temporal and spatial reality different from that established by the filmmaker's own footage.[68] As such, archival and
"found" footage are usually rejected because of their controlled quality.

Dziga Vertov, as noted earlier, rejected the direction and the script that are traditional
to both narrative and nonfiction cinema:

> Thoughts must be communicated from the screen directly, without being
> translated into words; words ought to be synchronized with thoughts, with-
> out any interference with the impression left by thoughts. The viewer must
> read and understand thoughts a priori, before they have been translated into
> words. This allows for the vivid interaction between the audience and the
> screen, a communication from one mind to another.[69]

Direct cinema filmmakers appear to have adopted Vertov's principle in guiding their
fundamental decision to place the film's meaning in all the cinematic properties of their
work. This principle is expressed through the selection of a complex subject for filming,
and through the structural arrangement of images into a model that re-presents rather
than re-creates that complexity. This decision rejects not only direction and script, but
also the usual patterns of problem and solution, linear development, cause and effect,
or even crisis situation and resolution. In direct cinema, meaning develops through a
process of accretion, in which the images grow and coalesce in the viewer's perception.
Often, however, the structure will superficially resemble familiar patterns used in the
traditional documentary film—the "day in the life" (SALESMAN, 1969), the labyrinth
(WELFARE, 1975), or the "job well done" (RUNNING FENCE, 1978)—to offer a self-contained microcosm of American life.

Direct cinema does not elude interpretation, but rather encourages it, making the
viewer aware of form and its value. In direct cinema, both the viewer and the filmmaker
establish the meaning. Frederick Wiseman noted:

> Since the reality is complex, contradictory, and ambiguous, people with dif-
> ferent values or experience respond differently. I think that there should be
> enough room in the film for other people to find support for their views while
> understanding what mine are. Otherwise I'd be in the propaganda business.[70]

Just as direct cinema refuses to impose direction during filming, and avoids subordi-
nating people and events to filming, so, too, it refuses to impose direct control over
meaning, and asks the viewer to interpret the inherent ambiguities in any subject.

The reliance on images to carry the film's meaning raises an important connection
between uncontrolled shooting and the structures that may be imposed through editing.
As Stephen Mamber emphasizes, direct cinema is not random filming, but a difficult
and disciplined approach to filmmaking.[71] The traditionally large amounts of footage
shot in the direct cinema mode involve a major expectation that the editing process will
find or create an inherent pattern while greatly reducing this footage.

MANY TYPES OF AMBIGUITY AND A SENSE OF "BEING THERE"

Direct cinema creates a highly structured model of reality that includes many types of
ambiguity. Here, ambiguity suggests richness of meaning—"plurisignation," as Philip

Wheelwright calls it.[72] Successful direct cinema makes the viewer more aware of the ambiguity inherent in the organic nature of reality than of the mechanisms by which cinematic structure is created. The viewer is similarly confronted with a more challenging task of seeing and interpreting, of seeing cinematic unity created through the juxtaposition of opposites, and of finding meaning in those disparate, contrary, and opposing elements. Direct cinema creates images that mean something in themselves, but it is only through understanding their interaction that the viewer arrives at the interpretive possibilities of the whole film. Thus, the inherent, organic tension between these images, and between the parts of the films, reinforces their multiple implications. Serious viewers know that the more they try to interpret any one "meaning" of a direct cinema film, the more elusive it will become.

Direct cinema is an active mode, recording active people, and appealing to audiences for whom film viewing is an active—interactive, in some cases—not passive, experience. What would at first appear to be its improbable fusion of directness and intimacy results in images that create for the viewer the sense of "being there," of immediate proximity in time and space in the filmed action. The immediacy and intimacy of the cinematography and "live" sound recording bring the viewer closer to the life being filmed and reaffirm the existential nature of all cinema.

Direct cinema affords a greater opportunity for the viewer willingly to suspend disbelief than any other mode of cinema, except perhaps horror, thriller, or pornographic films that shock audiences into a close emotional relationship with the action on the screen. The direct cinema approach increases the filmmaker's mobile and flexible framing, tightens the spatial and temporal relationship between the viewer and the images, and heightens, for the serious viewer, the possibilities and pleasures of interpretation.

The success of any direct cinema film depends on the genuineness of the subject, and the fidelity of the cinematographic observation and editing to the subject. Unlike the traditional nonfiction film, which frequently has the opinionated voice of a narrator to guide the viewer's interpretation, direct cinema speaks as/for itself. Direct cinema achieves its meanings through its sight and sound images, without the intervention of a narrator (or charts, or music) to tell us what to think. The cinematographer must have the agility to move quickly in many different situations, the stamina to record long takes, and an incisive eye for selecting and framing the right shot without a director's interference. It is no coincidence that among the most important direct cinema filmmakers are also outstanding cameramen (D. A. Pennebaker, Richard Leacock, Albert Maysles, Richard Leiterman, and William Brayne). In the absence of intrusive or interpretive narrative guides, the viewer becomes more involved with the pleasures of interpretation.

Use of Lightweight, Portable Equipment

Speculation arose that the development of lightweight, portable filmmaking equipment in the 1960s would revolutionize the nonfiction film. However, this speculation mistakenly invested inert machinery with unattainable expectations, confused the artists with their equipment, and fundamentally misread the creative process. In itself, there is nothing surprising in the belief that the resolution of technical problems will release the artist for creativity, but the belief remains naive when advances in technology may proceed so fast as to almost preclude their impact on aesthetic innovations, which inevitably follows at a much slower pace.[73] New equipment in the 1960s did provide "a new mobility for filmmakers intent on capturing images rather than creating them."[74]

The advantages offered by new developments in technology raised other issues, including the crucial issue of the effect a camera has on a person or an event. According to Richard Leacock, a pioneer in the development of advanced lightweight filmmaking equipment and in the integration of that equipment in the direct cinema process, the important point is not that the camera changes things, but how much it changes them.[75] Depending on the subject, the intimacy achieved between the filmmaker and subject may influence the finished product. In portrait films made about arts and entertainment personalities (e.g., JANE, 1962; A STRAVINKSY PORTRAIT, 1964; and DON'T LOOK BACK, 1967), the performer's appearance is often affected by an awareness of the camera and consideration of how to relate to it. In films about subjects whose lives are not lived before an audience, there is generally less awareness of the camera, and somehow we tend to trust more of what we see. However, this situation is not the case with the on-screen behavior of a person who at heart wants to be an actor (e.g., Paul Brennan in SALESMAN, 1969).

Camera and microphone presence is a critical issue in the production and interpretation of direct cinema, for the matter goes beyond the artistic freedom afforded by technical mobility to questions of the artist's morality and responsibility to himself, his subject, and his audience. The new equipment establishes a relationship to the subject that presupposes at least two conditions: 1) the filmmaker's willingness to get sufficiently close to the subject to re-present it, and 2) the subject's willingness to disregard the camera and microphone (insofar as it is possible to do so for a person who is a non-professional actor). This intimacy between filmmaker and subject implies a pre-established relationship, and raises a neglected topic of great concern: the boundary between coverage and exploitation. The issues involved include the rights of artists to choose their subjects, the rights of individuals as filmed subjects to be free of humiliation, and the rights of society to know more about people (public figures and others), especially in films that cover subject matter that is either unfamiliar or stronger than what some critics believe is suitable for the screen (e.g., TITICUT FOLLIES, 1967; WARRENDALE, 1966; HOSPITAL, 1970).[76]

DIRECT SOUND RECORDING

Direct cinema means live synchronous sound recording as well as long-take cinematography. While direct cinema may seem essentially a mode in which the editing of visual images takes precedence over everything else, the aural effect is actually very often stronger than the visual. Live sound recording provides freedom from the control of an off-screen narrator telling audiences what to think, and means "that we are able to hear people saying things that no one has told them to say."[77] Directional or omni-directional microphones permit the precision of audio coverage required by the filmmaker, including normal speech patterns and the natural sounds of the environments in which the recordings are made. The synchronized sound recording in direct cinema contributes to a more complex screen image, in which both synchronous and asynchronous sounds are present; as a result of more complex editing, this fusion of synchronous and asynchronous sounds can produce a contrapuntal effect.

PRIMACY OF EDITING OVER CINEMATOGRAPHY

Editing appears to be the most important cinematic element because it creates the complex form that sets direct cinema apart from all other filmmaking. The processes of shooting and editing—most often handled by different people in a traditional nonfiction film—are often undertaken by the same people in direct cinema. Seamlessly combined, cinematography and editing take on an almost parallel importance that is the equivalent of directing. The principle prevails, as far as possible, even when the editor has not been present at the shooting (e.g., Charlotte Zwerin and SALESMAN) by which footage is given form and suggests meaning on the screen. Direct cinema editing is both organizational and creative; the successful direct cinema editor is guided by a sense of integrity to re-presenting actuality as it was filmed. D. A. Pennebaker believes that "any attempt to distort events or remarks would somehow reveal itself and subject the whole to suspicion."[78]

PRIMACY OF FORM OVER CONTENT

In the final editing, if not in the shooting, the formal properties of direct cinema take precedence over subject matter. The direct cinema artist does not seek to make a film that is faultless in its factual re-presentation, but rather one that is consistent in both its re-presentation and persuasiveness. Nevertheless, while this strategy may result in a seamless "model of reality," it is not mistaken for reality itself. In direct cinema, form and subject are defined simultaneously: they are inextricably tangled, so much more than in the other approaches that they are probably the same thing. If they are different, the film's subject is its starting point, but not its destination—a direct cinema filmmaker cannot freely redispose the elements of his subject matter, as, say, a painter can, to construct a film that fits whatever conception he may have of the subject. Instead, he discovers his subject within the possibilities inherent in his medium (e.g., PRIMARY). If the broad scope of the subject refuses to re-compose itself economically within the limitations of the frame and other variables of a particular production, the filmmaker is free to contrive a different but compatible subject, composed of those elements necessary to create the model of reality he seeks (e.g., SALESMAN).

Major Direct Cinema Filmmakers and Films

The development of American direct cinema during the 1960s took place in five overlapping and interacting stages, each dominated by distinct personalities and approaches: first, Robert Drew and his associates; second, Richard Leacock; third, D. A. Pennebaker; fourth, Albert and David Maysles; and, fifth, Frederick Wiseman. Their belief in the spontaneous, uncontrolled cinematic recording of important events, issues, and personalities established an approach so strong that it dominated the further development of the form.[79] The pioneering work of all these filmmakers combined the unique properties of two mass communications media—journalism and the traditional documentary film—to develop a third, direct cinema.[80]

DREW ASSOCIATES   Robert Drew brought to nonfiction filmmaking a knowledge of journalism and still photography from ten years at *Life* magazine, and an awareness of the deficiencies of the traditional documentary film. He hoped to infuse the weakness of the latter with the excitement and directness of the former. With others experimenting with the nonfiction form during the post–World War II period, Drew astutely observed that the Griersonian documentary was little more than an illustrated lecture.[81] Drew believed that he and others could find ways to make it less one-sided, and more cognizant of reality. Drew was convinced that the future of the nonfiction genre lay in television, not in independent production. Hindsight confirms his correct assumption that documentary film's dullness was a function of historical precedent, not an inherent limitation in its form. However, Drew himself acknowledges his misjudgment in assuming that television would be the vehicle.[82] While television could theoretically provide a place for the new, experimental form of nonfiction film that Drew envisioned, it ultimately did not provide the regular air-time or programming environment necessary to establish the new form and to ensure the growth of audience understanding and acceptance.

In the earliest years, however, television was an appropriate environment for direct cinema development because of the establishment, by the Federal Communications Commission, of broadcasters' responsibility to address issues of general public interest through public affairs programming. ABC-television, the network that provided the creative climate for Drew's initial experiments, differed from CBS-television and NBC-television by accepting public affairs programming produced outside of its own news operations. Although ABC had the lowest ratings and the smallest share of the viewing audience, it had in the Bell & Howell Company a sponsor willing to support an incentive to try something different from traditional documentary film and ordinary television news programming. The difference was represented by Drew's approach, characterized principally by its sync-sound location shooting of uncontrolled events and its reliance on images, rather than a narrator, to present the subject.

These factors helped to emphasize an objectivity that was important to the network and its sponsor in addressing the FCC's "Fairness Doctrine," creating an impression of a disinterested network and a commercial company doing something valuable to raise the public consciousness by conforming to the prevailing political climate of consensus.[83] Nevertheless, while many factors seemed favorable for ensuring the successful development of Drew's approach, several did not, including the lack of general audience interest in both public affairs and direct cinema; the ABC network's tendency to slot a time for public affairs programming where it would be seen by the least number of people; television's primary reliance on the "talking head"; and the gradual absorption of many direct cinema methods into mainstream television news reporting.[84]

Robert Drew and his associates—among them, Richard Leacock, D. A. Pennebaker, and Albert and David Maysles—produced nineteen films of an astonishing variety.[85] A wide-ranging curiosity helped them to record and to reveal two of the most important events in the early years of the 1960s (civil rights and Vietnam), several personalities (Jawaharlal Nehru, John F. Kennedy, and Robert F. Kennedy) whose importance transcended their time, and several subjects (such as capital punishment, drug addiction, and school integration) that today remain potent public issues

The goal that Robert Drew Associates established for the "Living Camera" series was to present a crucial day, week, or month in the lives of their subjects, famous or unknown.[86] What they achieved represented an important step in bringing human insight to creative cinematography. Some of these films have a definite dramatic structure (e.g., EDDIE, 1961, and THE CHAIR, 1962) that is not imposed upon the material, but comes from within it, while others (PRIMARY, 1960, and CRISIS: BEHIND A PRESIDENTIAL COMMITMENT, 1963) are closer to the journalistic reporting of Drew's *Life* magazine background and rely more on the significance of people and events than on the shape and direction of circumstances. Of these, PRIMARY[87] is notable because it was the first, and CRISIS: BEHIND A PRESIDENTIAL COMMITMENT because it was the most controversial.[88] YANKI, NO! (1960)[89] or JANE (1962)[90] are notable because they fell short-

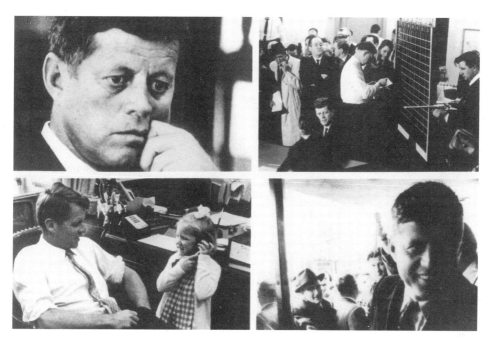

*Robert Drew made three landmark cinéma verité films on John F. Kennedy—*PRIMARY, CRISIS, *and* FACES OF NOVEMBER. *The left-side images of Kennedy* (top) *and his brother Bobby with daughter Kerry* (bottom) *are from* CRISIS. *The filmmaker is seen in the two right-side shots from* PRIMARY, *pointing a microphone at Kennedy from the far right* (top), *and holding up a microphone behind Kennedy* (bottom).

est of reaching any goal. THE CHAIR (1962) seems to have the most lasting value as an early demonstration of the antinomies inherent in the direct cinema style and the virtual impossibility of achieving objectivity about certain news events.[91]

Eventually, Leacock, Pennebaker, and others left Drew Associates to become independent filmmakers on their own, for reasons that included the rigidity of the television format, the crisis structure that was not suitable for all subjects, and the manipulative editing used to secure this dramatic framework. Disagreements like those that surrounded the making of THE CHAIR suggested that if direct cinema were to realize its potential, it would be an auteur's achievement, carrying with it the stamp of an identifiable and controlling artistic intelligence.[92] Since the early and valuable experiments of Drew Associates, direct cinema continued to develop into the 1970s and 1980s in two directions—represented by the collaborative approach of Albert and David Maysles and their associates, and by the individual approach of Frederick Wiseman. The outstanding achievements of each of these filmmakers confirm the value of both approaches.

RICHARD LEACOCK   Richard Leacock and D. A. Pennebaker worked with Drew Associates—most notably on PRIMARY (1960), EDDIE (1961), and THE CHAIR (1962)—and subsequently worked together as Leacock-Pennebaker on DON'T LOOK BACK (1967) and MONTEREY POP (1968).[93] Richard Leacock's early career in direct cinema includes directing for the landmark television show *Omnibus* (e.g., "Toby and the Tall Corn," 1954) and developing lightweight motion-picture production equipment.[94] His

most significant films during the 1960s were HAPPY MOTHER'S DAY (1963) and A
STRAVINSKY PORTRAIT (1964).[95] HAPPY MOTHER'S DAY, recording the reaction of a
small South Dakota town when a local mother gives birth to quintuplets, was Leacock's
first film after leaving Drew Associates. It is a masterpiece of objective observation and
ironic narrative, confirming Leacock's gift for balancing objectivity with intimacy.[96] Like
the Maysles–Zwerin SALESMAN (1969), the film succeeds in holding up a mirror to
American society and its values while not taking itself too seriously.

Leacock and Pennebaker also displayed a distinct penchant for filming music and
musicians. Separately and together they produced films about Geza Anda, Van Cliburn,
Susan Starr, Dave Lambert, Bob Dylan, and the performers at the Monterey Pop
Festival of 1967. Of these, the most revealing is Leacock's A STRAVINSKY PORTRAIT.
This film shows both the professional—Stravinsky creating, discussing, and conducting
his work—and the personal—Stravinsky revealing his humor, tenderness, and impelling
enthusiasm. It is a rare document, made possible by Stravinsky's candor and Leacock's
intimate camera work and sound recording. There is here a collaboration between two
artists—one on either side of the filmmaking equipment—with the camera and microphone serving as their mutual confidante.

D. A. PENNEBAKER   After leaving Drew Associates, Donn Alan Pennebaker reflected
his determination in his first work to make films that would reveal the "spiritual energy"
of the people he chose as subjects.[97] With DON'T LOOK BACK, he found in the folk
singer Bob Dylan the perfect subject for this approach. While the film has provoked

A portrait of the artist: Bob Dylan in D.A. Pennebaker's DON'T LOOK BACK (1965).

considerable controversy—some of Dylan's fans, for example, argue that the singer's camera-consciousness invalidates the portrait—its grainy photography, poor lighting, and inadequate sound recording provide what many people regard as the classic direct cinema style (even if these characteristics are more clearly associated with cinéma verité). DON'T LOOK BACK has as its focus a charismatic performer, a vital element lacking in two of its more technically proficient predecessors, Pennebaker's DAVID (1961) and JANE (1962). DON'T LOOK BACK is a touchstone for studying one of the most creative and enduring legends of 1960s pop culture.[98]

The first of the big rock festival films, Pennebaker's MONTEREY POP (1968), is all the more enjoyable because it avoids the simple-mindedness of WOODSTOCK (1970) as well as the obfuscation of GIMME SHELTER (1970). Preserving some memorable musical performances, it recalls today that such festivals were fun until violence ended them at Altamont, California (in GIMME SHELTER). Beyond its value as social document and the directness of its excellent color photography and sound recording, it also reveals Pennebaker's particularly strong admiration for music and musicians. While Pennebaker never achieves the cinematic intimacy with his subjects as, for example, Leacock does with Stravinsky, or the Maysles brothers, he is secure in his understanding and presentation of musicians.[99] His belief in the "spiritual energy" of his subjects, as noted earlier, confirms the underlying truth that unless a filmmaker emphasizes the strengths of a person and wins the sympathy of the audience, the film will probably fail.[100] And while Pennebaker's work lacks the originality to be as enduring as Leacock's, he makes an important contribution to the overall development of 1960s American nonfiction film with an intuitive approach to subject matter that is uniquely his.[101]

ALBERT AND DAVID MAYSLES Between 1959 and 1962, Albert Maysles worked as a cinematographer with Drew Associates on a number of films,[102] but, in 1962, with his brother David, he formed an independent film production company. Reflecting the influence of the Drew approach, their impressive body of work nevertheless has its own particular stamp.[103] Stephen Mamber, historian and critic, discussed the Drew influence:

> Like the Drew films, the Maysles films consistently maintain a personality-oriented structure, and while not dependent upon the same sort of crisis conditions, they do have a sense of people trying to prove themselves (or, at least, to survive) in pressure situations. In Maysles films, however, the pressure never lets up. The contest never ends.

That analysis remains accurate as an assessment of both the Drew influence and the Maysles brothers' approach. Fascinated by the creative process, they perfected a direct cinema approach in which form and content are seamlessly joined. Like Truman Capote's concept of the "nonfiction novel," which utilized fictional techniques to shape the reporting of actual events, the idea of joining form and content seamlessly in the cinema is another important influence on the Maysles' style. They appear, moreover, to have been the first filmmakers to use the term "nonfiction" in describing their work, as well consistently calling it "direct cinema," rather than cinéma verité.[104] Fascinated also by creative personalities, they made films that reveal the character of such unusually gifted, compelling, and eccentric individuals as Joseph E. Levine (SHOWMAN, 1963), the Beatles (WHAT'S HAPPENING! THE BEATLES IN THE U.S.A., 1964), Marlon Brando

(MEET MARLON BRANDO, 1965), Truman Capote (WITH LOVE FROM TRUMAN, 1966), and four Bible salesmen (SALESMAN, 1969).[105]

Unlike Frederick Wiseman, for example, who edits his own films, the Maysles brothers work closely with their editors, among them Charlotte Zwerin, Ellen Hovde, Muffie Meyer, and Susan Froemke. Since the Maysles (as well as Wiseman) shot without a formal script, following events as they occur, it is the editors, often working closely at the editing table with the filmmakers, who gave the footage its structure and rhythm.[106] Although the brothers acknowledge that the structure of their films is realized through editing, they differ from other great formalists, Eisenstein in particular, because they count on the "spontaneous juxtapositions in life itself."[107]

Of the Maysles' films made during the 1960s, the most important are SALESMAN and GIMME SHELTER, both of which reveal their sensitivity to their subjects as well as their creation for the audience of the feeling of "being there" in the action. SALESMAN, subtitled *A Film by Albert and David Maysles and Charlotte Zwerin,"* bears an early hallmark of their work—control of the tension between film form and content. It is evident both in the film and in the filmmakers' comments that they cared for the subject and felt deeply about the film's implications.[108] While SALESMAN ostensibly focuses on the activities of four door-to-door Bible salesmen, particularly Paul Brennan, it suggests larger themes about American society and its values. It is Zwerin's editing, moreover, that maintains this tension between the Maysles' affection for Paul Brennan and their desire to remain objective in filming. The result is the intelligent, direct, and often witty handling of a sensitive subject.[109]

Like all films by the Maysles brothers, SALESMAN provoked a lively critical debate. John Simon wrote that the Maysles were searching for "something quaintly unwholesome yet typical," but discovered instead, "something Swiftian, scandalous, frightening, and heartbreaking. They have stumbled on to . . . a condemnation—however fragmented, fortuitous, and even inept—of the human condition, of man himself, but also of a society plagued by superstition, idiot competitiveness, and stultifying materialism."[110]

GIMME SHELTER, a film about Mick Jagger and the Rolling Stones, is emblematic of the Maysles' approach and of the critical debate it engenders. Like WOODSTOCK, GIMME SHELTER is a social document of a phenomenon that originated in the 1960s, the rock music festival. Unlike WOODSTOCK, however, it brings us close to violence at the tragic Altamont concert (a confrontation between some members of the Hells Angels motorcycle gang and the audience, and the subsequent stabbing of a black man by a white man)—behavior that contradicts all that Woodstock was thought to symbolize. While the filmmakers seem genuinely to believe that they have made an objective film, GIMME SHELTER raises serious questions about their fidelity to actuality. They set the Altamont incident in a larger context of the Stones' career, and intercut scenes of the Stones on and off the stage with scenes of Jagger and others watching the Altamont footage on an editing table. By creating distance from the event and playing down the violence, the Maysles reaffirm the film's broad coverage, but the final result is unsatisfying precisely because it is so detached and thus overlooks the festival's significance as a major turning point of the decade. The film also raises the theme of art *v.* reality, an issue central to direct cinema. While the Maysles achieved something less than their usual pure direct cinema of observation and juxtaposition, some audiences and critics wanted even more—specifically, a film that would analyze, cite causes, and place responsibility.[111] Direct cinema had reached a critical juncture: some viewers recognized

The feeling of "being there" in the concert film Gimme Shelter *(filmed in 1969 and released in 1970) provoked lively critical debate. Sixties culture was not all about peace and love.*

it as art while they still seemed to yearn for the Griersonian interpretive viewpoint against which direct cinema developed.

FREDERICK WISEMAN   Among important American direct cinema filmmakers of the 1960s, Frederick Wiseman is the only one not to have begun with Drew Associates. Educated in law, Wiseman worked alone in developing his own unique and enduring approach that gave to direct cinema what the "new journalism" gave to the print and broadcasting media.[112] He stretches the dimensions of reportage; maintains a strong narrative control over his material; does not preach; does not appear in, nor does he narrate his films, either as a character or by accident; uses small, repeated experiences that represent the total experience; and shapes the form of his films with a logic so unobtrusive that interpretations of their content seem to arise only in the viewer's mind. Wiseman's art of direct cinema communicates its meaning not through a duplication of the real world, but through a selection that creates a model of it.[113]

A strong, inquiring intelligence, the hallmark of Wiseman's work, is generally implicit in his choice of subject, his shooting of sequences, and his editing.[114] He does not personalize one man; rather, his films concentrate on one institution, exploring its operations and concentrating on the workers, clients, their families, and others who are part of, or affected by, those operations. He defines an institution as "a series of activities that take place in a limited geographical area with a more or less consistent group of people being involved."[115] It became commonplace in some critical circles to debate the significance of this concern with institutions, specifically whether it implies his dislike or distrust of them.[116] However, both Pauline Kael and Michael J. Arlen admired Wiseman as a social reformer. "What he's doing," wrote Kael, "is so simple and so basic that it's like a rediscovery of what we know, or should know. . . . Wiseman extends our understanding of our common life."[117] Similarly, Arlen wrote: "For, despite Wiseman's by no means insincere self-explications of his interest in 'American institutions,' what he has been doing all along is to dare to show us ourselves without masks—to let the camera strip us bare, so that the camera may build us anew; in short, he has been working with the kino eye."[118]

In his choice and handling of subjects, Wiseman reveals an intensity and concentration that set him apart from both tradition and his contemporaries. Like Grierson, Wiseman is fascinated by the internal operation of institutions, but in addition to showing how and why they work, he also provides us with enough material to determine for ourselves the quality of that operation. Arlen finds evidence of "some of the same obdurate, against-the-grain, though ultimately passionate, quality in Wiseman's films that may be found in the work of the pioneer Soviet realist Dziga Vertov."[119]

Five films comprise the first period of Wiseman's work: THE TITICUT FOLLIES (1967), HIGH SCHOOL (1968), LAW AND ORDER (1969), HOSPITAL (1970), and BASIC TRAINING (1971).[120] The first, his most controversial, is also atypical; the others conform basically to a familiar pattern, and have not only been discussed extensively, but also achieved a substantial critical reputation.[121]

THE TITICUT FOLLIES, Wiseman's view of the Bridgewater State Hospital for the criminally insane in Massachusetts, was perceived as so disturbingly candid by the state's citizens and by the mainstream media that it triggered considerable political controversy, a bitter legislative hearing, and a court censorship case.[122] At issue was the propriety of the film's graphic footage of disturbing behavior (by inmates and guards alike) and its avoidance of narration and commentary. In setting out to expose injustice and inhumanity at Bridgewater, Wiseman reveals to us the ugly aspects of such institutions. Predictably, critics attacked, and Wiseman defended, the approach.[123] Also at issue was the question of responsibility—the state's, in permitting the foolish, degrading, and almost inhuman treatment of patients, and Wiseman's in recording it.[124] THE TITICUT FOLLIES, a determined filmmaker's polemic, is not altogether characteristic of direct cinema, but when a film of such directness and honesty provokes such a public outcry, it deserves full attention. Although many important critics disliked the film,[125] Vincent Canby praised it in the *New York Times* as "extraordinarily candid," while Richard Schickel stated in *Life* magazine that "when a film achieves that kind of power it must be regarded as art, however artlessly, or even crudely, it generates it."[126]

HIGH SCHOOL focuses on an institution that would at first appear to be at the opposite end of the social scale from Bridgewater State Hospital. The subject is Philadelphia's North East High School, an urban institution with a functionally modern campus serving a predominantly middle class, white student body. On the outside it seems a "model" school, and to parents and administrators it probably is; but to Wiseman, looking at it from the inside, it is a model of a very different reality. A common theme apparent in other Wiseman films, the rigid, mechanical nature of authority often insulated in a self-contained society, links the film's many incidents. In a shift away from the negative reaction to Wiseman's first film, the critical reception of HIGH SCHOOL was almost totally favorable, and similar acceptance of Wiseman's subsequent work more or less prevailed through almost two decades. In both the national magazines and newspapers, critics

One of the least disturbing moments in Frederick Wiseman's THE TITICUT FOLLIES (1967).

expressed an understanding of the formal complexity and resultant ambiguity of Wiseman's approach.[127]

With HIGH SCHOOL Wiseman had brought his style to maturity, and his films began to achieve the reputation for seriousness and quality that they deserved. The following year he released LAW AND ORDER (1969), which focuses on the interactions of the police department and citizens of Kansas City. Characterized by stylistic problems that would become a small, but relevant factor in the critical reception of his continuing work, LAW AND ORDER is weakened because it concentrates so much on individuals that it prevents the achievement of a comprehensive institutional portrait. Wiseman acknowledged that several of his stereotypes about the police were changed during filming; this suggests that preconceptions may have further weakened it. A lawyer by profession before becoming a filmmaker, Wiseman was familiar with both sides of the criminal justice system, but the advocacy here is a reflection of skepticism, even fear, at the implications of then-President Richard Nixon's "law and order" society. One year before the film appeared, there were riots in Chicago at the Democratic National Convention, and the film recalls that incident through the use of archival footage of one of Nixon's campaign speeches on the need for law and order. Although it shows various elements of society—blacks and whites, men and women, young and old, police and citizens—it seems (with Wiseman's PRIMATE, 1974), to advocate a position, rather than to present, as is characteristic of his other films, a collection of impressions to which the viewer gives meaning. Structural and thematic variations result in a depiction of the police as both tough and kind, and the camera's relation to individuals balances its point-of-view, but one sees in this film a confusion of purpose.

LAW AND ORDER was concerned with American society's shift to political conservatism, its emphasis on law and order at home, and its increasing armed aggression

Contrasting images and contrasting roles: a teacher in Frederick Wiseman's HIGH SCHOOL (1968).

abroad. The film should have received more attention from audiences and critics alike, yet even with a brief flurry over some censorship of obscenities from the film, it was scarcely noticed.[128] Perhaps, in the final analysis, Wiseman's 1960s films all try too hard to be objective, to balance scenes in presenting a multiple point of view; he neither succeeds in engaging our attention, nor in providing a fresh perspective on a subject about which most people have definite opinions. In LAW AND ORDER, concluded Stephen Mamber, "the expected ambiguity of possible responses typical in Wiseman's work is lost, along with contextual complexity. As happens only rarely in his films, experience looks oversimplified."[129]

Nonetheless, Wiseman was widely perceived to have recovered the original intention of his uncontrived cinematic model of reality in his films of the 1970s (HOSPITAL, 1970; BASIC TRAINING, 1971; MEAN, 1976; and CANAL ZONE, 1977). As David Denby noted, "Obviously the possibility for distortion and simplification in editing are endless, but Wiseman is unique in the complexity and ambivalence he leaves in."[130]

American Nonfiction Film Outside the Direct Cinema Movement

Although direct cinema was the most influential development in American nonfiction film during the 1960s, the independent nonfiction film, the mainstay of the American tradition, continued to flourish.[131] It was a period of diverse and creative accomplishment in both traditional and non-traditional modes. Filmmakers were concerned with the central issues of the decade—politics, society and family life, civil rights, Vietnam, foreign affairs, personalities, institutions, rock music, show business, drugs, sports, and art—and also with such issues as the new equipment, the threat of television, and the expanding opportunities for longer nonfiction films and theatrical showings. In the following discussion of films arranged by subject category, the emphasis is on those that, by their achievements, deserve continuing attention.

POLITICS

Considering the importance of politics in the 1960s, surprisingly few significant nonfiction films produced during the decade were concerned directly with the subject. The political film had a promising beginning with such Drew Associates works as PRIMARY (1960), about the 1960 Kennedy-Humphrey Democratic presidential primary in Wisconsin, and ADVENTURES ON THE NEW FRONTIER (1961), a film about President

An American overkill still from IN THE YEAR OF THE PIG *(1969).*

John F. Kennedy. CAMPAIGN MANAGER (1964; also titled REPUBLICANS: THE NEW BREED—A FILM BY RICHARD LEACOCK, NOEL PARMENTEL, AND NICK PROFERES), about Barry Goldwater's 1964 presidential bid, was notable as one of the few American films that looks at conservative politics.

Most lively and controversial political films—not necessarily the most significant or the most lasting—were those made by Emile de Antonio: OPERATION ABOLITION (1961), about the House Un-American Activities Committee;[132] POINT OF ORDER (1963), about the Army-McCarthy Hearings;[133] RUSH TO JUDGMENT (1967), a study of the Warren Commission Report on the assassination of President John F. Kennedy;[134] and IN THE YEAR OF THE PIG (1969), about the emergence of the protest movement on the nation's college campuses, among the most important political phenomena of the 1960s. Of the films that either treat fully or incidentally examine protests on college campuses, including REVOLT AT COLUMBIA (1968), the best is Arthur Barron's controversial THE BERKELEY REBELS (1965).[135]

SOCIETY AND FAMILY LIFE

Filmmakers paid about as little attention to American society and family life as they did to politics. However, unique subjects of Americana provide the focus of several important films, including two distinguished by the light-handed humor of Richard Leacock: ON THE ROAD TO BUTTON BAY (1962), about the fiftieth anniversary of the Girl Scouts,

Some of the small-town teenagers in Arthur Barron's SIXTEEN IN WEBSTER GROVES *(1966).*

and A HAPPY MOTHER'S DAY (1963), discussed earlier. Others include Arthur Barron's SIXTEEN IN WEBSTER GROVES (1966) and WEBSTER GROVES REVISITED (1967), a two-part study of attitudes of small-town teenagers toward parents, education, and family life. Kurt MacKenzie's SATURDAY MORNING (1971), another study of teenagers,[136] and Craig Gilbert's television series about the Loud family, AN AMERICAN FAMILY (1973), would follow these leads. Barron's FACTORY (1969), a study of a factory worker, his family, and friends, is particularly interesting and should be compared with Frederick Wiseman's MEAT (1976). In contrast to more serious film studies of American society, Francis Thompson's TO BE ALIVE! (1964), presented at the 1964 New York World's Fair and seen by millions, is a multi-screened, lyrical, and cheerful tribute to life.[137]

Perhaps the most conspicuous aspect of 1960s' society was the so-called counterculture, evidenced, in part, by radical campus movements and rampant anti-intellectualism, widespread use and abuse of marijuana and hallucinogenic drugs, colorful clothes, folk and rock music, and the peace movement. Thus, it is surprising that filmmakers did not make better use of what were abundant opportunities for recording footage that was both colorful and socially meaningful. While aspects of the counterculture could be seen in certain films on rock music and the youth culture (most notably MONTEREY POP, 1968, WOODSTOCK 1970, and GIMME SHELTER, 1970), no major nonfiction film made in the 1960s covered the subject as a whole. Similarly, the less colorful aspects of these activities received scant attention. Drug addiction, previously associated with junkies and outcasts, became associated by some during the 1960s with mental and spiritual enlightenment; spreading throughout society, it became a scourge that killed drug apostles, rock star idols, hard-core users, and innocents alike. The 1960s were marked by experimentation with drugs and with permissiveness in general, and, with few exceptions, producers, filmmakers, and audiences alike were not interested in films on the subject.[138]

CIVIL RIGHTS

In the view of many, Vietnam and the civil rights struggle were the most important social issues of the day and also inseparable. But filmmakers, even politically committed ones, seemed less interested in the civil rights struggle than in other social issues. Among the exceptions is an early film of Richard Leacock's, THE CHILDREN WERE WATCHING (1960), which presents the attitudes of the white New Orleans community toward school integration.[139] Even more interesting, historically and aesthetically, is Gregory Shuker's CRISIS: BEHIND A PRESIDENTIAL COMMITMENT (1963), which was made by Richard Leacock, D. A. Pennebaker, James Lipscomb, and Hope Ryden.[140] Focusing on court-ordered integration of the University of Alabama, CRISIS raised serious questions that were later to become mainstays of direct cinema criticism: the validity and reliability of nonfiction footage shot in compliance with the principals; the possibility that the camera exploits personalities and issues; the ethics of the direct, unedited recording of conversations, particularly those involving issues of domestic security; and the ethics of imposing a dramatic structure (such as the paradigm of a "crisis") on nonfiction footage. The film remains relevant, not only because it reminds us that racial integration continues to be a social dilemma for many people, but also because it depicts in action many officials important to the event and to the overall political history of the decade, including President John F. Kennedy, Attorney General Robert J. Kennedy, and Alabama Governor George Wallace. American nonfiction films concerned with civil rights include Haskell Wexler's BUS (1965), an account of the 1963 March on Washington that the film historian Arthur Knight assessed as being "charged with enormous meaning for our times,"[141] and Edward Pincus's and David Newman's BLACK NATCHEZ (1967), a portrait of the people and activities of the Mississippi Freedom Democratic Party that Robert Coles described as a "valuable historical document."[142]

VIETNAM

During the 1960s and into the 1970s, the most serious and most controversial social issue was the United States' undeclared war in Vietnam. Unlike World War II films—on military training, combat, and the effects of war—remarkable for their consistent support of the role of the United States and its allies, nonfiction films about Vietnam reflect divergent viewpoints and the polarization of American society into those who supported and those who opposed the war.[143]

The United States government position is best expressed in WHY VIETNAM? (1966), made by the Department of Defense.[144] Its name and its purpose allude to Frank Capra's "Why We Fight" series (1943–45), but, aggressive and pro-war as it is, it had as little in common with Capra's masterful achievement as the war in Vietnam had in common with World War II.[145] Like the Capra films, WHY VIETNAM? was produced to indoctrinate troops on their way to battle, to trace the historical background of the conflict, and to show actual combat footage interspersed with official comment (in this case, the remarks of President Lyndon B. Johnson). However, it is also essentially a distorted, deceptive (one might even say desperate) attempt to justify the war's escalation to the millions of Americans who saw the film on television.[146] Its effect was predictable: it convinced those who supported the war, and it outraged those who were against it.[147] Several years later, Peter Davis's THE SELLING OF THE PENTAGON (1971) exposed even further the government's attempts to propagandize a false justification of the escalation of the war.

Eugene S. Jones's A FACE OF WAR (1968), one of the best films made about Vietnam, takes a humanistic approach.[148] Through a record of the daily experiences of American soldiers in the Seventh Marine Regiment, Jones makes a strong anti-war statement—the enemy is not the Viet Cong, but war itself. Two films about North Vietnam, EYEWITNESS NORTH VIETNAM (1966, James Cameron) and INSIDE NORTH VIETNAM (1967, Felix Greene), gave Americans an insight into the people, the issues, and the society on the other side of the struggle.[149] Other films on the war, some less widely seen by the general American public, include the newsreel documentaries, NO VIETNAMESE EVER CALLED ME NIGGER (1968), and Joseph Strick's INTERVIEWS WITH MY LAI VETERANS (1970).[150] Strick's film confirmed the My Lai atrocities and, with WOODSTOCK, shared the Academy Award for best documentary film of 1970. The two films demonstrated the polarities of genocide and flower power.[151]

It took two courageous independent films to present what neither television coverage nor other films had done: a broad political, historical, and cultural analysis of the Vietnam conflict. The best of these is Emile de Antonio's IN THE YEAR OF THE PIG (1969), a "heartbreaking" (the critic Stanley Kauffman's word) account that goes back more than forty years and, in the view of another critic, "lets us see and hear for ourselves how our leaders led us to believe that the downward spiral was a forward march."[152] It is a complex film that uses brilliant cinematic manipulation to make its points.[153] What it lacks in serving the conventional responsibility of the nonfiction film, it gains in the sheer, outrageous, cumulative forcefulness of its case against both French and American involvement in Vietnam.

Foreign Affairs

Vietnam was not the only aspect of American foreign policy that attracted nonfiction filmmakers during the 1960s. Early in the decade, Lionel Rogosin's COME BACK, AFRICA (1960) exposed the atrocities of the South African policy of apartheid; an over-looked film, it deserves attention as a serious attempt to deal with a major issue of human rights.[154] YANKI, NO! (1960), a film by Richard Leacock with Albert Maysles and D. A. Pennebaker, aroused awareness of strong anti-American feelings in Latin America. Richard Leacock's KENYA, AFRICA (1961) offered an uneven political analysis of an emerging African nation.[155]

Portraits

A major genre of the 1960s nonfiction film is the film portrait, usually, but not necessarily, of a well-known personality. While portraits can be grouped into several categories, they all raise the question of whether a personality accustomed to performing for the

Jason, a homosexual hustler, in Shirley Clarke's PORTRAIT OF JASON *(1967).*

public can do anything but perform before the camera.[156] The most prevalent are the portraits of personalities from the arts and popular entertainment. Early efforts include SUSAN STARR (1962, Drew-Leacock), a portrait of a young pianist preparing for a competition; JANE (1962, Drew Associates), an uneven film portrait of the young film star Jane Fonda;[157] SHOWMAN (1963, Albert and David Maysles), a portrait of motion-picture mogul Joseph E. Levine; MEET MARLON BRANDO (1965, Albert and David Maysles); LENNY BRUCE (1967, John Magnuson), which reveals the comedian's self-indulgent mediocrity;[158] JOHNNY CASH! (1969, Arthur Barron); GERTRUDE STEIN: WHEN THIS YOU SEE, REMEMBER ME (1970, Perry Miller Adato); and two films discussed above, Leacock's A STRAVINKSY PORTRAIT (1964) and Pennebaker's DON'T LOOK BACK (1966).

Other films about personalities—some well known—in the public eye include Drew Associates' X-PILOT (1960), about the final test flight of the X-15 by pilot Scott Crossfield; THE AGA KHAN (1962); Albert and David Maysles' WITH LOVE FROM TRUMAN: A VISIT WITH TRUMAN CAPOTE (1966); PORTRAIT OF JASON (1967), Shirley Clarke's study of a black homosexual hustler;[159] and William Klein's FLOAT LIKE A BUTTERFLY, STING LIKE A BEE (1969), a portrait of boxer Cassius Clay/Muhammad Ali.[160]

Portrait films about political personalities include NEHRU (1962, Drew Associates); ELEANOR ROOSEVELT'S STORY (1965, Richard Kaplan),[161] and JOHN F. KENNEDY: YEARS OF LIGHTNING, DAY OF DRUMS (1966, Bruce Hershensohn), which, considering the subject and the impact of the assassination, is a surprisingly bland biography made by the United States Information Agency.[162]

Interesting film portraits of institutions include Bert Stern's lyrical and stylish JAZZ ON A SUMMER'S DAY (1960), about the Newport Jazz Festival,[163] and Pennebaker's ORIGINAL CAST ALBUM: COMPANY! (1970), documenting the recording session of the Stephen Sondheim musical. While at first it might be problematic to separate films about institutions from films about the personalities behind those institutions, Frederick Wiseman's HIGH SCHOOL (1968) marked the application of the pure direct cinema approach to such a study. Other films that focus on institutions or group efforts include KU KLUX KLAN: THE INVISIBLE EMPIRE (1965), a collaboration of Richard Leacock and David Lowe for *CBS Reports*, and CHIEFS (1969), a short, amusing film about a convention of police chiefs in Hawaii, by Richard Leacock and Noel Parmentel.[164]

ROCK MUSIC

Many films were produced about rock music, musicians, and festivals (beyond those listed dealing with personalities). Some of them became as important as the subjects they documented. Memorable titles include the Maysles' brothers' WHAT'S HAPPENING! THE BEATLES IN THE U.S.A. (1964) and Pennebaker's MONTEREY POP (1968) and KEEP ON ROCKIN' (1970).[165] The most significant and enduring of these are Michael Wadleigh's WOODSTOCK (1970) and GIMME SHELTER (1970), a film by Albert and David Maysles and Charlotte Zwerin. Both films were shot at 1969 rock festivals—the first records its zenith, the second its nadir—and each takes a different approach. WOODSTOCK is a lavish, lyrical poem capturing and celebrating a pastoral event. GIMME SHELTER is a tight, jolting record, observing a burned-out ritual. Each film represents an opposite extreme of the decade's social climate and of its approaches to the nonfiction film. WOODSTOCK, despite the complexities of its camera coverage and overall production, is fairly typical observation; GIMME SHELTER, less complex in production, is complex and controversial direct cinema.

SPORTS

Sports provide an excellent opportunity for nonfiction film coverage of both action events and the personalities involved in them, and while sports films could also be classified with "personality portrait" films, it is the action and excitement of sports action that distinguish them. Early Drew Associates sports films include ON THE POLE (1960) and EDDIE (1961), both made from footage about race car driver Eddie Sachs,[166] and FOOTBALL (1961).[167] As a study of the football rivalry between two Miami high schools, the latter successfully reflects the strengths of the "crisis" approach so closely associated with early direct cinema, and is a charming study of a classically American subject. Successful full-length theatrical releases about sports include Bruce Brown's ENDLESS SUMMER (1966), a lyrical film that gives a good portrait of the surfing cult.[168]

ART

American art during the 1960s and early 1970s developed in various directions (op art, pop art, earthworks, minimal art—to name a few). Of the many American nonfiction films recording the art and the artists, those of Michael Blackwood were the most numerous, authoritative, and reliable. Two films were released outside the chronological scope of this study, but deserve mention because they are retrospective studies of 1960s art. Blackwood's ART IN THE 1960s (1973) is an excellent survey, relating the post-Abstract Expressionist developments to the contemporary culture. Among his other films are documentary and interpretive accounts of some of the most important and influential painters and sculptors of the decade.[169] Emile de Antonio's PAINTERS PAINTING (1972) is a fascinating study of the lives and works of New York artists, dealers, and critics between 1940 and 1970.[170]

More traditional art and the traditional nonfiction film approach are represented in the work of such pioneers as Leo Hurwitz, whose JOURNEY INTO A PAINTING (1969), about Paul Cézanne's *Still Life with Apples*, is far from Hurwitz's typical concern with social issues. Wheaton Galentine, in collaboration with producer Willard Van Dyke, made THE CORBIT-SHARP HOUSE (1965). A short film, it is a beautifully photographed and sensitive record of the work of craftsmen, and especially important as one of the few films about American architecture. Other films about art and artists include two short pieces about avant-garde artist Jean Tinguely—D. A. Pennebaker's brief BREAKING IT UP AT THE MUSEUM (1960), and Robert Breer's HOMAGE TO JEAN TINGUELY (1961).

FILMS ON MISCELLANEOUS SUBJECTS

Of the hundreds of American nonfiction films made during the 1960s, the scope of this study permits mention only those that—by their choice of subject matter, or cinematic innovation, or influence (or, rarely, all three)—constitute the most significant corpus of achievement. Some films are difficult to classify. George Stoney's A CRY FOR HELP (1962), is a training film for police dealing with suicide cases and, like Stoney's classic ALL MY BABIES (1952), is a model of a genre that, in hands less sensitive than Stoney's, is potentially deadly. Robert Gardner's DEAD BIRDS (1963), filmed in New Guinea, is a model ethnographic film.[171] Two films about historical events call attention to the use of archival footage.[172] GUNS OF AUGUST (1965), Nathan Kroll's adaptation of Barbara Tuchman's study of Europe just before World War I, is particularly interesting because there is a scarcity of footage from that period.[173] Arthur Barron's BIRTH AND DEATH (1969) juxtaposes the emotional experiences in the weeks before a child's birth and a man's death; in the process, it raises the familiar issue of the extent to which ordinary people are conscious of the camera.[174]

TELEVISION

The years between 1947 and 1950 marked a critical juncture in the history of mass communications: television replaced the motion picture as the major mass visual force of the second half of the twentieth century.[175] By 1949, the years of experimenting with the medium's technical potentialities had ended successfully, and regular television broadcasting had begun throughout the country, offering the public popular entertainment at home and seriously threatening the motion picture industry.

Yet, ironically, television had a beneficial, even a profound effect on the nonfiction film.[176] It fostered the continuing development of the traditional nonfiction film, one advantage of which—in contrast to the "look" of early television—was the relatively pure "look" of the cinematic form. Moreover, television itself offered new formal properties and created a new audience for them, as well as for those already-existing modes of cinematic reportage developed by newsreels, factual films, and such series as *The March of Time* and *This Is America*.[177] Television also fostered growth by providing two supporting elements that had aided the development of the early British documentary movement—sustained sponsorship and a creative atmosphere in which a dedicated group could pursue a common journalistic aim.[178] Television brought the high standards of nonfiction reporting to major news programs, "specials," and series, exemplified by *See It Now*, *CBS Reports*, and *The Twentieth Century*.[179] To these achievements, television added what no filmmaker, independent or collaborative, had ever enjoyed: the attraction of a new medium of mass communications and a vast audience that could enjoy it for virtually no cost beyond the initial investment in a television receiver.[180]

Conclusion

While American nonfiction film of the 1960s reaffirmed its realistic tradition and explored its own aesthetic needs, it did not reflect the social dynamic of the decade to the extent that might be expected from the cinematic genre that has been historically committed to social issues and social change. It was traditionally identified with a strong social responsibility—as in the works of such filmmakers as Pare Lorentz, Willard Van Dyke, Leo Hurwitz, and Ralph Steiner. American nonfiction filmmakers began associating themselves with wider European and British experimental movements. During the 1960s they developed new cinematic equipment and explored new subject matter and new cinematic forms. Technological advances brought, in turn, artistic freedom. While the established independent tradition flourished, there were new efforts in collaborative filmmaking, in television, and in the feature-length nonfiction film. As aesthetic concerns replaced social concerns, the traditional relationship between the documentary and society was replaced by a new emphasis on the nonfiction film as art, and on the exploration of its alternate possibilities and uses.

Of the new developments, direct cinema was the most radical and most important achievement, representing both a break from the American tradition and a unification of American efforts with the various European nonfiction film traditions. Direct cinema did not, like the traditional nonfiction film, emphasize cinematic content over form; nor did it, like much experimental film, emphasize cinematic form over content. Rather, through an emphasis on how cinematic form and content work together for a re-presentation of reality, direct cinema brought a new awareness of the possibilities of the nonfiction film. What, then, did direct cinema mean to this rebirth of the nonfiction film and to its continuing development?[181]

Although direct cinema began as a group effort, with Drew Associates, it continued its development through the 1960s largely as the result of the efforts of independent filmmakers. Although the direct cinema pioneers were what Stephen Mamber defines as a "fairly cohesive group of filmmakers who see their work as opposing the dominant and more conventional film forms around them," they were not able to sustain a high level of creativity for more than a short time. There are several reasons for this. First, they did not have, nor did they seem to want, one consistent or coherent theory of direct cinema. Second, the technological improvements which made possible the aesthetic achievements of direct cinema were quickly incorporated into more traditional and commercial modes of filmmaking. Third, although direct cinema filmmakers were initially committed to working outside those traditional and commercial modes, they were ultimately forced to make either accommodation or concession to them, because of the necessities of financing, distribution, audience access, critical acceptance, and overall survival in the film industry. Robert Drew continued to make films for television, but with the exception of Frederick Wiseman, those involved in the early group effort—D. A. Pennebaker, Albert and David Maysles—have moved into other areas, primarily those concerned with the industrial, advertising, and public relations uses of nonfiction film.

Of this group only Albert and David Maysles enjoyed sufficient success as commercial and industrial filmmakers to enable them to finance and produce important films like GREY GARDENS that continue to expand the possibilities—both in form and content—of the nonfiction film. Their achievements and influence are significant factors in contemporary nonfiction film history. They pioneered in creating nonfiction film studies of serious topics in an expanded format; such film studies include Craig Gilbert's AN AMERICAN FAMILY (1973, 12 hrs.), a television production;[182] Louis Malle's PHANTOM INDIA (1968, 6 hrs.), and Marcel Ophuls' THE SORROW AND THE PITY (1971, 4 hrs., 20 mins.). The Maysles' work in developing portable and mobile equipment was continued by others in progressively sophisticated video equipment and processing methods. Direct cinema was born in the television broadcasting medium, and one measure of its influence is evident in the "look" of contemporary nonfiction video coverage.

Direct cinema was the most important achievement and the central style of the 1960s American nonfiction film, and very much a part of its period. There was also significant work in the American independent, reality-based, nonfiction film of Griersonian origins, and an increasing number of women nonfiction filmmakers. Women filmmakers, as they had traditionally done, found in nonfiction film opportunities for screenwriting, editing, and cinematography that were less frequently available to them in other areas of the film industry. Among the women nonfiction filmmakers of the 1960s were Perry Adato Miller, Shirley Clarke, Ellen Hovde, Charlotte Zwerin, Jill Godmilow, Barbara Kopple, Julia Reichert, Joyce Chopra, Muffie Meyer, Claudia Weill, Amalie Rothschild, Nell Cox, and Martha Coolidge—some of whom used film as an active political voice in the emerging feminist movement.[183]

Besides the talented and diverse group of filmmakers, both men and women, who helped to revitalize the 1960s nonfiction film, two other factors, audiences and critics, contributed to this rebirth. Earlier, during the 1930s and 1940s, the short nonfiction film had a place in theatrical showings along with feature films, cartoons, and newsreels. In addition, it reached a limited, but dedicated, audience through screenings in schools, colleges, and film study groups, often in public libraries. In the 1960s, feature-length nonfiction film replaced shorter films in commercial theatres, while the secondary pattern of distribution of short films continued in educational institutions as well as on television. Through this variety of screenings, the audience for nonfiction films grew in size as well as in sophistication.

The audience growth can be traced in part to a growing interest in all kinds of cinema, as well as to the influence of those critics who write perceptively about the nonfiction film. Most notable among those critics writing for the general reader was Stanley Kauffmann (*New Republic*); also influential were Pauline Kael and Penelope Gilliatt (*New Yorker*), Arthur Knight and Hollis Alpert (*Saturday Review*), Philip Hartung (*Commonweal*), Robert Hatch (*The Nation*), and John O'Connor and Jack Gould (*New York Times*). In addition, there were numerous scholarly articles, essays, and anthologies devoted to the history, theory, and criticism of the nonfiction film.

"What Went Wrong?": The American Avant-Garde Cinema of the 1960s

WALTER METZ

Authorship in the Study of the 1960s American Avant-Garde Cinema

Kenneth Anger, the avant-garde artist, marks the sign of his authorship at the beginning of each of his films with the brief phrase, "a film by Anger." His meaningful pun serves this chapter's argument and permits us to consider the academic traditions for studying the 1960s avant-garde as well as suggesting necessary correctives to this tradition. For "a film by Anger" indicates that an authorial subject named Anger is the motive force behind the film, but, more significantly, it also indicates a subjective state, that of emotional anger, from which the film's content and stylistic practices emanate.

For example, consider his film SCORPIO RISING (1964), one of the most familiar of the American avant-garde films of the 1960s.[1] It is constructed out of thirteen narrative segments, each presenting imagery that is, to varying degrees, juxtaposed against mainstream American popular songs, such as "Blue Velvet" and "Wipeout." On the one hand, Anger deliberately positions his own authorial presence within the film by tilting the camera down the back of a biker's jacket to reveal "Kenneth Anger" printed in sequins. On the other hand, the film's major project is to make ironic the fetishization of the biker culture that it is purportedly celebrating. For example, in the imagery that accompanies the film's second musical number, "Wind Up Doll," a little kid in a biker outfit winds up a toy motorcycle. At this precise moment, the song informs us about the behavior of its passive female protagonist: "Wind me up and I'll come straight to you." The film's radical juxtaposition of image and sound thus produces an angry critique of a patriarchal order in which a violent masculinity is celebrated in subaltern biker as well as in mainstream, popular culture.[2]

Long-range beefcake in SCORPIO RISING *(1963, Kenneth Anger).*

As evidenced by Anger's approach in SCORPIO RISING, American avant-garde cinema of the 1960s is defined by its aggressive style. While these non-classical stylistic practices of the avant-garde cinema are well known, a brief explication of their use will prove worthwhile to set up many of the analyses of films that follow. To begin, consider the four-minute-long FILM IN WHICH THERE APPEARS EDGE LETTERING, SPROCKET HOLES, DIRT PARTICLES, ETC. (1966, George Landow) as a case study. The film consists of an image of a woman dressed in a red shirt reproduced in three film stills running up the left and right sides of the picture. In between appear the sprocket holes of the filmstrip, with label lettering interspersed between the sprocket holes. This image of the woman in the red shirt does not change noticeably throughout the four minutes of the film, although as the viewer watches, it appears it must be changing. This is part of the playfulness inherent in nearly all avant-garde films. Because the viewer is so used to reading visual patterns in a movie, when confronted with a pattern-less film—or, more precisely, with a film in which the only representation is one pattern that does not change—a natural response is to begin to psychologically project change into the reading of the stable image.

In fact, the constantly changing lettering is the only movement in the film, but it proceeds so quickly that it is impossible to begin seeking patterns in this portion of the image and the dirt particles that were caught on the filmstrip as it was being filmed. However, we cannot tell those filmed dirt particles from the ones that are appearing because of the particular projection of Landow's film as the viewer watches it. At their core, almost all of the avant-garde films of the 1960s use these playful, aggressive aesthetic strategies to force their viewers to think about what it is we mean by cinema itself.

Of course, this playful avant-garde did not emerge out of a cultural vacuum, but instead originated in response to specific developments in film history. One of the most important influences on avant-garde American cinema of the 1960s was similar experimentation in Europe that was becoming more noticeable in the United States. The economic effects of the 1948 Paramount consent decree that ended ownership of movie theaters by the major Hollywood studios resulted by the end of the 1950s in increasing importation of European films, particularly the films of the French New Wave. Their influence can clearly be seen in HALLELUJAH THE HILLS (1963, Adolfas Mekas), the pre-eminent example of what Jonas Mekas labeled the "New American Cinema." The film, which concerns two soldiers, Jack and Leo, who are in love with the same woman, Vera, resonates with strategies common to the French New Wave of the late 1950s and early 1960s. For example, there is a direct reference to Jean-Luc Godard's BREATHLESS (1959); as Jack and Leo run down the street, having gotten drunk in response to their troubles with Vera, a superimposed title reads, "Breathless." The structure of the film itself—two men after the same woman—echoes François Truffault's JULES ET JIM (1962).[3] Finally, the film has an aggressive narrative structure where the temporal relationships between the images we are seeing and the story the film is relating are muddled beyond coherence, which constitutes an analytical description that is as much apropos of the puzzling French feature LAST YEAR AT MARIENBAD (1960, Alain Resnais) as it is of HALLELUJAH THE HILLS.

Discussion of these three films opens up a traditional approach to avant-garde cinema of the 1960s. Their aggressive aesthetic textual practices allow direct attribution to authorial intention. By focusing on representational strategies relating to intertextual and identity politics, rather than merely on the artistic geniuses (i.e., the individualistic filmmaker as "Romantic artist") and the historical traditions behind them, a deeper understanding of the avant-garde cinema in the 1960s is revealed. This process, in turn, opens new insights into the canonical experimental films of that decade while at the same time drawing our attention to films previously ignored or marginalized. Janet Staiger's essay, "Finding Community in the Early 1960s: Underground Cinema and Sexual Politics" (1999), suggests that we approach the 1960s American avant-garde cinema not from the standpoint of production, but instead from that of reception. Staiger emphasizes that both the making of, and the watching of, avant-garde movies in the 1960s served a community-building social function: "It is this same potential of finding others like oneself not only for identity but for community building that I believe the space of the underground cinema of the early 1960s provided."[4] Hence, the notion that the director of the avant-garde film of the 1960s is the principal point through which to understand experimental movies gives way to an array of social and cultural frameworks for seeing canonical films anew, as well as for appreciating lesser known avant-garde films.

While film cultures of other nations had engaged the notion in earlier periods and in different ways, it was with the avant-garde of the 1960s that the idea of film's "radical potential" was first advanced in the United States. This expression emphasized the potential for using the cinema apparatus in noncommercial, yet highly visible ways "as a means of political representation of persons, attitudes, and events traditionally excluded from commercial channels (of expression and communication)."[5] In a widely cited article published in *Film Quarterly* in 1968, Ernest Callenbach neatly summarized this view of the avant-garde by clarifying the connection of the "amateurism" of so many of the aesthetic practices of experimental filmmakers to the idea of its inherent value as social criticism and its importance as a form of resistance to "political domination."[6]

THE GEOGRAPHY OF THE 1960S AVANT-GARDE

Geography is the simplest way to initially comprehend the community-forming functions of the 1960s American avant-garde cinema. There were two flourishing avant-
garde film communities, one in New York City, and the other in the San Francisco Bay
area. The New York community is usually associated with the organizational work of
Jonas Mekas, who was instrumental in merging disparate filmmakers into a cohesive film
culture complete with a film journal, aptly titled *Film Culture*. With the foundation of
the Film-Makers' Cooperative in the late 1950s, a reasonably democratic institution
through which filmmakers could distribute their films was established.[7]

The notion of the New York City avant-garde community was further popularized
and commodified by Andy Warhol, whose "Factory" became an industrial structure unto
itself in American cinema of the 1960s.[8] Warhol began experimenting with cinema by
doing minimalist films featuring one or no characters, such as SLEEP (1963) and
EMPIRE (1964), which consist, respectively, of uninterrupted views of a sleeping male
and the Empire State Building. By mid-decade he was incorporating larger numbers of
his self-created celebrities—Paul America, Joe Dallesandro, Gerard Malanga, Ondine,

Andy Warhol with workers at the Factory in 1967.

Edie Sedgwick, Ingrid Superstar, and Viva—into his films such as VINYL (1965) and THE LIFE OF JUANITA CASTRO (1965). The culmination of this technique of filming a large cast using one camera position and a limited number of shots occurred with THE CHELSEA GIRLS (1966), a film that lasts 195 minutes and contains some eight plot lines. By the end of the decade, Warhol was attempting to parody Hollywood studio filmmaking and its genres, as in the gay-themed "western," LONESOME COWBOYS (1967). Throughout the mid to late 1960s, Warhol's films relied on their communitarian parody of the star system to achieve their assault on Hollywood, by focusing on such clearly dubious "stars" such as Viva and Joe Dallesandro.[9]

New York City and San Francisco had arisen in the late 1950s as the twin meccas of the "Beat Generation." The central literary figures of this movement, Jack Kerouac, Allen Ginsberg, and William S. Burroughs, traveled widely and each one, at different times, expatriated himself from the United States. The social locus and the identity of Beats, however, remained solidly in these two cities—centered around the City Lights Bookshop and the coffee houses of North Beach in San Francisco (with Berkeley as a distant precinct) and in the Greenwich Village clubs and coffeehouses of New York City (with a tiny Beat outpost surviving near Columbia University, where the three great Beat writers had first met).[10] Many of the earliest avant-garde films of the 1960s were made as conscious extensions of the Beat movement in attempts to express on celluloid its perspectives. In both New York City and San Francisco the Beat scene coexisted and intermingled easily with the gay and lesbian communities, the jazz and alternative theatre culture, the nascent rumblings of political activism, and with the emerging avant-garde cinema movement.

For this alternative subculture in New York City, taken as a whole, 1964 was a pivotal year. In preparation for the onslaught of tourists expected in the city for the opening of the World's Fair, authorities moved to polish Gotham's image by closing down clubs, coffeehouses, and porn theaters frequented by gays and lesbians, Beats, pot-heads, and other "subterraneans." Among these raids, one resulted in the arrest of Jonas Mekas of the Film-Makers' Cooperative for showing Jack Smith's FLAMING CREATURES (1963). His arrest and the seizure of this film, according to historian Paul Arthur, "placed avant-garde film on the cultural map, stimulating support from quarters previously oblivious or even hostile to the movement."[11]

Later in that same year, the appearance of the "Free Speech Movement" at the University of California, Berkeley, hearkened the impending integration of several alternative movements in the Bay Area. By the time that the "Summer of Love" brought together an international array of nonconformists in the Haight-Ashbury district of San Francisco in 1967, it was clear that various alternative perspectives, from gay liberation to avant-garde cinema, were perceived to be merging into a singular "counterculture" at the same time that the Beat scene was giving way to the Hippie Movement.[12]

By the mid 1960s, a similar community of avant-garde filmmakers began coalescing in the San Francisco Bay area around Bruce Baillie, whose film poems complexly celebrated the American landscape, but offered a different vision of the roles and responsibilities of an avant-garde cinema than what was being defined in New York. For example, CASTRO STREET (1966) simultaneously represents the gritty industrial machinery that allows a city to function while abstracting it into a poetic visual celebration. For the purposes of community-building, however, the mechanisms of organization in San Francisco were quite similar to those in New York City. On August 14, 1966, under the stewardship of its founder, Bruce Baillie, Canyon Cinema became an institutional venture that allowed for the screening and rental of films, giving people the opportunity to see the work of this group of West Coast avant-garde filmmakers.[13]

THE GREAT EXCEPTION: STAN BRAKHAGE

The great exception to this notion of a geographic locus of community in the avant-garde cinema of the 1960s is Stan Brakhage, who began working in New York City, but fled to Colorado to make intensely individual works. Interrogating the boundaries between the various modes of cinematic experience, Brakhage's films use the aggressive stylistic practices of the avant-garde to represent the material of the home movie, including the filmmaker's own household and family members. In CAT'S CRADLE (1959), for example, shots of the naked bodies of a man and a woman are edited in such a way that very little narrative sense can be immediately gleaned from them. As the film wears on, however, it becomes clear that the viewer is witnessing some form of domestic conflict and the intimacy that follows (or perhaps precedes) it.

Brakhage's work in the 1960s continued this interrogation of the relationship between the film image and its spectator. "Implicit in all of Brakhage's work as a filmmaker," the scholar Wheeler Winston Dixon argued, "is an empirical connection with the spectator-subject as the paradigmatic force within the film being screened, rather than the consumerist recognition of perceptual relativity which serves as the foundation of dominant consumerist moving image constructs."[14] To encourage such a complex spectatorial response to his images, Brakhage developed an aesthetic means of layering his images via the superimposition of one shot on top of the other. He used this technique in THE DEAD (1960s) to simultaneously present moribund shots of granite tombs and headstones at a cemetery and vibrant shots of people walking and talking. With DOG STAR MAN (1964) Brakhage put the superimposition technique to its most startling effect. In relating what Dixon describes as "his epic creation of the universe,"[15] Brakhage layers as many as four images at a time on top of one another.

While usually considered an apolitical filmmaker more interested in the mechanisms of cinema than in using cinema to make didactic political interventions, even Brakhage by the late 1960s was employing his unique cinematic techniques in the service of social critique. His LOVEMAKING (1968), while referring back to previous explorations of human relationships and sexuality like WEDLOCK HOUSE: AN INTERCOURSE (1959), also grappled with the social politics of sexuality. Brakhage described the film as "an American Kama Sutra and love's answer to filmic pornography."[16] However, the most precise example of Brakhage's political turn is his two-part collage film, 23RD PSALM BRANCH (1967), which juxtaposes its Biblical title against superimposed images of the horrific Vietnam War. Brakhage's film follows in the tradition of Bruce Conner, the collage filmmaker famous for his 1958 masterpiece, A MOVIE.

Brakhage's retreat to Colorado makes him an unlikely candidate to be emblematic of the communitarian nature of American avant-garde cinema in the 1960s. He is, in fact, the only experimental filmmaker from that era who continued to exert a visible public influence on the concept of the avant-garde film through the remainder of the twentieth century. Throughout the 1970s, for example, Brakhage flew back and forth between Colorado and the School of the Art Institute of Chicago, where he gave courses in avant-garde cinema history. These well-attended lectures—in halls packed with as many as 500 students—consisted mainly of Brakhage detailing his personal reminiscences of the important practitioners of American avant-garde cinema, including filmmakers whose

Stan Brakhage at work with a standard issue camera for the avant-garde.

influence he enthusiastically acknowledged, such as Maya Deren and Marie Menken. Brakhage's lectures were subsequently published in his book, *Film at Wit's End* (1989).

Ironically, during a long period in which the widespread avant-garde experimentation of the 1960s in film had been relegated to academia, Brakhage, arguably the most peripheral member of the New York and Bay area avant-garde film communities of that decade, became one of the avant-garde's most powerful chroniclers. He also maintained his viability as a creative and influential filmmaker. Whereas the minimalist films of Andy Warhol and the structural films of Michael Snow by the twentieth century's end were seen as anachronistic oddities, employing aesthetic strategies that were tried and failed, Brakhage settled into the one place left for avant-garde film makers. He continued to teach and make avant-garde films at the University of Colorado at Boulder through the end of the century.

Intertextuality and the 1960s Avant-Garde

While it is easy to fall into the fetishization of the genius auteurs of the 1960s American avant-garde—such as Mekas, Baillie, and Brakhage—it is most important to understand the extent to which the avant-garde cinema engaged the larger political debates of 1960s culture, beginning with the two most obvious of issues, sexuality and race. Well established in the analysis of 1960s avant-garde cinema are the many intertextual references between those works and mainstream feature films. The dialectical connections have been richly explored by David James in his seminal study, *Allegories of Cinema* (1989).[17] However, it must be appreciated more emphatically that the importance of the 1960s avant-garde cinema lies in the extent to which it contributed directly to the cultural

Michael Snow, structuralist filmmaker.

matrix of American life. Stan Brakhage's BLUE MOSES, for example, is not just the "Romantic author" exploring in synchronized sound production technique, but becomes far more meaningful in the broadest cultural sense because of its reworking of Plato's "Allegory of the Cave" from *The Republic*.

Rather than chronicle the 1960s achievements of a few major filmmakers, this chapter seeks an intertextual understanding. What light do various works cast on each other, on the various avant-garde communities, and on 1960s society as a whole? This intertextual method will be used to study films that exhibit aesthetic practices resolutely associated with the avant-garde: BLUE MOSES (1962, Stan Brakhage), as a meta-textual mediation on the nature of representation, and PULL MY DAISY (1959, Robert Frank and Alfred Leslie), and HALLELUJAH THE HILLS (1963, Adolfas Mekas) as a cinematic attempt at Beat poetry. The intertextual method will also reveal the linkages between the experimental and the Hollywood genre film: HOLD ME WHILE I'M NAKED (1966, George Kuchar) and LONESOME COWBOYS (1967, Andy Warhol) will be investigated as a parody of a classic melodrama. These films may represent the work of prominent American avant-garde auteurs, but their rich references to culture and to other texts yield insights that a strict auteurist approach would leave obscured.

BLUE MOSES   BLUE MOSES begins with its credits obscurely and mysteriously written onto rocks in a wooded area. Suddenly, there is a cut to a cave with a shack in front of it. This is the central intertextual image in the film, as it summons to mind the most famous cave in the Western intellectual and artistic tradition, that described by Plato in

Book VII of *The Republic*. BLUE MOSES will become, as framed by this image, a meditation on the nature of cinematic representation. The allegory of the cave has profound implications for the study of representation in cinema. In Plato's allegory, a number of helpless prisoners are chained inside a cave. A fire burning behind them is used by their captors to illuminate shadows on the wall in front of the prisoners. One day, one of the prisoners escapes and discovers, much to his amazement, that the two-dimensional shadows he has been looking at for so long are in fact merely projections of a real, three-dimensional world. He returns to his fellow prisoners to inform them of the news, to which they respond with angry violence. Essentially, the desire of these prisoners to believe in the two-dimensional world over the real goes a long way to explaining our intense engagement with the two-dimensional representations offered by the cinema, a phenomenon that is intricately explored in BLUE MOSES.

At the beginning of BLUE MOSES, a man dressed as a carnival barker is presented in front of a cave in a series of jump cuts. As if advertising a sideshow, he screams out, "ladies and gentlemen. . . ." Then, back at the woods where the credits were introduced, this narrator begins telling us about some tracks on the ground that he finds perplexing. In a voice that conspicuously imitates Orson Welles, the narrator informs us that, "I'm here to find out about the tracks." At this point, the film appears to begin again. In a wooded area the viewer again sees a rock with the title of the film painted on it. Next, the narrator re-appears in a manner suggesting Moses from the Bible. He makes a grandiose, melodramatic gesture with his staff, excitedly presenting us with "an eclipse, manufactured but not yet patented, for your pleasure." In an aesthetic gesture that illustrates the avant-garde cinema's play with the basic materials of cinema, an inserted section of black leader (not a typical Hollywood special effect) simulates the eclipse about which Moses speaks.

Suddenly, and for no apparent reason, Moses begins speaking in a badly performed, stereotypical Southern accent. He invites us to "Let's play house." However, at this moment, he steps out of character and asks us, "Do you see what I meant by all that? It was ridiculous." He continues by telling us that the film is really about us, the viewers, and not about all that nonsense that has already occurred. In the film's payoff to the reference to the allegory of the cave, the narrator tells the viewer that there is a filmmaker behind everything. At this moment, he requests that we "Don't turn around. It's useless." Thus, the film's narrator, himself representing a profoundly important Biblical character, tells us not to repeat the liberating gesture of the escaped prisoner from Plato's story. However, the film's self-conscious reference almost impels us to turn around to see the projector that is itself converting a strip of celluloid into a two-dimensional projection of a twice-removed natural world that was filmed long ago.

The film then collapses the distinctions between the filmmaker and the narrator by drawing attention to the conventions of the medium of cinema itself. The film we are watching is suddenly projected onto the narrator's bare back, so that he becomes not only a fictional presence in the film, but also part of the mechanism of the delivery of cinema itself. The film concludes with an emphasis on this metadiegetic reflection over and above any narrative sense-making function. The narrator returns to the wooded area and makes reference to "the woman . . . his wife, so to speak." He returns to the mysterious tracks, which turn out to have been a narrative red herring all along. Contributing no more narrative understanding, he turns away in disgust, grumbling, "those damn tracks." We cut back to the carnival barker at the cave, who takes a bow to end the film.

BLUE MOSES thus achieves an investigation into the mechanism of cinema through a complex pairing of the Bible and Plato's *Republic*, not for narrative, but instead for metacinematic purposes. This illuminates, of course, one of the commonly studied features of experimental cinema: the ability of the form to reflect upon the basic components of the medium itself. However, the intertextual method reveals this self-reflexivity as having roots in the history of ideas, dating all the way back to the birth of Western culture itself.

PULL MY DAISY and HALLELUJAH THE HILLS   Intertextual references illuminate another truism of the 1960s American avant-garde cinema—its birth in the literary traditions of Beat poetry—in PULL MY DAISY (1959). Starring Allen Ginsberg and featuring the voice-over narration of Jack Kerouac, it is an avant-garde adaptation of Kerouac's book *The Beat Generation*. The film tells the story of a family living on the Lower East Side of Manhattan.[18]

Focusing on masculinity through the character Milo, PULL MY DAISY ends with an affirmation of the Beats' belief that a feminized, domestic culture is stifling. Milo's wife yells at him, "All these Beatniks in the house," then begins to cry. Simultaneously, Beat characters holler up the staircase to Milo, who puts on his coat and leaves his wife. The film cuts to an image of an empty rocking chair, concretizing the stifling, traditional nature of the domesticity that Milo just barely escaped. Milo assures his Beat friends, "She'll get over it." Engaging in a Beat mantra, Milo ends the film, "Let's go. Go. Go. Go."

The film uses its engagement with Beat poetry to advance a very traditional male rejection of the stifling nature of feminine, domestic culture. The critique of traditional marriage in PULL MY DAISY is from the point of view of the male victim, but is couched in a critique of organized religion that is seen to be the motor force behind the ensnaring of the male within this conventional institution. Certainly, this is not the only way the American avant-garde cinema of the 1960s represented the domestic space of patriarchal marriage—witness the feminist films of Marie Menken and Joyce Wieland.[19] In this instance, however, through the intertext of Beat poetry, the domestic is seen as stifling a fundamental masculinity that is essential to creativity and which is held to be capable of finding its true expression only in the company of other men.

PULL MY DAISY, made on the eve of the 1960s, was followed by a more thoroughly misogynist production, HALLELUJAH THE HILLS (1963), which employs an overt plot structure emphasizing traditional femininity's threat to male independence. Making explicit reference to the silent melodramas of D.W. Griffith, including an homage to the ice flow scene of WAY DOWN EAST (1920), the film shows how traditional patriarchal culture forestalls the exploration of an Emersonian appreciation of liberating nature. Images of Jack and Leo frolicking in a snow-bound wilderness are intercut with scenes of them competing for the love of Vera in her suburban house. After many years of conventional rituals, Thanksgiving and Christmas dinners and the like, Jack and Leo are finally freed when Vera marries another man. Liberated from such rituals, Jack and Leo run out of their log cabin and scream "hallelujah" while prancing through the snow, nearly naked. As a reward, Jack and Leo encounter a forest full of women. In an orgy of libidinal release, they chase the women around the forest. Failing to catch any of them, they return to their jeep and drive away, shouting good-bye to the snowy woods, and to female companionship altogether. As perhaps a final reminder of what they have escaped, the film concludes with them driving past two escaped convicts, one of whom is played by Beat artist Taylor Mead, whose literal prison shackles resonate with the figurative gendered ones just shed by the two male protagonists.

HOLD ME WHILE I'M NAKED   The American avant-garde cinema of the 1960s also engaged complexly with the representational traditions of mainstream Hollywood. The avant-garde film that most clearly assaults traditional Hollywood genres, HOLD ME WHILE I'M NAKED (1966, George Kuchar), deconstructs the melodrama. It begins with an image shot through a chain-link fence of a well-dressed woman running through a dilapidated city lot. A man's voice-over tells her to keep running, that this is a great part to be playing. Excessively suspenseful music accompanies the image of her running. The film cuts to a man in a parka filming the scene through a cheap 8mm camera. He signals O.K. and shakes gleefully as the scene comes to an end. Thus, HOLD ME WHILE I'M NAKED begins by self-reflexively interrogating the making of a film, but the film being made is not another avant-garde film; instead it is a low-budget exploitation film. The low-budget sensibility of the avant-garde cinema is applied to the making of an exploitation film, both of which offer conspicuously different production standards than the Hollywood norms.

The credit sequence of HOLD ME WHILE I'M NAKED parodies Hollywood high-gloss filmmaking. The sequence is filmed with flares, giving the image an excessively glossy sheen as if to emphasize the star quality that Hollywood would give the film if it were not a low-budget avant-garde production. In this ridiculous and shlocky parody, however, cardboard cutout letters float across the screen spelling the actors' names. In another imitation of Hollywood glamour, a title indicates, "Miss Kerness' clothes by Hope Morris," a gesture that does little to impress the viewer, given that Hope Morris has just been revealed to us as one of the actresses in the film.

After a pause in the soundtrack, piano music returns as the director films a scene in which an actor and an actress expand from lengthy kissing into sex, as the director inexplicably films the scene through a stained-glass window. The director has the actors repeat the scene, this time with the actress taking off her top because, according to the director, "the mysticism of the stained-glass window and the profanity of the brassiere do not go well together." In this way, the film interrogates the lure of the cinema, as the actors will suffer whatever humiliations are necessary just to be in a movie, even a painfully bad one and nothing like the Hollywood product that seduces people to want to be in pictures in the first place.

The director tells the actors the scene was terrific. His outline of the scenes they will shoot tomorrow again emphasizes the exploitative nature of the film, as one of the scenes will involve a fallout shelter where the female character suffers radiation damage to her thigh. When the director leaves, the couple continue their lovemaking, indicating a further level of irony: the two actors are not seduced by the lure of Hollywood after all, but instead are simply aroused.

Later, an actress in the film leaves the production, telling the director, "I'm sick and tired of being naked in almost every scene." The director, Phillip, responds by interacting with a blow-up plastic doll of a woman. Then, Phillip phones the actress, begging her to finish the film. After she refuses, Phillip calls one of his friends, who has just met a woman with dark glasses and smoking a cigarette—a direct imitation of the classic Hollywood femme fatale. While talking with Phillip on the phone, the actor begins making out with the femme fatale and they move on to the shower. Phillip tries to call them again, desperate to get them to act in his movie. Phillip takes a shower himself, and the film intercuts the lovers in the shower and Phillip in his shower alone. Phillip bangs his head into the shower wall repeatedly, at first indicating his frustration over his woes in making this film. However, there is a sudden knock at the bathroom door, as Phillip's mother tells him to get out of the shower because he has been in there for over an hour. Thus, the film indicates that all of the preceding scenes have merely been Phillip's fantasy of being a film director.

The film ends with an explosion of bitter irony. Excessively melodramatic music plays on the soundtrack as we see Phillip sitting at the kitchen table in his robe. His mother places before him a plate of disgusting black goo that is supposed to pass for food. Phillip looks directly into the camera and says with an exceptionally funny, droll irony, "There's a lot of things in life worth livin' for, isn't there?" In this way, HOLD ME WHILE I'M NAKED questions the allure of Hollywood cinema—telling glamorous stories about beautiful people, and then violently juxtaposing that illusion with the reality of an awkward kid who has no more chance of being a Hollywood director than he does of having sex with a beautiful woman. As avant-garde art, the film constructs a violent juxtaposition between the grim realities of everyday suburban life and the image of filmmaking as a glamorous profession.

LONESOME COWBOYS   Hollywood genre conventions are also parodied and reworked in LONESOME COWBOYS (1967, Andy Warhol), a revisionist western. The film begins with an extended sex scene between neophyte cowboy Little Joe (played by Joe Dallesandro) and Ramona (played by Viva), the proprietress of the local bordello. Whereas the Hollywood western typically represents a world of repressed sexuality—as in HIGH NOON (1952, Fred Zinnemann), where Gary Cooper's love for Grace Kelly is constructed through glance-object cuts that convey a desire not spoken in the dialogue—LONESOME COWBOYS emphasizes sexuality as the motor force of the genre. This is carried even further, as the Warhol film camps the repressed homoerotic desire among men in the Hollywood western, as when the competition between John Wayne and Montgomery Clift for the same woman in RED RIVER (1948, Howard Hawks) is expressed as physical violence toward one another. LONESOME COWBOYS translates this directly to homosexual desire and fulfillment, as Little Joe becomes the desired object for not only Ramona, but also for a gang of gay cowboys.

The ways in which these five avant-garde films forged their respective critiques of Western cultural traditions (BLUE MOSES), contemporary cultural practices (PULL MY DAISY and HALLELUJAH THE HILLS), and Hollywood cinema (HOLD ME WHILE I'M NAKED and LONESOME COWBOYS), constitute one abiding passion of the social and cultural community of experimental filmmaking in the 1960s. Each of these films represents a frontal attack upon notions of tradition, concepts of civilization, and ideas of religious faith, as well as glamour and entertainment. These assaults on propriety and conventionality were at the core of the cultural unrest that was evident among the highly self-conscious groups of artists and students who fashioned themselves as resisting the banalities of mainstream American culture in the late 1950s and on into the mid 1960s. Such films, and the essentially benign forms of cultural resistance that they nurtured, were the precursor of the counterculture of the late 1960s that spread across the United States. It was, however, in that segment of the avant-garde cinema that directly engaged the American social landscape through its representation of nontraditional sexuality—in defiance of puritanical traditions and conventional repression—that a more explosive form of film experimentation emerged.

Identity Politics and the 1960s American Avant-Garde Cinema

It was during the 1960s that gay and lesbian sexuality in the United States first asserted an aggressive claim for recognition of these "deviances" as alternative lifestyle choices. Although far from being spread widely in American culture, the grounds for this assertion amounted to the basic claims of equal treatment in society and the recognition that such lifestyle choices were being advanced as a claim of civil rights. Homosexuals and lesbians first came out of the closet in the United States during the 1960s, and they did so in the two urban centers, New York City and San Francisco, where gay lifestyles were most evident and most confrontational toward mainstream American culture. New York City and San Francisco also happened to be where the avant-garde cinema of the 1960s was centered. The actual shift to a gay political activism may date from the "Stonewall Incident" in 1969, when New York City police conducted a brutal raid at a popular gay bar, but the visibility of a growing gay counterculture and a new gay consciousness were both evident in New York City and San Francisco much earlier in the decade.[20]

Two avant-garde films of the 1960s, FLAMING CREATURES (1963)[21] and BLONDE COBRA (1963), deserve special consideration for their aggressive representation of sexuality. FLAMING CREATURES is organized into seven major sections, beginning with an orgy behind which is presented the film's credits. This sequence is followed by a scene in which a drag queen puts on lipstick. Suddenly, two traumatic events are presented—a rape and an earthquake. The film continues with a scene featuring a drag queen vampire, a celebratory dance, and concludes with an orgiastic performance of the pop song "Be Bop a Loo."

FLAMING CREATURES   The film features the self-reflexive gestures that one would expect of an avant-garde film, yet these gestures are deliberately tied to the representation of scandalous sexual practices. The first shot of the film features a sultry woman playing with her hair. Then, another woman steps in front of her and begins mugging for the camera. The camera tracks past these women to reveal the film's title, not presented on a title card, but instead written on the wall behind the women. One of the women walks in front of and obscures the film's title, thus calling attention to the film's modernist strategy of constantly reminding us of the tenuous relationship between the diegetic and metatextual levels of the film's narration. On the soundtrack, a man whispers "Ali Baba comes today," evidently punning between the nature of the music being heard and the orgy that is being seen.

The camera begins to reveal more of this orgy in progress. Close-ups of men taking off their pants lead to hands fondling a flaccid penis. It is at this moment that the film begins to engage its radical representational practices: The viewer is now clearly in a representational space completely unavailable to the mainstream Hollywood cinema. As if to comment on this shocking discovery, the soundtrack at this moment features Miklos Rozsa-style rousing march music commonly heard in Hollywood action films of the classical period. FLAMING CREATURES is constructed as an epic in the tradition of the

Hollywood films of the period, but in such a way that emphasizes the differences between what it shows as compared to what Hollywood can merely allude; consider, for example, the sexual explicitness of FLAMING CREATURES as compared to the subtle allusions to gay sexuality in the "oysters and snails" scene from SPARTACUS (1960, Stanley Kubrick).

Even more nontraditional sexuality appears in the film when a drag queen is shown sniffing flowers. A woman in a black dress (who is about to be violently raped) vamps in front of the camera. On the soundtrack, a romantic, Spanish-style tune can be heard. FLAMING CREATURES takes great pains to show the normality of the events: the woman in the black dress and the drag queen hug and talk, innocently. The drag queen begins putting on lipstick as the film enters its second section, during which the very conventions of classical cinema will be assaulted. On the soundtrack, we hear a radio announcer extolling the benefits of a new brand of indelible lipstick. This is accompanied by a stereotypical romantic melody emphasizing an expected heterosexual romance narrative. Instead, one of the ribald partygoers contradicts the expectations produced by the soundtrack when he is heard to say, "Is there a lipstick that doesn't come off when you suck cocks? But how does a man get lipstick off his cock?" Suddenly, and very comically, the radio announcer replies, "A man is not supposed to have lipstick on his cock." Thus, as is expected of an experimental film of the 1960s, FLAMING CREATURES breaks down distinctions between diegetic experiential orders, in this case the world of radio advertising and a scandalous orgy. This aesthetic gesture presents sexual practices that the mainstream culture presumably would want to vilify by showing them on screen precisely as a radio announcer's voice on the soundtrack intones that all oral sex—not just between men—is condemned. However, the film refuses to endorse the announcer's Puritanism, and this section of the film ends with a man deliberately putting lipstick on a penis which he happens to discover resting on his shoulder.

As if to remind us of the source of the radio announcer's Puritanism, the third section of FLAMING CREATURES begins with an image of a Victorian woman standing immobile amidst the orgy. Suddenly, however, our expectations are again shattered. In the film's most frightening moments, the drag queen turns violent, grabbing the woman in the black dress. Other men join him and the rape scene begins. Rough hands pull her breasts out of the dress and we hear her screaming. Just as her genitals are revealed, a mysterious cut to a shaking black lamp follows.

Gradually, the viewer becomes aware that the fourth section of the film—the earthquake—has commenced. As if to construct a moral retribution against this act of rape, but not necessarily the orgy which preceded it, we are given an overhead shot of the rape continuing as debris from the crumbling ceiling begins falling on the rapists. The screams of the rape victim now become indistinguishable from those of the earthquake victims. The participants of the orgy are now again seen to be writhing, but whether that gesture is from pleasure or agony is not clear. A blonde woman in pearls intervenes, taking the woman in the black dress into another room. They begin kissing, and it seems as if lesbian sexuality becomes the curative for the vicious act of male violence that the woman in the black dress has just experienced.

This transition initiates the fifth section of the film, in which a blonde vampire suddenly arises out of a coffin. Comically, this generic image associated with the horror film is juxtaposed on the soundtrack with a country-western singer crooning "Honky Tonk Angels." The vampire proceeds to suck the blood out of the necks of the earthquake victims, expressing another image of retribution for the acts of violence previously witnessed. The vampire begins dancing with the drag queen, as the sixth section of the film—a kind of celebratory dance of death—commences. Again, these unfamiliar images of nontraditional sexuality are juxtaposed with old-fashioned dance music on the soundtrack, emphasizing the film's entire strategy of anachronism. Quick-paced tango music suddenly replaces the old-fashioned music as a man in drag with a flower in his mouth enters the frame. A cut to an overhead shot emphasizes the frantic dancing of all in the room. At this moment, it becomes clear that the earthquake has produced not just rubble and destruction, but a palpable sense of death as well. To concretize this sensibility, a drag queen in a white dress with blonde hair—who can only be a reference to Marilyn Monroe—dances, amidst the rubble, with a dowdy-looking woman wearing horn-rimmed glasses. Postwar Hollywood's quintessential sex goddess, Monroe died in 1962, the year before the completion of FLAMING CREATURES, and thus is used by the film as another image that conflates gender, sexuality, and death. This "dance of death" section of the film continues with a shot of a black-haired woman. A mysterious hand begins fondling her breast. However, she lies completely inert, quite literally dead to the sexual advance. Negative image shots of the dancing bring the section to a conclusion, emphasizing the macabre, death-laden aspects of the ending moments of FLAMING CREATURES.

The film concludes, ironically, with a performance of "Be Bop A Loo" on the soundtrack as the camera cranes downward past the revelers and reveals a title card stating, "The End." However, the orgy continues, and the film presents us with more close-ups of hands fondling breasts. The last image of the film, in fact, is of a male hand jiggling a woman's bare breast. The film thus concludes by indicating its deepening contradiction between ribald representations of sexual pleasure, which are coupled with the contradictory progression toward death and morbidity. The film indicts male violence against women in its Cecil B. DeMille-like earthquake scene, yet its stance on the political nature of the behavior of these "flaming creatures" is otherwise ambiguous. The film revels in its representations of sexual behavior that mainstream culture would deem scandalous. It is, however, by no means a facile representation, as FLAMING CREATURES very clearly portrays the idea that such sexual acts—in a Puritanical culture at any rate—occur under the specter of violence, death, and destruction.

FLAMING CREATURES thus represents, on the one hand, a typical avant-garde film: it uses radical gestures of representation to shock and motivate its spectators into a heightened state of awareness about the conventions of cinema. The juxtapositions between image and soundtrack, the breaking down of the diegetic and meta-diegetic worlds, the intertextual use of glamorous yet ill-fated pop stars like Marilyn Monroe all establish the film's experimental lineage. On the other hand, however, FLAMING CREATURES applies these avant-garde strategies to deliberate engagements with sexuality as an identity political issue. Male violence against women, most explicit in the rape scene but also present through the image of Monroe, is interrogated. Same sex relationships, both between men and between women, are represented by the film with resolute precision. Moreover, the stakes of these representational practices are constantly emphasized, as the film uses the epic destruction of the space of the orgy to illustrate how tenuous these experiences are in a homophobic and sexist culture.

BLONDE COBRA   BLONDE COBRA, the other significant 1960s American avant-garde film about sexuality, further develops ambiguities between a free expression of sexuality and a pervasive cultural climate of constraint and violence. The film begins with two off-screen narrators engaging in a conversation about American popular music. A man with a deep voice queries, "What are your favorite Gershwin songs?" and another man with a squeaky high-pitched voice replies, "I Got Rhythm" and "Wonderful." While this conversation engages a common motif in gay culture, the love of deeply ambiguous American pop tunes, the image track is resolutely imponderable, consisting in this moment of a still photograph of Jack Smith eating what appears to be a piece of fruitcake. While playfully indicating that Smith is some kind of a "fruit," the soundtrack replies existentially to this image, initiating the film's musical refrain from "Let's Call the Whole Thing Off." The film becomes more and more aggressive in using stretches of white film leader to indicate what cannot be represented through imagery.

Then, the film presents color footage of men, including a shot of one smoking a pipe, and another of Jack Smith wearing a suit and tie. As Smith suddenly slides into a bathtub, the high-pitched narrator begins singing, off-key, "we are drowning in a sea of nascience." BLONDE COBRA thus lays out its primary aesthetic strategy: as a found-footage filmmaker, Ken Jacobs includes parody voice-off narration that comments on these found images. In this case, an already campy image of traditionally masculine subjects (because we know one of the men is Jack Smith) is further rendered ironic by the absurd vocal commentary.

Keeping with the "imperfect cinema" aesthetic practices of most underground film of the 1960s, hand-drawn title cards introduce the viewer to BLOND COBRA.[22] Jack Smith holds a card that indicates we are watching "a philm by Bobby Fleischner," while the narrator sings a parody of "boop boop e doo," a la Betty Boop. After another sequence of inexplicably inserted white film leader, we are presented with images of a graveyard, as the soundtrack informs us, "This is New York. The city of opportunity . . . enjoy the benefits of democracy." Like FLAMING CREATURES, the film thus presents us with an ironic juxtaposition, between platitudes of the American Dream on the soundtrack and representations of death and decay in the image.

BLONDE COBRA connects its fixation on death and decay to the impossibility of a stable gay sexuality in what was still an intensely homophobic culture. A somber gospel hymn on the soundtrack is directly paired with an image in which Smith campily kisses his own mirror reflection. The linkage to morbidity is again enforced, as the high-pitched voice narrates, "ravish. . . ravish. . . ravish. . . I'm ravishing the corpse." In a bizarre imitation of Sid Caesar, he continues by singing, "necrophiliac longing. . . necrophiliac fulfillment," finally finishing in a grandiose melodic flourish, "Leprosy is eating a hole in me."

The film then explicitly denies the connection between image and sound by removing the image altogether. While watching black leader, which lasts for four minutes, the narrator tells us a story to the accompaniment of stereotypically melodramatic orchestral music. "There once was a little boy," the narrator begins archetypally, "who lived in an enormous house." The story begins to lay out the narrator's childhood as a site of Oedipal trauma. He wails "Mother" repeatedly on the soundtrack. He then proceeds to tell a story of burning his neighborhood friend's penis with a match. Thus, again, the conflation between alternative sexuality and homophobic culture is linked through the register of violence, and in this case, genital mutilation.

As the image returns, we see Jack Smith lying in bed, naked. The narrator responds, "Oh God. Oh Creator, I mean." The joke at the expense of formal religion opens up the next major section of the film, which concerns Madame Nascience, the Mother Superior of a convent. Jack Smith plays Madame Nascience in gaudy drag and red lipstick. The image track consisting solely of black leader again returns, as the narrator tells us the story of Madame Nascience's lesbian encounter with Sister Dexterity. Reflecting on the moral erasure of lesbianism in homophobic culture, Madame Nascience insists that Sister Dexterity's story of abuse (she purportedly receives 90 lashes with the rosary with her habit dropped down) is a lie. When Sister Dexterity decides to lie on the altar and give herself to God as atonement, the narrator comments on the sacrilegious nature of the story, "what a turgid dream, indeed."

The sacrilegious nature of the story begins to take its toll on the narrator, as he lapses into a hysterical insanity and relates the tale. As he is describing Madame Nascience paddling the other nuns with a silver cross, the narrator begins to laugh hysterically as the paddling is heard on the soundtrack. This initiates a new section of the film in which the narrator's insane narrative turns toward the notion of God's existence. He sings, "God is dead and man is abandoned." When he changes his mind, arguing—"God is not dead. He is just marvelously sick"—he resumes; his insane laughter at the absurdity of life.

This in turn initiates yet another section of the film in which the history of Hollywood cinema is explored. Footage of Jack Smith resumes; this time he is wearing a papal hat and holding a Barbie doll's plastic leg. To this image the narrator comments, "Maria Montez was admirable. For one thing, she refused to wear brassieres." By invoking a Hollywood star—Montez was famous for her exotic south seas melodramas, including COBRA WOMAN (1944), from which Jacobs' film's title must derive—BLONDE COBRA indicates the myth of beauty on which the mainstream American cinema is built, and which the project of Jacobs' film is to parody. Montez is a perfect figure through which to engage the parody of Hollywood. Born in the Dominican Republic, and thus useful for a racist Hollywood to construct as exotic, she parlayed her good looks into a modeling and then a film career. Her first big success was in the title role of THE INVISIBLE WOMAN (1941). Her follow-up role, as Scheherazade in ARABIAN NIGHTS (1942), would forever typecast her as the exotic woman, such that she would become associated with the star discourse, "Aladdin and His Wonderful Vamp." The late career of Montez, her decline and death, made her an apt appropriation for the camp strategy of BLONDE COBRA. As Montez's fame began to fade in the late 1940s, she entered a period of depression as she gained weight rapidly. Her second husband, the international art film star Jean-Pierre Aumont, took Montez to Europe to try to stage a comeback. In a desperate attempt to lose weight, Montez began a dangerous hot bath regimen, and during one of these baths she died of a massive coronary.[23]

In attempting to make sense of this decay of beauty toward death, the narrator of BLONDE COBRA pursues a series of quotations. First the narrator quotes the film's star: "Why shave when I can't even think of a reason for living. Jack Smith. 1958." The film thus places the existential futility confronted within its diegesis in a specific historical context. The next quotation—"Life is a sad business. Greta Garbo"—returns the film to its campy subtext, through its reference to another beautiful female star ground up by the Hollywood machine. The narrator responds to this example with desperate camp, singing "You say neither, I say neither. Let's call the whole thing off," as Jack Smith dances joyfully in front of the camera. The insertion of white film leader ends the song mid-verse. The film concludes this section with another quotation, "Life swarms with innocent monsters. Charles Baudelaire," which resonates with the Romantic mythology of the avant-garde cinema itself, but which is being used not so much to justify the greatness of the artist as to express the general despair of the human condition.

BLONDE COBRA enters its final section with Smith shown in drag smoking cigarettes with a man in a gangster outfit. Suddenly, a second man wearing a fedora hat pulls out a knife and stabs the man in the gangster suit in the chest. Again imitating Sid Caesar,

Smith recoils in parodic horror. A cut to a panning shot which moves up Smith's body reveals the knife mysteriously emanating out of his buttocks, to which the narrator humorously responds, "Sex is a pain in the ass." Thus, the film returns to the central motif of the American avant-garde film of the 1960s concerning sexuality, namely the connection between sexuality and morbidity that is caused by a Puritanical and homophobic culture.

As the film ends, the narrator returns to his Oedipal analysis, arguing that "A mother's wisdom has dragged me down to this: hunger, futility, despair." As Jack Smith holds the title card reading, "The End," the narrator desperately screams out, "What went wrong! What went wrong!" Thus, the film concludes with an existential despair that germinates from the inability of its subjects to find a satisfying sexual and interpersonal expression in the midst of a repressive culture.

THE COOL WORLD   While the representation of sexuality is the focal point of identity politics in the American avant-garde cinema of the 1960s, other issues of identity in contrast to the mainstream of American society are present as well. Films on racial issues are the most problematic, given the dearth of African American filmmakers in the 1960s avant-garde, yet many core films of the avant-garde grapple with issues of race. The first in this tradition is SHADOWS (1959, John Cassavetes), a ground-breaking experimental film about the politics of passing, analyzed in the relationship between a light-skinned African American woman and her Italian-American jazz musician boyfriend.

The independent films of the 1960s that most directly followed in the tradition of SHADOWS include THE COOL WORLD (1963, Shirley Clarke) and ONE POTATO, TWO POTATO (1964, Larry Peerce). ONE POTATO, TWO POTATO is a realist study of an interracial marriage. THE COOL WORLD engages in an aggressive, stylized presentation of the life of Duke, an African American boy who lives in Harlem, gets mixed up in crime, and is killed by the police.

The cases of THE COOL WORLD and ONE POTATO, TWO POTATO indicate that during the 1960s, an unprecedented breakdown between the various modes of cinema—in this case, mainstream narrative and avant-garde cinema—was underway. That is to say, the distinctions between a mainstream film, an independent film, and an avant-garde film began to collapse in a film-going environment where extremely experimental films like HALLELUJAH THE HILLS and THE COOL WORLD received theatrical releases. For this reason, rigid distinctions between avant-garde, experimental, underground, and independent films cannot be sustained historically.

Films like SHADOWS and THE COOL WORLD need to be discussed simultaneously with more unambiguously avant-garde films like THE QUEEN OF SHEBA MEETS THE ATOM MAN. SHADOWS has much in common with the films under scrutiny in this chapter, even though it was directed by John Cassavetes, who would subsequently direct more conventional independent features like FACES (1968), HUSBANDS (1970), and A WOMAN UNDER THE INFLUENCE (1974). Shot in 16mm and improvised, SHADOWS was forged out of a communitarian approach to filmmaking, in stark contrast to Hollywood production methods.

THE COOL WORLD was directed by Shirley Clarke, whom the scholar Lauren Rabinovitz labels one of the three most important women avant-garde filmmakers working in New York City. Shot in 16mm and aggressively mixing filmmaking styles by employing cinéma verité documentary techniques to present a fictional plot, THE COOL WORLD represents life in Harlem in impressively direct and confrontational political terms. The film actually begins with a boldly aggressive narrative gesture. The viewer is placed without warning in the midst of a Black Muslim's speech (shot in close-up) about how "the white devil" is ruining the African American community. We are forced to wonder what function this has in the overall narrative pattern of the film. It becomes clear that the film is interested in sociologically positioning the teen-aged protagonist Duke in relation to African American culture in Harlem and a larger white supremacist culture in general.

The film often makes these connections quite subversively. For example, a white teacher takes his black students from Harlem on a field trip to Wall Street. He drones on about the American Dream while standing in front of a statue of George Washington. The black students joke and smoke cigarettes, caring neither about the teacher nor his American Dream. THE COOL WORLD treats this lack of communication ironically by focusing on the statue of George Washington, who for the white teacher is an icon of freedom, but to black folks certainly must represent the legacy of eighteenth-century slavery. The moment's final contradiction occurs as the teacher hands each black student a pamphlet that reads "Own a Share in America." The slogan is an advertisement for Wall Street, but given the circumstances it is a bitter irony since "shares" of black folks like these kids were once owned by whites.

The film plays off this irony at its end, as Duke is gunned down by the white police. The last images of the film reveal a police car, sirens blaring, rushing to some other disturbance. On the film's soundtrack, a radio news report delivers the final irony as commentary about a communist stronghold in Vietnam is juxtaposed against a story on urban gang warfare. Thus, THE COOL WORLD asserts that its local plot about a gang member needs to be understood in the larger context of global politics, and that America is both a racist social regime and an imperialist power.

THE QUEEN OF SHEBA MEETS THE ATOM MAN   While THE COOL WORLD is one of a handful of highly unusual independent features in the tradition of SHADOWS, more thoroughly experimental films of the 1960s also grappled with issues of race. Most interesting in this tradition is THE QUEEN OF SHEBA MEETS THE ATOM MAN (1963), which concerns the tempestuous love affair between the Atom Man, a frail white man (played by Taylor Mead), and the Queen of Sheba, an enormous black woman (played by Winifred Bryan). The film begins with shots emphasizing the refuse-filled life in which the Atom Man lives without the Queen of Sheba. A poetic image of a crane picking up garbage is juxtaposed against a classical, symphonic soundtrack, and then the film cuts to the Atom Man's apartment, which is full of junk.

In a comedic gesture towards the drug culture, the Atom Man is revealed as a drug addict, storing his stash in a trash can labeled "heroin." He even feeds heroin to a rubber mouse he keeps beneath a sink. After burying his head in a can of heroin, he collapses to the floor. These images of drug-induced depravity are linked to our first encounter with the Queen of Sheba, beginning, as she is most often seen throughout the film, lying naked in bed. She awakens, immediately downs a glass of vodka, and then rings for her manservant to bring her more vodka. The images of the Queen of Sheba certainly link to the racist imagination, in which black folks are more connected to nature, and more earthy, although the film frames these images through such an excess that they could, even at this point, be read as parody of that very racist imagination.

The Atom Man arrives at the Queen of Sheba's apartment. He takes a mallet out of a violin case and begins gently tapping her nude body. He takes out an outrageously long

A scene from the independent, experimental film, THE QUEEN OF
SHEBA MEETS THE ATOM MAN *(1963).*

hypodermic needle and injects her, and she screams in pain. The film comically cuts to
a giant plaster foot squashing the Atom Man's face into the floor, perhaps an image of
the Queen of Sheba's violent reaction to his pseudo-medical torture of her body. The
two characters begin to play together with a string of pearls and a big metal hoop until
the Queen accidentally fall backwards on top of him, squashing the frail Atom Man.

Images of the grotesque, naked body of the Queen of Sheba are delicately juxtaposed
with the most poetic moments of the film in which the Queen walks around New York
City, dressed very conventionally in overcoat and purse.[24] A somber jazz score accompanies her stroll. She rides a subway train, and then takes a ferry ride across the river.
Glance-object cuts reveal the Queen looking at beautifully poetic shots of huge chunks
of ice floating in the river, accompanied by a somber prelude for piano by Frédéric
Chopin on the soundtrack.

Meanwhile, the Atom Man is also wandering around the city. He enters a museum,
where he touches a sculpture of a large black woman, drawing the film's own representation of the black female body into a larger context, including the realm of legitimate
art's representation of that body for the consumption of "sophisticated" art patrons. The
Atom Man's touching the sculpture emphasizes the false distinction between these types
of patron, sexualizing the response to the sculpture. This linkage to issues of nontraditional and "inappropriate" display of sexuality is furthered in the film's subsequent
moments, when the Atom Man enters the men's room and "accidentally" opens the toilet stall door on a man sitting on the pot. We then cut immediately to the Atom Man sitting in his apartment reading the book, *Diary of a Nymph,* and cracking up in front of
and mugging for the camera. It is this playful, self-conscious representation of sexuality
as a human act of pleasure that most distinguishes THE QUEEN OF SHEBA MEETS THE
ATOM MAN, whether it is in the representation of Taylor Mead's bisexuality, or in its
emphasis on a most intriguing interracial romance.

The combination of bisexuality and interracial romance is most forthrightly represented in the film's next major sequence, in which the Atom Man arrives at the Queen's

apartment, only to find her in bed with another white man. The scene begins with the man and the Queen in bed. Behind them, clearly emphasized in the *mise-en-scene,* is a photo of Marlon Brando dressed as Fletcher Christian from MUTINY ON THE BOUNTY (from the cover of an edition of *Life* magazine) pasted to her wall. At first, the Atom Man does not notice the Queen having sex with another man. The comic nature of this delay of discovery is enhanced when he responds to this betrayal with ridiculous, melo-dramatic gestures. He then playfully collapses onto the bed with them, deciding to join in rather than respond jealously. Inexplicably, in the next shot, the lover is seen lying on the floor, inert. The Atom Man and the Queen then engage in a post-coital bout of con-sumption, consisting of vodka and peanut butter. The film engages in a riotously funny parody of advertising culture: the Atom Man produces a product placement ad for the peanut butter, writing "Skippy Peanut Butter" in shaving cream on a mirror. Then, the two fall asleep.

In the next shot, Brando is re-constructed as an object of gay desire. The Atom Man reads the *Life* magazine article about Brando, stopping to lick and eat each page that features a photograph of Brando. After this consumption of the star image, the Atom Man reads another book, *Men,* by Taylor Mead, thus collapsing the distinction between star and character in the midst of representing a fan's erotic attachment with the star.

The film's radical collapse of such comic moments with deeply political moments is its most interesting narrative feature. For example, the Atom Man enters a liquor store and begins shoplifting. A policeman catches him and, in a scene that directly references a similar one in A NIGHT AT THE OPERA (1935) in which Harpo Marx is caught steal-ing, the Atom Man begins to give everything he has stolen to the cop. However, in the midst of this sight gag, the Atom Man unexpectedly steals the cop's gun and shoots him in the face. Footage from Anthony Perkins in THE TRIAL (1962, Orson Welles) running through narrow, brightly lit corridors, is inserted as the Atom Man desperately flees from the police. The scene ends with a Kafkaesque image, as the chase comes to a halt in front of a giant clock face. Hence, a slapstick comedy is transformed into a desperate political agenda; the Atom Man goes from instantaneously riffing on Harpo Marx to becoming a violent outlaw. Nonetheless, he is no romanticized outlaw in the tradition of Hollywood's BONNIE AND CLYDE (1967), but instead is a true existential renegade because of his nontraditional sexuality, as the intertextual linkage to the reputedly gay actor Anthony Perkins attests.

The film uses this radical intertextuality throughout to explore issues of sexuality. In the clearest example of this technique, the film parodies William Shakespeare's *Hamlet.*[25] This sequence begins as the Atom Man enters an art house cinema where Laurence Olivier's film adaptation of HAMLET (1948) is playing. The Atom Man sits and watches the ending sword fight between Hamlet and Laertes. Suddenly, the film cuts to a shot in the Queen of Sheba's apartment. A man holds a hand-drawn sign that reads, "Hamlet," an imperfect cinematic gesture in stark contrast to the elegant one-sheet for Olivier's film that the Atom Man looked at on his way into the revival house. The Queen of Sheba begins re-enacting the plot from Hamlet, pouring poison into a man's ear as if she were Claudius and the man were Hamlet's father. The Atom Man enters the scene anachronistically, skipping gleefully and waving a roll of toilet paper. Thus, his presence assaults the propriety of the canonical text, as there is no toilet paper in Olivier's version of the play, for this would ruin the aura around the work of art by reminding us that peo-ple must defecate even in Shakespeare. However, the Atom Man quickly gets into the swing of things, skewering a man hiding behind a curtain, as if he were Hamlet and his victim were Polonius. In an overhead shot, we see the Atom Man and the Queen of Sheba standing over the two dead bodies. The Atom Man quickly jumps on top of the Queen, and the two have sex amidst the dead bodies.

The adaptation of *Hamlet* within THE QUEEN OF SHEBA MEETS THE ATOM MAN is confusingly avant-garde. The moment is clearly about camp parody, especially in its exploration of the seeming incongruity of the toilet paper. However, the scene also grapples with issues of sexuality that are at play in *Hamlet*, although in different terms. Claudius murders Hamlet's father, in part for a sexual purpose—he wants Gertrude for himself—while Hamlet kills Polonius, albeit mistakenly, due to his jealousy over his mother's sexual union with Claudius. The terms of sexuality are thrown into utter chaos, however, in the avant-garde film's adaptation of this plot material. For, effectively, Hamlet (the Atom Man) and Claudius (the Queen of Sheba) end up having sex with one another. Thus, an incongruity in the adaptation is used to emphasize the film's unique Oedipal sexual union between the frail Atom Man and the excessively maternal Queen of Sheba, most prominently figured through her enormous breasts that repeatedly serve as the sites for male suckling.

Although not prominent in the *Hamlet* section of the film (except in terms of the undeniability of the Queen of Sheba's huge, naked black body), race figures throughout the film's penultimate section. Jack Smith, that perennial stand-by of the 1960s avant-garde scene, comes over to the Queen's apartment for an orgy. During the festivities, the Atom Man dons an African mask while dancing. In the meantime, Jack Smith drags the Queen of Sheba over to a couch by her bare legs and places a clock mask over her vagina. The Atom Man licks her genitals, sticking his tongue out of the eye-hole of the African mask. Thus, in addition to the nontraditional sexuality being represented during this sequence, the viewer is also confronted with the significance of race-related signifiers, as in the African mask that alters the Atom Man's persona while he engages in oral sex with the Queen of Sheba.

The film ends with an overtly politicized sequence emphasizing the public significance of the interracial relationship between the Atom Man and the Queen of Sheba. While they engage in playful sexual activity (the Atom Man jiggles the Queen's bare breast), some activists enter the apartment. They wear placards that state, "Peace must come from the people," "General strike for peace now," and "We must love one another and die." Taking the Atom Man, they leave the apartment and go to a bar that features a prominent sign, "No Dancing." As soon as the Atom Man begins dancing, a bouncer comes over and throws him out onto the street. The Queen of Sheba and the Atom Man return to the bar together. The Queen uses her immense heft to begin beating the bouncer. Suddenly, the bouncer changes his opinion, and he and the Queen begin dancing, with the "No Dancing" sign prominently in the background. Others in the bar join in dancing. Thus, the film ends with an act of communitarian transformation; the prohibition against dancing is overcome by the overthrow of authority in a defiant act of collective strength. Clearly, this is a central motif of the film as a whole: cultural taboos such as bisexuality and interracial romance can only be torn down by resistant acts, such as the representational practices of the film itself.

Go Go Go   The relationship between the Atom Man and the Queen of Sheba indicates one aspect of how completely issues of gender were explored in the American avant-garde cinema of the 1960s. This should not come as a surprise, given the appearance of the women's liberation movement during this period, which began crystallizing first in the rise of counterculture communities that began appearing not long after the publication of Betty Friedan's *The Feminine Mystique* in 1963. However, with the exception of Maya Deren, who herself is often characterized through a patriarchal lens as a kind of maternal figure for a younger generation of more accomplished avant-garde filmmakers, criticism has tended not to analyze in detail issues of gender in the 1960s American avant-garde cinema. One of the more interesting of the avant-garde films that promoted a feminist agenda in the decade was GO GO GO (1964, Marie Menken).

Menken's title itself clearly establishes her film as responding to one of the seminal American avant-garde films, PULL MY DAISY (1959). That film ends with Milo chanting, "Let's go. Go go go," as he escapes his domestic chains represented by his wife. The entire idea of Menken's GO GO GO frontally assaults the masculinist nature of the Beat imagery in PULL MY DAISY by subtly transforming the subject matter of the avant-garde film itself. Built out of home movie imagery, GO GO GO calls attention to the engendered nature of this mode of cinematic experience, thus hollowing out the patriarchal assumptions of both the home movie and the avant-garde film.[26] GO GO GO begins with its most obvious reminder that a differently gendered authorial voice is addressing its audience: The credits are written in bright red lipstick over a glass plate. The film then cuts to rapid tracking shots of New York City, recalling the city symphony films of Dziga Vertov and Walther Ruttmann from the 1920s. However, the film quickly moves away from this canonical avant-garde tradition, focusing instead on the home movie mode of experience. GO GO GO cuts to a graduation ceremony, rendered in fast motion. The home movie aesthetic, coupled with the fast motion, renders this ceremony ridiculous, stripped of its pomp and circumstance. The orderly rows of students receiving their diplomas, while controlled by officious men who are keeping them in line, is constructed to depict each of them as sheep rather than bright, individual minds.

These images of a male order are contrasted with shots of a men's bodybuilding competition and a girl's debutante ball. However, both of these sequences are also rendered in aggressive stylistic terms. The bodybuilding competition is shot from an extreme distance, while the debutante ball is filmed from behind some shrubbery. Thus, the film's mode of address emphasizes its own marginality, not its privileged status. In the case of the bodybuilding imagery, the film represents an alternative desire for the male body while at the same time ideologically critiquing such a desire via the absurd distance through which it is represented. Similarly, the images of the debutante ball construct an ambiguous relationship that exists in stark contrast to both the graduation ceremony and the bodybuilding competition. This debutante ball is a traditionally feminine space to which the filmmaker does not appear to have full access.

Such simultaneous playfulness with both traditional gender roles and their deconstruction constitutes the remainder of the film. Menken's pairing of seemingly incongruous images continues with more home movie footage, this time of a wedding, cut together with a man laboring at his typewriter, looking out his window at the cityscape and apparently searching for inspiration. In this way, the film interrogates the nature of traditional gender roles. The wedding indicates the appropriate behavior for a woman, while another stereotype, crucial for seeing the importance of the female authorship of GO GO GO, indicates the male struggle to create artistically.

In the penultimate pairing of images, we see a girl in a bikini kissing her boyfriend at the beach at Coney Island, and then nuns walking on the streets of Manhattan, reminding us of two traditional, although contradictory, roles for women. The film ends, however, with yet another pairing that assaults the earlier image of the man at the typewriter:

a poetic image of the sunset over New York's harbor is disrupted by a shot of a woman behind a glass screen on which "The End" is written in red lipstick. Her ambiguous gesture serves to interrogate this myth of male artistry by ending Go Go Go with an image of a woman character who does not create, but at least begins to gesture for more to come. That more to come, of course, is presented by the film's meta-diegetic circumstances: Marie Menken is the female response to that struggling male artist within the diegetic space of the film.

The Structural Avant-Garde Film

A much more complicated analytical site of a woman filmmaker working in the American avant-garde cinema of the 1960s is the case of Joyce Wieland. As the scholar Lauren Rabinovitz poignantly describes, Wieland has nearly always been overshadowed by her more famous structural filmmaker husband, Michael Snow.[27] It is with an emphasis on the films of Joyce Wieland, however, that gender as a political identity issue can be revealed even within the sub-genre of the structural film in the 1960s American avant-garde cinema. This is important, because by definition, structural films (or "pure cinema," as some practitioners and critics prefer to call it) are intended not to be contaminated by issues of any ideology, including gender. WAVELENGTH (1967, Michael Snow) or 1933 (1967, Joyce Wieland) are purportedly exercises in the functioning of cinema unhampered by distractions of narrative or character development. WAVELENGTH, for example, is a forty-five minute continuous zoom that begins in a long shot and ends in an extreme close-up of a photograph of a wave on the opposite wall of the room.[28]

Michael Snow's status as the most famous structural avant-garde filmmaker of the 1960s is uncontested. For example, the critic Wheeler Winston Dixon concludes his discussion of Snow with unbridled praise: "Working in cinema, sculpture, photography and video, Snow continues to create a torrent of original and captivating work which, for many, defines the essence of the experimental cinema of the 1960s."[29] The structural films for which Snow is famous include WAVELENGTH, a film built out of one zoom shot, and BACK AND FORTH (1969), a film consisting of increasingly rapid horizontal pans. Thus, these films become interrogations of the very building blocks of film language, each focusing on one aesthetic practice and emphasizing its operation in exquisite detail. Interestingly, Snow himself does not envision his structural filmmaking as a direct assault on classical Hollywood conventions. Discussing the narrative event in WAVELENGTH when a man (played by the experimental filmmaker Hollis Frampton) falls over and dies, Snow comments: "I absolutely *never* intended the film as a critique of 'Hollywood-style narratives.' There are thousands of 'narratives' in the film, some of them verbally indescribable. I simply included a 'peopling' of the space with implications of further continuity as one of the types of 'narrative' in the film."[30] Such tensions in the structural film, between the rigor of the aesthetic practice and the uncontrollable implications of narrative, lie at the core of Snow's work. In discussing the background images of WAVELENGTH, which consist of cars and people passing by outside the apartment window, Snow states: "WAVELENGTH is both carefully thought out, formally shaped and conscious and fortuitous and unconscious which is precisely part of its content."[31]

Similarly, Joyce Wieland's 1933 consists of ten images connected by white leader, constructing both a rigorous repetition and yet a haunting system of potentially mean-

The apartment in WAVELENGTH *(1967, Michael Snow).*

ingful differences. Each of the ten images is outwardly the same: a stable camera position at a high angle looks through an iron railing, down at a street scene. People walk on the street, passing the unmoving camera at various speeds. In some of the shots, "1933" in white letters is superimposed over the image, while in other shots this detail is missing. Thus, like most structural films, the strategy involves forcing the viewer to attempt to find meaning in patterns that may be developing in the images themselves, or in the internal rhythms that appear to be structuring the films. In fact, it is not until the fourth or fifth time the shot recurs that it becomes clear we are watching the same image again and again, rather than very similar images filmed at different times of day on the street. The film thus uses this repetition to construct an image of street life as creepy, alienated, lonely, and frightening.

At first glance, the structural strategy of 1933 seems perfectly in keeping with the other films in the tradition. There is a feminine specificity in the work of Wieland, however, that is not found in the work of Michael Snow. For like Menken's views in GO GO GO, 1933 presents a specific kind of passive alienation from the world going on around the camera. This passivity stands in stark contrast to the way in which WAVELENGTH addresses its viewer. In the Michael Snow film, women are directly represented. His film begins in a long shot of a loft apartment in the middle of a big city. Women enter the apartment and direct moving men to place a bookcase on a wall screen left. Shortly afterward, these two women return. One of them shuts the window, while the other turns on a radio. Each is involved in her own actions; these two never talk to one another. Thus, these women are in fact alienated, but specifically from one another. This

Rubber-gloved hand in Joyce Wieland's structuralist film, WATER SARK.

idea is further reinforced by the fact that the women leave the apartment one at a time, during which the camera is slowly zooming forward, in its inevitable progress toward the close-up of the photograph on the opposite wall.

Midway through the film, in its most notorious event, a man enters the apartment and stumbles, falling onto the floor, beneath the bottom of the film frame. The camera does not respond to this mysterious action, refusing to stop the progress of the zoom and look down to investigate why the man has fallen. The image itself responds, by flashing violently, and so does the soundtrack, which resumes an increasingly higher pitched whining hum. Thus, unlike 1933, in which there is never any choice but to inhabit the alienated, lonely, and frightening place behind the iron grillwork looking out over the street, WAVELENGTH makes a deliberate, intellectualized decision to deny the viewer the pleasure of narrative resolution, which in itself is a worthwhile distinction in terms of the relationship between narrative desire and the nature of gendered representations in these films.

A subsequent film by Wieland, CATFOOD (1968), even further emphasizes the importance of gender in the construction of her structural cinema. It consists of various close-ups of a cat consuming a dead fish. Unlike the importance of the murder or accidental death represented in WAVELENGTH, CATFOOD presents a perfectly innocent domestic situation rendered grotesque by the filmmaker's intervention into the material.

Early manifestations of Wieland's ideological reconstruction of the structural film resonate in the experiments at Andy Warhol's "Factory." In particular, a Warhol film like BLOW JOB (1963) indicates that the roots of structural cinema do not lie in pure cinema at all, but, instead, in a deep interest in the ideological nature of representation. BLOW JOB consists of a thirty-five-minute medium close-up shot of a blonde-haired man's face. He periodically leans his head back and shows an expression of elation. He frequently glances upward, wipes his forehead with his hand, and purses his lips together, all indicating to us that he is experiencing extreme pleasure. At the end of the film, he lights and smokes a cigarette in a state of extreme satisfaction.

However, nothing in the image indicates that he is receiving this pleasure from an act of oral sex. This interpretation is activated entirely through the information conveyed to the viewer via the film's title. BLOW JOB is a structural experiment in spectatorship, interrogating how linguistic phenomena (titles, in this case) relate to representational material within the diegesis. Thus, even from its earliest manifestations, the structural film was deeply imbued with ideological material. Besides playing with the structural nature of film representation, BLOW JOB relates to issues of gender as well as sexuality: it is not indicated whether the person performing fellatio is male or female, since we do not see the person performing the act.

Much as Warhol's film interrogates taboos against sexuality, Menken's female authorial voice in GO GO GO is used to counteract the misogyny of the Beat film, PULL MY DAISY, and Wieland's film reconstructs the structural film from a different gender perspective. WATER SARK (1965), another film by Wieland, begins with an intriguing credit sequence that relies on aggressive superimpositions and concludes with a cut to a reflection of a lamp's illumination in a pool of water. The film's production company, "Corrective Films," is apropos of its project of gender critique and we next see Wieland operating the camera in a mirrored reflection. The images of the domestic situation that motivated the structural analysis in CATFOOD are also present here, this time in the form of a dining table on which sits a glass of water, some fruit, and a blue teapot.

WATER SARK begins to sensualize these domestic images. The fruit is represented in distorted fashion through reflections in the mirror and the water glass. The images are already vaguely sensual, although nothing yet establishes that they are unambiguously sexual. However, these images are next intercut with a blurry and distorted picture that takes some time for the viewer to realize that the content has shifted from the domesticity of the fruit to female breasts and the sensuality of the female body. The film uses the image of water to express the fluidity of female sexuality in the literal shot of Wieland shaking the glass of water in front of her breasts.

Further clarifying its strategy of distorted images, the film reveals that these images have been shot through a prism, which for the first time the viewer sees clearly. A red filter, moreover, is used to further abstract images during this section of the film. Next, Wieland dons a plastic glove on her hand, which she uses to play with a plastic tugboat in the water. The plastic glove makes a more explicit reference to the domestic: such a glove might be used most appropriately to clean house. Wieland dips the glove into the water, examining the boat and the water itself. This is an image that conveys the denial of a tactile sensation and becomes an extended metaphor for women's domestic experience within a patriarchal society.

After the film lingers, under the abstraction caused by the prism and the red filter, on Wieland's naked body, a sudden transition occurs to a blue filtered image, in which Wieland is seen in a blue striped dress as she walks around her apartment. Entering this new phase, the film indicates that we have just witnessed the climax, perhaps literally, as Wieland's sensual experience with her own body has now come to an end. In this final phase of the film, Wieland wields a magnifying glass, using it to again shake and distort the image. This is WATER SARK's most provocative representation, for in direct conflict with the conventions of traditional cinema, in which the male role is that of investigator, here Wieland herself fulfills that role. As in CATFOOD, the magnifying glass is brought to bear on an image of the household cat, the feline serving metaphorically as the female. Wieland again turns the camera on herself, blinking grotesquely with the magnifying glass placed directly in front of her eye. The film thus playfully represents the female investigator not attempting to make sense of the outside world, but of her own body. More playful grotesquery ensues, as the film presents, in stop motion, Wieland examining her teeth with the magnifying glass and the film camera.

WATER SARK concludes with Wieland taking in her hand a toy tugboat that appeared during the middle of the film. She now plays with it in the water with an ungloved hand. A concluding title card reading "Corrective Films New York" reinforces the meaning of this image. The plastic glove associated with domestic constraint has been discarded, allowing the full experience of female sexuality. It is finally this "corrective" that the film has taken great pains to represent.

Conclusion: American History and Avant-Garde Cinema

There is no better example of an avant-garde film that explores its historical context than REPORT (1967, Bruce Conner), which uses the aggressive aesthetic and intertextual strategies of the avant-garde, as outlined above, in order to grapple with the trauma produced by the assassination of President John F. Kennedy. The film begins with television coverage of Kennedy traveling to Dallas and an announcer relating facts about the president's visit. The film begins to interrogate the nature of representation with the particular crisis of the Kennedy assassination as its backdrop. On the film's soundtrack, the announcer tells us that something has happened, but the film shows us no corresponding images. Instead, the motorcade is shown before the assault on the president's life. Ironic editing is employed, as a strip of film with the word "Finish" is presented. Thus, the very means of cinema meant to be hidden (such as film leader) are used to represent the most graphic event of the 1960s. The film denies what makes cinema special—the ability to render moving images in motion. Instead, the film gives us what is most moving emotionally solely on the soundtrack, suggesting that images cannot possibly capture this sort of trauma. Flickering white leader is all that is presented for three minutes, as the announcer describes the limousine rushing the president to the hospital.

Later, REPORT pursues its radical historiographical project by expanding outward from its core cinematic investigation into the Kennedy assassination. Chaotically mixing temporal locations, the presidential jet arrives in Dallas. The soundtrack tells us that "the doors (of the jet) fly open." In the accompanying image, however, the viewer sees a television commercial in which doors of a refrigerator fly open. Thus, the loss of President Kennedy is presented within a larger narrative of national tragedy in which advertising imagery contaminates the culture. REPORT then pursues its use of juxtapositional irony further, equating the devastating trauma of President Kennedy's death with the atomic bomb. As the viewer is presented with a stock footage image of the atomic mushroom cloud, a reporter tells us of the weather during Kennedy's visit to Dallas: "The weather couldn't be better. We have a brilliant sun at this moment." The film constructs this metaphor of reaping what one sows through imagery of the classical Hollywood horror film, FRANKENSTEIN (1931, James Whale). Dr. Frankenstein is seen firing up his generators, intercut with shots of Kennedy in his casket, which implies that the death of President Kennedy is to be comprehended as a monstrous consequence of the cold war and the atomic age. The film ends bitterly, directing its critique of an America that produced the assassination of President Kennedy against the nation's large corporations. Found footage of a woman operating an IBM electric stock trading device ends the film, as she pushes the button labeled, "Sell." Thus, an America that produced the assassination of its hero has been sold out—by the atomic age and by corporations. Hence, REPORT produces a complex historiographic analysis of America in the 1960s that far transcends its status as the experimental "found footage work" of an individualistic avant-garde artist, Bruce Conner, who might otherwise be considered as interested solely in a formalistic manipulation of film in order to heighten the viewer's awareness of cinema as a system of representation and expression.

A final note of importance concerns the ways in which 1960s American avant-garde cinema uses images of outer space. Both canonical and understudied avant-garde films of the 1960s are haunted by abstract imagery directly tied to the fascination with space in American culture throughout the 1960s. The fact that this fascination was the direct result of the space race is a little-appreciated facet in studying the avant-garde. From this point of view, DOG STAR MAN (Stan Brakhage, 1964) emerges as one of many cultural manifestations of the cold war-driven space race. To study the avant-garde of the 1960s from such a position is to directly challenge our understanding not only of the avant-garde, but of its relationship to 1960s culture writ large.

American avant-garde cinema in the early 1960s was marked by the extremely precarious financing for the films, most often drawn from personal funds. The origins of that cinema, moreover, were strongly alternative and remained focused in the Beat scene and counterculture communities of San Francisco and New York City. The decade's leading sustainer and promoter of this avant-garde, Jonas Mekas, has documented the various "showcases" he ran during the 1960s for experimental films of all sorts. The New Bowery Theater on St. Mark's Place in New York City, for example, was closed by police after the seizure of FLAMING CREATURES in 1964. Although many cinemas, especially in Greenwich Village, hosted such screenings from time to time during the 1960s, avant-garde films never truly found a sustainable home in the established exhibition venues of movie theaters—either in New York City or elsewhere.[32] Beyond screenings in clubs or coffeehouses, exhibition of avant-garde cinema became far more common in the museum and gallery world and eventually made inroads to college and university campuses, which significantly increased its cultural presence nationwide. The founding of the National Endowment for the Arts in 1966, and the subsequent establishment of arts councils in many states over the next several years, meant increased funding for avant-garde cinema production and exhibition from the public treasury, although most of this money quickly became earmarked for museums, rather than for individual artists and filmmakers. By that time experimental film—already attracting generous grants attention from the Ford Foundation and other private organizations— was well along the path of becoming institutionalized.[33] The American avant-garde cinema was at its most provocative and challenging in the early years of the decade, when its daring and radical alternative visions of human logic, sex, drugs, and cinema stood out so explosively against the background of a still quiescent mainstream culture.

To return to the chapter's opening, these films demonstrate that the avant-garde cinema of the 1960s emerged from a position of anger. Many different avant-garde films of the period emerge as being fueled "by anger," not just a film by (Kenneth) Anger, but by a multitude of others as well. From Duke's anger at racial oppression in THE COOL WORLD to that angry response to President Kennedy's assassination as explored in REPORT, we can see in the 1960s avant-garde a bilious frustration with the status quo in all forms. Such anger is given both social expression, as in GO GO GO's gendered reworking of the home movie, and textual expression, as in the cage-like aesthetic space of THE BRIG (1964, Jonas Mekas). To return to BLONDE COBRA's apocalyptic ending phrase, "What went wrong?," the answer lies in the breakdown of the American social order during the 1960s. The avant-garde's response was angry and refused to remain silent, choosing instead to engage aesthetically, thematically, and ideologically with a sense of wrong-ness that was not yet self-evident to mainstream Americans. The origins of these sentiments were most emphatically expressed in the experimental thinking and art of the avant-garde that rejected not only America's rigid cultural conventions and its misguided public posturing, but which also challenged the fundamental cultural assumptions of America at their core. In their attack upon the very logic of an entertainment cinema, and in their uncompromising creation of liberated visions of alternative realities, the avant-garde films of the 1960s constituted a challenge not only to the conventions of American culture but to its deeper purposes as well.

Conclusion

In Hollywood feature production during the 1960s, the aesthetics of a cinema of sensation that emphasized increasingly graphic visual depictions and effects began to coexist alongside the classic cinema of sentiment and spectacle. American feature films became faster-paced and more visceral visually, and less traditionally dramatic and dialogue-bound. Cinematographers experimented with grittier, more realistic looks and laid the groundwork for filming with decidedly lower light levels than had been demanded by classic three-point lighting for that sleek Hollywood look.

Widescreen possibilities and the more elongated rectangular aspect ratios of feature films meant that directors of photography had more space to fill in the frame. Overall, however, the wider formats and aspect ratios had less impact on the audience's perception of movies than critics often have claimed. Moreover, the principles of visual composition and visual storytelling were actually given less attention in the new aesthetics. The cinema of sensation was largely premised on the goal of creating sheer visual stimulation, even if such sensation was created at the cost of narrative consistency and dramatic continuity. Subsequently, for the remainder of the twentieth century after 1970, the aesthetic of sensation in the American feature film would be advanced at the cost of storytelling and character development. Hence, it was not the Hollywood techniques advanced in the 1950s—all of which were based on sheer size and power of the image, such as widescreen or a widened aspect ratio to the film image—that eventually appealed to the new, younger audience for movies in the 1960s. Instead, it was a shift through film editing techniques—toward pulsating and faster pacing and the increasing manipulation of time, not space—that defined the 1960s film aesthetic.

Socially, culturally, and politically, one might observe that the cinema of sensation which announced itself with PSYCHO in 1960 coincided chronologically with a sit-in protest against segregation at a lunch counter in Greensboro, North Carolina, by black students in February of 1960, the approval of the marketing of the birth control pill later that spring, and the election of John F. Kennedy to the presidency in November of that year. To note the timing of these events, however, reveals nothing necessarily or directly about the American cinema of the 1960s. Moreover, an analysis of the previous art of PSYCHO's director, that British-born veteran, Alfred Hitchcock, does little to explain the film's appearance and it subsequent effects. Finally, little that is telling or informative about the cinema of sensation is revealed by referring to the fact that its closest antecedent in the international history of film dated back to the opening minute of a 1927 avant-garde project made by the surrealist artist Salvador Dali and the Spanish filmmaker Luis Buñuel, UN CHIEN ANDALOU, in which a human eyeball filling the screen appears to be slit in two by a straight razor.

History is not deterministic, nor are the connections between art and society, nor between movies and their markets. Our perceptions of social and cultural development in relationship to the cinema must remain opaque in direct proportion to our capacity to acknowledge the complexity of all such relationships. By the end of the 1960s, Hollywood movies had become decidedly more adult and more provocative in terms of both their surface eroticism and their underlying thematic pessimism. The Hollywood Production Code was abolished and replaced by a ratings system enforced at movie theater box offices. Many of the traditional proprieties of conformist, middle-class America regarding sexuality and criminality were challenged through the movies by the end of the 1960s. "Downer" stories became a part of the Hollywood scene, at first as a refreshing alternative to classic Hollywood's over-resolved endings and stereotypically attractive and wholesome characters. Within a few years, however, most of these new thematic tendencies would become as formulaic as the predictable happy endings and the behavior of chaste characters had once been. Television, quite simply, had taken over the mass family audience and proved capable of indulging sentimentality if not better, then at least more inexpensively, than the movies. By the late 1960s television held this mass audience market so tight, in fact, that Hollywood theatrical movies, for awhile, would simply define themselves as being more distinctively mature in their graphic sexuality and violence in contrast to American television. Even the preservation of the classic formulas of sentimentality in feature films frequently demanded efforts at integrating them into movies strong on visual effects, or which successfully repackaged what could be considered older sentiments in combination with new situations and alternative characters. Portrayals of violence and sex became more graphic, paving the way for the future. In the long run, the graphic portrayal of violence on the screen more greatly influenced the future of Hollywood aesthetics. Television again lurked in the background as a strong, though indirect, influence. For it was after the introduction of color television in the United States in 1963, and the subsequent shift of nearly all Hollywood feature production to color over the next several years, that the aesthetics of a cinema of sensation in the American feature film became anchored. The triumph of color film, industry-wide, moreover, was tied directly to the rise of graphic portrayals of violence and disaster on the screen.

Politically and socially, the prevailing historical image of the 1960s is characterized by the rise of the New Left and of a counterculture related to it. Nonetheless, the most reliable assessment of the decade's political and social legacy recognizes the contradictions of the 1960s. Each of the three different presidential administrations in the 1960s reflected one set of these contradictions: John F. Kennedy exuded youth and pronounced a "New Frontier," but he was committed to cold war policies and the quest for American global superiority; Lyndon Johnson's Great Society domestic policies were dogged by his administration's escalation of the war in Vietnam that eclipsed his presidency; Richard Nixon pursued policies of Vietnamization of the war and the eventual U.S. military withdrawal from Southeast Asia while becoming the architect of rapprochement with Red China and détente with the Soviet Union.

Even more deeply and tellingly, the ethos of protest itself in 1960s America was from its inception deeply conflicted between communitarian and libertarian impulses. The answer as to how true revolutionary change in American society would occur remained elusive: Was it to come from a seizure of power by radicals who might then impose their enlightened will upon society through the apparatus of the state?; or, was true change possible only to the degree that individuals could change themselves and then craft their new-found personal liberty into a collective model for others? One ubiquitous slogan of the late 1960s, "Make love, not war," summed up the conflicting and problematic appeals of the counterculture. If you were in your dorm room smoking pot and having sex, what possible effect could that have upon U.S. foreign policy and getting the troops out of Vietnam? And even when the U.S. military intervention was ended in southeast Asia, how would that, in itself, necessarily further the pursuit of life, liberty, property, and happiness that the American Republic in its purist idealism promised its citizenry?

Hollywood feature films ignored Vietnam, except for THE GREEN BERETS (1968), a pro-war feature modeled on World War II formulas and directed by John Wayne and Ray Kellogg, or settled for allusions to the conflict, as in George Romero's low-budget NIGHT OF THE LIVING DEAD (1969). Feature films of the 1960s also skirted the civil rights movement: a handful of movies were produced that endorsed racial integration or exposed the continuing anachronistic institutions of the Deep South, with the hits starring Sidney Poitier remaining the most memorable among them. For critics and commentators who demanded "engaged art" or who expected feature films to respond directly to the great social and political causes of the age, Hollywood was a lost cause. Not surprisingly, although avant-garde films reached only limited numbers of viewers who understood their experimental aesthetics and who had access to their limited

On the set of THE GREEN BERETS *(1968) with co-director John Wayne. The film offered a counterpoint to the counterculture that was rallying against the Vietnam War.*

venues of exhibition, the avant-garde cinema advanced the only truly radical cinematic challenges to mainstream American culture with films of alternative gay sexuality, outrageous assaults on religion and middle-class lifestyles, and savage satires of social and political power. By contrast, American nonfiction cinema during the 1960s was less focused on social and political radicalism than on aesthetic and stylistic innovations. Documentary production was predominantly leftist in its overall political and social perspectives, of course, but the fundamental concept of the emergent "direct cinema" that dominated nonfiction work of the 1960s was observational—a quality that eventually had to be perceived as being inherently at odds with engaged and tendentious filmmaking. Philosophically, observational filming, of course, could be justified as a form of advocacy on the premise that it inevitably raised the consciousness of its viewers, but this also meant that the American nonfiction cinema of the decade was destined never to become a cinema of the barricades. To a large extent, this development was very much in keeping with the political and cultural realities of the United States.

American society lacked the ideological moorings of many other nations in the industrialized world. Protests at the Democratic National Convention in Chicago in August 1968, and the police response to them, for example, were not the equivalent of the revolutionary alliance of students and workers in Paris in May 1968 that paralyzed that nation. Even in such European centers of ideological clarity and engaged cinema practice, however, the role of documentarians was already becoming peripheral. 1968, after all, was no 1848, the year in which revolutions against the established governments of various nations spread across Europe. In the late 1960s, advanced industrial capitalism proved remarkably capable of effectively appropriating the anti-establishment rhetoric of the New Left. Documentary filmmakers found themselves marginalized, however, primarily because the capacity of television to provide nearly instantaneous coverage and commentary on political events and social processes from around the globe was already established.

While Hollywood features, in essence, never dealt directly with the social and political issues of the period, they frequently touched on the wellsprings of youthful malaise and rebelliousness against the "establishment" and mainstream American values that characterized the counterculture spawned by the post–World War II "baby boomers," who had been born between 1948 and 1955 and who matured into adolescence and young adulthood during the late 1960s. The production of such features films became pronounced in the last three years of the decade, but the themes of youthful rebelliousness, existential disillusionment, and protest traced all the way back to the mid 1950s. As the beatniks of the 1950s were predecessors to the hippies of the 1960s, so were movies from the mid 1950s about teenage malcontents and rock and roll culture the predecessors to Hollywood's movies of alienation and angst in the late 1960s.

Nonetheless, even in the 1960s Hollywood was not yet swallowed up whole by the shifting audiences for movies and the attempts to appeal to the values and tastes of younger Americans. The diversity of the American population and the growing affluence of that population in the decade translated into burgeoning demands for leisure and entertainment of all sorts. Feature production continued to offer classic movie fare aimed at audiences "from eight to eighty," and the cinema of sentiment continued to churn out reliable moneymaking movies through the decade. In hindsight, none of this should have been surprising. Hollywood's audience was global, and the dynamics of the growing youth audience in the United States was only a portion of the overall demographic puzzle with which producers had to deal. And, of course, even "youth cohorts" are not monolithic; the audiences in the age range eighteen to twenty-five still covered a welter of differences—urban, suburban, rural; male and female; social and economic class; "hip" and "square," liberal and conservative, engaged and detached, pro-war and antiwar, and so on. Moreover, there were still moviegoers of various ages and still a wide variety of tastes that could respond with large box-office turnouts to certain movies.

The major changes for American culture and the American movies occurred in the late 1960s, just as the major Hollywood companies were being taken over by larger conglomerates and corporations with staffs of young and savvy business school graduates. The takeover of Hollywood financing and distribution by the conglomerates and other large business entities, however, did not necessarily mean any monolithic new direction for the American feature film. Instead, film production actually entered a phase at the beginning of the 1970s in which various new directions were possible and a number of talents who often offered some alternative to the classic concepts of Hollywood film-making gained an opportunity to display their talents and pursue their ideas. Contrary to the claims of subsequent neo-Marxist criticism, the 1960s did not mark the disruption of American popular culture into the postmodernist disarray of late capitalism, but rather established the ascendancy of a popular culture that succeeded by being simultaneously pluralistic and global.[1] For alongside the civil rights movement and the antiwar movement, American culture during the 1960s was shaped by a burgeoning consumer movement. All three movements were democratizing in their essence and pluralistic in their nature, and their combined influence would, over time, become global.

The late 1960s in the United States was far more revolutionary culturally than it ever was politically. From a perspective anchored within an understanding of post–World War II American political, economic, social, and intellectual development, this appears a logical consequence of the "American way of life": by the late 1960s American society and culture, even among its most radical of youth, had already evolved beyond ideology. While many of the America's public mythologies were shaken during the 1960s with the assassinations of John F. Kennedy, Robert Kennedy, and Martin Luther King, Jr., and the criticisms that led to the increasing unpopularity of the Vietnam War, none of those events reversed the trend in the dominant culture of the United States toward increasingly non-ideological and apolitical responses to society. Indeed, American society was characterized by the transference of social and political conflicts in society, beginning in the late 1960s, to the combat field of America's "culture wars," which grew more passionate through the rest of the century. Nonetheless, there was a simultaneous growth of appreciation for the value of self-actualization asserted in the 1960s that continued to thrive at the very heart of American life through the twentieth century and which, most notably, aligned only uncomfortably with any specific ideological or political force.

Between the conflicting libertarian and communitarian impulses of the decade's counterculture there, finally, could be no closure. The New Left might have been dominant among those attending colleges and universities in the late 1960s, but lurking in the American political psyche was the equally rebellious voice of the "Young Americans for Freedom" who had supported Barry Goldwater and his nomination for president in 1964. In his interpretation of eros and civilization New Left guru Herbert Marcuse linked the structures of capitalism to sexual repression and portrayed an atomization in contemporary American society that denied an individual's self-actualization. By contrast, Ayn Rand's pro-capitalist messages about the self-positing individual who transcends guilt and bad conscience in the quest for self-liberation coexisted as a counter-argument. By the end of the 1960s, the ideological direction of the American nation, like the direction of the Hollywood feature film, was essentially up for grabs.

The changes of the 1960s constituted transformations of attitude, style, and direction, rather than institutional change. American culture absorbed rebelliousness and change, but there was never so much of a flicker of what might have become the second American Revolution. Hollywood's loss of innocence during the 1950s with the rise of television and the demise of the studio system preceded the American nation's loss of its post-World War II innocence with the assassination of President John F. Kennedy in 1963. In addition to television's competition, the American movie industry also had to give way to the rise of rock music and the new kind of rock music star whose popularity transcended that of any Hollywood screen star. Even for the "film generation" that Stanley Kauffmann trumpeted in the mid 1960s, rock music existed as a kind of "cultural cement" with which feature films could not compete. The proliferation of rock music, and the related forms of folk rock and soul, provided avenues of expression and protest for the youth culture, its social concerns, and the protest against the Vietnam War with which no form of film competed. It was also in the popular music of the late 1960s that African American performers began to appeal to white audiences in the United States

Janis Joplin, shown performing at the Monterey Pop Festival in 1967, became a symbol of the empowered woman and was far more popular than any female screen star of the 1960s.

in ways that movies with African American casts, and set in African American communities, did not. As women's consciousness was raised and a nascent women's liberation movement emerged among younger women in the 1960s, it was those powerful and self-positing images projected by female rock vocalists, like Janis Joplin, Grace Slick, and Aretha Franklin, who became far more important in American culture at the end of the decade than any image projected by a lead actress in Hollywood.

Nonetheless, in the history of the American cinema during the 1960s one finally discovers a far better microcosm and reflection of the nation as a whole than one might have expected. In its shifting toward new audiences, in the adjustment of its surface culture, rather than its essence, and in the ways in which its core, well-established institutions finally survived, the history of 1960s American cinema turned out to resemble the history of the United States. In the turbulence of the last years of the decade the importance of the American feature film for spreading the democratization of global youth culture around the world from 1970 to the end of the twentieth century was forged. The most important and overarching legacy of the 1960s, however, was the shift of the historic nature of culture itself. For in all societies previously, culture had been transmitted from generation to generation, handed down as a heritage that was to be preserved for the future. The traditional and historic structure of culture was vertical. By reason of the assumption that culture was carried on from one generation to the next, the essence of culture itself was defined by that dynamic of its linear transmission over time. In the 1960s in the United States, culture and art dramatically and definitively shifted toward a model that was horizontal. With the proliferation of forms of expression and entertainment, and the explosion of affluence and access to them by listeners and viewers, art and culture moved from being "handed down" to being "spread out."

The phenomenon of this pervasive shift in the transmission of culture has neither been well understood by academics nor by popular critics. Nonetheless, the results of this shift, even when not concretely acknowledged, have attracted resentment and hostility from both the ideological Left and the Right. In the closing decades of the twentieth century, the globalization of wave upon wave of cultural forms that appeal horizontally across audiences primarily recognizable as generational cohorts have come to the fore. The American feature film, which historically had based its production process and its international presence on a vertical model crafted during the studio era, was able to claw its way during the 1960s toward a new aesthetic and commercial presence in the emerging global culture that was integrated horizontally and, thus, to assure the reestablishment of the primacy of Hollywood movies by the late 1970s.

Appendixes

NUMBER OF FEATURE FILMS RELEASED BY THE SEVEN MAJOR DISTRIBUTION COMPANIES, 1960–1968, 1970

	COLUMBIA	MGM	PARAMOUNT	20TH CENTURY– FOX	UNITED ARTISTS	UNIVERSAL	WARNER BROS.	TOTAL
1960	35	18	22	49	23	20	17	184
1961	28	21	15	35	33	19	16	167
1962	30	21	17	25	36	18	15	162
1963	19	35	17	18	23	17	13	142
1964	19	30	16	18	18	25	18	144
1965	29	28	24	26	19	26	15	167
1966	29	24	22	21	18	23	12	149
1967	22	21	30	19	19	25	21	157
1968	20	27	33	21	23	30	23	177
1970	28	21	16	14	40	17	15	151

SOURCE: Christopher H. Sterling and Timothy R. Haight, *The Mass Media: Aspen Institute Guide to Communication Industry Trends* (New York: Praeger, 1978).

APPENDIX 2

NUMBER AND FREQUENCY OF THEATRICAL AND MADE-FOR-TV FEATURE FILMS ON U.S. NETWORK TELEVISION, 1961/62–1970/71

	THEATRICAL FILMS		MADE-FOR-TV FILMS	TOTAL FILMS ON NETWORK TV
	Number of Films Shown	Percentage of Films	Number of Films Shown	
1961/62	45	100	0	45
1962/63	72	100	0	72
1963/64	60	100	0	60
1964/65	85	100	0	85
1965/66	120	99	1	121
1966/67	142	93	11	153
1967/68	138	97	4	142
1968/69	141	89	17	158
1969/70	140	77	43	183
1970/71	113	69	53	166

SOURCE: Sterling and Haight, *Mass Media.*

APPENDIX 3

NUMBER OF MOTION PICTURE THEATERS IN THE UNITED STATES

	FOUR-WALL THEATERS	OUTDOOR THEATERS	TOTAL
1960	12,291	4,700	16,991
1961	15,000	6,000	21,000
1962	15,000	6,000	21,000
1963	9,250	3,550	12,800
1964	9,650	4,100	13,750
1965	9,850	4,150	14,000
1966	10,150	4,200	14,350
1967	13,000	4,900	17,900
1968	13,600	4,975	18,575
1969	9,750	3,730	13,480

SOURCE: Sterling and Haight, *Mass Media.* (The authors point out problems with these estimates, including identical totals for 1961 and 1962, which they call "improbable," and which likely influences the appearance of a horrendous drop between 1962 and 1963. Most likely, the 1962 figures are inflated. Nonetheless, the patterns for the decade remain clear.)

APPENDIX 4

CONSTRUCTION OF NEW MOTION PICTURE THEATERS IN THE UNITED STATES, BY TYPE

	SHOPPING CENTER THEATERS			OUTDOOR THEATERS		
	Completed	Started	Total	Completed	Started	Total
1963	46	97	143	34	46	80
1964	74	147	221	35	66	101
1965	100	138	238	45	55	102
1966	103	101	204	55	44	99
1967	98	92	190	31	40	71
1968	90	108	198	20	59	79
1969	92	133	225	39	59	98
1970	96	84	180	24	27	51

SOURCE: Sterling and Haight, *Mass Media;* as based upon reports of the MPAA and selected issues of *Box Office* magazine.

APPENDIX 5

MOTION PICTURE BOX OFFICE RECEIPTS IN THE UNITED STATES

	Box Office Receipts in Millions of Dollars	Receipts as a Percentage of Consumer Expenditure	Receipts as a Percentage of Recreation Expenditure
1959	958	0.31	5.6
1960	951	0.29	4.7
1961	921	0.27	4.4
1962	903	0.25	4.1
1963	904	0.24	3.7
1964	913	0.23	3.5
1965	927	0.21	3.3
1966	964	0.23	3.2
1967	989	0.22	3.1
1968	1,045	0.20	3.0
1969	1,099	0.19	2.9
1970	1,167	0.19	2.7

SOURCE: Joel W. Finler, *The Hollywood Story* (New York: Crown Publishers, 1988).

APPENDIX 6
RELEASES IN WIDESCREEN PROCESSES, 1960–1968

	1960	1961	1962	1963	1964	1965	1966	1967	1968
COLOR									
CinemaScope	32	31	25	8	7	8	7	2	0
Technirama	3	1	3	0	1	0	0	0	0
VistaVision	2	2	1	0	1	0	0	0	0
Panavision	5	8	13	23	19	29	36	38	37
BLACK & WHITE									
CinemaScope	10	4	5	3	4	3	0	0	0
Panavision	1	1	3	4	3	9	2	1	0

SOURCE: Finler, *Hollywood Story.*

APPENDIX 7
ACADEMY AWARD NOMINATIONS AND WINNERS (IN BOLD) FOR BEST PICTURE, 1960–1969

1960

THE ALAMO, Batjac Productions / United Artists; John Wayne, Producer
THE APARTMENT, The Mirisch Company; Billy Wilder, Producer
ELMER GANTRY, Burt Lancaster–Richard Brooks Prod., United Artists;
    Bernard Smith, Producer
SONS AND LOVERS, 20th Century–Fox, Jerry Wald, Producer
THE SUNDOWNERS, Warner Bros.; Fred Zinnemann, Producer

1961

FANNY, Mansfield Productions / Warner Brothers; Joshua Logan, Producer
THE GUNS OF NAVARONE, Carl Foreman Productions / Columbia Pictures;
    Carl Foreman, Producer
THE HUSTLER, Robert Rossen Productions / 20th Century–Fox; Robert Rossen,
    Producer
JUDGMENT AT NUREMBERG, Stanley Kramer Productions / United Artists; Stanley
    Kramer, Producer
**WEST SIDE STORY, Mirisch Pictures, Inc. and B. & P. Enterprises / United
    Artists; Robert Wise, Producer**

1962

**LAWRENCE OF ARABIA, Horizon Pictures (G. B.), Led. / Sam Spiegel–David
    Lean Productions / Columbia Pictures; Sam Spiegel, Producer**
THE LONGEST DAY, Darryl F. Zanuck Productions / 20th Century–Fox; Darryl F.
    Zanuck, Producer

Meredith Willson's THE MUSIC MAN, Warner Bros.; Morton Da Costa, Producer
MUTINY ON THE BOUNTY, Arcola Productions / MGM; Aaron Rosenberg, Producer
TO KILL A MOCKINGBIRD, Universal-International-Pakula-Milligan-Brentwood Productions, U-I; Alan J. Pakula, Producer

1963

AMERICA, AMERICA, Athena Enterprises / Warner Bros., Elia Kazan, Producer
CLEOPATRA, 20th Century–Fox, Ltd.–MCL Films / S.A.-WALWA Films / S.A. Productions / 20th Century–Fox; Walter Wanger, Producer
HOW THE WEST WAS WON, MGM and Cinerama; Bernard Smith, Producer
LILIES OF THE FIELD, Rainbow Productions / United Artists; Ralph Nelsom, Producer
TOM JONES, Woodfall Productions / United Artists–Lopert Picture; Tony Richardson, Producer

1964

BECKET, Hal Wallis Productions / Paramount; Hal B. Wallis, Producer
DR. STRANGELOVE, OR HOW I LEARNED TO STOP WORRYING AND LOVE THE BOMB, Hawk Films, Ltd. Productions / Columbia Pictures; Stanley Kubrick, Producer
MARY POPPINS, Walt Disney Productions; Walt Disney and Bill Walsh, Producers
MY FAIR LADY, Warner Bros.; Jack L. Warner, Producer
ZORBA THE GREEK, Rochley Ltd. Productions / International Classics; Michael Cacoyannis, Producer

1965

DARLING, Anglo-Amalgamated, Ltd. Productions / Embassy; Joseph Janni, Producer
DOCTOR ZHIVAGO, Sostar S.A.–MGM British Studios, Ltd.; Carlo Ponti, Producer
SHIP OF FOOLS, Columbia Pictures: Stanley Kramer, Producer
THE SOUND OF MUSIC, Argyle Enterprises Productions / 20th Century–Fox; Robert Wise, Producer
A THOUSAND CLOWNS, Harrell Productions / United Artists; Fred Coe, Producer

1966

ALFIE, Sheldrake Films, Ltd. / Paramount; Lewis Gilbert, Producer
A MAN FOR ALL SEASONS, Highland Films, Ltd. / Columbia Pictures, Fred Zinnemann, Producer
THE RUSSIANS ARE COMING, THE RUSSIANS ARE COMING, Mirisch Corporation of Delaware Productions / United Artists; Norman Jewison, Producer
THE SAND PEBBLES, Argyle-Solar Productions / 20th Century–Fox; Robert Wise, Producer
WHO'S AFRAID OF VIRGINIA WOOLF? Chenault Productions / Warner Bros.; Ernest Lehman, Producer

1967

BONNIE AND CLYDE, Tatira-Hiller Productions / Warner Bros.–Seven Arts; Warren Beatty, Producer

DOCTOR DOOLITTLE, Apjac Productions / 20th Century–Fox; Arthur P. Jacobs, Producer

THE GRADUATE, Mike Nichols–Lawrence Turman Productions / Embassy; Lawrence Turman, Producer

GUESS WHO'S COMING TO DINNER, Columbia Pictures; Stanley Kramer, Producer

IN THE HEAT OF THE NIGHT, Mirisch Corporation Productions / United Artists; Walter Mirisch, Producer

1968

THE FRANCO ZEFFIRELLI PRODUCTION OF ROMEO AND JULIET, B. H. E. Film / Verona Productions / Dino de Laurentis Cinematographica Productions / Paramount; Anthony Havelock-Allen and John Brabourne, Producers

FUNNY GIRL, Rastar Productions / Columbia Pictures; Ray Stark, Producer

THE LION IN WINTER, Haworth Productions / Avco Embassy; Martin Poll, Producer

OLIVER! Romulus Films / Columbia Pictures; John Woolf, Producer

RACHEL, RACHEL, Kayos Productions / Warner Bros.–Seven Arts; Paul Newman, Producer

1969

ANNE OF THE THOUSAND DAYS, Hal B. Wallis–Universal Pictures, Ltd. Production / Universal Pictures; Hal B. Wallis, Producer

BUTCH CASSIDY AND THE SUNDANCE KID, George Roy Hill–Paul Monash Productions / 20th Century–Fox; John Foreman, Producer

HELLO, DOLLY! Chenault Productions / 20th Century–Fox; Ernest Lehman, Producer

MIDNIGHT COWBOY, Jerome Hellman–John Schlesinger Productions / United Artists; Jerome Hellman, Producer

Z, Reggane Films–O.N.C.I.C. Production / Cinema V; Jacques Perrin and Hamed Rachedi, Producers

SOURCE: Richard Shale, ed., *Academy Awards: An Ungar Reference Book*, 2nd ed. (New York: Frederick Ungar, 1982).

APPENDIX 8

SELECTED AMERICAN AVANT-GARDE
FILMS OF THE SIXTIES, BY YEAR

PULL MY DAISY (Alfred Leslie and Robert Frank, 1959)
SHADOWS (John Cassavetes, 1959)
THE DEAD (Stan Brakhage, 1960)
THE CONNECTION (Shirley Clarke, 1961)
COSMIC RAY (Bruce Conner, 1961)
DRIPS IN STRIPS (Marie Menken, 1961)
FILMS BY STAN BRAKHAGE: AN AVANT-GARDE HOME MOVIE (Stan Brakhage, 1961)
BLUE MOSES (Stan Brakhage, 1962)
GUNS OF THE TREES (Jonas Mekas, 1962)
BLONDE COBRA (Ken Jacobs, 1963)
BLOW JOB (Andy Warhol, 1963)
BREATHDEATH: A TRAGEDEE IN MASKS (Stan VanDerBeek, 1963–1964)
FLAMING CREATURES (Jack Smith, 1963)
HALLELUJAH THE HILLS (Adolfas Mekas, 1963)
THE QUEEN OF SHEBA MEETS THE ATOM MAN (Ron Rice, 1963)
TO PARSIFAL (Bruce Baillie, 1963)
THE BRIG (Jonas Mekas, 1964)
DOG STAR MAN (Stan Brakhage, 1964)
GO GO GO (Marie Menken, 1964)
MASS FOR THE DAKOTA SIOUX (Bruce Baillie, 1964)
SCORPIO RISING (Kenneth Anger, 1964)
KUSTOM KAR KOMMANDOS (Kenneth Anger, 1965)
THE LIFE OF JUANITA CASTRO (Andy Warhol, 1965)
VIET-FLAKES (Carol Schneemann, 1965)
VINYL (Andy Warhol, 1965)
WATER SARK (Joyce Wieland, 1965)
CASTRO STREET (Bruce Baillie, 1966)
FILM IN WHICH THERE APPEARS EDGE LETTERING, SPROCKET HOLES, DIRT
    PARTICLES, ETC. (George Landow, 1966)
HOLD ME WHILE I'M NAKED (George Kuchar, 1966)
1933 (Joyce Wieland, 1967)
23RD PSALM BRANCH (Stan Brakhage, 1967)
ATMOSFEAR (Tom DeLay, 1967)
THE BIG SHAVE (Martin Scorsese, 1967)
DAVID HOLZMAN'S DIARY (Jim McBride, 1967)
LONESOME COWBOYS (Andy Warhol, 1967)
REPORT (Bruce Conner, 1967)
WAVELENGTH (Michael Snow, 1967)
THE BED (James Broughton, 1968)
CATFOOD (Joyce Wieland, 1968)
MAXWELL'S DEMON (Hollis Frampton, 1968)

PLUTO (James Herbert, 1968)
RAT LIFE AND DIET IN NORTH AMERICA (Joyce Wieland, 1968)
SNOWBLIND (Hollis Frampton, 1968)
BACK AND FORTH (Michael Snow, 1969)
MOON 1969 (Scott Bartlett, 1969)

Notes

INTRODUCTION

1. Gideon Bachman, "A New Generation of Critical Fans," *Variety*, June 1, 1960, p. 5.
2. Frederic Stuart, *The Effects of Television on the Motion Picture and Radio Industries* (New York: Arno Press, 1976).
3. Gerald Mast, ed., *The Movies in Our Midst: Documents in the Cultural History of Film in America* (Chicago: University of Chicago Press, 1982), p. 643.
4. Gerald Mast, *A Short History of the Movies*, 4th ed. (New York: Macmillan, 1986), p. x.
5. Jack C. Ellis, *A History of Film*, 2nd ed. (Englewood Cliffs, N.J.: Prentice-Hall, 1985), pp. 382, 383.
6. Thomas Schatz, "The New Hollywood," in Jim Collins, Hilary Radner, and Ava Preacher Collins, eds., *Film Theory Goes to the Movies* (New York: Routledge, 1993), p. 10.
7. Douglas Gomery, *Movie History: A Survey* (Belmont, Calif.: Wadsworth, 1991), pp. ix and 283–345.
8. David A. Cook, *A History of Narrative Film* (New York: W. W. Norton, 1981), pp. 413–444 and 623–635.
9. Ethan Mordden, *Medium Cool: The Movies of the 1960s* (New York: Alfred A. Knopf, 1990), p. 7.
10. Robert Brustein, "The New Hollywood," in Mast, ed., *The Movies in Our Midst.*
11. Peter Lev, *The Euro-American Cinema* (Austin: University of Texas Press, 1993), p. 15.
12. Frank C. Beaver, *On Film: The History of the Motion Pictures* (New York: McGraw-Hill, 1983), p. 469.
13. Mike Bygrave, "The New Moguls," in David Pirie, ed., *Anatomy of the Movies* (New York: Macmillan, 1981), p. 63.
14. Landon Y. Jones, *Great Expectations: America and the Baby Boom Generation* (New York: Ballantine Books, 1981), p. 250 ff.
15. Richard Reeves, *President Kennedy: Profile of Power* (New York: Simon & Schuster, 1993), pp. 459, 460, and 622–625.
16. Norman Cantor, *Twentieth Century Culture* (New York: Peter Lang, 1988), p. 270.
17. Angus McLaren, *A History of Contraception* (Oxford: Basil Blackwell, 1990), pp. 240 ff.
18. Terry Anderson, *The Movement and the 1960s: Protest in America from Greensboro to Wounded Knee* (New York: Oxford University Press, 1995), p. 91.
19. Jones, *Great Expectations*, p. 121.

CHAPTER 1 (HOLLYWOOD FACES NEW CHALLENGES)

1. Christopher H. Sterling and Timothy R. Haight, *The Mass Media: Aspen Institute Guide to Communication Industry Trends* (New York: Praeger, 1978), see especially their discussion of movie attendance, pp. 186, 187 ff.
2. Janet Wasko, *Movies and Money: Financing the American Film Industry* (Norwood, N.J.: ABLEX Publishing Corp., 1982), pp. 104 ff.; see also Tino Balio, "Introduction to Part I," in Tino Balio, ed., *Hollywood in the Age of Television* (Boston: Unwin Hyman, 1990), pp. 3 ff.
3. *Variety* (Weekly), January 6, 1960, p. 8.

4. Thomas H. Guback, "Film as an International Business: The Role of the American Multinationals," in Gorham Kindem, ed., *The American Movie Industry* (Carbondale: Southern Illinois University Press, 1982), pp. 336 ff.
5. *Variety* (Weekly), September 27, 1961, p. 1.
6. Jack C. Ellis, *A History of Film,* 2nd ed. (Englewood Cliffs, N.J.: Prentice Hall, 1985), p. 281.
7. *Variety* (Weekly), December 27, 1961, p. 3.
8. Peter McDonald, "Sun Never Sets on Global Empire U.S. Television Has Built for Itself," *Variety,* Special Anniversary Issue, October 1965, p. 5.
9. Guback, "Film as an International Business," p. 338.
10. *Variety* (Weekly), May 27, 1969, pp. 7, 8.
11. Interview with Jack Valenti in *Attenzione* (July/August 1981): 32–35.
12. I. G. Edmonds and Reiko Mimura, *Paramount Pictures and the People Who Made Them* (New York: A. S. Barnes & Co., 1980), p. 253.
13. Arthur Mayer, "Growing Pains of a Shrinking Industry," in Arthur F. McClure, ed., *The Movie, An American Idiom: Readings in the Social History of the American Motion Picture* (Fairleigh Dickinson University Press, 1971), p. 42.
14. Gary R. Edgerton, *American Film Exhibition and an Analysis of the Motion Picture Industry's Market Structure, 1963–1980* (New York: Garland, 1983), p. 48.
15. Richard Maltby, "'Nobody Knows Everything': Post-Classical Historiographies and Consolidated Entertainment," in Steve Neale and Murray Smith, eds., *Contemporary Hollywood Cinema* (New York: Routledge, 1998), p. 31.
16. *Variety* (Weekly), November 30, 1960, p. 3.
17. *Variety* (Daily), December 20, 1960, p. 1.
18. *Variety* (Weekly), March 9, 1960, p. 17.
19. *Variety* (Weekly), August 24, 1960, p. 3.
20. *Variety* (Weekly), June 1, 1960, p. 22.
21. *Variety* (Weekly), September 13, 1961, p. 4.
22. Charles Higham, *Hollywood at Sunset* (New York: Saturday Review Press, 1972), p. 144.
23. Robert W. Gilbert, "Foreign Film Subsidies," in A. William Bluem and Jason E. Squire, eds., *The Movie Business: American Film Industry Practice* (New York: Hasting House, 1972), pp. 70 ff. contains an excellent discussion of such subsidies and schemes.
24. *Hollywood Reporter,* June 17, 1998, p. 18.
25. Chris Musun, *The Marketing of Motion Pictures* (Los Angeles: Chris Musun Publishing, 1969), p. 103.
26. Meyer, "Growing Pains," p. 42.
27. *Variety* (Weekly), January 10, 1962, p. 2.
28. *Box Office,* April 24, 1961, p. 7.
29. Gene Moskowitz, "French Twist: Hollywood Films and Dollars Welcomed," *Variety,* Special Anniversary Edition, October 1967, pp. 13, 14.
30. Guback, "Film As an International Business," p. 340.
31. Richard Dyer MacCann, "Hollywood Faces the World," in Gerald Mast, ed., *The Movies in Our Midst: Documents in the Cultural History of Film in the United States* (Chicago: University of Chicago Press, 1982), p. 673.
32. Higham, *Hollywood at Sunset,* p. 144.
33. Aubrey Solomon, *Twentieth–Century Fox: A Corporate and Financial History* (Metuchen, N.J.: Scarecrow, 1988), p. 159.
34. *Hollywood Reporter,* January 20, 1964, p. 1.
35. Jerzy Toeplitz, *Hollywood and After: The Changing Face of American Cinema,* Boleslaw Sulik, trans. (London: George Allen and Unwin, Ltd., 1974), p. 38.
36. Guback, "Film as an International Business," p. 348.
37. Christopher H. Sterling and Timothy R. Haight, *The Mass Media: Aspen Institute Guide to Communication Industry Trends* (New York: Praeger, 1978), p. 372.
38. See the especially ambitious study of the Hollywood studios and their involvement in production for television, Christopher Anderson, *Hollywood/TV* (Austin: University of Texas Press, 1994), especially pp. 61 ff. and pp. 156 ff.
39. *Film Daily,* November 24, 1969, p. 1.

40. See the comprehensive discussion of these initiatives in Tino Balio, "Introduction to Part II," in Balio, ed., *Hollywood in the Age of Television*, pp. 264 ff. For an excellent article from the period on the Hollywood majors and pay-TV, see *Los Angeles Times*, September 9, 1962.

41. Robert R. Faulkner, *Hollywood Studio Musicians: Their Work and Careers in the Recording Industry* (Chicago: Aldine-Atherton, 1971), p. 25.

42. Cobbett Steinberg, *Reel Facts: The Movie Book of Records* (New York: Vintage Books, 1982), p. 66.

43. Douglas Gomery, *Shared Pleasures: A History of Movie Presentation in the United States* (Madison: University of Wisconsin Press, 1992), pp. 251, 252.

44. Robert Stanley, *The Celluloid Empire: A History of the American Motion Picture Industry* (New York: Hastings House, 1978), p. 247.

45. *Variety* (Daily), January 9, 1968, p. 9.

46. David F. Prindle, *The Politics of Glamour: Ideology and Democracy in the Screen Actors Guild* (Madison: University of Wisconsin Press, 1988), pp. 83, 84.

47. Charlton Heston, *In the Arena: An Autobiography* (New York: Simon & Schuster, 1995), see especially pp. 87 ff. and pp. 237 ff.

48. *Variety* (Daily), April 13, 1960.

49. Prindle, *The Politics of Glamour*, pp. 120, 121.

50. *Variety* (Weekly), April 14, 1965.

51. Robert Evans, "The Producer," in Jason E. Squire, ed., *The Movie Business Book* (Englewood Cliffs, N.J.: Prentice Hall, 1983), p. 15.

52. *Variety* (Daily), August 31, 1960.

53. John McTiernan, Director, Public Lecture, Montana State University, Bozeman, October 27, 1995.

54. Richard Zimbert, "Business Affairs and the Production/Financing/Distribution Agreement," in Squire, ed., *Movie Business Book*, p. 176.

55. For a good discussion of the star's rising influence in post-1960s Hollywood, see Norman H. Garey, "The Entertainment Lawyer," in Squire, ed., *Movie Business Book*, pp. 166 ff.

56. Tino Balio, "New Producers for Old: United Artists and the Shift to Independent Production," in Balio, ed., *Hollywood in the Age of Television*, pp. 175–177.

57. *Film Daily*, September 7, 1960.

58. *Variety* (Weekly), May 5, 1965.

59. *Variety* (Weekly), January 18, 1964.

60. Jack Lodge, John Russell Taylor, Adrian Turner, Douglas Jarvis, David Castell, *Hollywood: Fifty Great Years* (New York: Galahad Books, 1989), p. 350.

61. Aubrey Solomon, *Twentieth Century Fox: A Corporate and Financial History* (Metuchen, N.J.: Scarecrow, 1988), p. 147.

62. Paul Ryan, *Marlon Brando: A Portrait* (Emeryville, Calif.: Carroll & Graf, 1994), pp. 114 ff.

63. Lodge et al., *Hollywood: Fifty Great Years*, p. 351.

64. See Heston, *In the Arena*, pp. 239–241, pp. 273 ff.

65. *Los Angeles Times*, February 25, 1969.

66. Tino Balio, "New Producers for Old: United Artists and the Shift to Independent Production," in Balio, ed., *Hollywood in the Age of Television*, pp. 173, 174.

CHAPTER 2 (CHANGING PATTERNS OF PRODUCTION AND THE ARRIVAL OF THE CONGLOMERATES)

1. Janet Wasko, *Movies and Money: Financing the American Film Industry* (Norwood, N.J.: ABLEX Publishing Corp., 1982), p. 107.

2. Arthur Mayer, "Growing Pains in a Shrinking Industry," in Arthur McClure, ed., *The Movie, An American Idiom: Readings in the Social History of the American Motion Picture Industry* (Fairleigh Dickinson University Press, 1971), p. 45.

3. Wasko, *Movies and Money*, see pp. 111–119 for an excellent discussion of the majors' financing of "independent" productions.

4. "Summary of Studio Activities," *Variety*, October 25, 1960, p. 1 ff.

5. Frederic Stuart, *The Effects of Television on the Motion Picture and Radio Industries* (New York: Arno Press, 1976), p. 54.
6. "Summary of Studio Activities," pp. 22, 23.
7. *Variety,* May 18, 1960, p. 3.
8. David Pirie, "The Deal," in David Pirie, ed., *Anatomy of the Movies* (New York: Macmillan, 1981), pp. 56, 57.
9. *Los Angeles Herald Examiner,* February 18, 1988, p. 19.
10. Pirie, "The Deal," p. 57.
11. *Variety,* Special Anniversary Issue, October 1961, pp. 8, 9.
12. *Box Office,* May 8, 1961, p. 11.
13. Mitch Tuchman, "Independent Producers; Independent Distributors," in Pirie, ed., *Anatomy of the Movies,* p. 89.
14. Robert Stanley, *The Celluloid Empire: A History of the American Motion Picture Industry* (New York: Hastings House, 1978), p. 241.
15. Wasko, *Movies and Money,* p. 107.
16. See Kirk Bond, "For a New American Film Industry, There's No Evading Big Money," *Variety,* May 8, 1961, pp. 10, 11, where he engages in a lively written debate with columnist Gideon Bachman over the lack of "artistically significant" movies in the United States.
17. Quoted in Jack Carmody, "The Man Who Moves Movies," *Los Angeles Times,* November 13, 1966.
18. Quoted in Pirie, "The Deal," p. 47.
19. *Los Angeles Times,* July 15, 1962, p. 32.
20. *Hollywood Reporter,* January 2, 1964, p. 6.
21. Ed Naha, *The Films of Roger Corman: Brilliance on a Budget* (New York: Arco, 1982), p. 42.
22. *Variety* (Daily), September 7, 1966, p. 3.
23. Digby Diehl, "Roger Corman: A Double Life," *Action* (July/August 1969): pp. 27–29.
24. Wheeler Dixon, "In Defense of Roger Corman," unpublished paper, Film and Video Research in Progress, a Service of the University Film & Video Association (UFVA), 1985, p. 3.
25. Naha, *Films of Roger Corman,* pp. 66 ff.
26. Vincent LoBrutto, *Selected Takes: Film Editors on Editing* (New York: Praeger, 1991), p. 191.
27. J. Philip DeFranco, *The Movie World of Roger Corman* (New York: Chelsea House, 1979), p. 158.
28. *Film Daily,* August 24, 1967, p. 6.
29. Stanley, *Celluloid Empire,* pp. 238, 239.
30. Thomas M. Pryor, "A Year of Industry Ferment," *Variety,* Special Anniversary Issue, October 1966, p. 1 ff.
31. "Investigation of Conglomerate Corporations." Report by the Staff of the Antitrust Subcommittee on the Committee on the Judiciary, United States House of Representatives, 92nd Congress, 1st Session, 1971, p. 163. (Hereafter cited as "House Antitrust Subcommittee Report.")
32. Michael Korda, "The Last Business Eccentric: Why There Aren't Any More CEOs like Gulf + Western's Charles Bluhdorn," *New York* magazine, December 16, 1996, pp. 32 ff. See also Chris Welles, "Charles Bluhdorn: Collector of Companies," manuscript, undated, Files of the Academy of Motion Picture Arts & Sciences, Center for the Study of the Motion Picture, Beverly Hills, California. No source adequately explains why a plus sign replaced the original ampersand in the company's name soon after its founding.
33. Thomas Schatz, *Old Hollywood / New Hollywood: Ritual, Art, and Industry* (Ann Arbor: UMI Research Press, 1983), p. 172.
34. David F. Prindle, *The Politics of Glamour: Ideology and Democracy in the Screen Actors Guild* (Madison: University of Wisconsin Press, 1988), p. 89.
35. Dick Atkins et al., *Method to the Madness (Hollywood Explained)* (Livingston, N.J.: Prince Publishers, 1975), p. 42.
36. *Time,* January 1, 1965, p. 69.
37. Schatz, *Old Hollywood/New Hollywood,* p. 189.
38. *Time,* January 1, 1965, p. 69.
39. Robert Sklar, *Movie-Made America: A Cultural History of American Movies,* rev. ed. (New York: Vintage Books, 1994), p. 287.
40. Atkins et al., *Method to the Madness,* p. 42.
41. I. G. Edmonds and Reiko Mimura, *Paramount Pictures,* pp. 253, 254.
42. Charles Higham, *Hollywood at Sunset* (New York: Saturday Review Press, 1972), p. 165.

43. "House Antitrust Subcommittee Report," p. 196.

44. Ibid., p. 163.

45. Ibid., p. 196.

46. Ibid., p. 163.

47. Jerzy Toeplitz, *Hollywood and After: The Changing Face of American Cinema*, Boleslaw Sulik, trans. (London: George Allen and Unwin, Ltd., 1974), p. 31.

48. *Los Angeles Times*, July 11, 1979.

49. James Monaco, *American Film Now* (New York: Oxford University Press, 1979), p. 36.

50. Axel Madsen, *The New Hollywood* (New York: Crowell, 1975), p. 89.

51. "House Antitrust Subcommittee Report," p. 191.

52. Hollis Alpert, "Last of the New Tycoons," *Film International* (July 1975): 12–14.

53. Joe Hyams, "Poured in the Mogul Mold," *Los Angeles Times: West Magazine*, June 11, 1967.

54. Gerald Clarke, "Can Bob Evans Find True Happiness?" *Esquire* (February 1974): 72.

55. Robert Evans, "Confessions of a Kid Mogul," in Pirie, ed., *Anatomy of the Movies*, p. 84.

56. Alpert, "Last of the New Tycoons," p. 13.

57. Nancy Collins, "Arts and Pleasures," *Women's Wear Daily*, April 7, 1976.

58. Stanley Penn, "Focusing on Youth," *Wall Street Journal*, n.d., Cinema Collections of the Doheny Library at the University of Southern California.

59. *Variety*, May 3, 1961, p. 1.

60. Stanley, *Celluloid Empire*, p. 148.

61. Art Buchwald, "Let's Have a World-Wide Referendum on Our Cleo," *Los Angeles Citizen News*, April 20, 1962, p. 18.

62. William K. Zinsser, "Cleo, Liz, and Coincidence," *Show Business International*, January 2, 1962.

63. Walter Wanger with Joe Hyams, "The Trials and Tribulations of an Epic Film: CLEOPATRA," *Saturday Evening Post*, June 1, 1963, p. 28.

64. Wanger with Hyams, "Trials and Tribulations," p. 28.

65. Calvin Pryluck, "Front, Box Office, and Artistic Freedom," in Michael T. Marsden, John G. Nachbar, and Sam L. Grogg Jr., eds., *Movies as Artifacts: Cultural Criticism of Popular Film* (Chicago: Nelson-Hall Publishing, 1982), p. 50.

66. Joe Hyams, "CLEOPATRA: Hollywood's Most Expensive Girl Friend," *This Week Magazine*, November 25, 1962, p. 12.

67. *Los Angeles Times*, April 23, 1964, p. 38.

68. Thomas M. Pryor, "The Era of Great Discontent, or How's Life in the Executive Suite?" *Variety*, Special Anniversary Issue, October 1965, p. 2.

69. "Independents and Marketing/Distribution Innovations," in Jon Lewis, ed., *The New American Cinema*, (Durham: Duke University Press, 1998), pp. 66, 165–172.

70. Solomon, *Twentieth Century Fox*, p. 160; see also Thomas Schatz, "The New Hollywood," in Jim Collins, Hilary Radner, Ava Preacher Collins, eds., *Film Theory Goes to the Movies*, (New York: Routledge, 1993), p. 14.

71. Stanley, *Celluloid Empire*, pp. 238, 239.

72. Steinberg, *Reel Facts*, pp. 73, 74.

73. Robert Evans, "Confessions of a Kid Mogul," in Pirie, ed., *Anatomy of the Movies*, pp. 83, 84.

74. Gary R. Edgerton, *American Film Exhibition and an Analysis of the Motion Picture Industry's Market Structure, 1963–1980* (New York: Garland, 1983), p. 36.

75. Solomon, *Twentieth Century Fox*, p. 154.

76. Stanley, *Celluloid Empire*, p. 254.

77. Steinberg, *Reel Facts*, p. 82.

78. Gustafson, "What's Happening to Our Pix Biz? From Warner Brothers to Warner Communications," in Balio, ed., *Hollywood in the Age of Television* (Boston: Unwin Hyman, 1990), p. 575.

79. Stanley, *Celluloid Empire*, p. 263.

80. John Douglas Eames, *The MGM Story: A Complete History of Fifty Roaring Years* (New York: Crown Publishers, 1979), p. 9.

81. Leonard Quart and Albert Auster, *American Film and Society Since 1945* (New York: Praeger, 1984), p. 75.

82. Thomas M. Pryor, "The Decade of the Conglomerates," *Variety*, Special Anniversary Issue, October 1969.

83. *Box Office,* September 9, 1968, p. 1.
84. Stanley, *Celluloid Empire,* p. 258.
85. Madsen, *New Hollywood,* p. 69.
86. "House Antitrust Subcommittee Report," p. 186.
87. Michael F. Mayer, *The Film Industries* (New York: Hastings House, 1978), pp. 109, 110.
88. *Economist* (April 1972): see the entire edition.
89. Garth Jowett, *Film: The Democratic Art* (Boston: Little, Brown, & Co., 1978), pp. 428–457.
90. Schatz, *Old Hollywood/New Hollywood,* p. 194.
91. Clarke Taylor, "Hepburn's Off-Screen Intimacy," *Los Angeles Times,* March 26, 1986, p. 32.
92. William Fadiman, *Hollywood Now* (London: Thames & Hudson, 1973), p. 24.
93. Steinberg, *Reel Facts,* p. 43.

Chapter 3 (The Runaway Audience and the Changing World of Movie Exhibition)

1. *Variety* (Weekly), July 5, 1961.
2. Frederic Stuart, *The Effects of Television on the Motion Picture and Radio Industries* (New York: Arno Press, 1976), p. 12.
3. Robert Sklar, *Movie-Made America: A Cultural History of American Movies,* rev. ed. (New York: Vintage Press, 1994), p. 321.
4. Stuart, *Effects of Television,* p. 10.
5. Terry Christensen, *Reel Politics* (New York: Basil Blackwell, 1987), p. 112.
6. Douglas Gomery, *Shared Pleasures: A History of Movie Presentation in the United States* (Madison: University of Wisconsin Press, 1992).
7. Stuart, *Effects of Television,* p. 19.
8. Robert Stanley, *The Celluloid Empire: A History of the American Motion Picture* (New York: Hastings House, 1978), p. 237.
9. Landon Y. Jones, *Great Expectations: America and the Baby Boom Generation* (New York: Ballantine Books, 1980), p. 11, 12.
10. Gomery, *Shared Pleasures,* p. 28.
11. William Issel, *Social Change in the United States, 1945–1983* (New York: Schocken Books, 1985), pp. 87, 88.
12. Aubrey Solomon, *Twentieth Century Fox: A Corporate and Financial History* (Metuchen, N.J.: Scarecrow, 1988), pp. 147, 148.
13. *Variety* (Weekly), May 25, 1960.
14. Issel, *Social Change,* p. 100.
15. Gomery, *Shared Pleasures,* pp. 155–170; see "Movie Theaters for Black Americans."
16. Robert Brustein, "The New Hollywood," in Gerald Mast, ed., *The Movies: Documents in the Cultural History of Film in America* (Chicago: University of Chicago Press, 1982), p. 685.
17. *Time,* December 8, 1967, p. 72.
18. *Variety* (Weekly), February 24, 1960, p. 3.
19. *Variety* (Weekly), April 26, 1961, p. 1.
20. Emanuel Levy, *And the Winner Is . . . The History and Politics of the Oscar Awards* (New York: Ungar, 1987), p. 83.
21. Mason Wiley and Damien Bona, *Inside Oscar: The Unofficial History of the Academy Awards* (New York: Ballantine Books, 1993), p. 332.
22. Stanley Kauffmann, "The Film Generation: Celebration and Concern," in *A World on Film* (New York: Harper & Row, 1966), pp. 415–428.
23. Peter Lev, *The Euro-American Cinema* (Austin: University of Texas Press, 1993), p. 73.
24. *Variety* (Weekly), October 24, 1962.
25. William K. Zinsser, "Quo Vadis, Hollywood," *Look,* July 11, 1967, p. 14.
26. Mitch Tuchman, "Independent Producers; Independent Distributors," in David Pirie, ed., *Anatomy of the Movies* (New York: Macmillan, 1981), pp. 90–92.
27. *Time,* December 8, 1967, p. 66.
28. *Box Office,* May 29, 1961, p. 3.
29. Cobbett Steinberg, *Reel Facts: The Movie Book of Records* (New York: Vintage, 1982), p. 40.

30. A. D. Murphy, "Distribution and Exhibition: An Overview," in James E. Squire, ed., *The Movie Business Book* (Englewood Cliffs, N.J.: Prentice Hall, 1981), pp. 244, 245.

31. *Newsweek,* July 8, 1963, p. 54.

32. A compilation of excellent statistics on the number of "four wall" theaters and outdoor theaters in the United States between the 1920s and 1975 is found in Christopher H. Sterling and Timothy R. Haught, *The Mass Media: Aspen Institute Guide to Communication Industry Trends* (New York: Praeger, 1978), pp. 34, 35. See also Frederic Stuart, "The Effects of Television on the Motion Picture Industry," in Gorham Kindem, ed., *The American Movie Industry* (Carbondale: Southern Illinois University Press, 1982), pp. 263 ff.

33. Gary R. Edgerton, *American Film Exhibition and an Analysis of the Motion Picture Industry's Market Structure, 1963–1980* (New York: Garland Publishing Company, 1983), p. 32.

34. Albert E. Sindlinger, "Finding Lost Audiences," *Variety,* Special Anniversary Issue, October 1961, p. 12.

35. Suzanne Mary Donahue, *American Film Distribution: The Changing Marketplace* (Ann Arbor: UMI Research Press, 1987), p. 109.

36. Edgerton, *American Film Exhibition,* p. 33.

37. *United States Department of Commerce 1967 Census of Business: Selected Services, Motion Pictures* (Washington, D.C.: U.S. Government Publishing and Printing, November 1970).

38. *Variety* (Weekly), April 27, 1960, p. 1.

39. Edgerton, *American Film Exhibition,* p. 34.

40. *Variety* (Weekly), August 24, 1960, p. 3.

41. *Box Office,* May 29, 1961, p. 6.

42. John Belton, *Widescreen Cinema* (Cambridge: Harvard University Press, 1992), pp. 212, 213.

43. "Stanley H. Durwood Obituary," *Kansas City Star,* July 16, 1999.

44. Steinberg, *Reel Facts,* p. 39.

45. Edgerton, *American Film Exhibition,* p. 34.

46. *Hollywood Reporter,* January 13, 1966.

47. Steinberg, *Reel Facts,* p. 40.

48. *Box Office,* July 22, 1968, p. 2.

49. *Box Office,* September 30, 1968.

50. Gomery, *Shared Pleasures,* pp. 89–92.

51. Charles Higham, *Hollywood at Sunset* (New York: Saturday Review Press, 1972), pp. 175, 176.

52. *SMPTE* (Society of Motion Picture and Television Engineers Magazine), March 1960, p. 25.

53. Belton, *Widescreen Cinema,* p. 178.

54. Justin Wyatt, "From Roadshowing to Saturation Release: Majors, Independents, and Marketing/Distribution Innovations," in Jon Lewis, ed., *The New American Cinema* (Durham and London: Duke University Press, 1998), pp. 66, 67.

55. Belton, *Widescreen Cinema,* p. 179.

56. *Box Office,* September 30, 1968.

57. Jerry Lewis, "Observations of a New Motion Picture Producer," Academy of Motion Picture Arts & Sciences, Motion Picture Study Collection, n.d.

58. Gomery, *Shared Pleasures,* p. 101.

59. "Script for the 33rd Academy Award Ceremonies," Center for Motion Picture Study, Academy of Motion Picture Arts & Sciences, Beverly Hills, California.

60. Cecil Smith, "Oscar's Up for Grabs," *Los Angeles Times Weekly Magazine,* April 16–22, 1961, pp. 2, 3.

61. *Hollywood Reporter,* April 16, 1966, p. 6.

62. Rick DuBrow, "High School Gymnasium Next?" *Los Angeles Evening Lookout,* April 10, 1962, p. 22.

63. *Film Bulletin,* April 16, 1962, p. 2.

64. *Hollywood Reporter,* April 19, 1966, p. 19.

65. Academy Files, 39th Award Ceremonies, Center for Motion Picture Study, Academy of Motion Picture Arts & Sciences, Beverly Hills, California.

66. "Rules for the Conduct of the Balloting for the 40th Academy Awards," Center for Motion Picture Study, Academy of Motion Picture Arts & Sciences, Beverly Hills, California.

67. *Motion Picture Daily,* April 11, 1968, p. 4.

68. Paul Michael, *The Academy Awards: A Pictorial History,* 5th ed. (New York: Crown Publishing, 1982), pp. 142–144.

69. Lev, *The Euro-American Cinema,* p. 13.

70. Jacques Sichier, *Nouvelle Vague* (Paris: Editions du Cerf, 1961), p. 22.

71. Thomas Schatz, *Old Hollywood/New Hollywood: Ritual, Art, and Industry* (Ann Arbor: UMI Research Press, 1983), p. 175.

72. *Box Office,* September 30, 1968, p. 6.

73. Michael F. Mayer, *The Film Industries* (New York: Hastings House, 1978), p. 63.

74. *Variety* (Daily), September 6, 1963, p. 3.

75. Robert Gessner, "The Handwriting on the Screen," *Saturday Review,* October 10, 1964.

76. Hollis Alpert, "Cinema: The Global Revolution," *Saturday Review,* October 5, 1963.

77. *Film Daily,* June 4, 1965, p. 1.

78. *Film Daily,* September 9, 1965, p. 7.

Chapter 4 (The Waning Production Code and the Rise of the Rating System)

1. See the discussion of the competition posed by foreign films in this regard in Peter Lev, *The Euro-American Cinema* (Austin: University of Texas Press, 1993), p. 14.

2. See, for example, Raymond Moley, *The Hays Office* (New York: Bobbs-Merrill, 1945), or Gerald Gardiner, *The Censorship Papers: Movie Censorship Letters from the Hays Office, 1934–1968* (New York: Dodd, Mead, 1987). The original office was named after Hollywood's first choice for supervising this self-censorship board, Will Hays, a former Postmaster General with a sound reputation and a long string of political connections.

3. Stephen Faber, *The Movie Rating Game* (Washington, D.C.: Public Affairs Press, 1972), p. 12.

4. Gerald Mast and Bruce F. Kawin, *A Short History of the Movies,* 5th ed. (Boston: Allyn and Bacon, 1996), p. 310.

5. Robert Stanley, *The Celluloid Empire: A History of the American Motion Picture* (New York: Hastings House, 1978), p. 209.

6. Frank Miller, *Censored Hollywood: Sex, Sin, and Violence on the Screen* (Atlanta: Turner Publishing Company, 1994), p. 185.

7. *Hollywood Reporter,* January 11, 1960, p. 2.

8. *Variety,* May 17, 1961, p. 1.

9. *Variety,* August 30, 1961, p. 6.

10. Charles Higham, *Hollywood at Sunset* (New York: Saturday Review Press, 1972), p. 143.

11. Lev, *The Euro-American Cinema,* p. 13.

12. *Box Office,* May 1, 1961, p. 2.

13. Robert Frederich, "Film Ads? The Nose for News Is Blue," *Variety,* Special Anniversary Issue, October 1965, p. 20.

14. *Variety* (Daily), June 6, 1963, p. 1.

15. Miller, *Censored Hollywood,* pp. 202, 203.

16. *Los Angeles Times,* November 5, 1967.

17. Faber, *Movie Rating Game,* p. 13.

18. Lev, *Euro-American Cinema,* p. 95

19. Faber, *Movie Rating Game,* p. 10.

20. Jerzy Toeplitz, *Hollywood and After: The Changing Face of American Cinema,* Boleslaw Sulik, trans. (London: George Allen and Unwin, Ltd., 1974), p. 164.

21. *Variety* (Daily), June 13, 1967, p. 9.

22. Abe Greenberg, "Voice of Hollywood," *Los Angeles Citizen News,* April 9, 1968.

23. *Variety,* Special Anniversary Issue, October 1966, p. 5.

24. Faber, *Movie Rating Game,* p. 14.

25. Mayer, *Film Industries,* p. 122.

26. Faber, *Movie Rating Game,* p. 14.

27. Letter, Charles Wales to Jack Valenti, May 6, 1968, in Jack Valenti Biographic File, The Margaret Herrick Library, Center for Motion Picture Study, Academy of Motion Picture Arts and Sciences, Beverly Hills, California.

28. *Variety* (Weekly), February 21, 1968.

29. *Los Angeles Times,* December 20, 1968.

30. Faber, *Movie Rating Game,* p. 14.

31. Wayne Nagra, "Exhibitors Hold Key to 'Valenti Plan'," in *Los Angeles Times,* October 20, 1968.

32. *Film–Television Daily,* April 30, 1968.
33. *Hollywood Reporter,* August 27, 1971.
34. Michael Scragow, "The Wild Bunch," *Atlantic Monthly* (June 1994).
35. Lois R. Sheinfeld, "Ratings: The Big Chill," *Film Comment* (May/June 1986).

CHAPTER 5 (THE CAMERA EYE)

1. David A. Cook, *A History of Narrative Film,* 3rd ed. (New York: W. W. Norton, 1996), p. 462.
2. Emanuel Levy, *And the Winner Is . . .: The History and Politics of the Oscar Awards* (New York: Ungar, 1987), p. 7.
3. Roderick T. Ryan, *A History of Motion Picture Color Technology* (New York: Focal Press, 1977), p. 148.
4. Ibid., pp. 151–153.
5. Andrew Laszlo, "Recent Trends in Location Lighting," *American Cinematographer,* September 1968, pp. 666, 667.
6. Barry Salt, *Film Style and Technology: History and Analysis,* 2nd ed. (London: Starword, 1992), p. 252.
7. Ethan Mordden, *Medium Cool: The Movies of the 1960s* (New York: Alfred A. Knopf, 1990), pp. 115, 116.
8. Vincent LoBrutto, *By Design: Interviews with Film Production Designers* (Westport, Conn.: Praeger, 1992), p. 7.
9. *Variety* (Weekly), August 9, 1961, p. 19.
10. Todd Rainsberger, *James Wong Howe: Cinematographer* (San Diego: A. S. Barnes & Co., 1981), p. 242.
11. H. Mario Raimondo Suoto, *The Technique of the Motion Picture Camera* (Boston: Focal Press, 1982), pp. 78, 79.
12. The Academy of Motion Picture Arts and Sciences honored Pierre Angenieux for the design of the 10:1 zoom lens in 1964, although this recognition was challenged by the late Joseph B. Walker's heirs on his behalf.
13. LoBrutto, *By Design,* p. 25.
14. Ibid., pp. 78, 79.
15. Raimondo Suoto, *Technique of the Motion Picture Camera,* p. 233.
16. Kenneth Macgowan, *Behind the Screen: The History and Techniques of the Motion Picture* (New York: Delacorte, 1965), p. 486.
17. For a good, brief discussion of film aspect ration, see John Cantine, Susan Howard, and Brady Lewis, *Shot by Shot: A Practical Guide to Filmmaking,* 2nd ed. (Pittsburgh: Pittsburgh Filmmakers Media Arts Center, 1995), p. 11.
18. Salt, *Film Style and Technology,* p. 261.
19. John Belton, *Widescreen Cinema* (Cambridge: Harvard University Press, 1992), pp. 224, 225.
20. Film, of course, can be shot at 30 fps. This is rare and normally utilized only in a scene in which a picture is on a television and must be filmed so as to appear faithful to its TV image without any roll bars or flicker appearing on the screen. Digital television, mandated for introduction in the United States by the middle of the first decade of the twenty-first century provides for a more elongated TV picture, better resembling the aspect ratio in which film is projected theatrically. The field drop problem of 24 fps in transferring film to video (30 fps), however, will not be impacted.
21. ANDY WARHOL'S FRANKENSTEIN (1974), directed by Paul Morrissey, was a famous exception, as were several others, but generally 3-D was reserved for occasional horror, sexploitation, and "camp" movies after the 1950s. See the discussion in Gerald Mast and Bruce F. Kawin, *A Short History of the Movies,* 5th ed. (New York: Macmillan, 1992), pp. 300 ff.
22. Michael Z. Wysotsky, *Wide-Screen Cinema and Stereophonic Sound,* A. E. C. York, trans., annotated and introduced by Raymond Spotiswoode, ed. (New York: Hastings House, 1971), p. 57.
23. *Variety* (Weekly), April 3, 1968, p. 4.
24. For precise statistics on the decline of these processes year by year, see Joel W. Finler, *The Hollywood Story* (New York: Crown Publishers, 1988), p. 282.
25. Salt, *Film Style and Technology,* p. 260.
26. "Filmed in Panavision: The Ultimate Wide Screen Experience," publication of the Panavision Corporation, Woodland Hills, Calif., 1998.

27. Belton, *Widescreen Cinema*, pp. 155, 156.
28. Salt, *Film Style and Technology*, pp. 260, 261.
29. Belton, *Widescreen Cinema*, p. 179.
30. "Filmed in Panavision."
31. Quoted in Axel Madsen, *The New Hollywood* (New York: Crowell, 1975), p. 259.
32. Dennis Schaefer and Larry Salvato, *Masters of Light: Conversations with Contemporary Cinematographers* (Berkeley: University of California Press, 1984), p 135.
33. George A. Huaco, *The Sociology of Film Art* (New York: Basic Books, 1965), p. 15.
34. Schaefer and Salvato, *Masters of Light*, p. 144.
35. Ibid., p. 14.
36. Richard Shale, *Academy Awards: An Ungar Reference*, 2nd ed. (New York: Frederick Ungar, 1982), p. 455.
37. Salt, *Film Style and Technology*, p. 259.
38. Nathalie Frederik, *Hollywood and the Academy Awards* (Los Angeles: Award Publications, 1968), p. 164.
39. Leonard Maltin, *The Art of the Cinematographer: A Survey and Interviews with Five Masters* (New York: Dover, 1971), p. 44.
40. Peter Greenburg, "A Cinematographer Looks at Directors: Bob Surtees," *Action* (January/February 1976): 20.
41. Herb A. Lightman, "Cinematographer with a 'Split Personality'," *American Cinematographer* (February 1968).
42. Greenburg, "Cinematographer Looks at Directors."
43. Lightman, "Cinematographer with a 'Split Personality'."
44. Schaefer and Salvato, *Masters of Light*, p. 153.
45. Ibid., pp. 159, 160.
46. *Motion Picture Herald*, December 20, 1967, p. 11.
47. *Time*, November 22, 1967, p. 52.
48. Louis Gianetti and Scott Eyman, *Flashback: A Brief History of Film* (Englewood Cliffs, N.J.: Prentice-Hall, 1986), pp. 372, 373.
49. Maltin, *Art of the Cinematographer*, p. 41.
50. Schaefer and Salvato, *Masters of Light*, p. 258.
51. *American Cinematographer* (October 1968): 725.
52. John Simon, *Movies into Film* (New York: Dial Press, 1971), p. 78.
53. "Credits: Cinematographer Laszlo Kovacs," *Look*, November 3, 1970, p. 68.
54. Confirmed in an interview, Andrew Laszlo with Paul Monaco, October 3, 1999, Bozeman, Montana.
55. Andrew "Andy" Laszlo, Files of the Academy of Motion Picture Arts and Sciences, Center for the Study of the Motion Picture, Beverly Hills, California.
56. Interview, Andrew Laszlo with Paul Monaco, October 3, 1999, Bozeman, Montana.
57. Salt, *Film Style and Technology*, p. 251.
58. Schaefer and Salvato, *Masters of Light*, pp. 154–158.
59. Andrew "Andy" Laszlo, Files of the Academy of Motion Picture Arts and Sciences, Center for the Study of the Motion Picture, Beverly Hills, California.
60. Schaefer and Salvato, *Masters of Light*, pp. 154–158.
61. Ibid., p. 139.
62. Patrick McGilligan, "William Fraker's Magic Camera," *American Film* (April 1979).
63. Ken Dancyger, *The Technique of Film and Video Editing* (Boston: Focal Press, 1993), pp. 184, 185.
64. BULLITT grossed over $19 million in North American rentals alone, outranking such hits as EASY RIDER, MIDNIGHT COWBOY, and LAWRENCE OF ARABIA.
65. Herb A. Lightman, "The Five Best Photographed Motion Pictures of 1968," *American Cinematographer* (April 1969): 392–394.
66. *Hollywood Reporter*, October 23, 1968, p. 17.
67. *American Cinematographer* (February 1969): 204.
68. *American Cinematographer* (July 1969): 651.
69. Simon, *Movies into Film*, p. 83.
70. Joseph McBride, "The Man behind the Camera, a Name Out Front, Too," *Variety* (Daily), October 28, 1980, p. 10.

71. John Stanley, "The Art of the Cinematographer: Laszlo Kovacs," *Filmmakers' Newsletter* (July 1978): 4, 5.
72. Quoted in *Variety* (Daily), October 15, 1991, p. 3.

CHAPTER 6 (THE CUTTER'S ROOM)

1. Scott Mitchell, "Editing: The Kindest Cut," *Los Angeles Times,* March 21, 1990, pp. F-1, F-8.
2. Gabriella Oldham, *First Cut: Conversations with Film Editors* (Berkeley: University of California Press, 1992), p. 349.
3. Vincent LoBrutto, *Selected Takes: Film Editors on Editing* (Westport, Conn.: Praeger, 1991), p. 79.
4. Michael Webb, ed., *Hollywood: Legend and Reality* (Boston: Little, Brown, & Co., 1986), p. 143.
5. Karel Reisz and Gavin Millar, *The Technique of Film Editing,* 2nd ed. (New York: Hastings House, 1968), p. 327.
6. "Prime Cut: 75 Editors' Filmographies and Supporting Materials," *Film Comment* (March/April 1977): 25.
7. See the discussion of Godard's New Wave editing techniques, and an assessment of their influence, in Ralph Rosenblum and Robert Karen, *When the Shooting Stops . . . the Cutting Begins: A Film Editor's Story* (New York: Viking, 1979), pp. 143, 144.
8. "Prime Cut," p. 25.
9. Rosenblum and Karen, *When the Shooting Stops,* p. 12.
10. Ken Dancyger, *The Technique of Film and Video Editing* (Boston: Focal Press, 1993), pp. 150–152.
11. "Prime Cut," p. 25.
12. Allan Arkush, "I Want My KEM-TV," *American Film* (December 1985): 65, 66.
13. Barry Salt, *Film Style and Technology: History and Analysis,* 2nd ed. (London: Starword Press, 1992), p. 265.
14. Gerald Mast and Bruce F. Kawin, *A Short History of the Movies,* 5th ed. (New York: Macmillan, 1992), p. 434.
15. Rosenblum and Karen, *When the Shooting Stops,* p. 178.
16. Arkush, "I Want My KEM-TV," p. 65.
17. Salt, *Film Style and Technology,* pp. 264, 265.
18. *Variety* (Daily), December 12, 1967, p. 6.
19. Salt, *Film Style and Technology,* p. 261.
20. Ally Acker, *Reel Women: Pioneers of the Cinema, 1896 to the Present* (New York: Continuum, 1991), p. 225.
21. Frances Taylor, "The View from the Editing Room," *Los Angeles Times,* October 3, 1973, p. 43.
22. LoBrutto, *Selected Takes,* p. 77.
23. Acker, *Reel Women,* p. 226.
24. LoBrutto, *Selected Takes,* pp. 137, 138.
25. Leonard Quart and Albert Auster, *American Film and Society Since 1945,* 2nd ed. (New York: Praeger, 1991), p. 84.
26. LoBrutto, *Selected Takes,* p. 78.
27. Arkush, "I Want My KEM-TV," p. 66.
28. LoBrutto, *Selected Takes,* p. 78.
29. Acker, *Reel Women,* p. 226.
30. LoBrutto, *Selected Takes,* p. 86.
31. Rosenblum and Karen, *When the Shooting Stops,* p. 141.
32. *New Yorker,* April 4, 1965.
33. Arkush, "I Want My KEM-TV," p. 66.
34. Roy Paul Madsen, *Working Cinema: Learning from the Masters* (Belmont, Calif.: Wadsworth Publishing, 1990), p. 285.
35. Rosenblum and Karen, *When the Shooting Stops,* pp. 178, 179.
36. "Prime Cut," p. 25.
37. Rosenblum and Karen, *When the Shooting Stops,* p. 190.
38. Oldham, *First Cut,* p. 372.
39. Walter Kerr, "Films Are Made in the Cutting Room," *New York Times,* March 17, 1985.

40. Robert Osborne, "Good, Clean Cuts," *Hollywood Reporter,* "Craft Series," 1992, p. S-18.
41. Gene D. Phillips, *Alfred Hitchcock* (Boston: Twayne, 1984), p. 162.
42. Madsen, *Working Cinema,* p. 285.
43. David Bordwell and Kristin Thompson, *Film Art: An Introduction,* 4th ed. (New York: McGraw-Hill, 1993), p. 206.
44. Douglas Brode, *The Films of the Sixties* (Secaucus, N.J.: Citadel Press, 1980), p. 99.
45. Bordwell and Thompson, *Film Art: An Introduction,* pp. 254–257.
46. Oldham, *First Cut,* pp. 161, 162.
47. LoBrutto, *Selected Takes,* pp. 65, 66.
48. Oldham, *First Cut,* p. 165.
49. LoBrutto, *Selected Takes,* p. 66.
50. Oldham, *First Cut,* pp. 165, 166.
51. Michael Ryan and Douglas Kellner, *Camera Politica: The Politics and Ideology of Contemporary Hollywood Film* (Bloomington: Indiana University Press, 1988), p. 21. For a discussion of this sequence in THE GRADUATE as an "associational montage," see Stephen Prince, *Movies and Meaning: An Introduction to Film* (Boston: Allyn and Bacon, 1997), pp. 143–149.
52. *Variety,* May 8, 1968, p. 7.
53. Dennis Schaefer and Larry Salvato, *Master of Light: Conversations with Contemporary Cinematographers* (Berkeley: University of California Press, 1984), p. 133.
54. *Variety,* September 13, 1968, p. 5.
55. James Destro, "Movies on Tape," *Film/Tape World,* March 1989.
56. Webb, ed., *Hollywood: Legend and Reality,* p. 143.
57. *Variety,* April 3, 1968, p. 1.
58. Dancyger, *Technique of Film and Video Editing,* pp. 166, 167.
59. Oldham, *First Cut,* p. 209.
60. LoBrutto, *Selected Takes,* p. 129.
61. Dancyger, *Technique of Film and Video Editing,* p. 152.

CHAPTER 7 (SOUND AND MUSIC)

1. For a thorough discussion of this transition see Donald Crafton, *The Talkies: American Cinema's Transition to Sound, 1926–1931* (New York: Charles Scribner's Sons, 1997), especially part 2, pp. 271–380.
2. Karel Reisz, *The Technique of Film Editing* (Boston: Focal Press, 1964), p. 55.
3. John Belton, "The Technology of Film Sound," in Elizabeth Weis and John Belton, eds., *Film Sound: Theory and Practice* (New York: Columbia University Press, 1985), p. 66.
4. Marie Michel, "Le film, la parole, et la langue," *Cahiers du 20eme siecle* 9 (1978): 67–75.
5. Marc Mancini, "The Sound Designer," in Weis and Belton, eds., *Film Sound,* p. 361.
6. Vincent LoBrutto, *Sound on Film: Interviews with Creators of Film Sound* (Westport, Conn.: Praeger, 1994), p. xii.
7. John Belton, *Widescreen Cinema* (Cambridge: Harvard University Press, 1992), p. 151.
8. Stephen Handzo, "Glossary of Film Sound Technology," in Weis and Belton, eds., *Film Sound,* p. 419.
9. Michael Z. Wysotsky, *Wide-Screen Cinema and Stereophonic Sound,* A. E. C. York, trans., annotated and introduced by Raymond Spotiswoode, ed. (New York: Hastings House, 1971), pp. 145 ff.
10. LoBrutto, *Sound on Film,* pp. 44–46.
11. Wysotsky, *Wide-Screen Cinema,* pp. 148, 149.
12. Handzo, "Glossary of Film Sound Technology," p. 419.
13. Douglas Gomery, *Shared Pleasures: A History of Movie Presentation in the United States* (Madison: University of Wisconsin Press, 1992), p. 228.
14. Handzo, "Glossary of Film Sound Technology," p. 421.
15. Barry Salt, *Film Style and Technology: History and Analysis* (London: Starword, 1992), pp. 263, 264.
16. David Koester, *Guide to Production and Post-Production Sound Recording* (Bozeman: Montana State University, 1998), pp. 6 ff.

17. In fact, the Nagra remained standard technology for motion-picture sound production until the advent of digital recording and mixing with the DAT system of the 1990s. Even then, many professionals continued to consider the Nagra to be the equal in quality of digital recording.

18. Handzo, "Glossary of Film Sound Technology," p. 405.

19. Ibid., p. 405.

20. See LoBrutto, *Sound on Film,* pp. 55–58.

21. Ralph Hodges, "More on Movie Sound," *Stereo Review* (September 1988).

22. Wysotsky, *Wide-Screen Cinema,* p. 129.

23. LoBrutto, *Sound on Film,* p. 30.

24. David Bordwell and Kristin Thompson, *Film Art: An Introduction,* 4th ed. (New York: McGraw-Hill, 1993), p. 257.

25. Allan Arkush, "I Want My KEM-TV," *American Film* (December 1985): 65.

26. Martha Frankel, "It Came from the Screening Room," *American Film* (May 1989): 40, 41.

27. Bordwell and Thompson, *Film Art: An Introduction,* p. 217.

28. George Hickenlooper, *Reel Conversations: Candid Interviews with Film's Foremost Directors and Critics* (Secaucus, N.J.: Carol Publishing Group, 1991), p. 175.

29. Robert R. Faulkner, *Hollywood Studio Musicians: Their Work and Careers in the Recording Industry* (Chicago: Aldine-Atherton, 1971), p. 23.

30. Walter Scharf, *The History of Film Scoring* (Studio City, Calif.: Cinema Songs Publishing, 1988), p. 59.

31. Fred Karlin, *Listening to Movies: The Film Lover's Guide to Film Music* (New York: Schirmer Books, 1994), p. 201.

32. Ethan Mordden, *Medium Cool: The Movies of the 1960s* (New York: Alfred A. Knopf, 1990), p. 23.

33. Landon Y. Jones, *Great Expectations: America and the Baby Boom Generation* (New York: Ballantine Books, 1980), p. 73.

34. Mordden, *Medium Cool,* p. 10.

35. Christopher H. Sterling and Timothy R. Haight, *The Mass Media: Aspen Institute Guide to Communication Industry Trends* (New York: Praeger, 1978), p. 262.

36. Robert R. Faulkner, *Music on Demand: Composers and Careers in the Hollywood Film Industry* (New Brunswick, N.J.: Transaction Books, 1983), p. 213.

37. Mordden, *Medium Cool,* p. 24.

38. Tony Thomas, *Music for the Movies* (New York: A. S. Barnes & Co., 1973), p. 197.

39. "Interview with Henry Mancini," *Mix Magazine* (November 1988).

40. Tony Thomas, *Film Score: The Art and Craft of Movie Music* (Burbank, Calif.: Riverwood Press, 1991), pp. 199, 200.

41. *Hollywood Reporter,* June 15, 1994.

42. Thomas, *Film Score,* p. 200.

43. See the entry under "Bernard Herrmann" in Steven C. Smith, *The Film Composers Guide* (Los Angeles: Lone Eagle Publishing, 1991).

44. Colin Vaines, "Film Music and Composers," in David Pirie, ed., *Anatomy of the Movies* (New York: Macmillan, 1981), p. 196.

45. Robert Sklar, *Film: An International History of the Medium* (New York: Henry N. Abrams, Inc., 1993), p. 418.

46. Thomas, *Film Score,* p. 173.

47. Ibid., p. 292.

48. LoBrutto, *Sound on Film,* p. 20.

49. *Hollywood Reporter,* December 13, 1967.

50. Lo Brutto, *Sound on Film,* p. 17.

51. Faulkner, *Music on Demand,* p. 26.

52. Faulkner, *Hollywood Studio Musicians,* p. 18.

53. John Russell Taylor and Arthur Jackson, *The Hollywood Musical* (New York: McGraw-Hill, 1971), p. 98.

54. Faulkner, *Hollywood Studio Musicians,* p. 22.

55. Thomas, *Music for the Movies,* p. 195.

56. Taylor and Jackson, *Hollywood Musical,* p. 97.

57. Karlin, *Listening to Movies,* p. 244.

58. Taylor and Jackson, *Hollywood Musical,* pp. 97, 98.

59. Jon Mahoney, "MGM's Ice Station Zebra Cinerama Box Office Hit," *Hollywood Reporter,* October 23, 1968.
60. Thomas, *Film Score,* p. 288.
61. Vaines, "Film Music and Composers," p. 197.
62. Thomas, *Film Score,* p. 190.

Chapter 8 (The Twilight of the Goddesses:
Hollywood Actresses in the 1960s)

1. Mary Ellen O'Brien, *Film Acting: The Techniques and History of Acting for the Camera* (New York: Arco, 1983), pp. 29, 30.
2. See the excellent discussion on this point in Michael Kummel, *Manhood in America: A Cultural History* (New York: Free Press, 1996), pp. 269–272 ff.
3. Wendy Shalit, *A Return to Modesty: Rediscovering the Lost Virtue* (New York: Free Press, 1998), p. 248.
4. *Los Angeles Herald-Examiner,* January 8, 1961, p. 24.
5. Sidney Skolsky, "Tintypes: Doris Day," *Los Angeles Citizen News,* August 26, 1966, p. 28.
6. O'Brien, *Film Acting,* p. 43.
7. George Morris, "Doris Day: Not Pollyanna," in Danny Peary, ed., *Close-Ups: Intimate Portraits of Movie Stars by their Co-Stars, Directors, Screenwriters, and Friends* (New York: Workman, 1978), p. 78.
8. *Los Angeles Herald–Examiner,* March 6, 1963, p. 21.
9. Molly Haskell, *From Reverence to Rape: The Treatment of Women in the Movies* (New York: Holt, Rinehart and Winston, 1974), pp. 262–267.
10. Paul Kerr, "Stars and Stardom," in David Pirie, ed., *Anatomy of the Movies* (New York: Macmillan, 1981), p. 108.
11. *Variety* (Daily), January 18, 1968, p. 12.
12. *Variety* (Weekly), August 7, 1968, p. 1.
13. Michael Munn, *The Hollywood Murder Casebook* (New York: St. Martin's Press, 1987), pp. 18, 19.
14. Barbara Leaming, *Marilyn Monroe* (New York: Crown Publishers, 1992), p. 431.
15. *Variety* (Weekly), December 11, 1963.
16. Maureen Dowd, "Paul Newman and Joanne Woodward: A Lifetime of Shared Passions," *McCalls* (January 1991).
17. William Leonard, "They Love Liz Taylor, Shocks and All," *Chicago Tribune Magazine,* June 12, 1960.
18. *New York Times,* March 13, 1962.
19. Sibyl March, "The Intense Boredom of Elizabeth Taylor," *The Seventh Art* (Fall 1963).
20. Anthony Asquith, "A Director Views Liz," *Los Angeles Times,* September 1, 1963, p. 42.
21. See Maureen Turim, "Elizabeth Taylor: In the Public Eye," in Pirie, ed., *Anatomy of the Movies,* pp. 187, 188.
22. Foster Hirsch, *Acting Hollywood Style* (New York: Henry N. Abrams, Inc./AFI Press, 1991), p. 247.
23. Thomas Thompson, "While Burton Romances Rex, Liz Weighs Her Power and Her Future," *Life,* January 17, 1969.
24. The details of Wood's suicide attempt are discussed by the director Henry Jaglom, a close friend of hers, during an interview in the E-TV (Entertainment Television) documentary, *Natalie Wood,* first aired on E-TV, December 1997.
25. Simon Brett, "Audrey Hepburn," *Films and Filming* (March 1964).
26. *Los Angeles Citizen-News,* August 28, 1965, p. 25.
27. Anthony Holden, *Behind the Oscar: The Secret History of the Academy Awards* (New York: Simon & Schuster, 1993), p. 254.
28. *Hollywood Reporter,* June 20, 1965, p. 7.
29. Robert Windeler, *Julie Andrews: A Life on Stage and Screen* (Secaucus, N.J.: Birch Lane Publishing, 1997), p. 133.
30. Joyce Haber, "More Slippage for Julie's Image," *Los Angeles Times,* January 15, 1969.
31. Windeler, *Julie Andrews,* pp. 186, 187.

32. Bill Condon, "Shirley MacLaine: Early Rebel," in Peary, ed., *Close-Ups*, pp. 272, 273.

33. See Robert Stone, "Faye Dunaway: A Classic in Her Own Time," *Cosmopolitan*, May 1968, and James Monaco, *American Film Now: The People, the Power, the Money, the Movies* (New York: New American Library, 1979), p. 94.

34. Mason Wiley, "Faye Dunaway: Breaking the Id," in Peary, ed., *Close-Ups*, p. 545.

35. Charles Champlin, "Katharine Ross: A Seedling in Lotusland," *Los Angeles Times* (undated, in the files of the Center for Motion Picture Study at the Academy of Motion Picture Arts and Sciences).

36. Joe Morgenstern, "A Careful Comeback," *Elle* (March 1986): 102.

37. Quoted in Stephen Farber and Marc Green, *Hollywood Dynasties* (New York: Putnam, 1984), p. 238.

38. Hirsch, *Acting Hollywood Style*, pp. 158, 257.

39. Paul Kerr, "Stars and Stardom," in Pirie, ed., *Anatomy of the Movies*, p. 113.

40. Jeff Corey, "Jane Fonda: Actress with a Message," in Peary, ed., *Close-Ups*, pp. 283, 284.

41. O'Brien, *Film Acting*, p. 43.

42. Dorothy Manners, "Barbra Streisand's Solid Gold Highway," *Los Angeles Herald-Examiner*, May 19, 1967, pp. 32, 33.

43. Ira Mothner, "A Frantic, Brassy, Tender 'Funny Girl,'" *Look*, October 15, 1966. (The author offered the opinion that Streisand had "made life better for a helluva lot of homely little girls.")

44. Sidney Skolsky, "Fade Out, Fade In for Hollywood," *Hollywood Citizen-News*, November 21, 1968, p. 22.

45. Tom Ramage, "Barbra Transcends 'Funny Girl' Bonds," *After Dark*, September 25, 1968.

CHAPTER 9 (MALE DOMINATION OF THE HOLLYWOOD SCREEN)

1. Ethan Mordden, *Medium Cool: The Movies of the 1960s* (New York: Alfred A. Knopf, 1990), p. 62.

2. James Naremore, *Acting in the Cinema* (Berkeley: University of California Press, 1988), p. 205.

3. Jane Wilson, "What If My Eyes Turn Brown?" *Saturday Evening Post*, February 24, 1968, p. 29.

4. Lloyd Shearer, "Paul Newman: Politically Active Superstar," *Parade*, January 5, 1969, p. 10.

5. Al Morgan, "Paul Newman: New Breed of Screen Lover," *Show Business Illustrated* (February 1962): 17.

6. Sidney Skolsky, "Hollywood Is My Beat," *The Hollywood Citizen-News*, February 25, 1960, p. 24. (In this article, Skolsky labeled Newman as "A what does it mean? kinda guy!")

7. Cobbett Steinberg, *Reel Facts: The Movie Book of Records* (New York: Vintage Books, 1982), p. 60.

8. Richard A. Blum, *American Film Acting: The Stanislavski Heritage* (Ann Arbor: UMI Research Press, 1984), pp. 61–64.

9. Wilfrid Sheed, "Cool Hand Luke," *Esquire* (September 1967): 21.

10. Martin Quigley, Jr., and Richard Gertner, *Films in America, 1929–1969* (New York: Golden Press, 1970), p. 334.

11. Eric Lax, *Paul Newman: A Biography* (Atlanta: Turner Publishing, 1996), p. 124.

12. Shearer, "Paul Newman," p. 10.

13. David Pirie, "Deal," in David Pirie, ed., *Anatomy of the Movies* (New York: Macmillan, 1981), p. 45.

14. Lawrence Zuckenbill, "Oh, You Sundance Kid," *Esquire* (October 1970): 163.

15. Harry Clein, "The Robert Redford Renaissance," *Entertainment World*, April 13, 1970, p. 9.

16. Bob Thomas, "Robert Redford: A Hot New Star in a Period When Stars Are Cold," *Los Angeles Herald-Examiner*, August 26, 1970, p. 7.

17. Quoted in Graham McCann, *Rebel Males: Clift, Brando, and Dean* (New Brunswick, N.J.: Rutgers University Press, 1993), p. 168.

18. "Interview with Warren Beatty," *Films and Filming* (April 1961): 8.

19. Rex Reed, "Will the Real Warren Beatty Please Shut Up!" *Esquire* (August 1967).

20. William Lee Jackson, "Bye-Bye Beatty," *The Players* (Fall 1964): 56.

21. John Pym, ed., *Time Out Film Guide*, 4th ed. (London: Penguin Books, 1995), p. 468.

22. Louis D. Giannetti, *Masters of the American Cinema* (Englewood Cliffs, N.J.: Prentice-Hall, 1981), p. 381.

23. Thomas Thompson, "Under the Gaze of the Charmer," *Life*, April 26, 1968, p. 103.

24. *International Herald Tribune*, December 11, 1968, p. 12.

25. Biographical files, Steve McQueen, Center for the Study of the Motion Picture, Academy of Motion Picture Arts & Sciences, Beverly Hills, California.
26. Ann Lloyd and David Robinson, eds., *Movies of the Sixties* (London: Orbis Publishing, 1983), p. 65.
27. Graham McCann, *Rebel Males: Clift, Brando, and Dean,* p. 167.
28. John Hallowell, "McQueen," *Los Angeles Times Magazine,* November 23, 1969.
29. Mordden, *Medium Cool,* p. 65.
30. Judy Klemesrud, "Steve McQueen: Phi Beta Hubcap," *New York Times,* August 23, 1968.
31. Sidney Skolsky, "Tintypes: Gene Hackman," *Los Angeles Citizen-News,* March 31, 1968.
32. Pierce McDermott, "You Know Him as Mr. Tough Guy," *Coronet,* April 1972, p. 37.
33. Bridget Byrne, "Gene Hackman: A Brando for the Masses,"*Los Angeles Herald-Examiner,* December 12, 1970, pp. F-1, 2.
34. Vernon Scott, "Success Built on Ability," *Los Angeles Herald-Examiner,* December 19, 1971, p. F-9.
35. Michael Ritchie, "Gene Hackman: He Can't Get the Girl," in Danny Peary, ed., *Close-Ups: Intimate Portraits of Movie Stars by Their Co-Stars, Directors, Screenwriters, and Friends* (New York: Workman Publishing, 1978), p. 364.
36. Sidney Skolsky, "Tintypes: Gene Hackman," *Los Angeles Citizen-News,* March 29, 1968, p. 24.
37. Martha Weinman Lear, "Hoffman: The Man Behind the Smile," *Redbook* (September 1968): 147.
38. Quoted in Judy Michaelson, "The Bittersweet Taste of Success," *Pageant* (June 1968): 7.
39. Jane Wilson, "Dustin Hoffman," *Los Angeles Times Magazine,* July 13, 1969, p. 28.
40. David Zeitlin, "A Swarthy Pinocchio Makes a Wooden Role Real," *Life,* November 24, 1967, p. 114.
41. Steinberg, *Reel Facts,* p. 68.
42. Blum, *American Film Acting,* p. 67.
43. Richard L. Coe, "Sidney Poitier," *Washington Post,* April 21, 1967.
44. *Hollywood Reporter,* January 21, 1969, p. 7; also, *Film-TV Daily,* January 28, 1969, p. 4. (For example, Poitier's deferred earnings on To Sir, with Love [1966] alone exceeded $2,500,000.)
45. Hollis Alpert, "The Admirable Sidney," *Saturday Review,* July 8, 1967.
46. Clifford Mason, "Why Does White America Love Sidney Poitier So?" *New York Times,* September 10, 1967, p. D-21.
47. *Variety* (Daily), June 21, 1967, p. 1.
48. *Motion Picture Herald,* February 2, 1969.
49. Terry Christensen, *Reel Politics* (New York: Basil Blackwell, Inc., 1987), pp. 120, 121.
50. *Hollywood Reporter,* November 23, 1962, p. 4.
51. *Film Daily,* July 22, 1963, p. 10.
52. Jerry Lewis, "Observations of a New Motion Picture Producer," undated manuscripts, Collection of the Center for the Study of the Motion Picture, the Academy of Motion Picture Arts and Sciences, Beverly Hills, California.
53. "From Our Film Critic," *London Times,* January 23, 1965.
54. John Russell Taylor, "Jerry Lewis," *Sight and Sound* (Spring 1965): 77.
55. Ibid., p. 78.
56. *Film Daily,* March 22, 1965.
57. *Hollywood Reporter,* September 20, 1965, p. 4.
58. *Hollywood Reporter,* March 1, 1966, p. 11.
59. Axel Madsen, "Jerry Lewis Moonlights as Professor," *Los Angeles Times,* January 1, 1968, p. 28.
60. "Confessions of an Auteur: Interview with Mel Brooks," *Action* (November/December 1971): 17.
61. Ralph Rosenblum and Robert Karen, *When the Shooting Stops . . . the Cutting Begins: A Film Editor's Story* (New York: Viking Press, 1979), pp. 245 ff.

CHAPTER 10 (THE ESTABLISHMENT JUDGES: ACADEMY AWARDS FOR BEST PICTURE)

1. Pierre Norman Sands, *A Historical Study of the Academy of Motion Picture Arts and Sciences* (New York: Arno Press, 1973), pp. 31–35.
2. Rules for the Conduct of Balloting: The 33rd Academy Awards for 1960, Academy Awards File, Center for Motion Picture Study, Academy of Motion Picture Arts and Sciences, Beverly Hills, California.
3. Ralph L. Williams, "Oscar Win Worth $ $ $," *Los Angeles Citizen-News,* April 18, 1961, p. 12.
4. *Close-Up,* March 9, 1961.

5. Derek Monsey, "And I Name This Hollywood's Finest Comedy in Years," *London Sunday Express,* July 24, 1960, pp. 52, 53.

6. For a comprehensive and insightful study of United Artist's central role, beginning in the early 1950s, in leading the transition from studio-owned productions to financing independent producers, see Tino Balio, *United Artists: The Company That Changed the Film Industry* (Madison: University of Wisconsin Press, 1987); see also Balio's own chapters in Tino Balio, ed., *Hollywood in the Age of Television* (Boston: Unwin Hyman, 1990).

7. Judy Sloane, "Call Sheet: WEST SIDE STORY," *Film Review,* June 1994.

8. James A. Crenshaw, "Call for a Ghost in a Hurry," *Los Angeles Herald-Examiner,* February 17, 1963.

9. *Film Daily,* August 24, 1961, p. 7.

10. *Variety* (Daily), August 4, 1961, p. 18.

11. *Hollywood Reporter,* May 12, 1966, p. 12.

12. *Variety* (Daily), September 21, 1966, p. 1.

13. *Variety* (Daily), December 17, 1962, p. 2.

14. Cliff Rothman, "The Resurrection of LAWRENCE OF ARABIA," *Los Angeles Times,* January 29, 1989, p. 32.

15. Stanley Kauffmann, "LAWRENCE OF ARABIA: The Re-Release," *New Republic,* April 17, 1989, p. 60.

16. Glenn Collins, "LAWRENCE OF ARABIA the Way It Should Be," *Los Angeles Herald-Examiner,* December 21, 1989, p. F-1.

17. Angus McLaren, *The History of Contraception: Antiquity to the Present* (Cambridge, Mass.: Basil Blackwell, 1990), pp. 240, 241.

18. Stephen Holden, "An Angry Man Found Himself in TOM JONES," *New York Times,* August 21, 1994.

19. Paul Monaco, *Ribbons in Time* (Bloomington: Indiana University Press, 1988), pp. 50–54.

20. *Hollywood Reporter,* October 2, 1965, p. 2.

21. *Variety* (Daily), October 20, 1965, p. 4.

22. *Los Angeles Herald-Examiner,* October 29, 1964, p. 32.

23. THE SOUND OF MUSIC, Publicity File, 20th Century-Fox, the Center for Motion Picture Study, Academy of Motion Picture Arts and Sciences, Beverly Hills, California.

24. *Hollywood Reporter,* March 2, 1966, p. 19.

25. *Hollywood Reporter,* December 23, 1964, p. 6.

26. "THE SOUND OF MUSIC," unsigned review, *Saturday Review,* March 20, 1965.

27. *Variety* (Weekly), March 12, 1967, p. 10.

28. See her summary of negative criticism in Julia A. Hirsch, *"THE SOUND OF MUSIC": The Making of America's Favorite Movie* (Chicago: Contemporary Books, 1993).

29. Stanley Kauffmann, "Review: THE SOUND OF MUSIC," *New Republic,* March 20, 1965, p. 22.

30. John E. Fitzgerald, "The Hills Are Alive," *Our Sunday Visitor,* February 28, 1965, p. 3.

31. *Variety* (Daily), April 17, 1964, p. 7, and *Los Angeles Citizen-News,* July 20, 1964, p. 10. At various times, the motion-picture version of OLIVER!, which had opened on the London stage in 1960, was projected with Elizabeth Taylor and Richard Burton playing the leads and Peter Sellers cast as Fagin.

32. Philip K. Scheuer, "'Man' Becomes Profession Movie for All Seasons," *Los Angeles Times,* December 11, 1966, p. 39.

33. *Variety* (Weekly), April 12, 1967, p. 5.

34. Kenneth Turan, "Why Joe Buck and Ratso Live On," *Los Angeles Times Calendar,* February 20, 1994, p. 12.

35. Archer Winsten, "MIDNIGHT COWBOY," *New York Post,* May 26, 1969, pp. 52, 53.

36. *Los Angeles Herald-Examiner,* July 11, 1969, p. F-1.

37. See Justin Wyatt, *High Concept: Movie and Marketing in Hollywood* (Austin: University of Texas Press, 1995).

CHAPTER 11 (LANDMARK MOVIES OF THE 1960S AND THE CINEMA OF SENSATION)

1. *Time,* December 28, 1962, p. 58.

2. Art Seidenbaum, "The Low Cost of Quality," *Los Angeles Times,* February 17, 1963, p. 40.

3. *The Hollywood Reporter,* February 21, 1963, p. 7.

4. William Trombley, "Small Budget Triumph of DAVID AND LISA," *Saturday Evening Post,* March 16, 1963, p. 56.
5. Douglas Brode, *Films of the Sixties* (New York: Carol Publishing Group, 1980), p. 80.
6. *Time,* December 28, 1962, p. 58.
7. See Hazel Flynn, "Frank's CANDIDATE Among Best of the Year," *Los Angeles Citizen-News,* November 8, 1962, p. 10, and Philip K. Scheuer, "Frankenheimer's 'Candidate' a Big Winner," *Los Angeles Times,* October 28, 19?2, p. 28.
8. Richard Corliss, "From Failure to Cult Classic," *Time,* March 21, 1988, p. 72.
9. Jack Lotto, "Reds Jump on Sinatra Film," *Los Angeles Herald-Examiner,* December 15, 1962, p. 6; see also, *Variety* (Daily), December 18, 1962, p. 1.
10. *Variety* (Weekly), October 24, 1962, p. 12.
11. *Los Angeles Herald-Examiner,* November 23, 1962, p. 36.
12. Corliss, "From Failure to Cult Classic," p. 72.
13. Aljean Harmetz, "MANCHURIAN CANDIDATE: Old Failure Now a Hit," *New York Times,* February 24, 1988, p. 32.
14. *Los Angeles Times,* February 26, 1989. (The movie, it should be noted, was televised in local markets where its controversial nature was assessed to be less disquieting to substantial numbers of viewers.)
15. *Los Angeles Herald-Examiner,* April 29, 1988, p. F-2.
16. Brode, *Films of the Sixties,* p. 93.
17. *Hollywood Reporter,* June 17, 1998, p. 9.
18. Charles Maland, "DR. STRANGELOVE: Nightmare Comedy and the Ideology of Liberal Consensus," in Peter Rollins, ed., *Hollywood as Historian: American Film in a Cultural Context* (Lexington: University of Kentucky Press, 1982), p. 111.
19. *Digest of the University Film and Video Association,* (October/November 1998). (Interestingly, both the next two feature films from the 1960s to be selected were arguably really British productions: LAWRENCE OF ARABIA and 2001: A SPACE ODYSSEY.)
20. Terry Christensen, *Reel Politics* (New York: Basil Blackwell, 1987), p. 116.
21. Bosley Crowther, " DR. STRANGELOVE," *New York Times,* January 31, 1964, p. 44.
22. Brode, *Films of the Sixties,* p. 134.
23. Lawrence Suid, " DR. STRANGELOVE," in John E. O'Connor and Martin A. Jackson, eds., *American History/American Film: Interpreting the Hollywood Image* (New York: Frederick Ungar, 1979), p. 227.
24. Judith Crist, "MICKEY ONE," *Variety* (Daily), September 21, 1965, p. 2.
25. Ed Carter, "Notes to MICKEY ONE," the UCLA Festival of Preservation, Westwood, California, 1994.
26. *Hollywood Reporter,* August 11, 1965, p. 9.
27. *Cue,* October 2, 1965; see also *New Yorker,* October 2, 1965, p. 68.
28. *New Yorker,* April 1, 1961, p. 59.
29. Robert Sklar, *Film: An International History of the Medium* (New York: Harry N. Abrams, 1993), p. 463.
30. Harvey Mindess, "FACES," *Psychology Today* (June 1969): 16, 17.
31. "New Films," *Playboy* (September 1968): 81.
32. *Film Bulletin,* January 20, 1969.
33. Deac Rossell, "FACES Fills the Screen with Brilliant Reflections," *Boston Globe,* December 18, 1968, p. 38.
34. C. Robert Jennings, "Hollywood's Accidental Artist of FACES," *Los Angeles Times,* February 16, 1969.
35. Ray Carney, *The Films of John Cassavetes: Pragmatism, Modernism, and the Movies* (Cambridge: Cambridge University Press, 1994), pp. 23, 24.
36. Richard Schickel, "The Great Cassavetes Experiment," *Life,* January 17, 1969, pp. 39, 40.
37. Brode, *Films of the Sixties,* p. 281.
38. Hollis Alpert, "The Film of Social Reality," *Saturday Review,* September 6, 1969, p. 55.
39. Dennis Schaefer and Larry Salvato, *Masters of Light: Conversations with Contemporary Cinematographers* (Berkeley: University of California Press, 1984), p. 259.
40. Deac Rossell, "MEDIUM COOL: Wexler on Violence," *Philadelphia After Dark,* September 24, 1969, pp. 4, 5.

41. John Simon, *Movies into Film* (New York: Dial Press, 1971), p. 76.

42. Simon, *Movies into Film*, p. 78.

43. Stanley Kauffmann, "MEDIUM COOL," *New Republic*, September 20, 1969, p. 49.

44. Charles Champlin, "Medium with a Message," *Los Angeles Times*, September 21, 1969, p. 38.

45. The notion that young adults in the United States were unusually politicized in large numbers at the end of the 1960s is largely disparaged in books such as Landon Y. Jones, *Great Expectations: America and the Baby Boom Generation* (New York: Ballantine, 1981), see pp. 109, 110.

46. Schaefer and Salvato, *Masters of Light*, pp. 247, 248.

47. John Pym, ed., *Time Out Film Guide*, 4th ed. (Middlesex: Penguin Books, 1995), p. 462.

48. Murray Schumach, "Hollywood Flop," *New York Times*, August 19, 1962, p. 49.

49. Philip J. Sherry, "The Western Film: A Sense of an Ending," *New Orleans Review* (Fall 1990): 58 ff.

50. "Review: BUTCH CASSIDY AND THE SUNDANCE KID," *Motion Picture Exhibitor*, September 10, 1969.

51. "BUTCH CASSIDY AND THE SUNDANCE KID," *Cue*, September 27, 1998, p 38.

52. Jack C. Ellis, *A History of Film*, 2nd ed. (Englewood Cliffs, N.J.: Prentice-Hall, 1985), p. 400.

53. Brode, *Films of the Sixties*, p. 273.

54. *Motion Picture Herald*, September 17, 1969.

55. Kenneth M. Cameron, *America on Film: Hollywood and American History* (New York: Continuum, 1997), pp. 149, 150.

56. Winfred Blevins, "THE WILD BUNCH," *Los Angeles Herald-Examiner*, June 15, 1969.

57. Joel Resiner, "Art and Anti-Art," *Coast Magazine* (October 1969).

58. Kenneth Turan, "Bloody Marvelous Peckinpah," *Los Angeles Times Calendar*, February 26, 1995.

59. Arthur Knight, "Violence Flares Anew," *Saturday Review*, July 5, 1969, p. 60.

60. Joseph Morgenstern, "The Bloody Bunch," *Newsweek*, July 14, 1969, p. 50.

61. Leonard Quart and Albert Auster, *American Film and Society Since 1945* (New York: Praeger, 1984), p. 93.

62. Charles Champlin, "Violence Runs Rampant in THE WILD BUNCH," *Los Angeles Times*, June 15, 1969.

63. John Fleming, "Special Effects," in David Pirie, ed., *Anatomy of the Movies* (New York: Macmillan, 1981), pp. 186, 187.

64. Ray Greene, "Dead Reckoning," *Los Angeles Village View*, March 3–9, 1995.

65. Richard Schickel, "Sheer Beauty in the Wrong Place: COOL HAND LUKE," *Life*, November 3, 1967, p. 10.

66. Hollis Alpert, "On and Off the Beam," *Saturday Review*, November 11, 1967, p. 82.

67. Charles Champlin, "COOL HAND LUKE, Simple Tale with Truths to Tell," *Los Angeles Times*, October 30, 1967.

68. Quart and Auster, *American Film and Society Since 1945*, pp. 87, 88.

69. Alan Casty, *The Development of the Film: An Interpretive History* (New York: Harper Collins, 1973), pp. 375, 376.

70. Michael Ryan and Douglas Kellner, *Camera Politica: The Politics and Ideology of Contemporary Hollywood* (Bloomington: Indiana University Press, 1988), p. 20.

71. Abel Green, "How a Hit Pic Restores Tone," *Variety* (Daily), April 8, 1968.

72. Jacob Brockman, "Onward and Upward with the Arts: THE GRADUATE," *New Yorker*, December 30, 1967.

73. Thomas M. Pryor, "Year of Fevers," *Variety* (Anniversary Issue), October 1968.

74. Hollis Alpert, "SR Goes to the Movies," *Saturday Review*, March 16, 1968, p. 53.

75. "Letters to the Editor," written by Sandra A. Lonsfoote, Niskawaka, Indiana, *Saturday Review*, July 27, 1968.

76. Quoted in Edward Sorel, "THE GRADUATE," *Esquire*, May 1980, p. 81.

77. Andrew Sarris, " THE GRADUATE," *American Film* (July/August 1978). (In 1967, Nichols did not care for much of the criticism of his movie and angrily referred to film critics in general as being "like eunuchs watching a gang bang," as quoted in Brockman, "Onward and Upward with the Arts.")

78. Gene Vier, "TV Movies," in "TV Weekly," *New York Daily News*, January 23–29, 1983, p. 16.

79. John Simon, *Movies into Film* (New York: Dial Press, 1971), p. 106.

80. For a discussion of this review and others, see Lawrence L. Murray, "Hollywood, Nihilism, and the Youth Culture of the Sixties: BONNIE AND CLYDE," in O'Connor and Jackson, eds., *American History/American Film*, pp. 237–256.

81. *Films in Review* (December 1967).
82. *Variety* (Daily), December 13, 1967, p. 8.
83. Staff Report, "The New Cinema," *Time,* December 8, 1967, p. 51.
84. *Los Angeles Citizen-News,* August 23, 1967.
85. Pauline Kael, "BONNIE AND CLYDE," *New Yorker,* February 1, 1967, p. 61.
86. Charles Marowitz, "BONNIE AND CLYDE, Symptom and Cause," *Village Voice,* December 21, 1967, pp. 32, 33. For a further discussion of BONNIE AND CLYDE in its late 1960s context, see Paul Monaco, *Ribbons in Time: Movies and Society Since 1945* (Bloomington: Indiana University Press, 1987), pp. 96–102.
87. Quoted in Staff Report, "The New Cinema," *Time,* December 8, 1967, p. 51.
88. Cited in Morrden, *Medium Cool,* p. 189.
89. *Hollywood Citizen-News,* March 15, 1968.
90. *Hollywood Reporter,* August 27, 1968.
91. Peter Fonda interview, April 1997, Montana State University, Bozeman (videotaped by Matt Marshall).
92. See Mark Singer, "Whose Movie Is This? How Much of EASY RIDER Belongs to Terry Southern? A Countercultural Morality Tale," *New Yorker,* June 22 and 29, 1998, pp. 100–115.
93. Peter Fonda, *Don't Tell Dad* (New York: Hyperion, 1998), p. 152; also recounted by Peter Fonda in an interview, April 1997, Montana State University, Bozeman.
94. Richard Schickel, "EASY RIDER," *Life Magazine,* July 11, 1969, p. 10.
95. Stanley Penn, "Focusing on Youth: A New Breed of Movie Attracts the Young, Shakes Up Hollywood," *Wall Street Journal,* n.d., Files of the Academy of Motion Picture Arts & Sciences, Center for Motion Picture Study, Beverly Hills, California.
96. David Thomson, "Directors and Directing," in Pirie, ed., *Anatomy of the Movies,* p. 123.
97. "Notes to an Interview with Alfred Hitchcock," circulated at the Los Angeles County Museum of Art, May 22, 1982.
98. Editors of *Entertainment Weekly, Entertainment Weekly's Guide to the Greatest Movies Ever Made* (New York: Warner Books, 1994), p. 100.
99. Vincent Canby, "Chilling Truths About Scaring," *New York Times,* January 21, 1979, p. 38.
100. *Variety* (Weekly), July 27, 1960. (This marketing ploy caused particular havoc at drive-in showings of PSYCHO.) See also "Alfred Hitchcock: A Lesson in Psychology," *Motion Picture Herald,* August 6, 1960.
101. "PSYCHO," *Esquire,* October 1960.
102. See, for further consideration, Marc Shapiro, "Hitchcock's Throwaway Masterpiece," *Los Angeles Times,* May 27, 1990, p. D-3.
103. Raymond Durgnant, *Films and Feelings,* quoted in program notes to PSYCHO, University of Texas at Austin Film Series, January 23, 1975.
104. "THE BIRDS," *Variety* (Daily), March 28, 1963, p. 8.
105. "THE BIRDS," *Film Daily,* March 28, 1963, p. 4.
106. Pauline Kael, *I Lost It at the Movies: Film Writings, 1954–1965.* (Boston: Little, Brown, & Co., 1965), p. 10.
107. *Variety* (Weekly), November 29, 1961.
108. Tino Balio, "New Producers for Old," in Tino Balio, ed., *Hollywood in the Age of Television* (Boston: Unwin Hyman, 1990), p. 172.
109. *Newsweek,* March 7, 1994, p. 67.
110. Pym, ed., *Time Out Film Guide,* p. 742.
111. Vincent LoBrutto, *By Design: Interviews with Film Production Designers* (Westport: Praeger, 1992), p. 39.
112. See Thomas Schatz, *Old Hollywood/New Hollywood: Ritual, Art, and Industry* (Ann Arbor: UMI Research Press, 1981), pp. 191 ff.
113. Douglas Brode, *The Films of the Sixties* (Secaucus, N.J.: Citadel Press, 1980), p. 256.
114. Richard Schickel, "Crime Flick with a Taste of Genius," *Life,* November 22, 1968, p. 28.
115. James Destro, "Movies on Tape," *Film/Tape World* (March 1989).
116. Released as a British production in 1968, 2001: A SPACE ODYSSEY is nonetheless listed 22nd on the American Film Institute's assessment of the 100 Greatest American films.
117. Stanley Kauffmann, "Lost in the Stars," *New Republic,* May 4, 1968, p. 24.
118. "2001," *Variety,* April 3, 1968, p. 10.

119. *Hollywood Reporter,* March 1, 1968, p. 2.
120. "The Blockbuster," in Michael Webb, ed., *Hollywood: Legend and Reality* (Boston: Little, Brown, & Co., 1986), p. 170.
121. Stephen Chodorow, "Anybody Who Still Doesn't Dig *2001*?" *Inter/View* 1, no. 8 (August 1970) pp. 5, 6.
122. Morrdden, *Medium Cool,* p. 185.
123. John Russell Taylor, "On Seeing *2001* a Second Time," *New York Times,* September 22, 1968, p. 40.
124. Gene Youngblood, "Stanley Kubrick's *2001*: A Masterpiece," *Los Angeles Free Press,* March 19, 1968, p. 29.
125. Manohia Vargas, "Revival Pick of the Week: *2001*," *Los Angeles Weekly,* November 10, 1995, p. 5.
126. Quoted in Gary Crowdus, "A Tentative for the Viewing of *2001*," *Cineaste* (Summer 1968).
127. *Film and Television Daily,* March 3, 1968, p. 6.
128. *Variety* (Weekly), May 15, 1968, p. 22.
129. Christopher Finch, *Special Effects: Creating Movie Magic* (New York: Abbeville Press, 1984), pp. 114 ff.
130. John Fleming, "Special Effects," in Pirie, ed., *Anatomy of the Movies,* pp. 184, 185.
131. "Special Edition: 2001: A SPACE ODYSSEY," *American Cinematographer,* June 1968, pp. 886, 887. (See this entire issue for a complete discussion of the techniques created by the artistic personnel responsible for the camera work and special effects on *2001*.)
132. Louis Giannetti, *Masters of the American Cinema* (Englewood Cliffs, N.J.: Prentice-Hall, 1981), pp. 406, 407.
133. Fleming, "Special Effects," p. 280.
134. *Hollywood Reporter,* August 27, 1968.

CHAPTER 12 (THE NONFICTION FILM)

1. Standard histories of the genre are Paul Rotha, *Documentary Film* (New York: Hastings House, 1952); Richard M. Barsam, *Nonfiction Film: A Critical History* (Bloomington: Indiana University Press, 1992); and Erik Barnouw, *Documentary: A History of the Non-Fiction Film* (New York: Oxford University Press, 1974).
2. See William Alexander, *Film on the Left: American Documentary Film from 1931 to 1942* (Princeton: Princeton University Press, 1981); for anthologies of interviews with politically committed filmmakers, see G. Roy Levin, *Documentary Explorations: 15 Interviews with Film-Makers* (Garden City, N.Y.: Doubleday, 1971); Alan Rosenthal, *The New Documentary in Action: A Casebook in Film Making* (Berkeley: University of California Press, 1971); and *The Documentary Conscience: A Casebook in Film Making* (Berkeley: University of California Press, 1980).
3. Standard texts on the British documentary film movement include John Grierson, *Grierson on Documentary,* Forsyth Hardy, ed. (London: Faber, 1966); F. Hardy, *John Grierson: A Documentary Biography* (London: Faber, 1979); Rotha, *Documentary Film*; Alan Lovell and Jim Hillier, *Studies in Documentary* (London: Secker, 1972); Paul Rotha, *Documentary Diary: An Informal History of the British Documentary Film, 1928–1939* (New York: Hill, 1973); Elizabeth Sussex, *The Rise and Fall of British Documentary* (Berkeley: University of California Press, 1975); and Gary Evans, *John Grierson and the National Film Board: The Politics of Wartime Propaganda, 1939–45* (Toronto: University of Toronto Press, 1984). For information on alternative British approaches, see Don MacPherson and Paul Willemen, eds., *Traditions of Independence: British Cinema in the Thirties* (London: BFI, 1980).
4. André Bazin, "The Ontology of the Photographic Image," in *What Is Cinema?* (Berkeley: University of California Press, 1967), p. 12; for a useful group of readings on realist positions, forms, ideologies, aesthetics, and technology, see Christopher Williams, ed., *Realism and the Cinema: A Reader* (London: Routledge, 1980).
5. James Blue, "Thoughts on *Cinéma Verité* and a Discussion with the Maysles Brothers," *Film Comment,* 2, no. 4 (Fall 1964): 212–230. In *Quarterly Review of Film Studies,* 2, no. 2 (May 1977), see Ed Pincus, "New Possibilities in Film and the University," pp. 159–178, and William Earle, "Cinéma Banalité, and Surrealism," pp. 179–184.

6. See Robert C. Allen, "Case Study: The Beginnings of American Cinéma Verité," in Robert C. Allen and Douglas Gomery, *Film History: Theory and Practice* (New York: Knopf, 1985), pp. 213–241.

7. The major study of direct cinema is Stephen Mamber, *Cinéma Verité in America: Studies in Controlled Documentary* (Cambridge: MIT Press, 1974); see also Louis Marcorelles, *Living Cinema: New Directions in Contemporary Film-Making* (New York: Praeger, 1973).

8. Allen, "Case Study," p. 216.

9. See Richard M. Barsam, "Nonfiction Film: The Realist Impulse," in Gerald Mast and Marshall Cohen, eds., *Film Theory and Criticism,* 2nd ed. (New York: Oxford University Press, 1979), pp. 580–593.

10. See Charles Harpole, "What Is the Documentary Film? Some Problems in the Varying Definition of the Documentary Film," *Filmmakers' Newsletter* 6, no. 6 (April 1973): 25–27.

11. Kevin Brownlow, *The War, the West, and the Wilderness* (New York: Knopf, 1979) and John L. Fell, ed., *Film before Griffith* (Berkeley: University of California Press, 1983).

12. The Soviet formalist pioneers knew Flaherty's NANOOK, as Flaherty knew Eisenstein's BATTLESHIP POTEMKIN (1925) and Dovzhenko's EARTH (1930), which Flaherty once described as "the greatest of all films." See Arthur Calder-Marshall, *The Innocent Eye: The Life of Robert J. Flaherty* (New York: Harcourt, 1963), p. 130. But Flaherty seems not to have known the work of Dziga Vertov, who, in calling his work *kino-pravda* (film truth)—which, in French, became cinéma verité, a literal translation—placed an unwarranted burden of "truth" on films made in the cinéma verité or direct cinema modes.

13. Susan Sontag, *On Photography* (New York: Farrar, 1977), p. 87; see also Walter Benjamin, "The Work of Art in the Age of Mechanical Reproduction," in Mast and Cohen, eds., *Film Theory and Criticism,* 2nd ed. (New York: Oxford University Press, 1979), pp. 848–870.

14. Dai Vaughan, "Let There Be Lumière," *Sight and Sound* 50, no. 2 (Spring 1981): 127.

15. See Barsam, *Nonfiction Film: A Critical History,* chaps. 1–3.

16. Erik Barnouw, "Fragments," *Artsept,* no. 2 (April/June 1963): 20; see also Georges Sadoul, "Dziga Vertov," *Artsept,* no. 2 (April/June 1963): 19; see also Sadoul, "Actualite de Dziga Vertov," *Cahiers du Cinéma* 4, no. 144 (June 1963): 23–31, and "Bio-Filmographie de Dziga Vertov," *Cahiers du Cinéma* 25, no. 146 (August 1963): 21–29; "The Difficult Years of Dziga Vertov: Excerpts from His Diaries," trans. Vlada Petric, *Quarterly Review of Film Studies* 7, no. 1 (Winter 1982): 7–21.

17. Barnouw, *Documentary,* p. 57.

18. Some of Dziga Vertov's interests and achievements are in diverse areas unrelated to direct cinema as we know it. His theory and use of cinematic forms (among them, trick photography, multiple exposure, variable speeds, split-screen, photomicrography) are in many ways incompatible with direct cinema. Louis Marcorelles (*Living Cinema,* p. 36) puts even further distance between Vertov and direct cinema: "What Vertov considered cinéma verité, now, after all these years, seems merely a revolutionary determination to bear witness to the revolution by manipulating the revolutionary cinema."

19. James Monaco, "American Documentary Since 1960," in Richard Roud, ed., *Cinema: A Critical Dictionary* (New York: Viking, 1980), p. 51.

20. Film editor Patricia Jaffe recognizes the personal approach of Flaherty and others and its influence on direct cinema: Its "attempts to the rhythms and events of life are tied closely to the filmmakers' own ways of reacting and communicating with the world." See "Editing *Cinéma Verité,*" *Film Comment,* no. 3 (Summer 1965): 47.

21. Richard Leacock, "Remembering Frances Flaherty," *Film Comment* (November–December 1972): 39; for discussion of Flaherty as a realist, see "Descriptions of the Work of a Realist Film-Maker, Robert Flaherty," in Williams, ed., *Realism and the Cinema,* pp. 89–107.

22. Current Flaherty studies consist of a critical study, Richard Barsam, *The Vision of Robert Flaherty: The Artist as Myth and Filmmaker* (Bloomington: Indiana University Press, 1988); two biographies, Calder-Marshall, *The Innocent Eye* and Paul Rotha and Jay Ruby, *Flaherty, A Biography* (Philadelphia: University of Pennsylvania Press), p. xxx; and a bibliographical study, William T. Murphy, *Robert Flaherty: A Guide to References and Resources* (Boston: Hall, 1978).

23. Marcorelles, *Living Cinema,* p. 38.

24. Ted Perry, "The Road to Neo-Realism," *Film Comment* 14, no. 6 (November–December 1978): 7–13; Eric Rhode, "Why Neo-realism Failed," *Sight and Sound* 30, no. 1 (Winter 1960–61): 26–32.

25. Lindsay Anderson, "Free Cinema" and "Only Connect: Some Aspects of the Work of Humphrey Jennings," in Richard M. Barsam, *Nonfiction Film: Theory and Criticism* (New York: Dutton, 1976), pp. 70–74, 263–270; the first Free Cinema program, quoted in David Robinson, *The History of World Cinema* (New York: Stein, 1973), pp. 291–292; Gavin Lambert, "Free Cinema," *Sight and Sound* 25, no. 4 (Spring 1956): 173–177; Kenneth J. Robson, "Humphrey Jennings: The Legacy of Feeling," *Quarterly Review of Film Studies* 7, no. 1 (Winter 1982): 37–52; and Mary-Lou Jennings, ed., *Humphrey Jennings: Film-Maker, Painter, Poet* (London: British Film Institute, 1982). Stephen Mamber does not acknowledge this influence; another view of the changing British tradition is Jack C. Ellis, "Changing of the Guard: From the Grierson Documentary to Free Cinema," *Quarterly Review of Film Studies* 7, no. 1 (Winter 1982): 23–35; the many printer's errors in the Ellis article are corrected in the subsequent issue.

26. Peter Davis, "Lindsay Anderson Views His First Feature Film," *Chicago Daily News,* 28 July 1963, p. 21.

27. Jonas Mekas, "Cinema of the New Generation—Part One: Free Cinema and the Nouvelle Vague," *Film Culture* 21 (n.d.): 1–6.

28. Mamber, *Cinéma Verité in America*, p. 1.

29. See Ed Pincus, "One-Person Sync-Sound: A New Approach to *Cinéma Verité,*" *Filmmakers' Newsletter* 6, no. 2 (December 1972): 24–30; Edmund Bert Gerard, "The Truth about *Cinéma Verité,*" *American Cinematographer* 50 (May 1969): 474–475; Mike Waddell, "*Cinéma Verité* and the Documentary Film," *American Cinematographer* 49, no. 10 (October 1968): 754 ff.; Colin Young, "Three Views on *Cinéma Verité*: Cinema of Common Sense," *Film Quarterly* 17, no. 4 (Summer 1964): 26–29, 40.

30. As described by Robert C. Allen ("Case Study," p. 219): "Hollywood films run counter to the 'true nature' of the cinema in that they substitute a fictional illusion for reality. (2) The technical complexity of Hollywood filmmaking interposes an unnecessary barrier between filmmaker and subject and between subject and audience. (3) Hollywood films exist to make money for their producers, not to use the cinema for any higher purpose. (4) The social world of the Hollywood film is one of glamour, luxury, stars, and success. It ignores the 'real' problems of society: poverty, injustice, political struggle, and racism. (5) Whenever Hollywood films DO deal with social issues their artifice and conventions (the happy ending) render them merely one more 'unreal' fiction."

31. Monaco, "American Documentary Since 1960," p. 50; see also Allen, "Case Study," pp. 220–223.

32. Ibid., p. 221; see also James Wong Howe, "The Documentary Technique and Hollywood," *American Cinematographer* (January 1944): 10, and Philip Dunne, "The Documentary and Hollywood," in Barsam, *Nonfiction Film,* pp. 158–166. In its attempts to recoup the vast audience from television, Hollywood exploited the technological advantages that motion pictures had over television. While some of these developments, such as the various widescreen processes, were not integrated into the nonfiction film, some were, including the almost total conversion to the use of color film stock. For an excellent discussion of many aesthetic issues raised by the widescreen processes and other technological developments of the period, see Charles Barr, "CinemaScope: Before and After" in Mast and Cohen, eds., *Film Theory and Criticism* (New York: Oxford University Press), pp. 140–168.

33. Allen, "Case Study," p. 220.

34. Monaco, "American Documentary Since 1960," p. 50.

35. Allen, "Case Study," pp. 222–223.

36. Gerald Mast, *Film/Cinema/Movie* (New York: Harper, 1977), p. 158.

37. James Blue, "Thoughts on *Cinéma-Verité,*" p. 23.

38. Jay Ruby, "The Image Mirrored: Reflexivity and the Documentary Film," *Journal of the University Film Association* 29, no. 2 (Fall 1977): 3–12; two negative views, asserting a Hollywood position that the techniques of *cinéma verité* divert the audience's attention from what the filmmaker is saying, are Waddell, "Cinéma Verité and the Documentary Film," 754 ff., and Edmund Bert Gerard, "The Truth about *Cinéma Verité,*" *American Cinematographer* 50 (May 1969): 474–475.

39. James C. Lipscomb, "Correspondence and Controversy: *Cinema Verite,*" *Film Quarterly* 18, no. 2 (Winter 1964–1965): 62–63.

40. Erik Barnouw, *Documentary: A History of the Non-Fiction Film*, pp. 261–262.

41. Perrault's films include POUR LA SUITE DU MONDE (1963), LA REGNE DU JOUR (1967), LES

VOITURES D'EAU (1968), UN PAYS SAN BON SENS (1970), and L'ACADIE, L'ACADIE (1971); Koenig's films include LONELY BOY (1961).

42. Marker's many achievements include CUBA SI! (1961) and LE JOLI MAI (1963); Ruspoli is known for LES HOMMES DE LA BALEINE (1956), LES INCONNUS DE LA TERRE (1961), and REGARD SUR LA FOLIE (1961); Rozier, in such films as ADIEU PHILIPPINE (1963), joined, as did Jean Rouch, cinéma verité techniques with the more traditional techniques of fiction films.

43. There is also a connection between Rouch, Vertov, Flaherty, and the Italian Neo-Realists, but Rouch's work cannot be easily classified with theirs.

44. Jean-Andre Fieschi, "Jean Rouch," in Roud, ed., *Cinema*, pp. 901–909; Mick Eaton, ed., *Anthropology-Reality-Cinema: The Films of Jean Rouch* (London: British Film Institute, 1979); James Blue, "The Films of Jean Rouch (including interviews with Blue and Jacqueline Veuve)," *Film Comment* 4, nos. 2–3 (Fall and Winter 1967): 82–91.

45. That is but one source of the problem concerning the placement of Rouch's work in the history of nonfiction film. Another source is his comment that in *Chronicle of a Summer* he attempted to combine Vertov's theory and Flaherty's method. See "Table Ronde: Festival de Tours en collaboration avec l'UNESCO," *Image et Son* 160 (March 1963): 6.

46. Eric Rohmer and Louis Marcorelles, "Entretien avec Jean Rouch," *Cahiers du Cinema* 24, no. 144 (June 1963): 1–22.

47. "*Cinéma Verité* in France," *Film Quarterly* 17, no. 4 (Summer 1964): 36

48. Evoking the "nitty-gritty," a phrase indigenous to the 1960s, Henry Breitrose concludes that direct cinema should neither assume that there is a universal or absolute truth about objects or events nor assume that it could capture this real essence, the "nitty-gritty" of reality; see "On the Search for the Real Nitty-Gritty: Some Problems and Possibilities in *Cinéma Verité*," *Film Quarterly* 17, no. 4 (Summer 1964): 36–40.

49. Barnouw, *Documentary: A History of the Non-Fiction Film*, pp. 254–255.

50. See *Theory of Film: The Redemption of Physical Reality* (New York: Oxford University Press, 1960).

51. "Salesman," in Rosenthal, *New Documentary in Action*, p. 88.

52. "Grey Gardens," in Rosenthal, *Documentary Conscience*, p. 374.

53. Patricia Jaffe, "Editing *Cinéma Verité*," *Film Comment* 3, no. 3 (Summer 1965): 45.

54. Ian A. Cameron and Mark Shivas, "Interviews," *Movie* 8 (April 1963): 17.

55. The achievement of "total" cinema remains impossible, despite the efforts of those who have tried with technology to create what Bazin called "total cinema." What brings us close to it, however, is the direct cinema artist whose vision (both philosophical viewpoint and physical point of view) controls the representation of reality on film. See Andre Bazin, "The Myth of Total Cinema," in *What Is Cinema?* (Berkeley: University of California Press, 1967), pp. 17–22.

56. Monaco, "American Documentary Since 1960," p. 51.

57. To illustrate the international cross-pollination among these film movements, Jean-Luc Godard worked with Leacock, Pennebaker, and other Americans, as well as with a group he called the Dziga Vertov Group; see Richard Roud, "Jean-Luc Godard," in Roud, ed., *Cinema*, pp. 436–446.

58. For a different definition and interpretation of direct cinema, see Jean-Louis Comolli, "Detour par de direct: Un corps en trop," *Cahiers du Cinéma* 278 (July 1977): 5–16; for an English translation (with commentary by the editor), see Williams, ed., *Realism and the Cinema*, pp. 224–244.

59. My thinking here was influenced by M. H. Abrams, *The Mirror and the Lamp: Romantic Theory and the Critical Tradition* (New York: Oxford University Press, 1953), pp. 272–285.

60. Michel Marie, "Direct," in Eaton, ed., *Anthropology, Reality, Cinema*, p. 35.

61. Mamber, *Cinéma Verité in America*, p. 250.

62. Ibid., pp. 2–5.

63. Ibid., pp. 70–78.

64. Colin Young, "Three Views on *Cinéma Verité*: Cinema of Common Sense," *Film Quarterly* 17, no. 4 (Summer 1964): 26–29 ff.

65. G. Roy Levin, "Donn Alan Pennebaker," in *Documentary Explorations*, p. 228.

66. Among the excellent direct cinema achievements that combine a successful choice of subject matter, an apparent lack of control, and an accurate portrayal of the personality or atmosphere of a social issue are Pennebaker's DON'T LOOK BACK (1966), the Maysles brothers' SALESMAN (1969), Richard Leacock's A STRAVINSKY PORTRAIT (1964), Frederick Wiseman's HIGH SCHOOL (1968), and Perry Miller's ADATO'S PICASSO: A PAINTER'S DIARY (1980), the first successful attempt of many to be worthy of the subject.

67. Although not directly relevant to direct cinema, there is an excellent discussion of this issue in "The World at War," in Rosenthal, *Documentary Conscience,* pp. 35–88.

68. Archival footage is used with varying degrees of success in two later Maysles brothers films, GIMME SHELTER (1970) and GREY GARDENS (1975). Emile De Antonio and Cinda Firestone, two American filmmakers whose work is not really "direct cinema," have integrated archival footage as an essential part of their work; see Rosenthal, *Documentary Conscience,* pp. 205–226, 293–302.

69. "The Difficult Years of Dziga Vertov," p. 17.

70. "'You Start Off with a Bromide': Wiseman on Film and Civil Liberties, an Interview with Alan Westin," in Thomas R. Atkins, ed., *Frederick Wiseman* (New York: Monarch, 1976), pp. 49–50.

71. Mamber, *Cinéma Verité in America,* p. 250.

72. Wheelwright, Philip Ellis, *The Burning Fountain: A Study in the Language of Symbolism* (Bloomington: University of Indiana Press, 1954), p. 61.

73. For comments on these technical developments, see Charles Reynolds, "Focus on Al Maysles: The Man—How He Works," *Popular Photography* 54 (May 1964): 128–131; Pincus, "One-Person Sync-Sound," pp. 24–30; Del Hillgartner, "Super Serious-8: Leacock-MIT Super-8 System," *Filmmakers' Newsletter* 6, no. 12 (October 1973): 53–56, and 7, no. 1 (November 1973): 51–55; for various comments by filmmakers on equipment, see the interviews in Levin, *Documentary Explorations.*

74. Monaco, "American Documentary Since 1960," p. 50. For a good summary of equipment used, see Allen, "Case Study," pp. 222–223.

75. Leacock quoted in Marcorelles, *Living Cinema,* pp. 57–58.

76. Very little has been written on the ethics of the nonfiction film; see Calvin Pryluck, "Ultimately We Are All Outsiders: The Ethics of Documentary Filming," *University Film Association Journal* 28, no. 1 (1976): 21–29.

77. Mamber, *Cinéma Verité in America,* p. 127.

78. Pennebaker quoted in Marcorelles, *Living Cinema,* p. 25. Editor Ellen Hovde puts it another way. By emphasizing the collaborative process between cinematographer and editor, she equates making direct cinema with making a film about process, rather than events: "to take real people's lives, and the interactions between people, and make that interesting because it is psychologically interesting, and not because something is going to happen that you are waiting for." See *"Grey Gardens,"* in Rosenthal, *Documentary Conscience,* p. 384.

79. Three articles in *Film Quarterly* 17, no. 4 (Summer 1964) provide a comprehensive debate on the virtues and faults of early direct cinema: Henry Breitrose, "On the Search for the Real Nitty-Gritty: Problems and Possibilities in *Cinéma Verité,*" pp. 36–40; Peter Graham, *"Cinéma Verité* in France," pp. 30–36; and Young, "Three Views on *Cinéma Verité,*" pp. 26–29 ff. In *"Correspondence and Controversy,"* James C. Lipscomb, a member of Drew Associates, responds in an attempt to answer accusations that some scenes in Drew films were faked, to set the record straight, and to emphasize the collaborative nature of the group's work.

80. See Mamber, *Cinéma Verité in America,* pp. 23–114, and Allen and Gomery, *Film History,* pp. 213–241.

81. Allen, "Case Study," p. 223.

82. Richard Lacayo, "Why Are Documentaries So Dull?" *New York Times,* February 10, 1983, sec. 2, p. 29. See also "Television's School of Storm and Stress," *Broadcasting* 60 (March 6, 1961): 83.

83. For a discussion of these factors, see Allen, "Case Study," pp. 233–237. The "fairness doctrine" admonished broadcasters to "afford reasonable opportunity for the discussion of conflicting views on issues of public importance."

84. For information in this paragraph, I relied on Robert C. Allen's "case study" of direct cinema in Allen and Gomery, *Film History,* pp. 224–237.

85. Before joining with ABC-TV, they made PRIMARY (1960) and ON THE POLE (1960). For the ABC-TV "Close-Up!" series, they made four films: YANKI, NO! (1960), X-PILOT (1960), THE CHILDREN WERE WATCHING (1960), and ADVENTURES ON THE NEW FRONTIER (1961). Their work also included two specials, KENYA, AFRICA (1961), for ABC-TV, and ON THE ROAD TO BUTTON BAY (1962), for CBS-TV. For the "Living Camera" series they made EDDIE (1961), DAVID (1961), PETEY AND JOHNNY (1961), FOOTBALL (also titled MOONEY VS. FOWLE) (1961), BLACKIE (1962), SUSAN STARR (1962), NEHRU (1962), THE AGA KHAN (1962), JANE (1962), THE CHAIR (1962), and CRISIS: BEHIND A PRESIDENTIAL COMMITMENT (1962). See Mamber,

Cinéma Verité in America, pp. 29–30, on the question of authorship, and p. 265 on the division of responsibility in these films, as well as for critical discussion of most of them.

86. It was described in a typical news release that manages, in the mode of the carnival barker, to invoke Dziga Vertov: "It's unscripted, it's unrehearsed . . . for the first time the camera is a man. It sees, it hears, it moves like a man." Quoted in A. William Bluem, *Documentary in American Television: Form, Function, Method* (New York: Hastings House, 1965), p. 194.

87. Mamber (*Cinéma Verité in America,* pp. 30–42) offers a lengthy discussion of the film; a good discussion of its structural elements is William F. Van Wert, "Primary: Fictional Structures," *Film Library Quarterly* 7, no. 1 (1974): 17–22.

88. See Bluem, *Documentary in American Television,* pp. 128–124; for reviews, see Val Adams, "TV Filmed Kennedys in Alabama Crisis," *New York Times,* July 25, 1963, p. 49; part of the controversy can be seen in an editorial, "Not Macy's Window," *New York Times,* July 27, 1963, p. 16, and a letter responding to it, August 7, 1963, p. 32; John Horn, "Documentaries Score," *New York Herald Tribune,* October, 22, 1963, p. 35, and an editorial response, October 24, 1963; Jack Gould, "TV: Too Many Cameras," *New York Times,* October 22, 1963, p. 75, and "Behind Closed Doors," *New York Times,* October 23, 1963, p. 40.

89. For a perceptive review of YANKI, NO!, see Robert Lewis Shayon, "The Fuse in the Documentary," *Saturday Review* 43 (December 17, 1960): p. 29.

90. For an interview with Jane Fonda in which she comments on this film portrait, see "Jane," *Cahiers Du Cinéma* 25 (December 1963–January 1964): 182–190; see also Hal Seldes, "D. A. Pennebaker: The Truth at 24 Frames Per Second," *Avant-Garde* 7 (March 1969): 46–49, and Tony Rayns, "Jane," *Monthly Film Bulletin* 42 (August 1975): 177.

91. For an illustrated synopsis, see "The Chair," *Show* 4 (April 1964): 51–55; for discussions of the film, see Barsam, *Nonfiction Film,* p. 269 ff.; Louis Marcorelles, "Nothing but the Truth," *Sight and Sound* 32 (Summer 1963): 114–117; Jean-Luc Godard, "Richard Leacock," in "Dictionnaire de 121 Metteurs en scène," *Cahiers du Cinema* 25 (December 1963–January 1964): 139–140; Anthony Jay, "Actuality," *Journal of the Society of Film and Television Arts* 15 (Spring 1964): 5–7. Other useful sources include James Blue, "One Man's Truth: An Interview with Richard Leacock," *Film Comment* 3, no. 2 (Spring 1965): 15–23, and Ian Cameron and Mark Shivas, "*Cinéma Verité*: A Survey Including Interviews with Richard Leacock, Albert and David Maysles, William Klein, Jean Rouch, and Jacques Rozier," *Movie* 8 (April 1963): pp. 12–27.

92. For an excellent analysis of the problem of collaboration in direct cinema, see Mamber, *Cinéma Verité in America,* pp. 97–105, 122–123, 126–128.

93. For background information, see Robert Christgau, "Leacock-Pennebaker: The MGM of the Underground?" *Show* 1, no. 1 (January 1970): 34–37 ff.; Barsam, *Nonfiction Film,* pp. 252–267; and Mamber, *Cinéma Verité in America,* pp. 173–215.

94. Ernest Callenbach, "Going Out to the Subject," *Film Quarterly* 14, no. 3 (Spring 1961): 38–40, recognized that Leacock's ability to go out to the subject enabled him to get into it as well. James Blue, "One Man's Truth," pp. 15–23, conducts a lengthy interview with the filmmaker that covers the overall approach of his direct cinema style. Another interview is "Richard Leacock," in Levin, *Documentary Explorations,* pp. 195–221. For information on Leacock's technological innovations, see the two-part article by Del Hillgartner ("Super Serious-8") in *Filmmakers' Newsletter* 6, no. 12 (October 1973): 53–56, and 7, no. 1 (November 1973): 51–55; Louis Marcorelles, "Leacock at M.I.T.," *Sight and Sound* 18, no. 2 (Spring 1974): 104–107; and Pincus, "One-Person Sync-Sound," pp. 24–30.

95. For critical discussions of both of these films, see Barsam, *Nonfiction Film,* pp. 254–256, and Mamber, *Cinéma Verité in America,* pp. 192–204.

96. For comments on this film and on CHIEFS by Ed Pincus, see Levin, *Documentary Explorations,* p. 368.

97. For interview and filmography, see "Donn Alan Pennebaker" in Levin, *Documentary Explorations,* pp. 223–270; see also Barsam, *Nonfiction Film,* pp. 262–267, and Mamber, *Cinéma Verité in America,* pp. 173–191.

98. Penelope Gilliatt, "DON'T LOOK BACK," *New Yorker,* September 9, 1967, p. 116, says the film catches the "moving essence of being young now"; Andrew Sarris, "Films: I Dig Dylan," *Village Voice,* September 21, 1967, pp. 27–29, assesses Pennebaker's approach—"ugliness and awkwardness are subtly transformed from technical necessity to truth-seeming mannerisms"—and finds that the film records Dylan not as he is but how he "responds to the role imposed upon him by

the camera"—but concludes that this is a film where "the subject is everything, the style is nothing." Ed Pincus, "New Possibilities in Film and the University," *Quarterly Review of Film Studies* 2, no. 2 (May 1977): 159–178, in a good analysis of the history of direct cinema and what it has to offer for film production at the university level, considers the film as the best example for showing the aspirations and limitations of early direct cinema. See also D. A. Pennebaker, *Don't Look Back* (New York: Ballantine, 1968).

99. Ernest Callenbach, "Monterey Pop," *Film Quarterly* 23, no. 1 (Fall 1969): 52, does not appreciate the film's 35mm enlargement from the 16mm format and finds its treatment of the rock festival to be superficial and biased. Taking the other view, Penelope Gilliatt, in the *New Yorker,* March 22, 1969, p. 120, appreciates its ability to create the feeling of "being there" for the film's audience.

100. For another view, see William F. Van Wert, "The 'Hamlet Complex' or Performance in the Personality-Profile Documentary," *Journal of Popular Film* 3, no. 3 (1974): 257–263. In discussing *Don't Look Back* and *Gimme Shelter,* among others, Van Wert's main point is that "whenever a documentary is of the personality-profile variety, and whenever that performer being filmed is most aware of the camera filming him (live interview, live concert), we can be reasonably sure that we are witnessing a lie and not a reality, an artifice as opposed to the truth, a performance as opposed to a true personality."

101. For another assessment, see Merrill Shindler, "Donn Looks Back: *Cinéma Verité* with Dylan, Bowie," *Rolling Stone,* December 16, 1976, pp. 16 ff.

102. These include *Primary, On the Pole, Yanki, No!, X-Pilot, Adventures on the New Frontier, Kenya, Africa;* he also worked on *Eddie* in the "Living Camera" series. David Maysles is said to have worked as a reporter on *Adventures on the New Frontier* and on other Drew Associates films—see *Salesman* (New York, Signet, 1969), p. 125—although this contribution is not acknowledged in Mamber's more definitive filmography.

103. Hamid Naficy, " 'Truthful Witness': An Interview with Albert Maysles," *Quarterly Review of Film Studies* 6, no. 2 (Spring 1981): 155–179, provides an excellent interview in which the filmmaker claims that he and his brother are truthful observers or witnesses to real life; it covers their development of the direct cinema concept with Drew; their definition of direct cinema; the financing and distribution of their films; their selection of subjects; their editing and relationship with their editors. See also Calvin Pryluck, "Seeking to Take the Longest Journey: A Conversation with Albert Maysles," *Journal of the University Film Association* 28, no. 2 (Spring 1976): 9–16, and Bob Sitton, "An Interview with Albert and David Maysles," *Film Library Quarterly* 2, no. 3 (Summer 1969): 13–18. A seminal piece on subsequent articles on the Maysles is Blue, "Thoughts on *Cinéma Verité,*" pp. 22–30.

104. Albert Maysles explains this preference, as well as their working methods, in a dated, but important article—Maxine Haleff, "The Maysles Brothers and 'Direct Cinema'," *Film Comment* 2, no. 2 (Spring 1964): 19–23.

105. This continued in the 1970s with Mick Jagger and the Rolling Stones (*Gimme Shelter,* 1970), Christo (*Christo's Valley Curtain,* 1974, and *Running Fence,* 1978), and Edith and Edie Beale (*Grey Gardens,* 1975). For discussions of several of these early films, as well as *Gimme Shelter* and *Salesman,* see Barsam, *Nonfiction Film,* pp. 280–292; Mamber, *Cinéma Verité in America,* pp. 142–172, discusses several of these films as examples of, or departures from, the Drew Associates direct cinema approach and format. See also Kenneth J. Robson's excellent essay, "The Crystal Formation: Narrative Structure in Grey Gardens," *Cinema Journal* 22, no. 2 (Winter 1983): pp. 42–53, and Nancy Scott, "The Christo Films: Christo's *Valley Curtain* and *Running Fence,*" *Quarterly Review of Film Studies* 7, no. 1 (Winter 1982): 61–68.

106. See interviews with Charlotte Zwerin and Ellen Hovde in Rosenthal, *New Documentary in Action,* pp. 86–91, 372–387.

107. Robert Phillip Kolker, "Circumstantial Evidence: An Interview with Albert and David Maysles," *Sight and Sound* 40, no. 4 (August 1971): 183–186. See also Albert and David Maysles, "Direct Cinema," *Public Relations Journal* 38, no. 9 (September 1982): 31–33; "Financing the Independent Non-Fiction Film," *Millimeter* 6, no. 6 (June 1978): 74–75; and "Maysles Brothers," *Film Culture* 42 (Fall 1966): 114–115. For an account of their innovations in equipment and their shooting methods, see Reynolds, "Focus on Al Maysles," pp. 128–131. For a rambling interview, see "Albert and David Maysles," in Levin, *Documentary Explorations,* pp. 270–293.

108. See, for example, the interview with Albert Maysles in Rosenthal, *New Documentary in Action,* pp. 76–85.

109. Albert and David Maysles provide an excellent account of the difficulties they encountered in shooting, as well as technical and financial details of the production, in "GIMME SHELTER: Production Notes," *Filmmakers' Newsletter* 5, no. 2 (December 1971): 29–31.

110. "A Variety of Hells," *New Leader* 28 (April 1969). Harold Clurman in *Nation* 208 (March 10, 1969): 318, finds both comedy and tragedy in the film but says it is monotonous and too long; see also his introductory essay in *Salesman* (New York: Signet, 1969). Ernest Callenbach ("Monterey Pop," pp. 54–55) praises the film's honorable capturing of the human condition, but he finds that the ending is contrived and psychologically insufficient and that its organizing principle—curiosity—is not strong enough to sustain the film's length. Stanley Kauffmann, in the *New Republic* 160, no. 5 (April 1969): 24, finds that the fictional techniques obscure the filmmakers' point of view. Penelope Gilliatt in the *New Yorker*, April 19, 1969, p. 149, finds that the presence of the camera makes some of the behavior seem unnatural. Patrick MacFadden in *Film Society Review* 4, no. 6 (February 1969): 11–17, claims that SALESMAN represents "a turning point in the history of film." John Craddock in *Film Library Quarterly* 2, no. 3 (Summer 1969): 8–12, cites it as "a true actuality film."

111. Paul Schrader in *Cinema* 7, no. 1 (Fall 1971): 52–54, cites major faults: shallow intentions, aesthetics dictated by opportunism rather than necessity or moral commitment, artificially created suspense, montage clichés, irresponsible parallel cutting, and a bogus perspective created by the sequences in which Jagger and others watch the film within the film. Joel Haycock in *Film Quarterly* 24, no. 4 (Summer 1971): 56–60, sets it apart from other films exploiting or promoting rock stars; David Pirie in *Sight and Sound* 40, no. 4 (August 1971): 226–227, calls it a "definitive record of the hippie experience"; David Sadkin in *Filmmakers' Newsletter* 5, no. 2 (December 1971): 20–27, attempts to show that the "reality" was created by the editor and raises, but does not answer, the question of whether a restructuring of events means that a film can no longer be considered direct cinema.

112. See Liz Ellsworth, *Frederick Wiseman: A Guide to References and Resources* (Boston: Hall, 1979). An early, but still valuable, article that relies on extensive quotations from Wiseman about his approach is Beatrice Berg, "I Was Fed Up with Hollywood Fantasies," *New York Times*, February 1, 1970, pp. 25–26. For an anthology of articles, see Thomas R. Atkins, *Frederick Wiseman* (New York: Monarch, 1976).

113. Wiseman has defined this approach several times; see interviews in Levin, *Documentary Explorations*, pp. 316–317, and in Rosenthal, *New Documentary in Action*, pp. 66–75; see also John Graham, "'There Are No Simple Solutions': Frederick Wiseman on Viewing Film," *The Film Journal* (Spring 1971): 44–47.

114. In a perceptive study of Wiseman's work through 1971, Edgar Z. Friedenberg, "Ship of Fools: The Films of Frederick Wiseman," *New York Review of Books* 17, no. 6 (October 21, 1971): 19–22, discusses the institutions as well as the films and finds similarities in "the interlocking sets of social institutions, seldom useful in themselves, which provide roles for their members and sustain one another through a system of cross-referrals which serve to validate the raisons d'etre of all, using the clients who are supposed to benefit from their services as expendable counters in their own games." For other discussions of the individual and sociological nature of Wiseman's work, see Tim Curry, "Frederick Wiseman: Sociological Filmmaker?" *Contemporary Sociology* 14, no. 1 (January 1985): 35–39; Patrick Sullivan, "'What's All the Cryin' About?' The Films of Frederick Wiseman," *Massachusetts Review* 13, no. 3 (Summer 1972): 452–468.

115. Rosenthal, *New Documentary in Action*, p. 69.

116. For example, in *Nonfiction Film*, I wrote that "Wiseman clearly dislikes institutions, especially big, bureaucratic ones, but he does not pretend to suggest alternatives" (p. 271). After having seen another ten years of his astonishingly consistent films, I would not only substitute studies for clearly dislikes but also emphasize, more than before, the meticulousness with which his camera studies his subject and with which he edits the footage.

117. *New Yorker*, October 18, 1969, pp. 199–204.

118. *New Yorker*, April 21, 1980, p. 101.

119. Ibid., p. 96.

120. His subsequent films include ESSENE (1972), JUVENILE COURT (1973), PRIMATE (1974), WELFARE (1975), MEAT (1976), CANAL ZONE (1977), SINAI FIELD MISSION (1978), MANOEUVRE (1979), MODEL (1980), THE STORE (1983), and RACETRACK (1985). Of these seventeen films, thirteen have been broadcast by the Public Broadcasting System and seen by mil-

lions of viewers (more people have seen his films than any other nonfiction films in history) and then distributed widely through Wiseman's production company.

121. Analyses of these and other Wiseman films appear in Barsam, *Nonfiction Film,* pp. 271–280; Mamber, *Cinéma Verité in America,* pp. 216–249; and in Bill Nichols, *Ideology and the Image: Social Representation in the Cinema and other Media* (Bloomington: Indiana University Press, 1981), pp. 208–236.

122. For an excellent summary of its legal history and implications, see Carolyn Anderson, "The Conundrum of Competing Rights in Titicut Follies," *University Film Association Journal* 33, no. 1 (1981): 15–22. See also Elliot Richardson's letter and Wiseman's response, *Civil Liberties Review* 1, no. 3 (Summer 1974): 148–151.

123. Wiseman said that he provided "as complex a statement of the reality of the situation as possible" and that it is a "very polemical film" in Alan Sutherland, "Wiseman on Polemic," *Sight and Sound* 47, no. 2 (1978): 82.

124. For an excellent debate focusing on past abuses and patient rights, see Robert Coles, "Documentary: Stripped Bare at the Follies," *New Republic* 158 (January 20, 1968): 18, 28–30, and Ronald Kessler's response, " *New Republic* 158 (February 10, 1968): 35–36.

125. Andrew Sarris said the photography was crude and the editing awkward (he was correct about those aspects), that it "exploits reality as much as it reveals it, and . . . does not even begin to tell the whole story"; Robert Hatch said Wiseman took the horrible content out of its context; Wilfrid Sheed and Arthur Knight condemned its exploitation; and Brendan Gill called it "a sickening picture from start to finish." See Sarris, *Village Voice,* November 9, 1967, p. 33; Hatch, *Nation* 205 (October 30, 1957): 446; Sheed, *Esquire* 69, no. 3 (March 1968): 52, 55; Knight, *Saturday Review* 50 (September 9, 1967): 44; Gill, *New Yorker,* October 28, 1967, pp. 166–167.

126. Vincent Canby, "The Screen: Titicut Follies Observes Life in a Modern Bedlam," *New York Times,* October 4, 1967, p. 38; Richard Schickel, "Sorriest Spectacle: The Titicut Follies," *Life* 63 (December 1, 1967): 12.

127. Joseph Featherstone (*The New Republic*) discussed the merits of this "essay on emptiness"; Peter A. Janssen (*Newsweek*) praised it for capturing the truth about the "most anxiety-producing institution in modern society"; Pauline Kael (*The New Yorker*) identified its content (man's inhumanity to man) and lauded its form (particularly the feeling of "being there"); and Richard Schickel (*Life*) called it a "wicked, brilliant documentary." See Featherstone, "Documentary: HIGH SCHOOL," 160 (June 21, 1969), pp. 28–30; Janssen, "The Last Bell," 73 (May 19, 1969), pp. 102; Kael, "The Current Cinema," 45, No. 35 (October 18, 1969), pp. 199–204; Schickel, "A Verit, View of HIGH SCHOOL," *Life,* 67, No. 11 (September 12, 1969), n.p. Fred Hechinger, the education editor of the *New York Times,* criticized the film for being "too brutally selective," while William Paul (the *Village Voice*) claimed that "surface reality—which is all Wiseman ever presents us with—often has nothing to do with inner truth." See Hechinger, "A Look at Irrelevant Values" (March 23, 1969), sec. 4, p. 5; Paul, "HIGH SCHOOL: Documentary Follies," 15, No. 41 (October 8, 1970): 54, 64–65. Donald Robinson congratulated Wiseman for revealing "the unmistakable essence of the generation gap," while Susan Swartz, an alumna of North East High School, says Wiseman's lack of research and short shooting schedule prevented him from seeing the "real mess" in the school: "the track system that fostered a class system." See Robinson, "A Slanted, Cruelly Middle Class Debunking Film," *Phi Delta Kappa,* 51, No. 1 (September 1969): 47; Swartz, "The Real North East," *Film Library Quarterly,* 6, No. 1 (Winter 1972/73): 12–15. For the reaction of some teachers, see "Wiseman's Controversial Film— II: How Do Teachers React to HIGH SCHOOL," *American Teacher,* 54, No. 6 (February 1970): 13. In an analysis of the film according to contemporary theory, Jon Lewis studies fully what others have recognized: the "narrative" role of Wiseman's images. See "The Shifting Camera Point of View and 'Model of Language' in Wiseman's HIGH SCHOOL," *Quarterly Review of Film Studies,* 7, No. 1 (Winter 1982): 69–78.

128. For an account of his experiences in making the film, see Frederick Wiseman, "Reminiscences of a Filmmaker: Frederick Wiseman on LAW AND ORDER," *Police Chief,* 36, No. 9 (September 1969), pp. 32–35. For reviews, see George Gent, "Movie on Police Censored by NET: LAW AND ORDER Program Cut to Remove Obscenities," *New York Times* (February 27, 1969), p. 83. Reviews include Pauline Kael, "The Current Cinema," *The New Yorker,* 45 (October 18, 1969), pp. 199–204, and Gary Arnold, "LAW AND ORDER, *Washington Post* (March 7, 1969), Sec. C, p. 6.

129. Mamber, p. 224.

130. "Movies: Documenting America," *Atlantic Monthly*, 225 (March 1970): 139–142; included in these anthologies: Lewis Jacobs, ed., *The Documentary Tradition*, and Barsam, *Nonfiction Film Theory and Criticism*.

131. See Daniel Klughurz, "Documentary—Where's the Wonder," *Television Quarterly*, 6, No. 3 (Summer 1967): 38; W. Johnson, "Shooting at Wars: Three Views," *Film Quarterly*, 21, No. 2 (Winter 1967–68): 27–36; William C. Jersey, "Some Thoughts on Film Technique," *Film Comment*, 2, No. 1 (Winter 1964): 15–16; "Propaganda Films About the War in Vietnam," *Film Comment*, 4, No. 1 (Fall 1966): 4–22.

132. Representative reviews include Stanley Kauffmann, "OPERATION ABOLITION," *The New Republic*, 144 (March 27, 1961), n.p.; Dan Wakefield, "OPERATION ABOLITION," *The Nation*, 192 (January 28, 1961), p. 74; "OPERATION ABOLITION," *The National Review*, 10 (May 6, 1961), p. 277; "OPERATION ABOLITION," *Time*, 77 (May 17, 1961), p. 17.

133. Three background articles are Emile de Antonio, "The Point of View in POINT OF ORDER!," David T. Bazelon, "Background to POINT OF ORDER!," and Edward Crawford, "More Than Nostalgia," in *Film Comment*, 2, No. 1 (Winter 1964): 31–36. Representative reviews, which were almost consistently favorable, include Hollis Alpert, "POINT OF ORDER!," *Saturday Review*, 47 (January 25, 1964), p. 24; Brendan Gill, "POINT OF ORDER!," *The New Yorker*, 39 (January 18, 1964), p. 72; Philip T. Hartung, "POINT OF ORDER!," *Commonweal*, 90 (February 14, 1964), p. 601; Stanley Kauffmann, "POINT OF ORDER!," *The New Republic*, 150 (January 25, 1964), p. 29. A negative review is "POINT OF ORDER!," *National Review*, 16 (April 21, 1964), p. 325.

134. Background articles include Emile de Antonio and Mark Lane, "RUSH TO JUDGMENT: A Conversation with Mark Lane and Emile de Antonio," *Film Comment*, 4, Nos. 2–3 (Fall/Winter 1967): 2–18; and James J. Graham and Mark Lane, "RUSH TO JUDGMENT," *Commonweal*, 86 (April 21, 1967), p. 149. A representative positive review is Penelope Gilliatt, "RUSH TO JUDGMENT," *The New Yorker*, 43 (June 17, 1967), p. 95.

135. See interview with Arthur Barron in Alan Rosenthal, *The New Documentary in Action: A Casebook in Film Making* (Berkeley: University of California Press, 1971), pp. 131–148.

136. Stanley Kauffmann said its sincerity makes it depressing, "SATURDAY MORNING," *The New Republic*, 164, No. 24 (May 1, 1971), pp. 22+; see also "SATURDAY MORNING," *The New Yorker*, 47 (May 8, 1971), pp. 121–122.

137. For an article about Francis Thompson and Alexander Hammid, see "TO BE ALIVE!," *The New Yorker*, 40 (October 10, 1964), pp. 49–52.

138. The Drew-Leacock DAVID (1961) is about the efforts of a young jazz musician to free himself of hard drug addiction through the rehabilitation efforts of Synanon House in California. See Barsam, *Nonfiction Film: A Critical History*, p. 263; Stephen Mamber, in *America: Studies in Uncontrolled Documentary*, pp. 74–78; and G. Roy Levin, *Documentary Explorations: 15 Interviews with Film-Makers*, pp. 227–228. Martha Coolidge's very personal *David: Off and On* (1973) treats the drug problems of her brother.

139. A strongly-biased Canadian film on the subject is Douglas Leiterman's and Beryl Fox's *One More River* (1963).

140. Mamber (pp. 105–114) provides an excellent account of the film and its reception.

141. "BUS," *Saturday Review*, 48 (March 27, 1965), p. 43; see also Philip T. Hartung, "BUS," *Commonweal*, 82 (April 9, 1965), p. 84.

142. "BLACK NATCHEZ," *The New Republic*, 156 (February 18, 1967), p. 31.

143. See Erik Barnouw, *Documentary: A History of the Non-Fiction Film*, pp. 268–283; Philip Knightley, *The First Casualty* (New York: Harcourt, 1975); Michael Herr, *Dispatches* (New York: Knopf, 1977).

144. See Richard M. Cohen, "WHY VIETNAM?," *The New Republic*, 158 (June 8, 1968), p. 40; "WHY VIETNAM?," *The New Republic*, 155 (November 19, 1966), p. 6.

145. Robert K. Avery and Timothy L. Larson, "U.S. Military Documentary Films: A Chronological Analysis." (Dialog file ED178972, item CS502688) agree that WHY VIETNAM? is inferior to the Capra series.

146. In 1971, John Ford produced VIETNAM, VIETNAM for the U.S. Information Agency. I have not seen it, but, according to Alan Rosenthal, "the film was so highly distorted and extreme in its views that it became an object of ridicule and was eventually withdrawn from circulation" (*The Documentary Conscience: A Casebook in Film Making*, p. 12).

147. A typical review is Richard M. Cohen, "WHY VIETNAM?", *New Republic*, 158 (June 8, 1968), p. 40. Erik Barnouw comments that "revelations later published in *The Pentagon Papers* showed the

film to be even more deceptive than it had previously appeared to be" (*Documentary: A History of the Non-Fiction Film*, p. 272).

148. "A FACE OF WAR," *New Republic*, 158 (June 1, 1968), p. 26; Penelope Gilliatt, "A FACE OF WAR," *The New Yorker*, 45 (March 22, 1969), p. 152; Philip T. Hartung, "A FACE OF WAR," *Commonweal*, 88 (May 31, 1968), p. 336.

149. Hollis Alpert, "EYEWITNESS: NORTH VIETNAM," *Saturday Review* (December 10, 1966), p. 65; "INSIDE NORTH VIETNAM," *Nation* (December 25, 1967), p. 701.

150. Foreign films on the subject include Joris Ivens' THE SEVENTEENTH PARALLEL (1967) and THE PEOPLE AND THEIR GUNS (1970); Beryl Fox's THE MILLS OF THE GODS (1965), SAIGON (1967), and LAST REFLECTION ON A WAR (1968); Michael Rubbio's SAD SONG OF YELLOW SKIN (1970).

151. See Alan Rosenthal, *The Documentary Conscience*, pp. 205–244.

152. "IN THE YEAR OF THE PIG," *Newsweek* (November 10, 1969), p. 108; Pauline Kael, "IN THE YEAR OF THE PIG," *The New Yorker* (November 15, 1969), p. 177; Stanley Kauffmann, "IN THE YEAR OF THE PIG," *The New Republic* (December 13, 1969), p. 32. See also Emile de Antonio, "IN THE YEAR OF THE PIG," *Commonweal*, 90 (May 16, 1969), p. 250.

153. See Alan Rosenthal's marginally useful interview with de Antonio in *The Documentary Conscience*, pp. 206–226.

154. Representative reviews include Hollis Alpert, "COME BACK, AFRICA," *Saturday Review*, 43 (April 2, 1960), p. 26, and Stanley Kauffmann, "COME BACK, AFRICA," *The New Republic*, 142 (May 16, 1960), p. 22.

155. See Mamber, pp. 42–48, 57–62.

156. See Mamber, *Cinéma Verité in America*, pp. 89–96.

157. Filmmakers are D. A. Pennebaker, Richard Leacock, Abbot Mills, and Al Wirthimer.

158. Wilfrid Sheed said the film consists of Bruce reading a "bill of indictment against himself" in "LENNY BRUCE," *Esquire*, 68 (July 1967), p. 14.

159. Brendan Gill is more perceptive than usual in his review "PORTRAIT OF JASON," *The New Yorker*, 43 (October 14, 1967), p. 159; see also Arthur Knight, "PORTRAIT OF JASON," *Saturday Review*, 50 (September 9, 1967), p. 44.

160. *Newsweek* said the film provides "a strong sense of the prizefighter's fragrantly lunatic milieu," 74 (December 8, 1969), p. 122.

161. Among the excellent reviews were those in *The New Republic*, 153 (December 4, 1965), p. 34; *Esquire*, 64 (September 1965), p. 42; and *The New Yorker*, 41 (November 20, 1965), p. 231.

162. Because this film was released in the United States, it is listed here; however, this release was an exception to U.S.I.A. policy, which stipulated that the agency's films were to be made only for release outside of the United States. A good review is "JOHN F. KENNEDY: YEARS OF LIGHTNING, DAY OF DRUMS," *Newsweek*, 67 (April 18, 1966), p. 109.

163. The uniformly positive reviews included Philip T. Hartung, "JAZZ ON A SUMMER'S DAY," *Commonweal*, 72 (April 8, 1960), p. 40; Robert Hatch, "JAZZ ON A SUMMER'S DAY," *The Nation*, 190 (April 30, 1960), p. 392; and "JAZZ ON A SUMMER'S DAY," *Saturday Review*, 43 (March 12, 1960), p. 70.

164. Penelope Gilliatt, "CHIEFS" *The New Yorker*, 45 (March 22, 1969), p. 121.

165. See Mamber, *Cinéma Verité in America*, pp. 187–191.

166. In *Nonfiction Film: A Critical History*, pp. 258–259, I mistakenly suggested that these two films were one and the same. They are two separate and different films. The first half of EDDIE was taken from material shot for ON THE POLE. Stephen Mamber, *Cinéma Verité: Studies in Uncontrolled Documentary*, provides full discussions of both films.

167. The film is also known as MOONEY VS. FOWLE.

168. "ENDLESS SUMMER," *Newsweek*, 68 (August 1, 1966), p. 84.

169. Either as director or producer, Blackwood's many films include CHRISTO: WRAPPED COAST (1970), CHRISTO: FOUR WORKS IN PROGRESS (1971), ISAMU NOGUCHI (1971), LARRY RIVERS (1972), ROBERT MOTHERWELL (1972), THE NEW YORK SCHOOL (1973), PHILIP GUSTON (1973), ANDY WARHOL (1973), CLAES OLDENBURG (1975), and SAM FRANCIS (1975).

170. A later film about Robert Scull, America's most important collector of the art of this period, is Susan and Alan Raymond's AMERICA'S POP COLLECTOR (1974).

171. See Robert Gardner, "Chronicles of the Human Experience: DEAD BIRDS," *Nonfiction Film Theory and Criticism*, ed. Barsam (New York: Dutton, 1976), pp. 342–348, and Karl G. Heider, *The Dani of West Irian: An Ethnographic Companion to the Film DEAD BIRDS* (Andover, Mass.: Andover Modular Publications, 1972).

172. For an historical and theoretical study of the compilation film, see Jay Leyda, *Films Beget Films: A Study of the Compilation Film* (New York: Hill, 1964).

173. Representative reviews include Brendan Gill, "GUNS OF AUGUST," *The New Yorker*, 40 (January 16, 1965), p. 74, and "GUNS OF AUGUST," *The New Republic*, 152 (January 16, 1965), p. 27.

174. See Richard Corliss, "BIRTH AND DEATH," *Film Quarterly*, 22 (Spring 1969), pp. 38–40.

175. See A. William Bluem, *Documentary in American Television: Form, Function, Method* (New York: Hastings House), 1965.

176. In writing about this relationship between television and the status of the documentary film in the postwar period, A. William Bluem observed that "television has given the documentary film its greatest impetus; it has all but rescued an ailing patient in extremis" (p. 7). Bluem further observed that there was something almost historically inevitable in this relationship between television and the "documentary idea" (as defined first by Grierson and subsequently refined by others): "television is mass communication, and in this lies its strength as a documentary instrument" (p. 16). For an account of the relationship between the documentary film tradition and early television, see Vance Kepley, "The Origins of NBC's 'Project XX' in Compilation Documentaries," *Journalism Quarterly*, 61, No. 1 (Spring 1984): 20–21. See also Paul Rotha, "Television and the Future of Documentary," *Film Quarterly*, 9 (Summer 1955): 366–373, and Burton Benjamin, "The Documentary Heritage" in *Nonfiction Film Theory and Criticism*, ed. Barsam, pp. 203–208.

177. See Raymond Fielding, *The American Newsreel: 1911–1967* (Norman: University of Oklahoma Press, 1972) and *The March of Time, 1935–1951* (New York: Oxford University Press, 1978), and Richard Barsam, "'This Is America': Documentaries for Theaters, 1942–1951," *Cinema Journal*, 12, No. 2 (Spring 1973): 22–38.

178. For comments on the collaborative nature of early direct cinema, see James Lipscomb, "Cinéma Verité," *Film Quarterly*, 18, No. 2 (Winter 1964): 62–63.

179. Bluem, pp. 278–296, offers a list of significant early television documentaries. An excellent study is Richard C. Bartone. "A History and an Analysis of *The Twentieth Century (1957–1966) Compilation Series* (Diss., New York University, 1985).

180. For a later and more pessimistic view of the future for independently produced television documentaries, see Patricia R. Zimmerman, "Public Television, Independent Documentary Producer and Public Policy," *Journal of the University Film and Video Association*, 34, No. 3 (Summer 1982): 9–23.

181. I am indebted to Stephen Mamber for providing me with a copy of his unpublished paper, "Whatever Happened to Cinéma Verité."

182. In *Film Comment* 9:9 (November–December 1973), see Eric Krueger, "AN AMERICAN FAMILY: An American Film," pp. 17–19; "Pat Loud: An Interview with Melinda Ward," pp. 20–23; "The Making of AN AMERICAN FAMILY: Susan Raymond, Alan Raymond, and John Terry Interviewed by Melinda Ward," pp. 24–31.

183. See Julia LeSage, "The Political Aesthetics of the Feminist Documentary Film," *Quarterly Review of Film Studies* 3, No. 4 (Fall 1978): 507–523; Sharon Smith, *Women Who Make Movies* (New York: Hopkinson, 1975); and E. McGary, "Documentary Realism and Woman's Cinema," *Women and Film* 2, No. 7 (1975): 50–59.

CHAPTER 13 ("WHAT WENT WRONG?" THE AMERICAN AVANT-GARDE CINEMA OF THE 1960S)

1. In fact, Juan A. Suarez, *Bike Boys, Drag Queens, and Superstars: Avant-Garde, Mass Culture, and Gay Identities in the 1960s Underground Cinema* (Bloomington: Indiana University Press, 1996), pp. 141 ff., argues that SCORPIO RISING is "the most representative film of the 1960s American underground cinema."

2. Anger's authorial pun is especially significant when read against the backdrop of the major academic works of criticism of the 1960s American avant-garde cinema. The birth of this tradition can be directly traced to P. Adams Sitney's 1974 book, *Visionary Film: The American Avant-Garde* (New York: Oxford University Press, 1974). Drawing upon the work of the literary critic Harold Bloom, Sitney uses Romanticism as his framework for understanding the American experimental cinema of the sixties. For example, in the midst of his analysis of SCORPIO RISING, Sitney argues:

"After his own ritual costuming to the sound of 'Hit the Road, Jack,' ending in his putting on rings quite like the opening of Inauguration [of the *Pleasure Dome*], Scorpio takes a sniff of cocaine. Here we have an exultant image of Romantic liberation when the most interiorized of the songs in the film, 'Heat Wave,' is combined with an image on the television of birds escaping from a cage, and then, amid two frame flashes of bright red, a gaudy, purple picture of Dracula. We see in one or two seconds of cinema the re-creation of a high Romantic, or Byronic myth of the paradox of liberation (p. 119)."

Sitney assumes that American avant-garde filmmakers, through their belief in the ideologies of individualism and liberation, exist in an artistic line that can be traced back to such libertine poets as Byron. Subsequently, it is this unyielding belief in the Romantic artist that has been the lynchpin for every serious consideration of the American avant-garde cinema of the sixties. Given this premise, it is in no way surprising that Sitney's book is organized around individual filmmakers' idiosyncratic contributions to the experimental cinema. For example, his chapter "The Magus" is devoted to the films of Kenneth Anger, whereas "Major Mythopoeia" focuses on the sixties work of Stan Brakhage (pp. 93 ff.; pp. 211 ff.).

Historical writing and criticism of the sixties avant-garde cinema have maintained the Romantic organizational structures of Sitney's work, even while purportedly questioning those assumptions. Three otherwise exceptionally valuable books participate in this procedure: David James's *Allegories of Cinema,* Lauren Rabinovitz's *Points of Resistance,* and Juan Suarez's *Bike Boys, Drag Queens, and Superstars.* While each of these books provide post-structuralist critiques of humanism, individualism, and Romanticism, each one also contradictorily adopts essentially the same organizational structure as Sitney's approach.

3. It is not at all certain that Mekas would have seen such a recently released European film by the time filming began on HALLELUJAH THE HILLS. However, the argument asserted here merely relies on an historical and social confluence between the narrative structures of the two films, not on any claims grounded in authorial intention.

4. Janet Staiger, "Finding Community in the Early 1960s: Underground Cinema and Sexual Politics," in Hilary Radner and Moya Luckett, eds., *Swinging Single: Representing Sexuality in the 1960s* (Minneapolis: University of Minnesota Press, 1999), p. 39.

5. Paul Arthur, "Routines of Emancipation: Alternative Cinema in the Ideology and Politics of the Sixties," in David E. James, ed., *To Free the Cinema* (Princeton: Princeton University Press, 1992), p. 19.

6. See Ernest Callenbach, "Looking Backward," *Film Quarterly* 22, no. 1 (1968). Also, Annette Michelson, "Film and the Radical Aspiration," in *Film Culture Reader* (New York: Praeger, 1970), pp. 404–421.

7. See Arthur, "Routines of Emancipation," p. 28.

8. Warhol's "factory" was in fact modeled on the concept of the artist's studio, imported from the traditional art world. Nonetheless, Warhol was invoking the discourse of mass production as an assault against the Hollywood studio system's Taylorist mode of filmmaking.

9. For more on the work of Andy Warhol, see Stephen Koch, *Stargazer: The Life, World and Films of Andy Warhol,* rev. ed. (New York: Marion Boyars, 1991).

10. For a good discussion of the Beats and their geographic moorings, see Dennis McNally, *Jack Kerouac, the Beats, and America* (New York: Random House, 1979).

11. See Arthur, "Routines of Emancipation," pp. 28, 29.

12. Arthur Marwick, *The Sixties: Cultural Revolution in Britain, France, Italy, and The United States, c. 1958–c. 1974* (New York: Oxford University Press, 1998).

13. Mark J. Huisman, "Canyon Cinema: A History Worth Remembering," *Independent* (July 1998): 36–41.

14. Wheeler Winston Dixon, *The Exploding Eye: A Re-Visionary History of 1960s American Experimental Cinema* (Albany: SUNY Press, 1997), p. 29.

15. Ibid.

16. Quoted in ibid.

17. James states, "[This book] argues the need to jettison the essentialist binary notions between the aesthetic and the political avant-gardes and between those avant-gardes and mass culture that film history has inherited from art history and from the ideology of modernism in general" (*Allegories of Cinema: American Film in the Sixties* [Princeton, N.J.: Princeton University Press, 1989], p. 4).

18. For more on the Beats, see David Sterritt, *Mad To Be Saved: The Beats, the '50s, and Film* (Carbondale: Southern Illinois University Press, 1998), and *The Rolling Stone Book of the Beats: The Beat Generation and American Culture* (New York: Hyperion, 1999).

19. The Marie Menken films that I have studied closely are DRIPS IN STRIPS (1961) and GO GO GO (1964); for Joyce Wieland, WATER SARK (1965), 1933 (1967), and CATFOOD (1968).

20. For a detailed, personal account of how the sixties served as the cultural soil for the Stonewall revolution, see Martin Duberman, *Stonewall* (New York: Dutton, 1993). For a more academic take on the differences between the East Coast and West Coast gay communities in the sixties, see John D'Emilio's chapters in *Sexual Politics, Sexual Communities: The Making of a Homosexual Minority in the United States, 1940–1970* (Chicago: University of Chicago Press, 1983). Chapter 9 explores the New York City–based community whereas chapter 10 examines the San Francisco Bay area community.

21. FLAMING CREATURES is probably the most notorious of the 1960s American avant-garde films. The prime organizer of the New York city avant-garde scene, Jonas Mekas, was arrested for exhibiting it, and Susan Sontag devoted an entire essay to the film in her renowned collection of cultural criticism, *Against Interpretation* (New York: Laurel Publishing, 1966).

22. I take the term "imperfect cinema" from Nelson Pereira dos Santos, the South American filmmaker. In his explication of Italian Neo-Realism's influence on Brazil's "Cinema Nuovo," dos Santos argues: "Neo-realism taught us, in sum, that it was possible to make films in the streets; that we did not need studios; that we could film using average people rather than known actors; that the technique could be imperfect, as long as the film was truly linked to the national culture and expressed that culture." Quoted by John King in *Magical Reels: A History of Cinema in Latin America* (London: Verso, 1990), p. 107. I believe this concept, referring to all cinemas that resist high gloss Hollywood studio style, similarly applies to the American avant-garde cinema of the sixties as represented by a film like BLOND COBRA.

23. The two major biographies of Maria Montez were published in her native country of the Dominican Republic: Pablo Clase, *Maria Montez: mujer y estrella* (Santo Domingo de Guzman: Editorial del Nordeste, 1985) and Margarita Vicens de Morales, *Maria Montez, su vida* (Santo Domingo: Editoia Corripio, 1982). No biographies of Maria Montez are available in English, although a short biography of her appears in Thomas G. Aylesworth and John S. Bowman, *The World Almanac of Who's Who of Film* (New York: Pharos, 1987). Montez's star image spoke to some gay male spectators in the sixties because, tragically, she abused her body to meet absurd patriarchal and heterosexist standards of beauty and success. Richard Dyer studies a similar phenomenon using the case of Judy Garland in his book, *Heavenly Bodies: Film Stars and Society* (New York: St. Martin's Press, 1986), p. 141. These images are directly linked to the international history of the avant-garde cinema, most particularly to the "city symphony" films, such as BERLIN: SYMPHONY OF A GREAT CITY (1927) and MAN WITH A MOVIE CAMERA (1929).

24. Shakespeare is a frequent intertextual referent in American avant-garde cinema of the sixties. For example, LONESOME COWBOYS (1967, Andy Warhol) uses the nurse from ROMEO AND JULIET in its intertextual reworking of the Hollywood Western.

25. In this sense—the avant-garde movie as a critical variant of the home movie—the work of Stan Brakhage is heavily influenced by Marie Menken.

26. Both Michael Snow and Joyce Wieland are Canadians. However, they both did their work in the avant-garde cinema of the 1960s while living in New York City, and that work is considered correctly to be a part of American cinema. The Museum of Modern Art's Circulating Film Catalog, for example, lists Snow's films of the late-1960s with the United States as the national designation.

27. For more on Michael Snow and structural cinema, see Scott Macdonald's chapter on WAVELENGTH in *Avant-Garde Film/Motion Studies* (New York: Cambridge University Press, 1993); Teresa DeLauretis's analysis of Michael Snow in *Alice Doesn't: Feminism/Semiotics/Cinema* (Bloomington: Indiana University Press, 1982); William Wees, "Balancing Eye and Mind: Michael Snow," in *Light Moving in Time: Studies in the Visual Aesthetics of Avant-Garde Film* (Berkeley: University of California Press, 1992); and James Peterson's "Rounding Up the Usual Suspects: The Minimal Strain and Interpretive Schemata," in *Dreams of Chaos, Visions of Order: Understanding the American Avant-garde Cinema* (Detroit: Wayne State University Press, 1994). P. Adams Sitney coined the term "structural cinema" in his seminal 1969 essay "Structural Film," *Film Culture* 47 (Summer 1969): 1.

28. Dixon, *Exploding Eye*, p. 158.

29. Michael Snow, unpublished Letter to Paul Monaco and Charles Harpole, April 6, 1999, p. 2.
30. Ibid.
31. Jonas Mekas, "Showcases I Ran in the Sixties," in James, ed., *To Free the Cinema,* pp. 323, 324.
32. See the excellent discussion and criticism provided in Lauren Rabinowitz, "Wearing the Critic's Hat: History, Critical Discourses, and the American Avant-Garde Cinema," in James, ed., *To Free the Cinema,* pp. 268–283.

CONCLUSION

1. See the argument, for example, advanced by Fredric Jameson in "Post-Modernism, or the Logic of Late Capitalism," *New Left Review* (July/August 1984), that a new wave of American economic and military aggression coincides with the rupture of the modernist tradition in bourgeois society that is reflected in post-modern culture. (Jameson's argument was subsequently published as a book, *Postmodernism, or the Cultural Logic of Late Capitalism* [Durham: Duke University Press, 1991].)

Selected Bibliography

Abrams, Morris H. *The Mirror and the Lamp: Romantic Theory and the Critical Tradition.* New York: Oxford University Press, 1953.

Acker, Ally. *Reel Women: Pioneers of the Cinema, 1968 to the Present.* New York: Continuum, 1991.

Alexander, William. *Film on the Left: American Documentary Film from 1931–1942.* Princeton: Princeton University Press, 1981.

Alkin, E. G. *Sound with Vision: Sound Techniques for Television and Film, American Film Institute Screen Education Yearbook: 1967.* Los Angeles: AFI, 1967.

Allen, Robert C., and Douglas Gomery. *Film History: Theory and Practice.* New York: Knopf, 1985.

Amyes, Tom. *The Technology of Audio Post-Production in Video and Film.* Oxford: Focal Press, 1993.

Anderson, Christopher. *Hollywood/TV: The Studio System in the Fifties.* Austin: University of Texas Press, 1994.

Anderson, Terry H. *The Movement and the Sixties: Protest in America from Greensboro to Wounded Knee.* New York/Oxford: Oxford University Press, 1995.

Atkins, Thomas R., ed. *Frederick Wiseman.* New York: Monarch Publishing, 1976.

Aylesworth, Thomas G., and John S. Bowman. *The World Almanac Who's Who of Film.* New York: Pharos, 1987.

Balio, Tino. *United Artists: The Company That Changed the Film Industry.* Madison: University of Wisconsin Press, 1987.

———, ed. *Hollywood in the Age of Television.* Boston: Unwin Hyman, 1990.

Balmuth, Bernard. *Introduction to Film Editing.* Boston: Focal Press, 1989.

Barnouw, Erik. *Documentary: A History of the Non-Fiction Film.* New York: Oxford University Press, 1974.

Barsam, Richard M. *Nonfiction Film: Theory and Criticism.* New York: Dutton, 1976.

Bartone, Richard C. *A History and an Analysis of the Twentieth Century (1957–1966) Compilation Series.* Dissertation: New York University, 1985.

Bazin, André. *What Is Cinema?* Berkeley: University of California Press, 1958.

Belton, John. *Widescreen Cinema.* Cambridge, Mass.: Harvard University Press, 1992.

Bendazzi, G. *The Films of Woody Allen.* London: Ravette, 1987.

Bernard, Bernard L. *Basic Motion Picture Technology.* Boston: Focal Press, 1971.

Bluem, A. William. *Documentary in American Television: Form, Function, Method.* New York: Hastings House, 1965.

Bogdanovich, Peter. *The Cinema of Alfred Hitchcock.* New York: Museum of Modern Art, 1963.

Bohn, Thomas W., and Richard Stromgren. *Light and Shadows: A History of Motion Pictures.* Port Washington, NY: Alfred Publishing Co., 1975.

Bordwell, David, Janet Staiger, and Kristin Thompson. *The Classical Hollywood Cinema: Film Style and Mode of Production to 1960.* New York: Columbia University Press, 1985.

Braithwaite, Bruce. *Heroes of the Movies: Marlon Brando.* Surrey: LSP Books, Ltd., 1982.

Brode, Douglas. *Films of the Sixties.* New York: Carol Publishing Group, 1988.

Brodsky, John, and Nathan Weiss. *The Cleopatra Papers: A Private Correspondence.* New York: Simon & Schuster, 1963.

Brown, Peter H., and Jim Pinkston. *Oscar Dearest: Six Decades of Scandal, Politics, and Greed Behind Hollywood's Academy Awards, 1927–1986*. New York: Harper and Row Publishers, 1987.

Buscombe, Edward. "Sound and Color." *Jump Cut*. No. 17, 1978, pp. 23–25.

Calder-Marshall, Arthur. *The Innocent Eye: The Life of Robert J. Flaherty*. New York: Harcourt, 1963.

Cameron, Evan William, ed. *Sound and the Cinema: The Coming of Sound to American Film*. Pleasantville, N.Y.: Redgrave, 1980.

Cameron, Kenneth M. *America on Film: Hollywood and American History*. New York: Continuum Publishing, 1997.

Cantor, Norman. *Twentieth Century Culture: Modernism to Deconstruction*. New York: Peter Lang Publishing, 1988.

Cassady, Ralph. "Impact of the Paramount Decision on Motion Picture Distribution and Pricing." *Southern California Law Review* 31 (1958): 50–180.

Casty, Alan. *The Development of Film: An Interpretive History*. New York: Harper Collins, 1973.

———. *The Films of Robert Rossen*. New York: Museum of Modern Art, 1969.

Christensen, Terry. *Reel Politics*. New York: Basil Blackwell, 1987.

Clase, Pablo. *María Montez: Mujer y estrella*. Santo Domingo de Guzman: Editorial del Nordeste, 1985.

Collins, Jim, Hilary Radner, and Ava Preacher Collins, eds. *Film Theory Goes to the Movies*. New York: Routledge, 1993.

Conant, Michael. *Antitrust in the Motion Picture Industry*. Berkeley: University of California Press, 1960.

Cook, David A. *A History of Narrative Film*. 3rd ed. New York: W. W. Norton and Co., 1996.

Daley, Ken. *Basic Film Technique*. New York: Focal Press, 1980.

Dancyger, Ken. *The Technique of Film and Video Editing*. Boston: Focal Press, 1993.

Denby, David, ed. *Always in the Dark: An Anthology of Film Criticism, 1915 to the Present*. New York: Vintage Books, 1977.

Dickstein, Morris. *Gates of Eden: American Culture in the Sixties*. New York: Basic Books, 1977.

Donahue, Suzaane Mary. *American Film Distribution: The Changing Marketplace*. Ann Arbor: UMI Research Press, 1987.

Dyer, Richard. *Heavenly Bodies: Film Stars and Society*. New York: St. Martin's Press, 1986.

Eames, John Douglas. *The MGM Story: A Complete History of Fifty Roaring Years*. New York: Crown Publishers, Inc., 1979.

Edmonds, I. G., and Reiko Mimura. *The Oscar Directors*. San Diego: A. S. Barnes, 1980.

Ellis, Jack C. *A History of Film*. 2nd ed. Englewood Cliffs, N.J.: Prentice-Hall, 1985.

Ellsworth, Liz. *Frederick Wiseman: A Guide to References and Resources*. Boston: Hall, 1979.

Entertainment Weekly, editors of. *The Entertainment Weekly Guide to the Greatest Movies Ever Made*. New York: Warner Books, 1994.

Farber, Stephen, and Marc Green. *Hollywood Dynasties*. New York: A Delilah Book, Putnam Publishing, 1984.

Faulkner, Robert R. *Hollywood Studio Musicians: Their Work and Careers in the Recording Industry*. Chicago/New York: Aldine-Atherton, 1971.

———. *Music on Demand: Composers and Careers in the Hollywood Film Industry*. New Brunswick, N.J.: Transaction Books, 1983.

Fell, John L. *A History of Films*. New York: Holt, Rinehart and Winston, 1979.

Feuer, Jane. *The Hollywood Musical*. Bloomington: Indiana University Press, 1982.

Fielding, Raymond. *The American Newsreel: 1911–1967*. Norman: University of Oklahoma Press, 1972.

———. *The March of Time, 1935–1951*. New York: Oxford University Press, 1978.

Finch, Christopher. *Special Effects: Creating Movie Magic*. New York: Abbeville Press, 1984.

Finler, Joel. *The Hollywood Story*. New York: Crown Publishers, 1988.

Frayne, John G. et al. "A Short History of Motion Picture Sound Recording in the United States." *SMPTE Journal* 85, no. 7 (July, 1976): 515–528.

Fredrik, Nathalie. *Hollywood and the Academy Awards*. Los Angeles: Award Publications, 1968.

Giannetti, Louis. *Masters of the American Cinema*. Englewood Cliffs, N.J.: Prentice-Hall, 1981.

Gitlin, Todd. *The Sixties: Years of Hope, Days of Rage*. New York: Bantam Books, 1993.

Gomery, Douglas. *The Hollywood Studio System.* New York: St. Martin's Press, 1986.
———. *Movie History: A Survey.* Belmont, Calif.: Wadsworth Publishing, 1991.
———. *Shared Pleasures: A History of Movie Presentation in the United States.* Madison: University of Wisconsin Press, 1992.
Gorbman, Claudia. "Bibliography on Sound in Film." *Yale French Studies.* no. 60 (1980): 269–286.
Graham, Sheila. *Hollywood Revisited: A Fiftieth Anniversary Celebration.* New York: St. Martin's Press, 1985.
Hardy, Forsyth, ed. *Grierson on Documentary.* London: Faber, 1979.
Haskell, Molly. *From Reverence to Rape: The Treatment of Women in the Movies.* New York: Holt, Rinehart Winston, 1974.
Heston, Charlton. *In The Arena: An Autobiography.* New York: Simon & Schuster, 1995.
Higham, Charles. *Hollywood at Sunset.* New York: Saturday Review Press, 1972.
Hirsch, Foster. *Acting Hollywood Style.* New York: Heney N. Abrams, Inc./AFI Press, 1991.
Hirschhorn, Clive. *The Columbia Story.* New York: Crown Publishers, 1989.
Holden, Anthony. *Behind the Oscar: The Secret History of the Academy Awards.* New York: Simon & Schuster, 1993.
Honore, Paul M. *A Handbook of Sound Recording.* New York: A. S. Barnes and Company, 1980.
Horowitz, Daniel. *Betty Friedan and the Making of the Feminine Mystique: The American Left, the Cold War, and Modern Feminism.* Amherst: University of Massachusetts Press, 1999.
Houston, Penelope. *The Contemporary Cinema.* Baltimore: Penguin, 1963.
Hubatka, Milton C., Frederick Hull, and Richard W. Sanders. *Audio Sweetening for Film and TV.* Blue Ridge Summit, PA: TAB Books Inc., 1985.
Issel, William. *Social Change in the United States, 1945–1983.* New York: Schocken Books, 1985.
Jacobs, Lewis, ed. *The Documentary Tradition.* New York: Hopkinson, 1970.
James, David E. *Allegories of Cinema: American Film in the Sixties.* Princeton, N.J.: Princeton University Press, 1989.
Jamison, Andrew, and Ron Eyerman. *Seeds of the Sixties.* Berkeley: University of California Press, 1994.
Jowett, Garth. *Film: The Democratic Art.* Boston: Little, Brown, & Co., 1976.
Kael, Pauline. *I Lost It at the Movies: Film Writings, 1954–1965.* Boston: Little, Brown, & Co., 1965.
———. *Kiss, Kiss, Bang, Bang.* Boston: Little, Brown, & Co., 1968.
Karlin, Fred. *Listening to Movies: The Film Lover's Guide to Film Music.* New York: Schirmer Books, 1994.
Katsiaficas, George. *The Imagination of the New Left: A Global Analysis of 1968.* Boston: South End Press, 1987.
Kindem, Gorham, ed. *The American Movie Industry: The Business of Motion Pictures.* Carbondale: Southern Illinois University Press, 1982.
King, John. *Magical Reels: A History of Cinema in Latin America.* London: Verso, 1990.
Kobal, John. *John Kobal Presents the Top 100 Movies.* New York: NAL-Dutton, 1988 .
Kummel, Michael. *Manhood in America: A Cultural History.* New York: Free Press, 1996.
Leaming, Barbara. *Marilyn Monroe.* New York: Crown Publishers, 1992.
Lev, Peter. *The Euro-American Cinema.* Austin: University of Texas Press, 1993.
Levin, G. Roy. *Documentary Explorations: Fifteen Interviews with Film-Makers.* Garden City, N.Y.: Doubleday, 1971.
Levy, Emanuel. *And the Winner is . . .: The History and Politics of the Oscar Awards.* New York: Ungar, 1987.
Lewis, Jon, ed. *The New American Cinema.* Durham and London: Duke University Press, 1998.
———. *The Road to Romance and Ruin: Teen Films and Youth Culture.* New York: Routledge, 1992.
Light, Paul C. *Baby Boomers.* New York: W. W. Norton & Co., 1988.
Lipton, Lenny. *Foundations of the Stereoscopic Cinema: A Study in Depth.* New York: Van Nostrand Reinhold Co., 1982.
LoBrutto, Vincent. *By Design: Interviews with Film Production Designers.* Westport, Conn.: Praeger, 1992.
———. *Selected Takes: Film Editors on Editing.* New York: Praeger, 1991.
———. *Sound-on-Film: Interviews with Creators of Film Sound.* Westport, Conn.: Praeger, 1994.

Lyons, Paul. *New Left, New Right: Legacy of the Sixties.* Philadelphia: Temple University Press, 1996.

MacCann, Richard Dyer. *Hollywood in Transition.* Boston: Houghton-Mifflin, 1962.

Macgowan, Kenneth. *Behind the Screen: The History and Techniques of the Motion Picture.* New York: Delacorte, 1965.

Madsen, Axel. *The New Hollywood.* New York: Crowell, 1975.

Madsen, Roy Paul. *Working Cinema: Learning from the Masters.* Belmont, Calif.: Wadsworth Publishing, 1990.

Malkiewicz, Kris, assisted by Barbara J. Gryboski. *Film Lighting: Talks with Hollywood's Cinematographers and Gaffers.* Englewood Cliffs, N.J.: Prentice-Hall, 1986.

Maltin, Leonard. *The Art of the Cinematographer: A Survey and Interviews with Five Masters.* New York: Dover, 1971.

Mankovsky, V. S. *Acoustics of Studios and Auditoria.* London: Focal Press, 1971.

Manvell, Roger. *Theater and Film.* Fairleigh-Dickinson Press, 1979.

Marmorstein, Gary. *Hollywood Rhapsody: Movie Music and IRS Makers, 1900 to 1975.* New York: Schirmer Books, 1997.

Mast, Gerald, ed. *The Movies in Our Midst: Documents in the Cultural History Film in America.* Chicago: University of Chicago Press, 1982.

Mast, Gerald, and Bruce F. Kawin. *A Short History of the Movies.* 5th ed. New York: Macmillan, 1992.

Mast, Gerald, and Marshall Cohen, eds. *Film Theory and Criticism.* 2nd ed. New York: Oxford University Press, 1979.

McBride, Joseph, ed. *Filmmakers on Filmmaking: The American Film Institute Seminars on Motion Picture and Television.* Los Angles: J. P. Tarcher, Inc., 1983.

McCann, Graham. *Rebel Males: Clift, Brando, and Dean.* New Brunswick, N.J.: Rutgers University Press, 1993.

Michael, Paul. *The Academy Awards: A Pictorial History.* New York: Crown Publishers, 1978.

Miller, Frank. *Censored Hollywood: Sex, Sin, and Violence on the Screen.* Atlanta: Turner Publishing Company, 1994.

Monaco, Paul. *Ribbons in Time: Movies and Society Since 1945.* Bloomington: Indiana University Press, 1988.

Mordden, Ethan. *The Hollywood Musical.* New York: St. Martin's Press, 1981.

————. *MEDIUM COOL: The Movies of the 1960s.* New York: Alfred A. Knopf, 1990.

Mott, Robert L. *Sound Effects: Radio, TV, and Film.* Boston: Focal Press, 1990.

Musgrave, Peter. "The Dubbing of Sound." *American Cinematographer.* (March 1962): 168, 169.

Naremore, James. *Acting in the Cinema.* Berkeley: University of California Press, 1988.

Neale, Steve. *Cinema and Technology: Image, Sound, Colour.* Bloomington: Indiana University Press, 1985.

Neale, Steve, and Murray Smith, eds. *Contemporary Hollywood Cinema.* New York: Routledge, 1998.

Nelson, Thomas Allen. *Kubrick: Inside a Film Artist's Maze.* Bloomington: Indiana University Press, 1982.

Nichols, Bill. *Ideology and the Image: Social Representation in the Cinema and Other Media.* Bloomingtom: Indiana University Press, 1981.

Nisbett, Alec. *The Technique of the Sound Studio.* London: Focal Press, 1962.

O'Brien, Mary Ellen. *Film Acting: The Techniques and History of Acting for the Camera.* New York: Arco Publishing, Inc., 1983.

O'Connor, John E., and Martin A. Jackson. *American History/American Film: Interpreting the Hollywood Image.* New York: Frederick Ungar Publishing, 1979.

Ogar, Christine. "The Audience for Foreign Film in the United States." *Journal Of Communication* 40, no. 4 (autumn 1990): 59.

Oldham, Gabriella. *First Cut: Conversations with Film Editors.* Berkeley: University of California Press, 1992.

Paglia, Camille. *THE BIRDS.* London: BFI Publishing, 1998.

Peary, Danny, ed. *Close-Ups: Intimate Portraits of Movie Stars by Their Co-Stars, Directors, Screenwriters, and Friends.* New York: Workman, 1978.

Phillips, Gene D. *Alfred Hitchcock.* Boston: Twayne, 1984.

———. *John Schlesinger.* Boston: Twayne, 1981.

Pirie, David, ed. *Anatomy of the Movies.* New York: Macmillan, 1981.

Prindle, David F. *The Politics of Glamour: Ideology and Democracy in the Screen Actors Guild.* Madison: University of Wisconsin Press, 1988.

Quart, Leonard, and Albert Auster. *American Film and Society Since 1945.* 2nd ed. New York: Praeger, 1991.

Rabinovitz, Lauren. *Points of Resistance: Women, Power, and Politics in the New York Avant-Garde Cinema, 1943–71.* Urbana: University of Illinois Press, 1991.

Radner, Hilary, and Moya Luckett, eds. *Swinging Single: Representing Sexuality in the 1960s.* Minneapolis: University of Minnesota Press, 1999.

Raimondo Suoto, H. Mario. *The Technique of the Motion Picture Camera.* 4th ed. Boston: Focal Press, 1982.

Rainsberger, Todd. *James Wong Howe: Cinematographer.* San Diego: A. S. Barnes & Co., 1981.

Ray, Robert B. *A Certain Tendency of the Hollywood Cinema, 1930–1980.* Princeton, N.J.: Princeton University Press, 1985.

Reeves, Howard E. "The Development of Stereo Magnetic Recording for Film: Part II." *SMPTE Journal* (November 1982): 1087–1090.

Reisz, Karel, and Gavin Millar. *The Technique of Film Editing.* 2nd ed. New York: Hastings House, 1968.

Robertson, Joseph F. *The Magic of Film Editing.* Blue Ridge Summit, Pa.: TAB Books, 1983.

Robinson, David. *The History of World Cinema.* New York: Stein and Day, 1981.

Rosen, Marjorie. *Popcorn Venus: Women, Movies, and the American Screen.* New York: Coward, McCorum, and Geoghegan, 1973.

Rosenblum, Ralph, and Robert Karen. *When the Shooting Stops . . . the Cutting Begins: A Film Editor's Story.* New York: Viking, 1979.

Rosenthal, Alan. *The New Documentary in Action: A Casebook in Film Making.* Berkeley: University of California Press, 1971.

———. *The Documentary Conscience: A Casebook in Film Making.* Berkeley: University of California Press, 1980.

Roud, Richard, ed. *Cinema: A Critical Dictionary.* New York: Viking, 1980.

Russel, Louise. *The Baby-Boom Generation and the Economy.* Washington, D.C.: Brookings Institution, 1982.

Ryan, Roderick T. *A History of Motion Picture Color Technology.* New York: Focal Press, 1977.

Salt, Barry. *Film Style and Technology: History and Analysis.* 2nd ed. London: Starword, 1992.

Sands, Pierre Norman. *A Historical Study of the Academy of Motion Picture Arts and Sciences.* New York: Arno Press, 1973.

Sarris, Andrew. "After THE GRADUATE." *American Film* (July/August 1978).

Schaefer, Dennis, and Larry Salvato. *Masters of Light: Conversations with Contemporary Cinematographers.* Berkeley: University of California Press, 1984.

Scharf, Walter. *The History of Film Scoring,* Studio City, Calif.: Cinema Songs Publishing, 1988.

Schickel, Richard. *Second Sight: Notes on Some Movies, 1965–1970.* New York: Simon & Schuster, 1972.

Shale, Richard, ed. *Academy Awards: An Ungar Reference.* 2nd ed. New York: Frederick Ungar, 1982.

Sheniel, Sidney, and M. William Krasiolvsky. *The Business of Music.* 5th ed. New York: Billboard Publications, Inc., 1985.

Sherry, Philip J. "The Western Film: A Sense of an Ending." *New Orleans Review* (fall 1990).

Simon, John. *Movies into Film.* New York: Dial Press, 1971.

Sitney, P. Adams. *Visionary Film: The American Avant-Garde.* New York: Oxford University Press, 1974.

Sklar, Robert. *Film: An International History of the Medium.* New York: Henry N. Abrams, Inc., 1993.

———. *Movie-Made America: A Cultural History of American Movies.* Rev. ed. New York: Vintage Books, 1994.

Smith, Steven C. *The Film Composers Guide.* Los Angeles: Lone Eagle Publishing, 1991.

Solomon, Aubrey. *Twentieth Century Fox: A Corporate and Financial History*. Metuchen, N.J.: Scarecrow Press, 1988.

Sontag, Susan. *Against Interpretation and Other Essays*. New York: Farrar, Straus & Giroux, 1966.

Squire, Jason E., ed. *The Movie Business Book*. Englewood Cliffs, N.J.: Prentice-Hall, 1983.

Stacy, Jan, and Ryer Syvertsen. *Rockin' Reels: An Illustrated History of Rock & Roll Movies*. Chicago: Contemporary Books, 1984.

Stanley, Robert. *The Celluloid Empire: A History of the American Motion Picture Industry*. New York: Hastings House, 1978.

Steinberg, Cobbett. *Reel Facts: The Movie Book of Records*. New York: Vintage Books, 1982.

Sterling, Christopher, and Timothy Haight. *The Mass Media: Aspen Institute Guide to Communication Industry Trends*. New York: Praeger, 1978.

Stern, Stewart. *No Tricks in My Pocket: Paul Newman Directs*. New York: Grove Press, 1989.

Stuart, Frederic. *The Effects of Television on the Motion Picture and Radio Industries*. New York: Arno Press, 1976.

Suarez, Juan A. *Bike Boys, Drag Queens, and Superstars: Avant-Garde, Mass Culture, and Gay Identities in the 1960s Underground Cinema*. Bloomington: Indiana University Press, 1996.

Taylor, John Russell, and Arthur Jackson. *The Hollywood Musical*. New York: McGraw-Hill, 1971.

Taylor, Philip. "The Green Berets." *History Today* (March 1995): 21–25.

Thomas, Tony. *Film Score: The Art and Craft of Movie Music*. Burbank, Calif.: Riverwood Press, 1991.

———. *Music for the Movies*. New York: A. S. Barnes & Co., 1973.

———. *The Films of Marlon Brando*. Secaucus, N.J.: Citadel Press, 1973.

Vicens de Morales, Margarita. *Maria Montez: Su Vida*. Santo Domingo, Dominican Republic: Editoria Corripio, 1992.

Villchur, Edgar. *Reproduction of Sound*. New York: Dover, 1965.

Vineberg, Steve. *Method Actors: Three Generations of an American Acting Style*. New York: Schirmer Books, 1991.

Walter, Ernest. *The Technique of the Cutting Room*. Boston: Focal Press, 1973.

Wanger, Walter, with Joe Hyams. *My Life with CLEOPATRA*. New York: Bantam Books, 1963.

Wasko, Janet. *Hollywood in the Information Age*. Austin: University of Texas Press, 1995.

———. *Movies and Money: Financing the American Film Industry*. Norwood, N.J.: ABLEX Publishing Corp., 1982.

Webb, Michael, ed. *Hollywood: Legend and Reality*. Boston: Little, Brown, & Co., 1986.

Weis, Elizabeth. *The Silent Scream: Alfred Hitchcock's Sound Track*. Rutherford, N.J.: Farleigh Dickinson University Press, 1982.

Weis, Elizabeth, and John Belton, eds. *Film Sound: Theory and Practice*. New York: Columbia University Press, 1985.

Whitaker, Rod. *The Language of Film*. Englewood Cliffs, N.J.: Prentice-Hall, 1970.

Wiley, Mason, and Damien Bona. *Inside Oscar: The Unofficial History of the Academy Awards*. New York: Ballantine Books, 1993.

Williams, Christopher, ed. *Cinema: The Beginnings and the Future*. London: University of Westminster Press, 1996.

———. *Realism and the Cinema*. London: Routledge, 1980.

Windeler, Robert. *Julie Andrews: A Life on Stage and Screen*. Secaucus, N.J.: Birch Lane Publishing, 1997.

Wysotsky, Michael Z. *Wide-Screen Cinema and Stereophonic Sound*. A. E. C. York, trans., annotated and introduced by Raymond Spotiswoode, ed. New York: Hastings House, 1971.

Young, Freddie, and Paul Petzold. *The Work of the Motion Picture Cameraman*. New York: Hastings House, 1972.

MAJOR FILM JOURNALS, POPULAR MAGAZINES, AND
NEWSPAPERS CONSULTED FOR THE PERIOD 1960–1969

American Cinematographer
Box Office
Commonweal
Cue
Esquire
Film Comment
Film Library Quarterly
Film Quarterly
Filmmakers' Newsletter
Hollywood Reporter
International Herald-Tribune
Journal of Popular Film
Life
Los Angeles Citizen-News
Los Angeles Times

Motion Picture Herald
Nation
National Review
New Republic
New York Times
New Yorker
Newsweek
Quarterly Review of Film Studies
Saturday Review
Sight and Sound
Time
University Film Association Journal
Variety (Daily)
Variety (Weekly)
Village Voice

Picture Sources

Kobal Collection. Pages: 4 (20th Century Fox), 7 (Warner Bros.), 14 (Hawk Films Production/Columbia), 124 (United Artists/Seven Arts), 126 (Warner Bros.), 137 (Columbia), 158 (United Artists), 185 (Warner Bros.), 263 (Batjac Productions).

Collection of the Museum of Modern Art. Pages: 14, 61, 64, 75, 96, 108, 169, 213, 214, 217, 219, 220, 221, 222, 225, 232, 238, 250, 255.

Library of Congress. Page: 13.

Collections of the Academy for Motion Picture Arts & Sciences. Pages: 19, 22, 25, 31, 34, 53, 59, 77, 87, 89, 95, 99, 100, 111, 113, 115, 123, 131, 134, 136, 141, 143, 144, 159, 165, 171, 173, 175, 176, 177, 187, 189, 192, 193, 195.

Columbia Pictures. Pages: 21, 79, 114.

United Artists. Pages: 129, 150, 192, 193.

Courtesy of Mr. Roger Corman. Page: 28.

American International Pictures. Page: 29.

Archive Photos. Page: 43.

Corbis. Pages: 47 (© Jim McDonald/Corbis), 118 (© Bettman/Corbis), 266 (© Ted Streshinsky/Corbis).

Kansas City Star. Page: 48.

Anthology Film Archives. Pages: 55, 237.

The Lyndon Baines Johnson Presidential Library. Page: 60.

Warner Bros. and Seven Arts. Page: 63.

Courtesy of Panavision, Mr. Frank Kay. Page: 73.

National Screen Services Corp. Page: 83.

Warner Bros. Pages: 91, 101, 128, 146, 181.

Landau Company. Page: 93.

Universal Pictures. Page 97.

Courtesy of the Nagra Corporation. Page: 105.

20th Century-Fox. Pages: 132, 164.

Embassy Pictures Corp. Pages: 148, 183.

York Productions and Jerry Lewis Enterprises. Page: 153.

Samuel Goldwyn Company. Page: 162.

Continental Distributing, Inc. Page: 169.

PBS. Page: 191.

Andy Warhol Films, Inc. Page: 234.

General Index

Italic numerals signify illustrations.

Index of Films

Italic numerals signify illustrations.